SKETCHES OF SOME DISTINGUISHED ANGLO-INDIANS

Yours very sincerely,

SKETCHES OF SOME DISTINGUISHED ANGLO-INDIANS

INCLUDING

LORD MACAULAY'S GREAT MINUTE
ON
EDUCATION IN INDIA

WITH
Anglo-Indian Anecdotes and Incidents

W.F.B. LAURIE

GYAN

Published by

Gyan Publishing House
5, Ansari Road
Daryaganj, New Delhi-110002
Phone: 011-47034999, 9811692060
E-mail: books@gyanbooks.com

Distribution Network
gyanbooks.com
India, USA, Canada, UK, Australia, France

ISBN : 978-81-212-4033-8 (PB)
First Published, London, 1888

2nd Impression 2020

Printed at: Gyan Press, Delhi.

Sketches of Some Distinguished Anglo-Indians
Author: W.F.B. Laurie

SKETCHES OF SOME

DISTINGUISHED ANGLO-INDIANS:

INCLUDING

LORD MACAULAY'S GREAT MINUTE ON EDUCATION IN INDIA;

WITH

Anglo-Indian Anecdotes and Incidents.

BY

COLONEL W. F. B. LAURIE,

AUTHOR OF

"SKETCHES OF SOME DISTINGUISHED ANGLO-INDIANS," "OUR BURMESE WARS," "ASH PYEE, THE EASTERN OR FOREMOST COUNTRY," ETC.

"An statuas et imagines, non animorum simulacra, sed corporum, studiose multi summi homines reliquerunt: consiliorum relinquere ac virtutum nostrarum effigiem nonne multo malle debemus, summis ingeniis expressam et politam?"—CICERO.

"So might we talk of the old familiar faces."
CHARLES LAMB.

LONDON:
W. H. ALLEN & CO., 13, WATERLOO PLACE,
PALL MALL, S.W.

1888.

Yours very sincerely,
G. B. Malleson.

PREFACE

TO

THE SECOND SERIES.

In presenting a Second Series of "Distinguished Anglo-Indians" to the public, I have been actuated by the desire to leave my work in a more finished condition than on the first occasion. Besides, more than half of the former volume had been published before; while the present one may lay claim to chiefly new matter. One London critic of the *First Series* did me the honour to say that it "is now a fairly complete 'Indian Men of the Time';" another, that "the book is right-minded and high-minded;" and a third, that it ought to "find its way into the library of every one interested in the history and welfare of India." Surely the force of praise to an old Anglo-Indian author could no further go; and there is great satisfaction in hoping that the Series now given will afford a better title to deserve it. The principal sketches are far less numerous than in the former Series, and some of them, perhaps, of not so highly important a character. But they are all of men who have done really good work for, and deserved well of, their country. In the majority of cases, the "Distinguished" have been put in order according to date of appointment or commission. This was not attempted in the *First Series*, where simply personal sketches, with historical incidents relative to the First War in Afghanistan, the great Indian Mutiny, Burma, Indian and Eastern Railways, form the chief subjects of public interest. I am still well aware that many deserving Anglo-Indian heroes are not mentioned in this work, and that there are various glorious achievements or heroic episodes omitted. But in the wide range of Indian history they are done full justice to by other writers. One might have dwelt with pride and pleasure on the gallant Defence of Jellalabad—the very name bringing to mind "Fighting Bob"* (Sir Robert) and the heroic Lady Sale, also the vivid picture of Dr. Brydon, the solitary white-faced horseman who, "clinging to the neck of his horse in the extremity of mortal weakness," alone escaped to that famous fortress†—and on a minor, less known, yet hardly less glorious episode of the First Afghan War, the defence of Kahun, by Captain Lewis Brown; and another notable incident at the same time, that of the defence of Quetta by Captain Bean.

Something might also have been said of that grand fact in Indian history, the relief of the garrison of Arrah, at an early period of the Indian Mutiny, by the brave and heroic artilleryman, Major Vincent Eyre. And thus my book would have been flooded with glorious deeds, by distinguished Anglo-Indians of undying fame, placing other sketches at a discount, though among the subjects of them, in a more

* *See* also sketch of General J. R. Becher, C.B.

† Alluded to in "The Defence of Kahun" (prior to Jellalabad), by Charles Reynolds Williams, p. 8. This most interesting and graphic little work is well worthy of attentive perusal.

peaceful way, there are also incidents which, like the minor relief of Arrah and the greater of Lucknow, can never die!

The mention of railways in India leads one to think of telegraphs—together the ever-active levers of civilization and order. And here I cannot help alluding to the remarkable error made by the critic in a well-known London journal. In my sketch (*First Series*, page 281) of a distinguished servant of Government—who has done so much and so well for Indian railways—it is incidently noted that, as a commencement, a line of telegraph "had been actually laid and worked between Calcutta and Kedgeree, at the mouth of the Hooghly river." On this the above self-satisfied, but generally well-informed and able reviewer, was pleased to remark that the first telegraph line in India "extended from Calcutta to Saugor Island, and not only to Kedgeree." Now the line at first opened was simply from Calcutta to Kedgeree. The information—however slight—was not given without careful research, which the British public, in all cases, have every right to expect.

The despatch from Lord Dalhousie to the Court of Directors, dated April 23, 1852 (in Parliamentary Return No. 243, dated May 16, 1855), begins :—"We have the honour to transmit the accompanying report from the Government of Bengal, announcing the completion, by Dr. W. B. O'Shaughnessy,* of the line of electric telegraph from Calcutta to Kedgeree." Saugor Island, at that time, was only thought of or mentioned as the eventual terminus. There are a few other matters, including a misprint or two in the *First Series*, (not to dwell on two at the beginning of the review in question, where the very titles of two of my works

* Afterwards Sir W. O'Shaughnessy, and eventually Sir W. Brooke.

on Burma are wrongly given,) a slip of the author's pen, and so forth, which probably influenced this notice by my "candid friend," and which, had it been advisable, I should have liked to discuss with him, as he is evidently one who can be pleasant as well as instructive, when not too critical; these qualities, in the exercise of the liberal and humane art, only ranking second to what are justly considered its chief requisites—information and impartiality. But, as an old Anglo-Indian critic, I am anxious to stand well with a journal which did me the honour to say, while noticing "Our Burmese Wars and Relations with Burma"—with the matter of my two previous volumes, forming the only authoritative standard of reference on the Second Burmese War—that the "narrative of the events of 1852," in which I took "an active part, is spirited and correct." I should like my "Distinguished Anglo-Indians" to be considered at least equally "correct."

There is one novel feature which will be observed in this Second Series. A considerable space has been devoted to the great subject of Education, considered by Lord William Bentinck, as before remarked, "the first want, the second, and the third want of India."* And, perhaps, we never were so near a good and useful system as at present. The names of Lord Macaulay and Mr. Woodrow stand prominently forward as our most influential working Indian educationists. The latter well styles the former "the first master of the English language;" and, no doubt, had his Lordship been alive when Mr. Woodrow first collected his "Minutes," or, as stated elsewhere, "rescued them from the white ants," the "Nestor of Education in Bengal" would

* "Sketch of Anglo-Indian Periodical Literature," p. 334, *First Series.*

have received a hearty shake of the hand, and that generous help and praise which ever flowed, when well deserved, from England's brilliant historian, unrivalled critical essayist, popular orator, and classic poet. In addition to some unpublished particulars regarding the "Minutes," I have been able to give the "Great Minute" on Education in India entire; a performance hardly inferior to some of the immortal Essays which Lord Macaulay has left behind. Some "Extracts" from "Unpublished Minutes" will be found in an Appendix. Repeating what is said elsewhere, it may here be remarked that Mr. Woodrow discovered the late Lord Macaulay's educational "Minutes" scattered among the records at the office of the Director of Public Instruction, Calcutta (1862), and caused fifty copies, for private circulation, to be printed at his own expense. For this he received the thanks of Lord Canning—a fact alone showing that the "Minutes" should have been more extensively published long ago. The Appendices, as in the former Series, contain a fair share of varied and sometimes highly useful information. "Brief Notices of Distinguished Anglo-Indians" form another new feature in the work. The sketches greatly vary in length, as the subjects do in merit, although they are all "distinguished." A few Anglo-Indian anecdotes and incidents also take the place of Anglo-Indian and sporting periodical literature in the *First Series;* so I trust that the entertainment now offered will be pleasant as well as profitable to all readers, especially true friends of India, who may honour these pages with a perusal.

W. F. B. L.

LONDON, *December*, 1887.

POSTSCRIPT.—While the year is fast drawing to a close,

it has been pointed out by good authority that disquieting doubts and uncertainties are causing the "war spectre" to stalk over Europe—in which case he generally takes a steady look at India also—or that the political atmosphere is thick with fears and rumours of that seeming inevitable result in the history of great nations—war; but which we all trust may be averted in the new year, because it is that last process which is force, allowed and prescribed by the law of nature "for justice sake," when every other remedy fails. Peace under any circumstances, however, must come at last, not being, like restoring the dead, impossible. Turning for a moment from nations to individuals, this forces a thought of two eminent men sketched in the *First Series,* who have passed away during the year,* and a few words on the distinguished veteran Anglo-Indian administrator, just departed (December 28), who was only second to the immortal Lawrences in the Punjab. Sir Robert Montgomery was one of the foremost of that famous class of Anglo-Indian civilians who wisely understood the uses of war, but whose watchword, or guiding star, was peace. With a disposition "sweet as summer," he was not of that impracticable sentimental school of statesmen who could see no good come out of a well-conducted war; a war of strategic skill in a good cause; and for that very reason he was the stern advocate of peace during his long and able Punjab rule. Peace with Sir Robert, in the country of the five rivers—a famous land which produced the direst and bravest foe England ever had in the East, the almost invincible Khalsa army—there as nearly found rest as she ever did in our great Eastern

* Sir William Andrew, C.I.E., the eminent Eastern and Indian railway engineer and strategist, died in London, 11th March, 1887, in his 81st

Empire. And now the hard-working, warm-hearted Irishman—in the sunset of life, revered in his own loved county, Derry—is at rest himself.

Writing of peace, a graceful poet of the last generation sang :—

> "Nowhere finds she rest with men,
> Or only with the dead!"

But, as finely expressed by another poet, as if alluding to a lasting fellowship among Anglo-Indians, there is the pleasing hope to sustain them, when "the old familiar faces" are removed from the world's stage one by one :—

> "We shall all meet again,
> Not in the wood or plain,
> Nor by the lake's green marge.
> The past shall be lived o'er
> By a far greener shore,
> With our souls set at large."*

* From the new "Faber Birthday Book." *To a Lake Party.*—POEMS.

CONTENTS.

—o—

APPENDICES.

In Memoriam.

DISTINGUISHED ANGLO-INDIANS.

SAMUEL DAVIS, B.C.S., F.R.S.;

AND THE

DOMESTIC THERMOPYLÆ AT BENARES.*

> "I talk not of mercy, I talk not of fear;
> He neither must know who would serve the VIZIER."
>
> *Byron.*†

THE first appearance of Mr. (afterwards Sir John) Davis's short but most strange and eventful "History" was in 1844. The whole impression was soon exhausted, and a renewal, with additions, was supplied in 1871 for the use of private friends and relatives. The principal details were gathered by the author from a very distinguished Anglo-Indian, the Hon. Mountstuart Elphinstone, appointed, on his first arrival in India, to assist Mr. Davis's father, the Judge and

* The greater portion of the following sketch originally appeared under the head of a "Supplement," by the Rev. John Lockwood, Rector of Kingham, Oxon., to a most interesting chapter in British Indian History, entitled "Vizier Ali Khan, or the Massacre of Benares."

The title of "The Domestic Thermopylæ" may be either attributed to the author of the "Chapter," Sir John Davis (son of the hero), or to Lord Valentia—probably the coinage (most appropriate) of the latter's fanciful brain. (*See* Note 1; also Benares, Appendix I.)

† The couplet above quoted appears on the titlepage of the more lengthy Narrative.

Magistrate of Benares, and who was present at the time of the revolt. True enough, there were episodes in the great Indian Mutiny like those here recorded; and the author, in his preface, comes to the inevitable conclusion of all candid men who have studied the subject, that, had the first outbreak at Meerut, in 1857, been as speedily quenched, and the mutinous regiments prevented from marching to Delhi, "the perils of that crisis might have been greatly diminished."*

The story of Vizier Ali Khan, the spurious child of a King of Oudh, of course derives all its interest from the terrible massacre at Benares, which took place nearly ninety years ago. This is indeed a long time to go back for a sketch; but the subject is one little known to readers of Indian history and the British public; while reviewing the gallant deeds of distinguished men of the past is often of great use in teaching us how to act in the present under similar, or nearly similar, circumstances. To think of an Anglo-Indian like Samuel Davis, with stout heart and strong arm, with a firmness and courage worthy of Leonidas, defending the gorge in his house against the fierce assailants who were pressing upwards to destroy him, is an ennobling thought for every Englishman to dwell on. To this may be added the glowing words of the *Calcutta* reviewer (No. 1, 1844,) of Lord Teignmouth's Life and Correspondence. For nearly an hour and a half did "the British gentleman bid defiance to the ruthless gang of murderers who were pressing on to his destruction—for nearly an hour and a half did he successfully defend his life, and, dearer than life, his wife and children, who were looking on with terror and dismay. His courage and constancy prevailed at last." And what was the weapon used on this momentous occasion? Not a gun or musket, not a sword or bayonet, not a deadly Moplah or

* At page 98 of First Series of "Sketches," of General Beatson, it is thought not improbable that, had he been in command at Meerut, 10th and 11th May, at the first outbreak of the Mutiny, he would have headed a party of horse, galloped off, and not left the saddle till he had done his utmost to secure the mutineers on their way to Delhi, and bring them back, under a strong guard, to their proper station.

Coorg knife or dagger, but simply a spear—some say a hog-spear, others a spear of ceremony, as will be seen in the narrative—which Mr. Davis had providentially seized in the flight to the roof of his house. Had there been a "Victoria Cross" in his time, beyond a doubt, such a brave and vigorous defender would have had his reward.

The story of Vizier Ali,* it may here be remarked, belongs to the administration of Sir John Shore (Lord Teignmouth); but the sequel to the tale—a tragic one—comes under that of his successor, Lord Mornington (the Marquess Wellesley).

The former had no sooner returned to Calcutta from Lucknow than he embarked to return home, where his measures regarding Vizier Ali were entirely approved of by the British Government and the Court of Directors. Even before quitting Lucknow Sir John Shore had received advices from England, announcing the appointment of Lord Mornington, and his own elevation to an Irish peerage. He embarked at Calcutta early in March, amidst the highest possible enthusiasm and admiration of the inhabitants. Lord Mornington arrived in India in May, 1798, when his attention was immediately occupied by the threatening aspect of affairs in Mysore. Having now, we trust, excited a little interest in the "Domestic Thermopylæ at Benares," let us proceed to the relation of events, as given in their proper course.

In the year 1798, the East India Company deposed Vizier Ali from the throne of Oudh (to which he had succeeded as the reputed son of Asoph-ud-dowlah), on account of his vices and cruelty; but gave him a splendid pension, and permitted him to take up his residence in the large and beautiful city of Benares, where he lived in almost regal splendour. It is said that he spent whole days and nights with the lowest associates, in revelry and drunkenness; on one occasion, enraged at a fall from a favourite horse, he ordered it to be burnt alive. To his great profligacy and

* He was eventually conveyed to Calcutta; and died a wretched prisoner in Fort William, May, 1817. At his burial, a constabulary force was present to keep the peace.

cruelty, as is often the case with Orientals, he added great cunning; and perceiving among the chiefs of India a jealousy at the increasing power of the English, he determined to make use of it to regain, if possible, the throne from which he had been deposed.

He carried on his intrigues with great secrecy, and obtained promises from many of the most powerful of the native princes, that they would render him assistance as soon as he should have commenced such a revolt against the English as would hold out any prospect of success. Relying on these promises, he increased his troops and retainers, and watched his opportunity to unfurl the standard of rebellion. But notwithstanding the secrecy with which he carried on his plans, Mr. Davis, the Chief Magistrate of Benares, discovered that he was engaged in plots against the English, and wrote to the Governor-General, to advise that he should be immediately removed from Benares, where he was surrounded by chiefs and people of doubtful loyalty, and where he was so near the kingdom from which he had been deposed, as to be able to keep up a constant communication with it; and that he should be ordered to reside at Fort William, where all attempts to tamper with the fidelity of the Native Princes, or to spread discontent among the people, might be easily frustrated.

In consequence of this communication, an order was dispatched to the Vizier to leave Benares and proceed to Calcutta. He no sooner received this communication than, seeing that there was no time to be lost, he determined at once to put his plans into execution, and to commence his long-meditated rebellion; for he knew that if he once left Benares, the scene of action, and removed to Calcutta, he would be watched, cut off from his friends, and lose all hopes of success.

At that time there were many English residents at Benares, either as officials of the East India Company, or engaged in different branches of trade and commerce. The chief of these were Mr. Cherry, the Resident, and Mr. Davis, the Judge and First Magistrate, whose houses were about a mile without the city gates; and three miles, again, beyond them, were large cantonments, containing a brigade of the Anglo-Indian army.

On the 14th January, 1799, soon after his order of removal, the Vizier commenced his revolt. Leaving a large force in the city, he proceeded, with 200 chosen men, to the house of Mr. Cherry, under the pretence of paying him a friendly visit, but with the real purpose of putting him to death; and on his way thither he fell in with Mr. and Mrs. Davis, returning from their usual morning ride on an elephant. The instant he saw them he held a short consultation with his friends, whether he should at once attack and kill them on the spot, or should leave them for the present; and it was decided that as they did not appear to have any suspicion of his intentions, it would be better to proceed first to the house of the Resident, which was farthest from the city, and take them in his way back.

Mr. Davis at once perceived that the Vizier was engaged in some treacherous and hostile design, but thought it best to conceal his opinion; and having received and returned the salutation of the party with apparent indifference, he hastened home, and immediately despatched a messenger to Mr. Cherry, to warn him of some impending danger. But it was too late. Already had the unfortunate Resident and his friends fallen beneath the swords of the Vizier and his soldiers; and before any escape could be effected, or any preparation be made for defence, they were seen hastening towards Mr. Davis's house. What was to be done? Who were to be trusted? Were the native servants in the plot? Should they resign themselves at once to despair, and perish without a struggle? Mr. Davis possessed a bold and master spirit; but what could the courage of one man, however resolute, without a weapon, avail against two hundred troops armed to the very teeth? It was a moment of agony; but Mr. Davis at once perceived the only hope of safety, though that hope was a forlorn one.

In India the roofs of the houses are flat, and ascending to the roof of his own house was a narrow spiral staircase, with a trap-door at the top made with strong bamboo and thick matting, which let down upon the entrance. Up this staircase he urged his trembling wife and a Portuguese nurse, with one of his two little children * in her arms—but where was the other? His wife ventured down to seek for it, but was soon obliged to return, having scarcely escaped the pursuit of armed men. But what was her joy when she met, at the top of the stairs, the child whom she had sought at the peril of her life? Mr. Davis soon followed, taking with him a long and formidable spear, which he had snatched from the hands of a native servant, whose office it was—according to Eastern custom—to wait with it before his master's door, ready to accompany any of the family in their palanquin.

The Vizier, after searching the lower part of the house without finding the inmates, ordered some of his men to mount the spiral staircase. On the roof, at the top of the stairs, stood Mr. Davis, the trap-door partially lifted up, and the spear in his hand; and, the instant the first man turned the angle, with a vigorous thrust—to which the fearful peril of his position added energy—he threw him wounded down the stairs. Another and another followed, forced on by the Vizier, but with the same result; firing their pistols up the stairs in hopes of hitting the brave defender. But, fortunately, the thick matting of the trap-door proved to be bullet-proof. Unable to gain the roof, the Vizier now paused; but presently ordered one of his strongest men to watch his opportunity and seize the spear. He did so. But, by making a prop of the trap-door, Mr. Davis, with a sudden jerk, drew it back, almost cutting in two the man's hands with the sharp sides. Another pause ensued; and the nurse, venturing to look over the parapet to discover the cause, received a bullet in her arm; for men had been placed in different situations, with orders to fire at any one they could catch sight of on the roof. Nearly an hour had now passed since the Vizier had entered the house; when presently a well-known voice was heard on the stairs, and an old grey-headed native servant ascended with the news that the Vizier and his men were gone. The first impression upon Mr. Davis was that the old man had been

* Of whom the present Sir J. F. Davis was one.

forced to act a traitor's part, and that from behind him would rush armed men; but, being convinced of his fidelity, he admitted him to the roof, as well as some others who had come from their hiding-places. It was now ascertained that the Vizier had withdrawn his men to a little distance, and had despatched some of them to the city, no doubt for the purpose of obtaining ladders to scale, or materials to fire, the house.

The only hope now of the besieged was that the news of the revolt had reached the cantonment, and that assistance would arrive before it was too late. It was a state of fearful suspense; but before long they heard the distant trampling of horses. Was it the Vizier returning, or was it their friends coming to their rescue? Mr. Davis shut down the trap-door, and approached towards the parapet; and a burst of joy proceeded from the whole party as they perceived a regiment of cavalry, headed by English officers, galloping towards the house.

It appears that Mr. Cleves, a deputy judge, seizing the opportunity while the Vizier was at Mr. Davis's, mounted his horse, and by a circuitous route, to avoid meeting any of the conspirators, reached the barracks in safety, just as a regiment of cavalry were returning from their morning exercise. Not an instant was to be lost. Major Shubrick, who commanded, gave the order, and immediately the whole force turned their horses' heads, and hastened to the rescue, leaving Mr. Cleves to make his communication to the General, who instantly ordered out the troops; and a considerable force soon marched from the encampment, taking the road towards Mr. Davis's house, where they left, on their arrival, a guard, and then proceeded onward to the city. In their way thither they were attacked by the Vizier, who had been joined by his forces, and had taken up his position in a wood to the left; but, being dislodged by artillery, he retreated to the town, and proceeded to his own residence, called Mahdoo Doss's Garden, which had previously been fortified, and prepared against attack. The English followed, and suffered considerable loss, from being fired at from the houses. But they soon made a breach in the walls, and the gates also being forced, they entered the courts of the garden just as the sun set.

The Vizier made a precipitate retreat, accompanied by a large body of troops. With these he entered the district of Betoul, where he collected an army of some thousands; but being attacked by the English, and defeated, he fled to Rajpootana, and took refuge with the Rajah of Jeypore. By the Rajah he was given up to the English, on condition that his life should be spared, and that he should not be bound by fetters. He was brought down to Calcutta, and was placed in what could hardly be called otherwise than an iron cage, where he died.*

But to return to Mr. Davis. On descending from the roof of the house, he found the furniture of the lower rooms destroyed; the mirrors, which were of considerable value, broken; and the table-cloth, which had been laid for breakfast, awaiting his return from his morning ride, covered with blood from the wounds of the discomfited invaders of the roof. And without the house, to his great grief, he found three faithful native servants, either dead or dying of their wounds; with two old horses (which had formerly belonged to Warren Hastings, but were given to Mr. Davis, with a request that he should take care of them, as old and favourite servants) lying dead before the stables, where they had been shot by the Vizier; the other horses being conveyed away.

The painful task now fell upon Mr. Davis, as Judge and Chief Magistrate, to enter into an investigation of the conspiracy, and see how far it had extended, and what native princes had been engaged in it. He found that the plan of the Vizier had been, first, to murder the Resident and the Judge, with their households, so that none could escape to make known the revolt to the English army; and then to massacre the English residing within the city, and closing the gates, arm the townspeople; and the city once in a state of defence, and the English inhabitants destroyed, he

* Mr. Lockwood says that, after a time, he was removed to the fort at Vellore (Madras), where he died. But this is a mistake, as will be seen from a Note at the commencement of this sketch.

thought it would give such hopes of success that the native princes would be induced to fulfil their promises, and join his standard. But the long delay at Mr. Davis's disconcerted all his plans, and brought the English forces upon him before his scheme was sufficiently well prepared.

Many native princes and nobles were found to be implicated in the conspiracy, and long lists were discovered of forces which were to have been sent to his assistance; and had not Vizier Ali been prevented carrying his plans into execution by the brave defence of Mr. Davis, it is impossible to say what might have been the result—with the French ready to take every advantage, and the Mahomedan princes anxious to regain their power and expel the infidel from the land. But, as is often the case, because the rebellion was so soon terminated, men looked not beyond; and he who by his bravery saved the settlement of Benares, and arrested a conspiracy that might have spread like wildfire and jeopardized the whole of our Indian possessions, only received (in the absence of Lord Wellesley at Madras) a cold letter of thanks from the Council at Calcutta. But to this day, among the natives, the affair of Benares, and the disappointment of the Mahomedan princes, is still fresh in remembrance; and when the natives would show the effects of bravery, and that, however great the odds, none should despair, they relate how Davis sahib and his spear kept at bay 200 armed men with a prince at their head.

And having now brought this history to a conclusion, it only remains to give a brief sketch of the career of the brave man who played so conspicuous a part in it.

Mr. Davis went out to India as an engineer officer in the Company's service, but with the privilege, occasionally granted in those days, of leaving the army if he wished it, and becoming a civilian. The first station he went to was Madras; and here he became Aide-de-Camp to the Commander-in-Chief, and went with him to Calcutta, where, soon after his arrival, he was appointed, from his known talents for surveying, to accompany Mr. Turner in his embassy to Thibet. During this expedition he made a large collection of excellent plans and coloured drawings, the latter of which are still valuable, not only as accurate representations of that country, its temples and buildings, but as beautiful works of art.

On his return to Calcutta, thinking that the Civil Service afforded more prospect of advancement, he left the army, and obtained the appointment of Collector of Burdwan; and while in this situation he married Henrietta, daughter of Mr. Boileau, of Dublin, whose ancestor—of the ancient family of the Barons de Castelnau, in Languedoc—had left his native country at the Revocation of the Edict of Nantes, and settled in Ireland. He had not been long at Burdwan before he was removed to Benares, to act in the position of Judge and Chief Magistrate over that district. And being an excellent linguist and astronomer, he no sooner took up his residence in the holy city of the Hindus than he became acquainted with the Brahmins of the highest caste; and particularly with one who gave him much valuable information respecting both the ancient religion and astronomy of the Hindus. This Brahmin was afterwards proved by undoubted testimony to have been actively engaged in Vizier Ali's rebellion, and was brought up for judgment before Mr. Davis. The Judge, seeing his old friend, could not contain his emotion, and the tears fell from his eyes as he heard the proud Brahmin express his readiness to die, but entreat that he might not be degraded, or anything done to him unworthy of his high caste and station.

Shortly after this he was summoned to Calcutta, to carry into execution some plans connected with the public revenue; and when he had accomplished these, he left for England, having formed an intimate friendship with the three most distinguished men connected with India during his residence there—Warren Hastings, Sir W. Jones, and the Marquess Wellesley. The latter of these showed in what high esteem he held his memory, by the autograph inscription* written in a copy of his Despatches, which he presented to the widow of his friend.

Soon after his arrival in England he entered into the

* *See* Note 2.

Direction of the East India Company;* and, being requested by a Committee of the House of Commons to draw up a report upon the state of the revenues of India, he wrote that very able treatise known as the Fifth Report. But the labour of finishing this in a perfect state, within the limited period, accelerated a disease already latent in his constitution; for not long afterwards he was taken ill, and, gradually growing weaker under the effects of a painful disorder, he died the 16th day of June, 1819, at his house at Croydon, in the fifty-ninth year of his age.

Bengal civilians cannot but be proud of having had in their ranks such an admirable and intrepid member as Samuel Davis. Not even in the records of the military profession, where are to be found so many mighty men who have performed deeds of valour, appears a more splendid example of individual bravery; and the conduct of our Indian civilians during the Mutiny showed that there were yet many Davises among them. We have alluded to their determined bravery during "India's severest trial" in our First Series of *Sketches,*† their chivalrous and high-souled heroism still being fresh in the minds of those who were in India throughout the deadly rebellion. Davis was certainly a fine English gentleman of the olden time; and his grand performance of duty may be considered of inferior value by those who only think of glorious deeds of more modern and recent date. Still, with many, the famous defence of the house at Benares will, we trust, after their perusal of the foregoing sketch, sink deep into their minds, and into those of their children's children; for, in the noble Bengal civilian, with his spear, his devoted wife, and say one faithful attendant, as if in answer to the request so finely rendered in our poetry by Lord Byron, appeared to have

* In the valuable "Record" of the Madras Civil Service, by the author's late valued friend, Mr. Charles Campbell Prinsep, page xii., it is stated that Mr. Samuel Davis was a Director of the East India Company from 1810 to 1819. His death is there given as having taken place in July of the latter year.

† Page 179.

been granted "THREE, TO MAKE A NEW THERMOPYLÆ!" Domestic this time, doubtless; but still eliciting high admiration from the reader, as, after perusing this brief narrative, it is to be hoped he will think of a line in the *Giaour*—

"Say, is not this Thermopylæ?"

To lovers of Indian history, it may be interesting to add to this sketch some particulars of the period, from *Lord Teignmouth's Narrative,* given by the present Sir John Davis, F.R.S., who, in 1844,* held the appointment of Governor of Hong Kong. "In the progress of this revolution," wrote Lord Teignmouth, "many circumstances occurred to create doubt and anxiety. The failure of the post, the interception of my letters, any irresolution on the part of Saadut Ali, or accident in the course of his journey to Khanpoor might have involved me in serious embarrassments. As it was, I had a difficult task to amuse all parties, so as to prevent the discovery of my plans. The confidence which I was obliged to place in many was in no instance violated; and the declaration of my intention to place Saadut Ali† on the musnud, after his arrival at Khanpoor (Cawnpore), was a surprise to all who were not in my confidence. But, above all, I owe unbounded gratitude to Providence, which enabled me to accomplish so great a revolution without the loss of lives, and contrary to the expectations of almost all who knew my plans. Assassination, contempt of the English, and the power of Vizier Ali to resist them, were the common topics of conversation amongst the desperate crew who attended the confidential hours of Vizier Ali. It was a surprise to all that they did not succeed in instigating him to some act of desperation, with a view to avail themselves of the confusion to plunder the town. The Vakeel of Ambagee, a Mahratta

* As John Francis Davis, F.R.S.

† We may explain that Saadut Ali, a claimant of the throne, was brother and next-of-kin to the deceased Nabob Vizier; and the Governor-General deemed it both just and expedient to consider the claims of this man, who, for some time, had been living a pensioner at Benares! After being conveyed secretly to Cawnpore, he went to Lucknow. As the rightful Nawaub, he was there proclaimed without opposition on the 21st January, 1798.

chieftain, who arrived at Lucknow on the 15th of the month, had an opportunity of learning the projects entertained by the adherents of Vizier Ali—viz., to raise a commotion, plunder the city and retire with the spoils into the Mahratta frontier. They were heard to remark that if a single shot were fired it would be sufficient, and that thousands would be sacrificed. Every street in Lucknow was filled with armed men; and the accumulation of them on the 19th and 20th was observed by several Europeans. During the three successive days from the 21st great numbers were seen returning from the town, and passing the English camp in the neighbourhood. The consequence of an armed opposition in such a town as Lucknow would have been shocking. It is computed to contain 800,000 inhabitants; and the streets are, for the most part, narrow lanes and passages. Ibrahim Beg had under his charge about 300 pieces of ordnance, of which sixty or seventy were fit for immediate use; they were served by 1,000 Gole andages,* or native artillerymen; and the number of artillery drawn out for apparent opposition consisted of thirty pieces, so posted that they could not be seized without great slaughter. Ibrahim Beg, the commandant, was a violent and hotheaded Mogul, regardless of any authority, fearless of his life, and careless of the lives of others. The single accident which happened had, in all probability, no connection with the revolution. The successful accomplishment of it was to me a relief from more anxiety than I ever before experienced."

* Golundauz, as they are generally styled.

SIR JOHN FRANCIS DAVIS, F.R.S.

We cannot do better than close this sketch with a few brief remarks on the "highly respectable and able gentleman" to whom we are indebted for one of the most tragic chapters in British Indian history, the son of Mr. Davis, the Benares Judge and Magistrate, whose gallant defence has now been chronicled. For these we have to thank his nephew,—grandson of the great Samuel,—Mr. John Henry Rivett-Carnac, B.C.S., C.I.E., who, as if destined to remain associated with a city which gave his family immortality, is at present (1887) opium agent at Benares. Sir John Davis is now a venerable statesman, of ninety-two. His father was F.R.S. some twenty years before himself, and furnished a "Memoir" on Hindu astronomy, which was printed in the *Philosophical Transactions.* He has no written memoir of his father; but we are reminded that he was attaché as a young man to Captain Turner's Embassy to Thibet, and was not allowed to proceed on account of his skill in drawing, which excited jealousy and suspicion. He was afterwards Accountant-General at Calcutta. Sir John never having kept any diary during his long and eventful life is a matter of great regret to many true friends; for his early experiences in China would be valuable and interesting. Lady Davis entertained the hope, during the long winter evenings, of being able to take notes of her distinguished husband's experiences and reminiscences; for Sir John's memory is still wonderfully good. Such an eminent nonagenarian is not often to be found in English biography. Sir John's most popular work is "The Chinese: A General Description of China and its Inhabitants,"*—replete with information, research, and common sense, regarding the flowery land and the ever-wonderful and energetic Celestials.

* In three volumes, of which a new popular edition, enlarged and revised, was published by Charles Knight in 1844.

NOTES.

I.—The Domestic Thermopylæ.

"I examined the staircase that leads to the top of the house, and which Mr. Davis defended with a spear for upwards of an hour and a half, till the troops came to his relief. It is of a singular construction, in the corner of a room, and built entirely of wood on a base of about four feet. The ascent is consequently so winding and rapid that with difficulty one person can get up at a time. Fortunately, also, the last turn by which you reach the terrace faces the wall. It was impossible, therefore, to take aim at him while he defended the ascent with a spear; they, however, fired several times, and the marks of the balls are visible in the ceiling. A man had at one time hold of his spear, but by a violent exertion he dragged it through his hand, and wounded him severely. This gallant defence saved the settlement, as it gave time for the cavalry, which were quartered at Beetabur, about ten miles from Benares, to reach Secrole, and oblige Vizier Ali to retire with his followers to his residence in Mahdoo Doss's garden."—Lord Valentia, vol. i. p. 108.

II.—Lord Wellesley and the Defender.

Lord Wellesley, who was Governor-General of India at the period of the insurrection of Benares, but absent for the time on a visit to Madras, subsequently expressed his sense of the defence made by Mr. Davis in a letter, wherein he attributed the safety of the English residents, and the salvation of the city from pillage, to the "successful issue," as his lordship termed it, "of that arduous trial of his prudence, activity and resolution." The subsequent removal of that gentleman to Calcutta, the seat of supreme government, to fill offices of higher trust and importance, led to a personal friendship, which lasted through life, and was acknowledged by Lord Wellesley, shortly before his death, in a copy of the five volumes of his official despatches, which that distinguished statesman sent to the widow of his late friend, with this autograph inscription (*see* page 75 of Sir John Davis' "Short History"): "To Mrs. Davis, as a testimony of sincere respect and regard; and also a memorial of attachment, founded upon long intimacy, to the honourable and virtuous memory of her deceased husband; from her faithful friend and servant,—Wellesley."

GENERAL SIR ROBERT J. H. VIVIAN, G.C.B.

—o—

THERE are few better examples to be found of a sterling Anglo-Indian's military career than that exhibited by the late General Sir Robert Vivian, G.C.B.*

In him we have an admirable specimen of one of the old East India Company's Officers. He was born in 1802; and, having been educated at Burney's École Militaire, obtained a Cadetship in the Madras Army at the age of sixteen. He went out to India with the determination to work his way in his profession, and to seize every opportunity of seeing service. He had not long to wait for the gratification of his wishes. When the first Burmese War broke out, in 1824, his regiment, the 18th M.N.I., was ordered to Burma, and he was actively engaged during the two years' campaign which followed. He was present at the fall and occupation of Rangoon, the assault of various stubborn stockades, especially Kemmendine, and at the attack on and capture of the stockades of Thantabain, the attacks on the lines at Rangoon, where he was wounded, the action of Kokain, the capture of Timbike, the storming of Malown and the battle of Pagammew. Wherever there was fighting to do or enterprises to attempt, we may be sure young Vivian was a ready volunteer. After this activity there was a lull. His regiment returned to Madras, and the ordinary duties of a regimental officer occupied his attention. We hear of no particular service until 1841, when having obtained his majority he commanded a small force which captured the Fort of Nipanee, held by a

* For nearly all the particulars we are much indebted to a distinguished Anglo-Indian.

body of insurgent Arabs. For the part he took on this occasion he received the thanks of the Commander-in-Chief, and of the Government. Under the strict seniority system of the East India Company's Army promotion was generally slow, while the duties and responsibilities of the officers were, from the nature of the service and the conditions of the country, of a higher and more onerous character than those usually performed by officers in the Queen's service. The training and early experience thus gained had the effect of making the Indian officer ready of resource and fearless of responsibility. Having passed with credit and distinction through the various grades of his regiment, of which he had been Adjutant, Colonel Vivian was appointed Adjutant-General of the Madras Army in 1849, and held the post until 1854. His services in this capacity showed that his military and administrative qualities were of a high order; and when an officer was required to take the command of a force of 20,000 Ottoman troops, which had been placed at the disposal of the British Government, by the Sultan, to act as a contingent to the Allied Army in the Crimea, he was selected for the post by H.M.'s Government, on the recommendation of the Court of Directors of the East India Company. In accordance with the usual custom of those days, General Vivian was entertained at a banquet* by the Court of Directors before his departure. The Prime Minister, Lord Palmerston, attended on the occasion, and there were also present the Duke of Argyll, Lord Panmure, then Minister for War, the Turkish Ambassador, Lord Vivian, General Sir George Pollock, and many other distinguished persons. Colonel Oliphant, the Chairman of the day, presided, and when proposing General Vivian's health announced that, within three days after it had become known that the Turkish contingent was to be formed, and that Vivian had been appointed to the command, 200 officers had volunteered to serve. "The service," he added, "into which they enter is one of no ordinary character, and requires talents of a peculiar description. The troops they were to command differ from them in language and in customs; but H.M.'s

* On the 10th March, 1855.

Government have selected a Commander for this service in whom the gallant men who have volunteered have every trust and confidence that he will ably, zealously, and faithfully perform the task he has undertaken." M. Musurus, the Turkish Ambassador, on the same occasion made the following graceful allusion to the mutual confidence, which he knew would subsist, between officers and men in the force. "J'ai la certitude que, de même que les soldats Ottomans s'estimeront heureux d'avoir été confiés à la direction et aux soins d'un si brave général, de même le général sera fier d'avoir commandé des troupes si valeureuses."

Among those who served with him were Colonel Crewe, the Adjutant-General of the force; Colonel Neill, who afterwards gained undying renown for his energy and valour during the Mutiny; Lieutenant-Colonel Brett, of the 11th Hussars; and Major (now General Sir Frederick) Goldsmid, K.C.S.I., C.B. Colonel (afterwards Sir Edward) Wetherall, K.C.B., was Vivian's Quartermaster-General. Colonel John (afterwards Sir John) Michael, K.C.B., was also with him; and Captain (now Sir John) Lukes, R.E., K.C.B., had command of the Royal Engineers.

It is unnecessary now to discuss the question which was raised at the time, as to whether General Vivian was the fittest man for the command in question. The result fully justified the choice. But so also did his antecedents. The general orders by the Commander-in-Chief, and by the Governor in Council at Madras, on his resignation of the appointment of adjutant-general, exceeded the usual complimentary notice, dwelling on the zeal and ability with which the duties of the office had been discharged, and distinctly pointing him out as an officer who should be entrusted with high command on some future occasion. The earnest hope was expressed "that should Colonel Vivian return to India, an early opportunity may occur for his re-employment in some situation in which his superior military qualifications may be made of still further use to the State and to the army, of which he is so distinguished a member." The sympathy of the outside world was also not wanting. "The late Adjutant-General," said a local paper, "had the rare faculty of making friends of all with whom he came in contact; and whilst he upheld the discipline of the army, he never forgot that private soldiers were his countrymen, and his brother officers his equals." In February, 1855, when a discussion took place in the House of Lords, in consequence of some remarks made by Lord Ellenborough on the subject of his appointment, Lord Panmure bore testimony to his qualifications, and thus alluded to his training: "In early life, while connected with the Indian Army, no man in his position in the subaltern or inferior ranks of the army ever displayed more courage, or a more gallant bearing on the plains of India, than did Major-General Vivian."

The Turkish contingent was formed under a convention between Her Majesty and the Sultan, for the employment of a number of Turkish troops in the British service, one object being "to give the Sultan the advantage of our greater skill and larger pecuniary means in forming and training a force for the defence of his dominions."* General Vivian and his staff proceeded at once to Constantinople, and arrived there on the 11th April, 1855, but unforeseen delays occurred in the formation of the contingent, owing to many of the troops which were intended for the force having been suddenly and unexpectedly summoned by Omar Pasha to the seat of war. The disappointment was great, and the patience of the British commander was sorely tried. The Turkish authorities professed anxiety to remedy the state of affairs, but were not rapid in their movements. Their first proposition was to recall a certain number of the troops sent to Omar Pasha, but H.M.'s Government did not feel justified in encouraging any step which might weaken the force at the seat of war. It was considered preferable to withdraw troops from the army of the Danube; and this having been done, the contingent was formed, and encamped a few miles from Constantinople, at the head of the Bosphorus. The desire of the General and his staff was to join the army at Sebastopol, and to be in the thick of the fray; but this was not their destiny: and in June the contingent was ordered to take possession of Kertch. The position was an

* Lord Granville.

important one, commanding as it does the entrance to the Sea of Azof, and stretching along the coast for a length of about ten miles, with a fortress at each end. At this time the contingent consisted of about 14,000 Ottoman troops, obtained from different sources, and with various degrees of military training and experience, together with a detachment of the 10th Hussars and 700 men of H.M.'s 71st Highlanders, a few Chasseurs d'Afrique, and some French Marines. Its attitude during the year it occupied Kertch was one of watchfulness and defence. It was not opposed when it seized the peninsula; it fought no battle when in occupation, and had no opportunity of being engaged in any serious action. Only once was it threatened with an attack by the Russians; and on that occasion an officer, Captain Sherwood, who had been sent to reconnoitre, met his death in a skirmish. The enemy retired, and no further attempt to attack was made. The force was steady, and discipline and contentment were preserved. The skill, however, of Vivian, as a general in command of an army in the field, was not put to the test. But his tact and judgment under very difficult circumstances were fully tried, and he maintained his character as an able commander and administrator. At the conclusion of the war Kertch was evacuated, and restored to the Russians on the 22nd June, when an exchange of courtesies between British and Russians took place, the Russian band accompanying the English troops to the port of embarkation.

On his return to England, General Vivian was appointed a Knight Commander of the Bath, and was nominated a Director of the East India Company by the Queen. In 1858, when the Government of India was transferred from the East India Company to the Crown, Sir Robert Vivian was appointed a Member of the Council of the Secretary of State for India. In this position he took an active part as an adviser in military matters, and was subsequently appointed Chairman of the Military Committee of the Council. His old friend, General Sir Thomas Pears, was Military Secretary at the India Office, and the two worked earnestly and cordially together. The first very important question which had to be considered after the abolition of the East India

Company, was the discontinuance of the local Indian army as a separate force from the Queen's army. There were, of course, reasons for and against the measure. Besides being a question of military organization, it involved important financial and political considerations. Hitherto India had maintained her own army and her own military system, which had been supplemented by regiments of cavalry and of the line from the Queen's army, according to the requirements of the time, as signified by the Government of India. It was agreed that, by amalgamating the two armies, and placing the directing and controlling power exclusively in the hands of the military authorities in this country, the interests of India might suffer. The Indian Council, which included such men as Sir John (afterwards Viceroy of India and Lord) Lawrence, Sir H. Durand, Sir James Hogg, Sir H. Rawlinson, Sir Bartle Frere, and Mr. Pollard Willoughby, were opposed to the abolition of the local army, and Sir Robert Vivian joined them in strenuously endeavouring to preserve it. It is unnecessary now to discuss the question. It is sufficient to say that the decision of the highest power in the land was that there should be no separate Indian army; and this conclusion having been arrived at, Sir Robert Vivian loyally exerted himself, with other competent men, to carry out the best arrangements for securing as thoroughly efficient a system as could be established. The result was the creation of an Indian Staff Corps, and a system of reliefs. There are some who still regret the change; but many who opposed it are ready to acknowledge that their fears were exaggerated, and that the abolition of the local army was the inevitable consequence of the demise of the old glorious and munificent East India Company. Sir Robert continued in the Council till 1875, taking a warm interest in all Indian affairs, and a leading part in those relating to the Army. He then retired into private life. Successive Secretaries of State acknowledged the value of his advice, and the important services which he had rendered. He was once, we believe, offered the command of the Bombay army, but felt it his duty to decline. He was promoted to the rank of General in 1870, and in 1871 was appointed a Knight Grand Cross of the Bath.

He had been a keen sportsman all his life, and advancing age did not prevent his enjoying a day's shooting. On one occasion, some fifteen years before his death, a shot from a companion's gun glanced from a tree, and piercing the pupil of the eye, destroyed the sight; but he would not allow the day's sport to be interfered with; nor was he deterred from enjoying his favourite recreation in subsequent seasons, although cataract had formed in the other eye. After his retirement he lived for a few years at Torquay. Here he and Lady Vivian went through severe family troubles, losing their only daughter and a sailor son. They afterwards transferred their residence to Brighton, where he died on the 3rd May, 1887, at the age of eighty-five, within four days after the death of his wife, which event no doubt accelerated his own. Husband and wife were buried at the same time, in the same grave with their children at Torquay.

It has been seen that, although as a subaltern, Sir Robert Vivian was in many engagements, as a general officer he never had the opportunity of commanding an army in the field of battle; but he showed both in India and in the Crimea that he had all the qualities necessary for high military command, and that he was a worthy successor of his distinguished relative.* Strict as a disciplinarian, he had warm sympathies and a keen perception of character. Prompt to decide, he was quick to act, and his judgment was usually clear; but, if he found that it had been formed hastily, or from imperfect information, nobody was more ready to acknowledge that he had been mistaken and to correct the error. Generous, open-hearted, and naturally possessing high spirits, he was in private life a genial companion and a warm friend. The better he was known, the more he was beloved; and he died leaving many life-long friends.

Truly, a noble military career; a really useful, not, as is too often the case, a merely ornamental retirement; and the close—in shorter periods of existence no uncommon occur-

* Lord Vivian—Sir Richard Hussey, who served with distinction under Wellington at Waterloo.

rence—after such an eventful life's long day, darkened by family troubles.

Considering what he must have gone through, the age of eighty-five, which he attained, must be thought wonderful. In Sir Robert Vivian, a healthy mind ever assisted the vigorous and energetic body; and work for good, in some way or other, would appear to have been the guiding star of his long and, in some respects, brilliant term of service. One can imagine the General saying, on his retirement, "I have done all that I came into this world to do. I have worked task-work, and have the rest of the day to myself."* Even with the rest of the day to himself, it is the nature of a genuine, worthy Anglo-Indian never to be idle. Thus he has rightly learned to live. "Up and doing," chiefly in sunny climes, with him heroism occasionally becomes linked with longevity, from the early time, or, as with the subject of our sketch, from the beardless ensign of sixteen, down to the gallant and highly-respected General of eighty-five!

* *Essays of Elia.*

GENERAL JOHN REID BECHER, C.B., R.E.

—o—

It is pleasing to an author when he can rest assured that a sketch to which he invites general attention will be a favourite one with the public; and in the present instance he most decidedly feels this assurance. Here we have "real" and "earnest" life in the highest sense. There are men whose lives should be recorded, less perhaps as a pious debt to their own memory, than as a valuable and suggestive pattern to those who come after them. This may truly be said of the brave and conscientious officer over whom the grave closed on the 11th July, 1884, and whose whole career was characterized by a noble and uncompromising sense of duty. His father was Colonel George Becher, who served many years with honour in India, and left ten sons, all of whom (excepting two who died young) followed their father's vocation. John Reid Becher, the eighth of these, was a born soldier, and entered with true martial spirit into his future career. When leaving for India, a mere boy fresh from Addiscombe, he remarked to a young companion, "You'll hear of me one of these days left slain on the field of glory;" and his prediction was very nearly verified, for he *was* left at Sobraon, if not "slain," with a bullet through his cheek, resulting in the gain of an honourable scar (which he carried to his grave) such as embellishes and not disfigures a soldier's face.* Whether as a subaltern or a commander, in a military, judicial, or diplomatic capacity, John Becher was always found true to himself and to his

* "Paint me as I am!" said Cromwell to Sir Peter Lely; "if thou leavest out a single scar, I will not pay thee one penny."

traditions; always bringing to bear on the work committed to him, of whatever nature, all the force of his energies and all the discrimination of his shrewd intelligence and unprejudiced judgment, with an alacrity and courage, determination and perseverance, the outcome of a disinterested and noble character. His public dealings were directed by the calm, temperate, and matured decisiveness of a well-balanced mind; he was severe with no one but himself, and in the relations of private life, if his heart was tender and forbearing, it was also as true as steel and as generous as true. No wonder, then, that he won not only the fast and enduring friendship of the most distinguished of his brother officers, but the unreserved confidence of the highest in office, and so endeared himself to those under whom he served, that he remained till their respective deaths, equally the friend of Lord and of Sir Henry Lawrence. Such men would probably give precedence to military virtues over social qualities; at the same time there is no doubt that to them, as to others, the freshness and originality of his mind, and the vigorous independence of his opinions, the natural purity of his taste and cultivated appreciation of literature and art, joined to a peculiar simplicity and charm of manner, were irresistibly attractive. From the time he received his commission in the Bengal Engineers, in 1838, to that when nearly thirty years later a terrible attack of fever absolutely compelled him to abandon his labours, service in India was no sinecure; and of the many brave fellows who devoted themselves to the complicated interests of their country in that trying climate, he was one of the most indefatigable, and also of the most modest as to his own value. Among his many and varied services, he took part in the campaign in 1842 in Afghanistan, assisted at the forcing of the Khyber Pass by his uncle, Sir George Pollock, for which he received the medal; and four years later, he was actively engaged in the Sutlej Campaign, fighting at Sobraon, where, as already stated, he was severely wounded, and received the medal and clasp.

In 1854 he succeeded Major (afterwards General and C.B.) James Abbott in the civil and military charge of

Huzára, under Sir Henry Lawrence; and in 1857, during the Mutiny Campaign, his services and operations against the mutineers at Huzára, and also on the Eusofzai (Yusufzai) frontier were mentioned in the despatches. Besides these and other valuable war services, John Becher was (some time after the first Sikh War) actively employed in civil positions of difficulty and trust, having been appointed Boundary Commissioner to settle the frontier between Bekaneer (Bikaner) and other states; and, eventually, when Colonel James (Sir Herbert Edwardes's successor) left Pesháwar, he was advisedly selected to succeed him in his important duties there as Commissioner. Though the frequent mention of John Becher was necessarily inevitable in Bosworth Smith's what has been styled "magnificent biography," or "Life of Lord Lawrence," with whose work and whose pre-occupations as Governor-General he was so intimately and confidentially associated, it has, according to one of Becher's truest friends, been remarked by many practically conversant with the details of that period of British Indian history, that "scarcely the barest justice has been done him in these volumes, to the information in which, however, he largely contributed; they afford no idea of the responsible and anxious share which fell to his lot, nor of the valuable help he was able to give throughout to the Governor-General." And the same eloquent authority concludes in the following strain:—"We are justified in adding, that wherever the history of British India is read, the name of Becher will be found largely intermingled with its annals, and more than one of the gallant officers who have illustrated that honourable name has deserved well of his country." General Becher never recovered his health after his return from India in an apparently dying state. Brighton was his favourite resort, and he only left it for Southampton to be temporarily near his greatest friend, General Sir Neville Chamberlain. He was brought through several serious illnesses by the persevering care of his brothers. In the last, which caused him seven weeks of intense suffering, no human skill or care could avail, though his three brothers (General Sir Arthur, Septimus, and

Colonel Decimus William Becher) watched him with unremitting devotedness; and his career of simple and unobtrusive purposefulness terminated on the 9th of July. The brief and pathetic epitaph, more eloquent than pages of panegyric, on the gravestone of his "most approved master and friend," as he was wont to call Sir Henry Lawrence, epitomizes the history of John Becher's life—

"HE TRIED TO DO HIS DUTY." *

In truth, this single word DUTY is the mainspring of *real* distinction in the history of the British in India: it is the precious jewel which has given England an undying name among nations; and, so often well performed, it is the true source of her wealth and grandeur.

To the foregoing brief yet faithful memoir of a distinguished and admirable Anglo-Indian, we shall now add, with a few details, various remarks on, and give some interesting extracts from, an excellent and instructive pamphlet which has been presented to us by a valued and accomplished lady-friend of the departed General.† The brochure ‡ is entitled: "A Sketch of the Career of General John Reid Becher, C.B., of the Royal Engineers (Bengal). By an Old Friend and Brother Officer." This is followed up by a most appropriate stanza from Spenser's *Faerie Queene*, which, being applicable to so many noble and heroic subjects of the Queen-Empress, who have lived and died for India, we make no apology for quoting:—

"He was there knight, ne was there lady found
In Faerie Court, but him did deare embrace
For his fair usage and conditions sound:
The which in all men's liking gayned place,
And with the greatest purchast greatest grace:
Which he could wisely use, and well apply,
To please the best, and th' evill to embase;
For he loath'd leasing and base flattery,
And loved simple truth and stedfast honesty."—

* *See* also "Sketches," First Series, Sir Henry Lawrence, page 17.

† To this lady we are mainly indebted for the previous memorial.

‡ Printed for private circulation, 1884.

No wonder, after such a power of graphic description, Southey told Rogers, the "banker-poet," that he had read Spenser through about *thirty* times!

And now let us accompany the modest, amiable, and accomplished author who is "going to try," while sketching Becher's career, to set forth "the events in which he took a part, and the part itself which he played," which "were both distinguished." General Becher's biographer, however, evidently wishes us to keep well in mind that the subject demands "the portrait of a character rather than a narrative of events." Too little of the former, and an excess of the latter, are frequently unavoidable among the biographical craft.

John Reid Becher was born at sea in 1819. His father, Colonel John Becher, belonged to the Bengal Cavalry; and eight out of his ten sons entered various branches of the East India Company's service. John was brought up by an uncle at Chancellor's House, Tunbridge Wells, "well-known still as having been inhabited by Judge Jeffreys." He was partly educated at Bruce Castle—a school of which the famous Sir Rowland Hill, of Post-Office celebrity, was one of the originators. He entered Addiscombe early in 1836, and passed out at the end of 1837, "the head of the largest team (sixty-five in number) ever known at that Institution." To give an idea of how "grudgingly" Engineers' commissions were given in those days, it may be noted that only two cadets out of the sixty-five entered the great scientific corps—the remaining brain-power certainly not being equitably distributed in the way of commissions for the Artillery—sister scientific branch—Cavalry and Infantry. The Company's Engineer cadet at Chatham, fifty years ago, was accidentally treated with a slight disrespect, as to his title or rank; for there he was styled a "local and temporary ensign," instead of being a second-lieutenant like his Royal brother. The modesty of the greatest trading and political Company the world ever saw (or ever will see) in so dubbing their most scientific men, while going through the practical course of their profession, almost reminds one of an Ordnance aspirant, when officers were scarce in India, being styled Acting Temporary

Deputy Assistant Commissary! Colonel (afterwards General Sir Charles) Pasley, on being remonstrated with by the writer of the sketch on the above inequality of local rank, with a usual gesture, and after "a minute's pondering," replied: "Well! I don't remember what the reason was, but I have no doubt it was a very good reason."* It may now be mentioned that, out of the sixty-five cadets of Becher's term, "the best known to Indian fame, besides himself, were Sir Arnold Kemball, William Anderson, whose touching death, along with Vans Agnew at Mooltan, was the signal of the war that ended in the annexation of the Punjab, William Mayne, the great *sabreur* of Jellalabad and the Sutlej, and James Travers, who died recently General and V.C." The Indian officers at Chatham were Turnbull, Alfred Godwyn, Becher, Alexander, Yule, Boileau. Of these six the author of the biographical sketch under notice alone survives. This writer's own "most valued friend of over five-and-forty years, Major-General T. B. Collinson," Becher's former "closest friend and associate at Chatham," writes to him concerning the "loved and lost," after the funeral, showing, as his accomplished biographer observes, "how our impressions of young Becher coincide":—"My knowledge of Becher (intimate knowledge), as you know, was confined to those early days; but I feel as if I knew him as well as if we had been together all our lives. I suppose the real character of a man comes out in those early days, though we do not perceive it at the time; or perhaps he and I understood each other better than most do. But every one of his contemporaries at Chatham admired and respected Becher. His lively spirit, his frank and genial nature, his simple open character, his great intelligence and imagination, and his thoroughly innocent and gentlemanly

* This was Pasley to the life. There was something very genuine about this gifted Royal Engineer, who did so much good service at home for the East India Company. The author of this work recollects, when studying fortification (as a direct Artillery cadet) at Chatham, examination-day at length arrived (5th November, 1841); and, after praising our work, and a rough pen-and-ink sketch of Louis Quatorze, he said to us, as if thinking of his favourite Royal George, as well as the Plot: "Now, you are all blown up, and sent forth to-day!"

ways, made every one of us, of all sorts and characters, wish to be his friend and companion. Not one who was there then but would always remember with pleasure his lithesome figure and bright expressive face, crowned with the golden hair."

Regarding some play-acting—nothing better in the life of a soldier to "drive dull care away"—General Collinson also writes:—"When we perpetrated the enormity of acting these plays in the absence of our guide and ruler, I believe it was very much the winning character as well as the clever performance of our two leading artists, Becher and Tylden,* that softened the practical heart of Pasley when he came to hear of it." The biographer's sketch of Becher is even more pleasing than that of General Collinson, which is saying a great deal:—"He was from boyhood one of the most winning of mankind. He was an accomplished amateur artist; but he had gifts far more rare. Even as a cadet at Addiscombe, and as a 'local and temporary ensign' (think of that!) there was in him a gaiety, a brilliancy, a play of fancy in his conversation, which attracted men and women equally, and which, in combination with his bright, chivalrous aspect, his open blue eye, and silken hair of ruddy gold, have left on me an impression of Becher as he was in youth, absolutely unique in its kind; whilst the charm of his society and his sweet nature only grew with time, and the old impression constantly recurred during our too rare meetings in his later years."

Becher reached India in October, 1839, and joined the headquarters of the Bengal Sappers at Delhi. He did not at first take kindly to Indian life. In October, 1841, he was ordered to proceed "to Firozpur, then our frontier station in the N.W." His detachment was probably intended to join the "Kabul garrison"; and it was hastened across the Punjab, with Wild's brigade of Native Infantry, which Mr. Clerk (the Governor-General's agent on that frontier) "took on himself to start off at once for Peshâwar." Those were

* Like Collinson, a young Royal Engineer officer at Chatham, Tylden, as Brevet-Colonel and C.B., died from wounds received in the assault of the Redan at Sebastopol, 18th June, 1855.

not times for standing "upon the order of going"—which has frequently caused so much disaster in our civil and military administration, East and West. No one understood this better than the "still surviving in honour," Sir George Clerk, G.C.B., after having been twice Governor of Bombay, and once Governor of the Cape, and who then, "and throughout the imperial crisis which ensued, showed himself a diplomatist of the true English stamp—undaunted in difficulties, and resolute to maintain the honour of his country." * Such are the truly distinguished men for England, of whom she has sent so many to India, who, fearless of responsibility, in a great crisis, or in troublous times, resolve to act, or "go at once!" Wild's brigade was accompanied by Henry Lawrence as political officer; and two better men at this anxious time for India than Clerk and Lawrence it is impossible to conceive. And no doubt here John Becher first caught the glorious infection from the ever-ready-to-act-school of politicals. "Job's messengers in quick succession met the brigade as it crossed the plains of the Punjab; their tidings culminating after its arrival at Pesháwar (28th December), in the news of the murder of the envoy, Sir W. Macnaghten, and in the convention with his murderers." The insurrection at Cabul and murder of Sir Alexander Burnes had taken place nearly two months before (2nd November, 1841).† It is now stated:—"The utmost that was then contemplated by the high authorities in India was to facilitate the retirement of Sale's brigade from Jalálábád, and of the survivors of the Cabul force." Only a few artillery details, but no guns, were with Wild; and these were to be "petitioned from the Sikhs at Pesháwar." The Sikh gunners, like true artillerymen, would not allow their pieces to be lent to the English, with whose projects and prowess they were as yet imperfectly acquainted. Eventually, Henry Lawrence got four old guns out of them—probably one or two of them honey-combed, and as

* Sir H. B. Edwardes, in his "Life of Sir Henry Lawrence," quoted by Becher's biographer.—For Sir George's "Services," *see* First Series of "Sketches," p. 387.

† *See* also "Sketches," First Series, Sir Alexander Burnes, p. 14.

dangerous to the gunners as to their enemies. Then, according to Becher, the Sikh troops "strode insolently among our tents, and derisively asked our Eastern soldiers if they ever expected to return from the darkness of those passes." From this delay at Pesháwar, within view of "the jaws of the Khyber," it is said, dates the first symptoms of "that evil infection" among the British sepoys which came to a climax in 1857.

It should be mentioned that, at first, General Avitabile, a Neapolitan, the Governor under the Maharaja, was willing to help, but "he dared not *order* against the will of his troops." The introduction of this military adventurer's name gives Becher's biographer—ever ready to catch hold of something of interest for his readers—an opportunity of sketching his character from the materials at hand :—"Avitabile's apparent good-will to our people, and his open hospitality to the officers gathering at Pesháwar, obtained for him a more favourable character than he deserved; he was a strong and able man, but a ruffian of the first water." Becher says, "I was asked to a grand entertainment by General Avitabile, an Italian in the service of the Sikh Government, shrewd, and the only man who can control the very rebellious population, made up of Afghans, Khyberries, and a thousand other unruly tribes. He is a very monster, making nothing of hanging men without trial, or of the most cruel tortures, and is, besides, a complete satyr."—(*Letter to Collinson*, dated Jellalabad, May 12th, 1842.)

Of this man Edwardes writes: "More than once has the author heard citizens of Pesháwar tell how a follower, who had insulted some inmate of the General's harem, was forthwith ordered to be hurled down from the top of a minaret. The wretch was hurled, but halfway down caught hold of a projecting cornice, and thence screamed aloud to Avitabile for 'Mercy, for the sake of God!' Avitabile, unmoved, replied, 'God may have mercy on you if He likes, but I'll have none. Throw him off the ledge!'"—(Life of Sir Henry Lawrence, vol. i. p. 292.)

After such an awful scene, so repugnant to civilized views of human nature, our readers will perhaps not be angry with us if, leaving the subject of our sketch, we detain them a little longer at this stage to listen to an anecdote of what happened some years before the Sikh invasion of British India (1845–46), which we take from a first-rate narrative of that momentous event in our Indian history, furnished to the *Calcutta Review* by Sir Herbert Edwardes,*—an anecdote in its very wildness fully illustrative of those eventful and unruly times:—General Avitabile, whose character and habits have been drawn to the life in the pages of "The Adventurer in the Punjab," had a daughter (the child of some favourite beauty in his harem) on whom he doted. He brought her up and watched over her with jealous care, in a cloister-like building which may still be seen in the garden of the general's house, now occupied by Colonel Courtlandt. Here she spent the years of her youth, and grew up a lovely girl. So carefully was all access to her guarded, that even her meals were conveyed to her from without by means of a *tour*, such as are used at convent gates. The very shadow of a man had never crossed the threshold of her retreat. And for what high and romantic destiny does the reader think this fair recluse was reserved? Does he picture to himself some young Sikh warrior, who had heard the tale, crouching solitarily, night after night, among the roses beneath the windows of her prison, and singing in low, melting voice the charms of liberty and love, until she forgot her father, and fled with her lover to his fort? Does he hear that shout for "a horse and sword!" and see those fifty iron cavaliers spurring madly after one who seems to press a damsel to his broad breast and bid her be not afraid? The old leader of the fifty, far, far in front, with grey hair streaming in the wind, and his Italian eyes lit up with the prospect of revenge,

* Number XI., Sept. 1846. In the *second* and *third* numbers of this famous *Review*, on which its founder, Sir John Kaye, expended so much time and talent, Sir Henry Lawrence described the rise and progress of the Sikh power. In the *eleventh*, the reviewer, Sir Herbert Edwardes, had to tell of its "decline and fall."—At this period the *Calcutta* boasted some great names among its contributors, such as Drs. Marshman and Duff (for some time Editor), the Rev. Thomas Smith, Sir Henry Lawrence, Sir Herbert Edwardes, and others of less note.

comes nearer at every bound. The gallant beast on which the young warrior rides sinks deep into the sand at every step beneath his double burden; but, mad with the spur, still staggers on. But fifty yards, and the Raví is gained. The old man draws his sword. It flashes in the moonlight, bright, cold and merciless as him who wields it. Not a word is spoken; there is not time to curse or pray; not a horse's length between pursuer and pursued; and ten yards further to the river. The old man strikes his heel into his horse; they are together; his left hand drops the reins, and reaches out greedily towards the foe; his right is in the air; another moment and—a scream—a plunge—they have missed the ford;—the young warrior and the old man's daughter are deep beneath the swift waters of the Raví!—Is this, we say, our reader's dream of Avitabile and his daughter? Alas for Romance! Alas, too, for *fact! he married her to his cook*—a young Mahomedan, to whom he also gave with her a large dowry of money, jewels and precious stones. Time passed on; Avitabile had returned to Europe to receive a jewelled sword from the Honourable East India Company, and many honours from the Kings and Princes of the civilized world. The cook and his bride had sunk into private life; wishing for nothing more than to be left in quiet to enjoy their wealth. But they lived in times when the Government being poor, it was *lèse Majesté* in a subject to be rich. To hunt out traitors of this kind, and confiscate their property, was a favourite branch of Pundit Julla's administration. The story of our little heroine and her culinary spouse, therefore, soon reached his ears, and excited his cupidity. In the service of General Avitabile there had been a Kashmir Brahman, named Jodha Ram. He was a handsome, dark-featured man, with ability enough to rise to be the General's Dewan; in which capacity he continued for many years; and when Avitabile returned to Europe, succeeded to the command of his battalions, and became a general. By a sort of Punjab propriety he was now selected by the Minister as the fittest person to plunder his patron's daughter; and the Pundit seems not to have been mistaken in his man. The spoilt, petted, prisoned, ill-used daughter of Avitabile was stripped of her jewels and robbed of her riches. But retribution soon overtook the ungrateful servant. Pundit Julla was murdered, and Jowahir Singh sat in his place. Jodha Ram gave offence to the new Minister, and was given over to one of those cruel sentences which Runjit Singh was accustomed to call mercy.* But Jodha Ram was a Brahman, and no Hindu would do the deed which would secure to himself damnation through a hundred generations. The Kotwal of the City of Lahore,—a Mussulman, and no very particular person, who had for years been the municipal instrument of violence,—was therefore ordered to cut off the ears and nose of the wretched man. He too refused; and we blush to record that the only man in Lahore who could be found to execute the barbarous decree was a European. Mr. Gardener, or Gordana, in the Sikh Artillery, took a razor, and with his own hands, in cold blood, without personal enmity of any sort, inflicted the punishment which Sikhs, Hindus, and Mussulmans had shrunk from with disgust. But then he was made "*a Colonel*"; and, as Walpole observed, "Every man has his price. The only thing is to find it out."

We now return to Becher, who writes of Sir Henry Lawrence:—"At this time, although I was only a subaltern, and necessarily unacquainted with political arrangements, I used to meet Henry Lawrence, because the few artillery and engineer officers lived together, and he frequently joined our mess. We all recognized in him the leading man of the camp. He was always sanguine and ardent for an advance," to which all the Sepoys were equally averse. Becher also gives a capital account of the crisis among the Sepoys. Wild had determined that all the troops were to parade "to coerce these scoundrels."

The gunners got ready the Sikh cannon, and "we marched off, sappers and artillery." But Lawrence pre-

* "The culprits, bleeding as they were were driven out; 'Sharp work, Bellasis,' observed the King, as I looked after the mutilated thieves, 'We do not take life, but we punish.'"—"Adventurer in the Punjab," Chapter I. —In the end of 1839, Runjit Singh died, leaving a Kingdom formed by himself, and kept together solely by his talents and energy.

vented the mutineers from being blown to pieces, and the next day they accepted their pay. Becher had thus a grand lesson—probably his first—in moderation from a great military political. His biographer now gives vent to the following eloquent remark, calling back our attention to the immortal Gordon at Khartoum. "All this time Sale was calling for relief, and vainly fancying every day it was coming—much as a greater than Sale is doing now (1884) on the Upper Nile."

At length the Afridis attacked Ali Masjid (now a pass well known to our readers), and Wild determined to advance. After what Becher styles, in his letter to Collinson (May, 1842), "a fearful example not to divide a small force," produced by a retreat, a return, and a numerous list of casualties, it was "judiciously resolved to wait for a larger force, as the garrison of Jalálábad could hold out." On the 6th February, General Pollock—the renowned Bengal gunner, afterwards Field Marshal, and our hero's uncle by marriage—arrived at Pesháwar. The advance was soon made with a splendid force. Lieut. Becher on this grand march to Jalálábad was prominently brought to the notice of Government for the very essential services rendered by him as Field Engineer in clearing passes of impediments with wonderful alacrity, "notwithstanding their strength and difficulty of removal," eliciting the warmest admiration of the General. But Major (afterwards Sir) Frederick Abbott, and another senior officer joined at Jalálábad, thus superseding the young engineer; however, as remarked by his biographer, "there was no special work for them in the further advance to Kabul." Yet Becher was well to the front, and most honourably mentioned. After the return of the army he was employed on occasional surveys, and as an Engineer of Public Works—very different occupations from the dreams of martial youth at Chatham, which painted the glories to be achieved by carrying out the famous plans of engineers greater than Pasley or Burgoyne, such as Vauban, and Cormontaigne. During the year 1844, while his biographer and brother-officer was leading "a very solitary life on the West Jumna Canals," he was rejoiced by a visit from Becher, and "his delightful talk left a pleasant aroma behind for days after." Truly there is a brotherhood in the army—especially in a country like India—which may droop or fade a little, but can never die. Sometimes a friendship springs up which lasts, and travels beyond the grave. After what is forcibly styled "two years of seething restlessness beyond the Sutlej," came the passage of that "quasi-frontier" by the Sikh legions—the Sikh invasion of British India, already alluded to—and the "battles of Moodkee and Firozshah, succeeded by a general sweep of engineers from roads, canals, and plaster to the front." Becher arrived with his friend, Major F. Abbott, at the headquarters before Sobraon; "and on the memorable 10th of February, 1846, he was joined with Captain Baker (the late Sir William Baker, of dear and honourable memory) in conducting the leading attack by Sir Robert Dick's division." A way had been at length forced into the Sikh intrenchment; but now a serious check occurrèd; "and," writes his biographer, "whilst Becher, with others, was rallying the troops he received a severe wound from a bullet in the left cheek and mouth. His gallant conduct on this great occasion was honourably mentioned in the Commander-in-Chief's despatches; and in the G. O. of the Governor-General—the renowned hero of Albuera—Sir Henry (afterwards Viscount) Hardinge, who says:—"To Captain Baker and Lieut. Becher, of the Engineers, the G. G.'s acknowledgments are due for leading the division of attack into the enemy's camp. These officers well maintain the reputation of their corps whenever gallantry and science may be required of it." If ever true and eloquent words were written, here they are; for, throughout our most important Indian Campaigns, the science and bravery of the Engineers have gone hand-in-hand together.

Becher's glorious scar has been alluded to in the introductory sketch. "The honourable mark of Sobraon," his biographer now informs us, he "carried to his dying day; but it did not destroy the sight of an eye," as stated in the obituary notice. There is now an allusion to "the wounded man under a most hospitable roof at Firozpúr"—that of a friend and brother-officer, Lieut. Alfred Goodwyn, who had distinguished himself in the days preceding Firozsháh, and at the *Waterloo of India*, or the great battle there. "Not even a Sikh bullet in his mouth seemed capable of checking Becher's glee and fancy, though it certainly for a time impeded its utterance."

There were now three of the greatest Indian battles that had ever taken place for the friends to talk about—Moodkee,* Firozsháh, and Sobraon; the first and second having been fought on the 18th and 22nd December, 1845, respectively. Both of them well-read men, they probably alluded with the pride of Englishmen to perhaps the most striking passage in Napier's splendid "Military History," at Albuera, where, as Colonel Hardinge, the Governor-General had been so distinguished, when the rain flowed "in streams discoloured with blood, and eighteen hundred unwounded men, the remnant of six thousand unconquerable British soldiers, stood triumphant on the fatal hill."†

At Múdkí our loss was not nearly so severe as at the other battles. The grand total of killed and wounded was 872. Among the former was the brave General, Sir Robert Sale, known among the soldiers of his old regiment (H.M. 13th Light Infantry) as "Fighting Bob," and in the page of history as "the hero of Jallálábad." It may also be added, regarding this famous battle—fought just a week after the enemy crossed the Sutlej, and invaded British India—that the loss on the enemy's side has never yet been known. The Commander-in-Chief, Sir Hugh (afterwards Viscount) Gough, thought they brought into the field from 14,000 to 20,000 infantry, about the same force of cavalry, and forty guns. Sir Robert Peel estimated the Sikh force at "treble the amount" of the British; and this would make them upwards of 40,000. The late Sir Herbert Edwardes insisted on the fact that *the charge of the British Cavalry* was the turning point of the battle of Múdkí. The British loss in the battle of Ferozshah—or Firozsháh—was 694 killed, and 1,721 wounded; total, 2,415. "Foremost among the dead,"

* *See* "Distinguished Anglo-Indians," *First Series*, pp. 331-32,—the march, "a picture at Múdkí," &c.

† "History of the Peninsular War," Vol. III., p. 170.

wrote Edwardes, of one of the most distinguished Anglo-Indians that ever lived, "as he was ever foremost among the living, let us weep over GEORGE BROADFOOT, with whose life there left this earth one of the noblest spirits that ever lit upon it."

At Sobraon, on the side of the British there were killed 320, and wounded 2,063. Among the former was the gallant General, Sir Robert Dick, for some time officiating as Commander-in-Chief of the Madras Army, and a thoroughly good soldier.* At this famous battle, in which Becher distinguished himself, Sir Hugh Gough's plan of attack was as follows ; and it may be of interest to our brave Volunteers who have just (April 12th, 1887) been engaged in milder attacks in the well-managed but bloodless campaigns at Eastbourne, and near Dover.† The chief orders ran thus :—The heavy guns were to commence operations by a cannonade upon the entrenchment, into which, crowded as it was with upwards of 30,000 men, their fire was expected to carry confusion and dismay. Sir Robert Dick's division, on the extreme left of the British line, was then to advance and storm the right, or western corner of the Sikh position ; General Gilbert's (Sir Walter Raleigh) division on the centre, and Sir Harry Smith's on the right, were simultaneously to make false attacks, with the view of diverting the enemy's attention from the real attack of Sir Robert Dick. Brigadier Cureton, with a brigade of cavalry and a troop of Horse Artillery, was directed to threaten the fort of Hurrikí Puttan, about a mile distant from the eastern corner of the entrenchment, on the opposite bank of which the enemy's cavalry were posted. The battle fairly commenced about seven A.M., when the artillery opened. The attack was led by Brigadier Stacey with Her Majesty's 10th and 53rd Regiments,‡ sup-

* *See* also First Series of "Distinguished Anglo-Indians," p. 298.

† Nothing can be better for teaching the art of war than this annual working out a "general idea" of attacking an invading enemy. What would engineers or strategists like Pasley, Burgoyne, or De Jomini have said to this year's new feature in war—Cyclist Corps sending out their Cyclist scouts with advantage? Such a sight would certainly have startled the Sikhs at Sobraon.

‡ Also the 49th and 53rd N.I.

ported on the flanks by Colonel Lane's troop of Horse Artillery, and Captains Horseford and Fordyce's batteries. On one occasion their bridge having broken down, as graphically described by the Commander-in-Chief, in the Sikh "efforts to reach the right bank of the Sutlej, through the deepened water they suffered from our Horse Artillery a terrible carnage." At half-past ten o'clock A.M. "not a Sikh soldier was left alive upon the British bank of the Sutlej: and thus, in little more than four hours, was fought the bloodiest battle with the worthiest foe, and gained the *completest* victory recorded in our Eastern annals. *Thus ended also, in awful and disastrous tragedy, the Sikh Invasion of British India!*" There are few pictures of war grander than what it produced—hardly excepting those at Waterloo, "the battle of giants." It is impossible to admire too much the patriotism and determined courage of the Sikhs. As at Ferozshah, where the furious cannonade on both sides had such a deadly effect, the rapid discharges from the "red artillery," resounding through the country far and wide, so it was a crisis at Sobraon, as well said, before the conclusion of the former victory, where the existence of the Anglo-Indian Empire depended upon the Sikhs being not only beaten, but utterly overthrown and routed; and, again, after the Waterloo of India, that such battles will ever be "memorable in history as the nearest approach which the army of any native power has yet made to a victory over the English in India in a fair stand-up fight." We have thus been led to dwell a little on the Sikh invasion of British India, as the very remarkable battles which first repelled it are too apt to be forgotten by those who were living at the time; and they become almost matters of new interest to the present generation—sensational reading and varieties in political and social life having driven sober English and Indian history, in a great measure, out of the market. But the real friends of India, who are continually interested in its welfare, will, while musing over the first great battles on the Sutlej, feel that to retain for ever our wonderful Indian Empire, and *to keep the Russians out of India*—should they ever be so rash as to think of going there—it is our wisest policy to keep up the strongest friendship with the brave inhabitants of the Punjab, so carefully fostered by such sound administrators as the Lawrences and Montgomery, and less distinguished, though not less patriotic Anglo-Indians, such as James Abbott, and the subject of our sketch—John Becher.

We come now to what is styled "a turning point in Becher's career." Henry Lawrence had been attracted to him on the Kabul campaign; and, through the influence of the political artilleryman, the highly deserving engineer entered on employment in the Punjab. In 1847 he was employed in a revenue survey in the Jullunder Doab, "the only part of the Punjab annexed after the first war." This brings us to one of the most graphic and interesting passages in the whole sketch:—"This would bring him into close relation also with John Lawrence, who was Commissioner there. General Maclagan writes to me of very lively days at Subáthoo, in October, 1847, when he was staying in Hodson's house (Hodson, afterwards of Hodson's Horse, whom some have held up as the model of a Christian soldier, and others as the type of a seventeenth century buccaneer, but whom all agree in acknowledging to have been a first-rate soldier and most accomplished man). Among the guests and constant visitors were Becher, Napier (Field Marshal Lord Napier of Magdala), F. Abbott (Sir Frederick), and Lieut. Edwardes (Sir Herbert), a brilliant company certainly."

From the Jullunder, Becher was sent by Lord Hardinge on special duty as Commissioner, "for the adjustment of the boundaries between the Mohammedan state of Baháwalpur, on the Lower Sutlej, and the Rajpoot desert states of Bekaner and Jessulmer, as well as of those between Khaorpúr and Jessulmer."* About this time Sir Henry Lawrence —always fertile in resource for the good of India—proposed to raise the Punjab Corps of Guides, which afterwards

* On the reports being sent in (1851), the Marquis of Dalhousie wrote to Becher that he had conducted his inquiries "in the same spirit of caution, research, and impartiality, which has hitherto marked all your previous labours."

famous corps he suggested that Becher should command; but this appointment, for good reasons, never took place. Truly he might say, "There's a divinity which shapes our ends." During the Second Sikh War he was still engaged on the Rajputana boundary question; but on his return to the Punjab, after the annexation (1849), he was employed for two or three years under Sir Henry Lawrence. He was employed on reporting on the *Jaghirs* (*jagirs*), and other rent-free holdings of native chiefs. Becher's kindly feeling towards the natives of every class, and sympathy for them as a conquered people, made him admirably adapted for this important duty. To the liberal and kindly spirit of Becher's recommendations, we are told, Sir Robert Montgomery attributed "no small influence on the peace of the Punjab, and on the loyalty of the chiefs in 1857." This sympathetic feeling towards the Punjabis, beyond a doubt, was most valuable during the eighteen or twenty years Becher was employed in the Punjab. There is a capital story, taken from the "Life of Lord Lawrence," about Becher's recommending a settlement very much in favour of the "jagheerdar." It should have been remarked that his amiable disposition made him especially congenial to Sir Henry. "He would take the case first to the President (Sir Henry Lawrence), who was working in one room of the Residency, and who always countersigned his recommendations; he then took it to John, who was working in an adjoining room, and who would say, with a merry twinkle in his eye, which no one appreciated more than John Becher himself, 'Ah! I see you want to get over me, and let these lazy fellows waste the public money. No. I won't have it; sweep it away!' Becher then took the case to Montgomery, who generally agreed with John. Thus it happened, as Richard Temple once acutely remarked to Herbert Edwardes, 'That in these matters, while each brother was a salutary check upon the other, they, at the same time, confirmed each other's faults!'"* Becher was fond of accom-

* "Henry was more lavish in his proposals, because he thought that John would attempt to cut them down, whatever their nature; and John was more hard and economical upon parallel reasoning." Such Chancellors of the

panying Sir Henry Lawrence about the Punjab on those extensive tours in which the great soldier and administrator delighted more than in office details at Lahore. This was like taking a leaf out of the book of some of our most distinguished Bengal and other civilians, or following the advice of such men as the "big collector," Mr. Thomason (N.W.P.), and Holt Mackenzie (alluded to in our First Series).* As there recorded, the latter's advice to the collectors was, "*Take your gun in your hand, and go among the people!*" Without even the aid of a bottle of "Bass," or "a good bottle of claret," Sir Henry and his younger friend, Becher, frequently did this—the only way for a revenue officer to gain practical knowledge.

In 1852 after finishing his work at Lahore, Becher was appointed Deputy-Commissioner of Batála (west of Umritsur); and Mr. C. Raikes, in his "Notes on the Revolt, &c.," writes of this period: "I had the happiness of being associated with John Becher, who served under me as Deputy-Commissioner of Batála, when I was Commissioner of Lahore. When he left Batála for Hazára, the people followed him in crowds, weeping and invoking blessings on his head." In a letter, written in August, 1884, he is described by the same high authority as "dear John Becher," the district officer in the Punjab in 1853. "He was about the first specimen," writes Mr. Raikes, "of Henry Lawrence's '*Old Staff*' in the Punjab that I came across. I looked at him and at his work with curiosity, wonder, and admiration." In fact, he was a noble specimen of India's "hard-working administrators and fine soldiers," who were entirely devoted to the service of the people, "and from morning to night went in and out amongst the people, who crowded their rooms and gave them no respite." Of such splendid stuff were the men of Sir Henry Lawrence's *Old Staff* composed, both before and after the annexation of the country, that nothing more seemed to be desired. Such lessons in kind administrative excellence in our Eastern Empire are apt to make

Exchequer would have instructed and amused the present House of Commons in England.

* Pages 57–59.

the present writer turn to a very different region in every respect, and behold his late friend—the greatest Indo-Chinese or Burmese administrator that ever lived—the unrivalled Sir Arthur Phayre, who made Pegu—at Rangoon, with his tall figure standing at his high desk, surrounded by the respectful Mongolian varieties of mankind, with a smile for man, woman, and child, and a heart ever ready to do them all ample justice. Such are the men wanted to rule our millions in the East!

In the end of 1853, Becher was appointed to the charge of Hazára, which he held for six years. This district, first occupied by British officers after the First Sikh War, was, his biographer tells us, in the character of its population, "the wildest" in the Punjab. And again, we have the following interesting and instructive passage:—"It is the last territory on the North-West, abutting on those dark regions of the Indus which lie immediately below the great north-western elbow of that river, and into which no European has ever penetrated. The valleys of Hazára are shut in on the north by alpine peaks of 11,000 feet in height, and abound in magnificent forest scenery, whilst the tribes inhabiting them had been, during the native *régime*, constantly engaged in wars with one another, or in fierce revolt against the Sikh Government." Hazára was "part of the territory made over to Raja Guláb Singh along with Kashmír, under the Treaty of Lahore; but he found it very unmanageable; an exchange was made, and Hazára reverted to the Lahore Government." We now come to a famous Anglo-Indian, already named, Captain James Abbott, of the Bengal Artillery, who was deputed by the Resident to take over charge. Like the gallant and admired "Fred Burnaby" of a later day, some seven or eight years before arrival at Hazára, he had made a daring and adventurous journey to Khiva, "where he arranged for the release of captive Russians (who were afterwards conducted to Russian territory by his brother-officer, the late Sir Richmond Shakespear)." Abbott, doubtless, greatly admired Becher, his younger friend, "the heir of his authority, and of the essential characteristics of his administration." It should be noticed that, on the outbreak of the Second Punjab War, the people of Hazára "stood by Abbott against the Sikhs, and in that remote and wild tract he was able to hold his ground for many months, until freed by the crowning victory at Gujrát." The Artilleryman and Deputy-Commissioner—a position which he enjoyed from the annexation in 1849, till 1853—in his own way, won as great a victory in Hazára as his brother artillerymen did in this decisive battle—the most famous during the Second Sikh War.* In the latter year, Abbott—one of Lord Dalhousie's best men—left the Punjab, which he had so adorned by his administration. His work in Hazára immortalized the man. "He left it amidst the unfeigned regret of the people. During his rule exiles, driven out by the Sikhs twenty, thirty, forty years before, had flocked back again . . . . Hazára had passed from a desolation to a smiling prosperity." Abbott appears to have petted the children of his district as much as the amiable author of "The Deserted Village" did those of his own land; for to Uncle Abbott (or "Kaka Abbott," as they called him) they would go, "whenever their mouths watered for fruit or sugar-plums." Spending all his substance on the people, he is said to have left Hazára with only his month's pay!† Was ever more splendid self-denial heard of among our Eastern administrators? Our most entertaining biographer,

* The battle of Gujrát (or Guzerat) was fought on the 21st of February, 1849. It was indeed a glorious victory. The Sikh army, estimated at 60,000 men, with fifty-nine pieces of artillery, and a powerful auxiliary force of Afghan cavalry, was completely routed. The victory of Gujrát proved to be complete and decisive. "Once more," writes the historian, "the van of the British army had maintained its ground on this remote border of British India until reinforcements could be brought up, and then, trying the strength of the opposing power on a well-fought field, victory had unequivocally declared for the conquerors of the East. The fruits of this battle were the entire surrender of the Sikh army, including their commander, Rajah Shere Singh, his father, Chuttur Singh, his brothers, and most of the principal sirdars and chiefs." Forty-one pieces of artillery were unconditionally surrendered.

† Note by Sir Herbert Edwardes, written in 1857. Before this the author of the sketch under notice well remarks: "The story of Abbott in Hazára is one which no Anglo-Indian, no Englishman surely, can read without a glow of pride." Page 22.

like Sir Herbert Edwardes, puts Abbott before us, as he does Becher, with a force or strength of word-painting akin to what portrait-painters like Sir Joshua or Raeburn might have handed down to us on the ca .vas. And this, after all, is the desired object in full biography, and even more so in a biographical sketch.

We now learn that Edwardes himself was the immediate successor of the "chivalrous and benevolent" Abbott in Hazára; but, on the murder of Colonel Mackeson, Commissioner of Peshâwar, which happened soon after, Becher was appointed by Lord Dalhousie. The great Proconsul characterized the loss of Colonel Mackeson as one "which would have dimmed a victory."

Of Becher, Edwardes also writes:—"John Becher is James Abbott's successor, and is to Hazára all that Abbott *was*. High praise! His *cutcherry* is not from 'ten till four' by the regulation clock, but all day, and at any hour of the night that anybody chooses—the *barahduree* system of administration—the living in a house with twelve doors, and all open to the people." Here the author of the sketch mildly corrects the writer of a book styled "The Indian Empire," who mistakes *Bahaduree* (summer-house) for the foregoing word—thus, in a passage, substituting the administration of *swagger* (*bahháduri*) for the administration of accessibility!" Becher was in Hazára during the terrible Mutiny of 1857—alluded to at some length in our early sketches of Sir Henry Lawrence, John Colvin, and Neill. He gathered the principal men of his district around him, assured them of his reliance on their loyalty, and endeavoured to dispel the alarming rumours which would be sure to come among them. Being so far away also from the various scenes of the damnable action of the mutineers, greatly increased the seriousness of Becher's position. "It was doubtless to be apprehended that invasion might be attempted by the turbulent tribes and fanatics in Yusufzai; but eventually the chief danger to the district proved to be from the mutineers escaping from Peshâwar, who broke away from the north into Swat, and thence across the Indus into Hazára, necessarily avoiding the high road by Attok and Ráwal

Pindi; a large body of the 55th N.I. especially took this line, but the Deputy-Commissioner's plans had been effectually laid beforehand." Major John Becher's conduct of matters at this time is highly appreciated by Mr. Bosworth Smith, in his interesting "Life of Lord Lawrence"; he obtained "high recommendation from those under whom he served, and when honours came to be distributed a brevet promotion and C.B. (civil) fell to his lot."

Towards the middle of 1858, Becher was employed in an expedition, under Major-General Sir Sidney Cotton, against Mahomedan fanatics and promoters of rebellion in the Yusufzai hill-country, north of our Peshâwar frontier, and on the west of the Indus, opposite Hazâra; "in fact on the northern spurs of Mahâban, the mountain-site which has been identified by Lieutenant-General Abbott, with great force of argument, with the Aornoz of Alexander's historians."* This expedition—considered as a prototype of the Umbeyla one which took place against the same determined body of fanatics five years later—was very successful. Sir S. Cotton takes good care to note in his despatch the admirable conduct of Major Becher and his troops—a tight little force (which should never be less for such hill-service), consisting of two 12-pounder howitzers, one 3-pounder gun of Hazâra Mountain Train, 300 of 2nd Sikhs, and 750 men selected from 6th and 12th Punjab Infantry. The Chief highly commended Major Becher for the disposition of his troops, proving that the Deputy Commissioner was as good with the sword as with the pen. Colonel Edwardes (Sir Herbert), of the same stamp of distinguished Anglo-Indian, who accompanied the General as Commissioner of Peshâwar, also wrote:—"I cannot conclude this report without again acknowledging the services, civil and military, of Major Becher."† In the spring of 1860, we find him at home on furlough. The Anglo-Indian is often a strange fish-out-of-

* Page 25.

† Edwardes particularly alludes to Becher's wise and kindly management, to which he ascribes the valuable co-operation of the Otmanzyes of Kubbul, and to his military arrangements for the seizure of Upper Sitana.—*Calcutta Gazette*, June 15, 1858.

water during the lights and shadows of his furlough-life. The pleasures of going home are, perhaps, the best part of it; and, on this occasion, Becher had as his companion "the late gallant and devout Major-General Edward Lake, R.E.," who had also been an early protégé of Sir Henry Lawrence's, and had served in the Punjab as soldier and administrator ever since the victories on the Sutlej; and since, with some scratch levies, he helped Edwardes and Van Cortlandt to beat Múlraj in two battles, and drive him within the walls of Múltán."

On return (1862), Becher was appointed Commissioner of the Doraját, where, as usual, taking kindly to the people, he nevertheless missed his old Hazára friends. And we are now also informed by his amiable biographer, that changes "in the fashions of administration went against the grain." *Non-regulation* had been too much converted into *regulation*, till at length there was a distinction without a difference; or, as it was cleverly put by the author of the biographical sketch (1884), "rules and checks accumulate till we are reminded of the witty Frenchman, who some years ago defined non-intervention: 'La *non-intervention* est une expression de la haute politique, qui veut dire enfin à peu-près la même chose que *l'intervention*.'" The comparative utility of *non-regulation* and *regulation* has never been better defined than by the statement that the former "government requires men above the average, such as the Punjab had in its early days; when you come down to the average man you need to set him rules to keep him tolerably straight." Taking a wide survey of history, it may almost be said that all the famous actions of mankind have been performed by *non-regulation* men, men who never hesitate for a moment, *when they see their way forward*, to incur any amount of responsibility! In India this has been the case more than in any other portion of the dominions of the Queen-Empress. With Clive and Warren Hastings it began; and, if we would hold India strongly, it must go on till time shall be no more!

In 1863, we find Becher writing to his constant friend, Abbott, from Dera Ismail Khan:—"I feel in a constant treadmill, and have no time to see the people; no time to look broadly and composedly out, and survey the general administration. As for social life, I never go out; from early morning till dark I work, and seldom see any one; scarcely ever take exercise. Can you wonder, then, if I feel morbid?" And again, as if his spirits had got up a little, with the mercury:—"You will have been glad to see Chamberlain made a K.C.B. and Sir Neville. One Sunday I could not resist trying my hand at some doggrel on the occasion, which I sent to the *Lahore Chronicle.*" This is really a fine little poem, well and forcibly written, on a most distinguished Anglo-Indian; so we present three out of the four verses to our readers:—

"CHAMBERLAIN.

Honoured by England—in his grave—
  In the old Abbey, where she keeps
The memory of the great and brave,
  The Lion-hearted Outram sleeps.

. . . . .

And India looks around, to call
  Another champion to her side,
Whose crest gleams in the front of all,
  To whom may she that sword confide?—
Lofty, compassionate, and just,
  Knight without fear, and without stain,
A foe to dread, a friend to trust—
  Ride forth, SIR NEVILLE CHAMBERLAIN!" *

Doubtless, such a good judge of a brave knight as Sir Walter Scott would have greatly admired the above lines, which have a chivalrous ring about them, not often heard in an age when an exhibition of prosy sentimentality has, in a great measure, driven soul-inspiring verses out of the market.

In 1864, Becher went on a short leave to Simla, on a visit to Sir John Lawrence and his family. Sir R. Pollock was then sent to relieve him at Dera Ismail Khan. His visit to

* This well-known Officer is alluded to in the *First Series* of "Distinguished Anglo-Indians," page 298—"Some Madras Commanders-in-Chief." Sir Neville Bowles Chamberlain rose in the Bengal Native Infantry; became General in 1877, and is a G.C.B. as well as a G.C.S.I.

the renowned Viceroy, if only for health's sake, was, as his biographer remarks, "urgently needed"; for, beyond a doubt, he had been working too hard. Even hard-working city men will hardly believe that Becher worked twenty hours out of the twenty-four. In fact, his whole life and soul were in his *work*.

Sir R. Pollock writes:—"His patience was inexhaustible, and it need hardly be added that his arrears were heavy! life being too short for the sort of inquiry that he considered necessary in each case." Even in 1853, Sir John Lawrence had told Becher not to "work too hard." On this the author of the biographical sketch naïvely remarks:—"Did Lawrence ever tell any other man not to work too hard?"

A vacancy having occurred in the Commissionership of Pesháwar, through the death of Colonel James, Becher was sent to succeed him. But his "health was already greatly undermined"; and that alone rendered him unfit for "a charge like that of Pesháwar, with its heavy political anxieties and burden of far-reaching questions." Another Umbeyla campaign had just terminated successfully; but on the border and beyond it "towards Kabul," there was matter of intense anxiety for the Commissioner of Pesháwar. However, Becher carried on his onerous duties for nearly two years, when "his health broke down utterly, and he had to quit the scene of his duties for ever." In the spring of 1866, he had accompanied, as Commissioner, a force under Brigadier-General Dunsford, C.B., to "coerce certain villages on the northern Yusafzai border." The objects of the expedition were attained without conflict; and Colonel Becher reported favourably on this his last active work in the cause of order. It would be well if *coercion* were as easily managed elsewhere.* "When I conferred with him at Murree, in July or August 1866," his friend and successor, Pollock, writes, "I should never have dreamt of his surviving till 1884." This friend also added, with genuine good feeling and admiration, "that of all the prominent Punjab

* *Quere?*—the Irish Coerçion or Crimes Bill, while in Committee (May 1887).

officials there was certainly none more loved and respected than Becher. His only failing was a virtue carried to excess. In his anxiety to do full justice he paused so long sometimes in over-elaborating, that people suffered unnecessarily." We have frequently met with men in India like this; and, although they seem an evil or a drawback at the time, much good comes forth in the lives of such men. They are a check upon hasty decisions of every kind; they bring you face to face with facts; they explain results; and, above all, they show that conscience is not that unmeaning thing which our countrymen often take it to be in England as well as in India. At the same time this "canny" quality in public men is often injurious to the exercise of that great and useful virtue, decision of character. And yet Becher must have had a good share of this valuable attribute in his composition to have played his various and many parts so well. His health, then, had now entirely given way; the end of his career had arrived, for the spring of life was broken. Still, he lived to spend eighteen years in England, after his return. To a man so mentally, and at one time so physically, energetic as Becher, this *inertia* must have been frequently very galling. He had really compressed a long and useful life into a small number of years, during which, with his duty, he was always working and happy. The drones o society can never understand this; but, in reality, such nonentities never *live* at all, and never will *live*, till they have something to live for!

General Becher is now described as "a man greatly beloved by a few friends, including his brothers, to whom he was very dear, and who tended him through several dangerous illnesses, including the last."* As a fish out of water, of course he never settled anywhere. He lived in an hotel or in lodgings in Brighton or Hastings, Eastbourne or Southampton; and now and then he visited London, where the writer of the sketch found him located for many weeks at the Cannon Street Hotel! It is pleasing to read that, although of secluded habits, he was "by no means always

* Page 32 of "Biographical Sketch."

depressed"; and "old familiar faces" were ever dear to him; while old friends found him "as delightful as ever." Few "distinguished Anglo-Indians," or few distinguished public men at home, have been so fortunate in their biographers as General Becher. His friend is not content with exhibiting all the fine qualities of his hero to the reader, but cites Bosworth Smith (Lord Lawrence's eminent biographer), whose acquaintance Becher made in latter years.

He writes:—"I often grieved over him. He was a delightful man. Of all the Indian celebrities with whom I have conversed during the last few years, I do not think I got more pleasure from any one than from him. He was much more intellectual than most Anglo-Indians. He had also very delicate feelings and keen sympathy, combined with a touch of humour. His conversation was suggestive, and many of his hints I have worked out in the book (Life of Lord Lawrence) with, I trust, excellent result."—This liberal praise from Bosworth Smith hardly agrees with what is said in the preliminary brief sketch regarding the biographer's not doing full justice to one of the great Viceroy's most approved workers. It is remarkable about Becher that he appears to have left a strong impression on every one with whom he came in contact. His refinement and cultivation charmed gifted ladies; and his friend, Sir Richard Pollock, gives a reminiscence of how he once astonished Sir William Boxall, R.A., by his knowledge regarding the pre-Raphælite school. The author of the sketch follows this up, in his own admirable way, by a passage containing names of distinguished Anglo-Indians, fairly well known to the world, whose portraits, with others, may adorn some future Anglo-Indian gallery in London:—"The splendid body of the early '*Punjabees*' embraced a vast variety of strong and gifted characters, among whom there were inevitably at times deep rifts and schisms, but all loved Becher. The names among the departed, of Edwardes, Lake, Sir Donald Macleod, of the Punjab wrathful Achilles, Nicholson himself, come up before us; and, among men still spared to us, of Sir Neville Chamberlain, of Lord Napier of Magdala, of Sir R. Montgomery, of General James Abbott,—all these have been his friends, bearing him no ordinary affection, till their death or his." *

It is interesting to learn, at this concluding stage of such an excellent career, that the occasional divisions between the illustrious brothers, Henry and John Lawrence, had no effect whatever upon John Becher. He was equally attached to both; and he had served them faithfully and well. He said of John Lawrence, "His roughnesses were those of a big Newfoundland—no, let me say of a St. Bernard dog." The "rough man," we also read, "even in days when he *was* rougher than in the mellow autumn of his life," was strongly attached to our hero. "'I don't much care for many fellows,' he said to Becher, when the latter was returning to India, in 1861–2, '*but you are one of them.*'" † It is well worthy of note that neither of the great brothers ever said a harsh word to him. His even temperament would have just suited the views of an eminent London magistrate, who, in the glorious Jubilee year, wisely remarked in Court, that no officer or official should ever lose his temper!

At the end of May, 1884, General Becher was taken with a serious, painful, and tedious illness at Southampton. He had gone there to be near his friends, Sir Neville and Lady Chamberlain, and his elder brother, General Sir Arthur Becher, K.C.B., who "took part in almost every campaign in India from 1839 to 1858, and was severely wounded at Delhi, when serving as Quartermaster-General of the army." In brave and noble company, then, our distinguished Anglo-Indian—patient during approaching death as he had been in busy life—at length passed away, on the 9th of July, 1884, and was buried at Southampton on the 11th.

His "Old Friend and Brother Officer," as well as his

* We had the pleasure of seeing at the house of the accomplished lady before mentioned miniature portraits of Generals John Becher and James Abbott, C.B., both excellent likenesses and well painted. There was also a miniature of General Sir Travitt Phillips (Beng. Cav.), by the same versatile hand.

† Page 34, where, in referring us to the "Life of Lord Lawrence," I., 506–7, the author of the biographical sketch says: "Becher is the person in question, though not named there."

many friends, on his departure, probably thought of the following beautiful verses, by the Poet Laureate :—

"His memory long will live alone
In all our hearts, as mournful light
That broods above the fallen sun,
And dwells in heaven half the night.

. . . . .

"Sleep till the end, true soul and sweet,
Nothing comes to thee new or strange!
Sleep full of rest from head to feet;
Lie still, dry dust, secure of change!"

COLONEL G. B. MALLESON, C.S.I.

—o—

AFTER the lamented death of that great gun in Anglo-Indian literature, Sir John Kaye *—an artillery metaphor will be excused, as we were both actual gunners, though, in a literary sense, differing so materially in calibre—the founder of the *Calcutta Review*, the writer of immortal histories and biographies, the smart journalist and sometimes brilliant essayist, who looked every inch a Knight Commander of the Star of India, but who, sad to think, died with so many "Unaccomplished Purposes" (the title of one of his last essays) on his mind—the distinguished man who had written so much and so well to awaken England out of her deadly or dangerous lethargy (still apt to hover near her) regarding Indian affairs—his mantle could not have descended on the shoulders of a successor more gracefully, as an appropriate gift, than on those of Colonel Malleson.† As is not unfrequently the case in the arena of politics, or of science, the vacant high place was soon filled up; or, as in war, when the thunder of the artillery had ceased, and the deadly charge was over, there arose but slight delay in responding to the piercing cry which rent the air—"Another man to take the colours!" It almost seems, then, that Colonel Malleson had been born to succeed Sir John Kaye in his literary labours. And both had the same innate desire to excel in Anglo-Indian literary work.

* 24th July, 1876.

† Colonel Malleson is the second son of the representative of the junior branch of one of the old Cumberland families.

We have had the good fortune to read two biographical sketches of the gallant and learned officer, now to be added to the list of *Distinguished Anglo-Indians;* and his name and his works have been familiar to us for so many years that, even if he did not fill the worthy chair in Anglo-Indian literature of Sir John Kaye, it would be impossible not to feel interested in him. Moreover, he arrived in India in the same year as the present writer (1842); and both have made a portion of the same literary ground their study —that of the French struggles for Empire in the East.

Born in 1825, Colonel Malleson was educated at Wimbledon and Winchester; and, in 1842, he obtained a cadetship in the Bengal Army. He was, like so many other distinguished Anglo-Indians, not an Addiscombe, but a "direct" cadet; and, before leaving for India, he had every advantage for a first-rate education. In 1841 he was sent on the Continent, to perfect or improve his acquaintance with the French and German languages; which linguistic attainments, though not of any practical use to a cadet of Bengal Native Infantry, greatly assisted his literary labours in after life. In 1852, having qualified himself for the staff, so much more in accordance with his proclivities than the often dull routine of military duty, he was appointed to the Commissariat Department, where he remained till 1856. Notwithstanding its vast utility, this is a peculiarly dry service for the active-minded Indian officer—almost as dry as the firewood served out to the troops; yet, strange to say, some of the cleverest men in our splendid dominion have belonged to it. Of course, a high standard of proficiency in the native languages is necessary for the strict performance of the various Commissariat duties, which partly accounts for its select nature; and we have known in this department clever artists, well-read men, and masters of five or six different Oriental tongues. Colonel Malleson was next specially selected to fill a vacancy in the department of Military Finance; and while occupying this official position the deadly Mutiny—India's fearful trial—broke out; and ruthless Sivas (destroyers) were overrunning once fair and smiling lands. Hell was indeed "empty" in Bengal, and "all the devils" were there—no very suitable time for the commencement of a financial career. Whether the Government was utterly incapable, or not, of coping with the serious crisis which had arisen, is necessarily a matter of opinion.

According to one able authority—most interesting to quote, as we also have in his strictures an excellent sketch of the origin of the famous "Red Pamphlet":—"The pusillanimity which marked every action of the Government of India in the suppression of the rebellion, the want of appreciation of its really national character, and the importance accorded to the maintenance of the doctrine of 'India for the Civil Service,' rather than attention being solely directed to the extinction of the Mutiny, at length aroused the spirit of the local press to indignant remonstrance. However, the Government thought by the passing of the Gagging Act of 13th June, 1857, that it had effectually closed the mouth of importunate criticism. But the hour at last had come; and with it came the man! Animated with the sole thought that Englishmen had a right to be enlightened as to the extent of the national disaster, and the progress made to its rectification, Colonel (then Captain) Malleson sent home an account of the Mutiny—of its rise and its development. It was intended as a magazine article; in response, however, to advice, it was published in pamphlet form, under the title of 'The Mutiny of the Bengal Army.' But in the hands of the late Lord Derby, whose constant reference to its pages in the House of Lords sorely tried the temper of the Government, it suddenly acquired notoriety, and from the colour of its cover it obtained the well-known name of the 'Red Pamphlet.'" *

While serving in the Department of Military Finance, Colonel Malleson was associated with that ever energetic and able second edition of Joseph Hume, the redoubtable General Sir George Balfour—now an old M.P., and one of the best-known Anglo-Indians in the House of Commons—and from the sweeping reforms of such an eminent administrator and financier he gained a fair insight into the workings of the

* *St. Stephen's Review*, March 1, 1884, p. 13.—No. xxxii. of "St. Stephen's Portraits."

economical school. After the "Red Pamphlet," his valuable services could not possibly be dispensed with. The tremendous exigencies of the time would not permit of it, although there was no want of inclination to shelve him for his literary audacity; so he was appointed Assistant to the Controller-General of Military Finance. He held this appointment with much advantage till his nomination by Lord Lawrence to succeed Sir John Strachey at the head of the Sanitary Department, which office he successfully administered for four years. His marked success in public business now pointed him out as no ordinary man. Colonel Malleson also presided for a short time as Controller-General of Military Finance. He had already visited Europe on furlough; but, at length, on his return from leave (this time spent on a trip to the Himalayas), he found himself appointed guardian to the young Rajah of Mysore, then only six years of age. On the arrival in India of Lord Mayo, as Viceroy and Governor-General (September, 1868), the attention of the Government had been called to the state of Mysore and the young potentate destined to rule over it.—"A young prince," says an able writer, "not six years old, had been declared heir to the dominions of the predecessor who had adopted him, and who for more than thirty years had been debarred from the exercise of ruling powers. To bring up that royal boy in a manner which would enable him at a maturer age to steer clear of the evils which had fatally tempted his predecessor, and to introduce amongst the nobles of the country a manly and healthy tone, required the services of an officer upon whom the Government could fully depend. Lord Mayo, whose strong point was perception of character, selected Colonel Malleson for that task."*

Before the honoured preceptor's departure, the chivalrous and admirable Lord Mayo thus addressed him, in the style which made the lamented Viceroy such a general favourite: "I have, unasked, selected you, Colonel, for this difficult position, as it is one requiring great temper and judgment, and one calling for the services of an officer upon whom the

* *The Army and Navy Magazine: a Monthly Service Review*, No. 24, October, 1882.—Pp. 481-82.

Government can confidently depend." The results amply justified the choice; and Colonel Malleson remained in Mysore seven years. The Bengal officer had come into a famous historical province of the Madras Presidency, some 30,000 square miles in extent, or about the size of Scotland. Enclosed on three sides by high ranges of mountains, it has in many parts dense forests of teak, ebony, sandal-wood, and bamboo; and the elevation of the country varies from 1,000 to 6,000 feet. Tigers, cheetahs, elephants, and other wild animals, dear to the Indian *Shikarrie*, abound in the forests. Mysore is also noted for having the best draught oxen in India; and before the batteries of artillery were horsed, the long-horned noble creatures, though sorely trying a gunner's temper on critical occasions, on the whole did their work wonderfully well. After his studies, and the imposition of some literary task on the future hope of the country, we may safely imagine the energetic Colonel being off to *shikar* (in which he is an expert), or to the romantic isolated hills or droogs for a change of air, beside masses of granite about two miles in circumference; or it may have been an occasional trip to the adjoining rugged and mountainous region of Coorg, more than 3,000 feet above the sea's level, and where the fire-fly's light is, perhaps, grander, or more extensive, than in any other country of the East.* With a strong love of historical research, doubtless, the downfall of the house of Tippoo Sultan in 1799, the erection into a separate State, under a rajah of the ancient Hindu dynasty, by Lord Mornington (Marquess Wellesley), with the battles, sieges, and scenes of horror and persecution enough for a hundred

* A natural phenomenon. The yearly appearance of the fire-fly on the April and May nights of Coorg, is thus graphically described:—"A scene of strange beauty is spread below. Shrub and bush and tree, as far as the eye can reach, burn with magic light. The ground, the air, teem with lustre, every leaf seems to have its own fairy lamp. The valley at your feet, the wooded hills to your right and left, the dark distant forest, all are lit up, and gleam in ever-varying splendour, as if every star had sent a representative to bear his part in this nightly illumination of the poor, dark Earth. . . . . Now they flash up brighter than ever, as if this world of phosphoric lustre was animated by pulsations keeping regular time."—*Coorg Memoirs*, by Rev. H. Moegling.

tragedies, also occupied Colonel Malleson's attention. But Lord William Bentinck's injunction, *Educate! Educate! Educate!* must have been the action uppermost in his thoughts during those long seven years! He founded a large public school on the model of Winchester, having already given an English tone to the native society of Mysore, from which the best results were expected; and he placed there, "under competent native masters, the boy prince and the boy nobles of the country." The system of classes and promotion by merit may be truly said to have astonished the intelligent natives. And so our distinguished Anglo-Indian, even for this innovation alone, deserved well of Mysore.

It is highly pleasing to read that, by the inculcation of principles of honour and right feeling, as well as by the maintenance of a manly and healthy tone—to which the great public schools of England owe nearly all their celebrity—in the new Academy for the rising generations of Mysoreans, Colonel Malleson was enabled to effect results of the most satisfactory nature in the training of the young Prince* and his too often vain and flighty followers. The indefatigable Colonel's object was in a great measure attained by the encouragement of athletic sports, in which he was a rare adept. By the old Anglo-Indian hospitable system of keeping open house, he did much to popularize the young Rajah's rule in the country; and his preceptor and adviser certainly succeeded in winning a large share of goodwill from native landowners and others by his wise and liberal administration. Few, if any, Anglo-Indians ever before had such an opportunity for distinction as this; and that he was able to do so much good while in Mysore at once showed the wisdom of Lord Mayo's choice. Colonel Malleson may well be proud of the Address which hangs in his study, drawn up by some of the principal native inhabitants of Calcutta and its neighbourhood, and dated April 2, 1877,

* According to the writer in the *Army and Navy*, "an article in *Blackwood's Magazine* for January 1874 describes in accurate terms the training at this royal college—a training the results of which are manifested in the admirable conduct of the Prince, now that he worthily administers the dominions of his ancestors."

"expressive of the high appreciation of all that he had done for the natives of India during his service of thirty years." As in the case of the late Sir William Andrew, in a totally different walk (that of Indian railway pioneer and strategist), it is impossible not to wonder how so much excellent work, in life's calm evening, has received so few honours! But, to the end of time, such apparent neglect will often occur towards men of real merit. But it must be noted that the Colonel received one honour from the State, chiefly for his services in Mysore, having, in May, 1872, been admitted to the dignity of a Companion of the Star of India.

The following information will be of special interest to Anglo-Indians—probably the best and most enthusiastic sportsmen on the face of the earth! The Colonel's chief amusement, after the discharge of his official duties, "was the breaking in and training of the young Prince's horses, of which there were generally over eighty; and here, and in the Ootacamund Hills [the Neilgherries, or Blue Mountains], where narrow paths and precipices abound, he was in the constant habit of driving a four-in-hand of wild native ponies, whose spirit and temper required a 'whip' of no mean order. Indeed, sport in any form is dear to him, whether with gun, rod, or spear. Over the doors of the rooms at his house in Kensington, the antlers of deer of various breeds are placed; the heads of two huge 'grizzlies' supporting a hat-rail, frown at you in the vestibule, and the head of a solitary 'bull-bison' adorns the entrance to the drawing-room. The mention of these wild animals suggests a reference to a *wag-nuck*, or 'tiger's claws,' which Colonel Malleson shows you—a most unpleasant-looking weapon. It is worn inside the hand, by placing the fingers through the perforated plate, fixed firmly over four steel claws. This one on the mantelpiece is the *fac-simile* of that by which Sivaji, the Maratta chief, slew his Mahomedan enemy, Afzul Khan, in 1659, treacherously embracing him after the fashion of Orientals, whilst striking the *wag-nuck* deep into his bowels."*

From such rude language, let us now proceed to that of

* *St. Stephen's Portraits*, No. xxxii.

ferns and flowers. We also read, without surprise, of "a fernery beyond the study." The love of ferns and flowers is strong in the genuine Anglo-Indian. In such a country as India he must occasionally be refreshed with something, or he would die of old age, like Addison's "Rake," at (say a little older than the time given) five-and-thirty! With reference to this fernery, while reading of the "pleasant splash of dripping water, and the trickling sound of hidden streamlets amongst the cool green foliage of fern and lichen," denoting the love of verdure which makes England so dear to Anglo-Indians, at the risk of trying the reader's patience, having alluded to the Ootacamund Hills, or to the delightful Blue Mountains (nearly 8,000 feet above sea-level), while Colonel Malleson is, in our imagination, again driving his team of wild ponies in dangerous places, let us touch for a moment, having a strong recollection of them, on the flowers and ferns of the Neilgherries; approaching which sanitarium all sick and feverish from the plains, surrounded by shrubs and flowers, and, as you ascend through the winding ghauts, hearing the running of cooling streams, and the sweet songs of birds, is a far higher state of "Elysium on earth" than any of which Moore so sweetly sings. The *Flora* of the Neilgherries might have been honoured with the praises of all the best poets who have written on flowers. Burns and Campbell of our own land, and Bryant, Percival, and Longfellow of America; each of them might have sung of flowers on the Blue Mountains,—

"Beautiful things ye are, where'er you grow!"

and derived a moral from each of them. The favourite primrose in such a romantic spot would, doubtless, have given some happy thought to reflective minds like those of Wordsworth and Lord Beaconsfield. Even Mr. Gladstone, in the "sunset of his genius and his days,"* if possible, escaping from a dry budget or an endless debate on the Coercion Bill, could refresh himself with a flower or a nosegay on the Hills. Here the *geranium* attains great perfection. Whole

* See *First Series* p. 202.

hedges of it are to be seen around some of the dwellings—the bright colours affording a most exhilarating aspect. The *heliotropes* here are superb. The wild roses and the cluster roses—the former very abundant—are also remarkably beautiful. The *fuschia* blooms in full beauty here; and with violets, carnations, heartsease, primroses (at home grown into the ladies' *party* flower), sweet-peas, wall-flowers, and other *flora* of the English garden, the invalid of taste can indeed revel among the flowers. Ferns of various kinds attain great perfection on the Hills. The giant or tree-fern abounds on the ghauts, and the bracken here is not to be surpassed—except, perhaps, by some of those in the Colonel's fernery at Kensington.

And now we look around the study, beholding celebrities most of whom have long passed away. Engravings of Bolingbroke and Chatham, of Strafford, Burke, Pitt, and Canning; and, among Indian heroes, Clive, Warren Hastings, and the Marquess Wellesley, live again by the power of Art; while Art itself and Literature are represented by Molière, Byron, Voltaire, and Benvenuto Cellini. There are also portraits of the late Lord Beaconsfield, by Weigall, Sir Francis Grant, and by the clever and versatile Count D'Orsay. From 1844, when Colonel Malleson enrolled himself under his banner, the intellectual preceptor of the Mysore Rajah *in esse* was a strong admirer of the great Conservative statesman,* whom, when Mr. D'Israeli, the eloquent but abusive Daniel O'Connell once styled "the lineal descendant of the impenitent thief," and of whose tongue, when in political combat, we well recollect a most distinguished and learned member of the House of Lords saying that it "out-venomed all the worms of Nile!"

In the evening of life, when in the House of Lords, Lord Beaconsfield's style—always sarcastic in an encounter—became much subdued, and his speeches were admired by young and old. Having studied the characters of heroes in every kind of strife, their virtues and their failings, their weakness and strength of speech and action, their wishes or

* Until the death of Lord Beaconsfield, Colonel Malleson maintained correspondence with him, and had several interviews.

prophecies, sometimes verified but oftener unfulfilled, it is not difficult to imagine a man like Colonel Malleson taking a strong interest in the brilliant writer of "Vivian Grey" * and "Tancred," and in the rising, but too often scorned, politician who told the House of Commons that *they would one day be forced to listen to him!* Nearly twenty years had elapsed between the publication of the above novels—the latter appearing not long after the subject of our sketch reached India. We also, not long emerged from a state of *griffinage* (1844–45), when life promised to be happy, at the famous historical rock of Trichinopoly—so admirably defended by a distinguished Anglo-Indian of old, that gallant and able officer, Captain Dalton † (1752–53) — recollect devouring "Tancred" with an interest only second to that felt in the immortal works of Sir Walter Scott. The vivid descriptions contained in the three political novels, "Coningsby," "Sybil," and "Tancred," were more entertaining to various readers than the Tory principles so fully developed in them. In the day of our reading "Tancred," many of us thought of no other politics than those of obeying orders and doing our duty—perhaps the best kind for military men in general. But, probably, the young Bengal officer, who was eventually to distinguish himself, took a different view, and at once became an ardent politician, to the occasional edification of his brother officers at the mess or *chota haziree* (small breakfast).

In maturer years he steadily followed the strong "National" Premier in his foreign and colonial policy (which even Liberals were sometimes forced to admire), till, having received all the honours which England could bestow, Lord Beaconsfield died at the ripe age of seventy-seven. Although, not having a seat in Parliament, doubtless the present state of parties often affords reflection for the Colonel's mind; and such a lover and writer of history we can imagine declaring, beyond fear of contradiction, that there never was a more extraordinary political state of affairs than at present. Mr.

* In the year 1826 Mr. Benjamin Disraeli published this, his first, novel.

† See "Memoir of Captain Dalton," H.E.I.C.S. By Charles Dalton, F.R.G.S. (1886).

Disraeli, many years ago, said at a public dinner: "I am a Conservative to preserve all that is good in our Constitution, a Radical to remove all that is bad." * This is, or should be, the strict Conservative view at the present day; and even the ladies, through wearing the primrose, give their favourite Earl an annual resuscitation, and become politicians in spite of their fair selves! And now, while writing this sketch (middle of May), comes forth the very last and briefest description of the policy of the Liberal Party—a definition worthy of Lord Rosebery, one of our most able and rising statesmen: "To give the largest possible satisfaction to local aspirations." Surely, after this, the force of political ambition can no farther go. Yet, looking closely at the idea, it is "your only peace-maker," *if it could be carried out!*

But we are wandering from Colonel Malleson, to whom as a literary man, we now return from what must, in some degree, be considered a digression. It is curious to note that when at Winchester his memory was bad, and, to improve it, when in India he set himself to the task of learning Disraeli's speeches by heart, and, in 1884, he still retained them. It is likely that, from this circumstance—this intense deference to "Dizzy's opinion"—his admiration of the great statesman has been styled "an infatuation." Two facts now become apparent, that of his possessing a good memory during his literary career, coupled with extraordinary industry.

Colonel Malleson is best known as a writer and as an historian of Indian subjects. The "Red Pamphlet" has been already adverted to; and we now learn that its literary success occasioned an eager competition among the editors of the Calcutta press to secure the author's "exclusive services," so that on his return from Europe he was soon making a handsome income by contributing to the *Calcutta Review*,† *Englishman*, and *Friend of India*. He also held the appointment of

* "A Sketch of the Public Career of the late Earl of Beaconsfield." By F. A. Hyndman. P. 6.

† For matter pertaining to this Indian Quarterly (founded May, 1844), see *First Series*—sketches of Sir Henry Lawrence, Sir John Kaye, and of *Anglo-Indian Periodical Literature.*

Times correspondent. But more lasting than comparatively transitory effusions, the dignity of Indian History had at length found in him a valuable accessory, and he availed himself of the position with surprising zeal and ability. In 1868 he issued "The History of the French in India," on which interesting subject, just twenty-three years before, after a residence in Pondichery (the Paris of the East), we had written two little works.* On the appearance of the new "History," therefore, giving a very correct account of the contest waged by the East India Company against French influence, it was pleasing to think that François Martin (who purchased Pondichery in 1683), Dupleix, Labourdonnais, Lally, Bussy, Clive, and Lawrence, were not altogether strangers to us, having travelled over so many of the scenes of their ambitious aims and battles, and minor operations, and having enjoyed French society at Pondichery, where almost another Clive would have been hospitably received, even although, like the great original, he had annihilated their dreams of Empire in the East, and then coolly walked off to Paris to learn dancing, in order to please the French ladies! Dupleix, at Chandernagore, running about the streets of the chief French settlement in Bengal with a lot of wild young fellows, one of whom, while their fickle chief played the fiddle, held an umbrella over the future Governor's head—Dupleix, who, when Director-General, threatened to dethrone the Mogul, and reduce Madras and Calcutta to their original state of fishing towns; and the renowned French statesman and gallant admiral, Labourdonnais, who was Governor of Mauritius, where the scene of the beautiful story of "Paul and Virginia" is laid; and Bussy's intrigues in the Dekhan; and Lally's blowing Brahmans from guns—showing a sad want of the conciliating policy of the Marquess Wellesley—all again came vividly to memory when we sought for the new work on the French in India. The high-minded book was so well received by the French nation that it caused the "Société du Bien Nationale" of France to award Colonel Malleson a silver medal, and to grant him their diploma,

* "Notes on Pondichery; or, The French in India," and "A Brief View of the French in India," both published in Calcutta.

which in a frame adorns the wall of his study. As may be recollected by readers of our first series of "Sketches," it was regarding a work on "The French in India" that Lord (then Mr.) Macaulay wrote to the author that he did not conceive there was much public curiosity about the French in India, but that any subject might be made attractive through "eloquence and vivacity."* These are just the qualities we should attribute to Colonel Malleson, of which we shall leave the reader to judge from a passage in the work just brought under notice. We allude to the summary of the treatment Dupleix received from his countrymen :—
"His arrival" (that of Dupleix) "in France was looked upon in the light of a misfortune, and it appeared for some time not improbable that he might even be reinstated in his post. He was, therefore, well received and flattered with hopes of a settlement of his claims. As soon, however, as the intelligence of the disgraceful peace made by Godcheu reached France, and the disagreements with England were regarded as settled, the Ministry began to treat Dupleix as a man from whom nothing more could be hoped, but who, on his part, would importune them with claims. They therefore at once changed their manner towards him, and absolutely refused to take his accounts into consideration. In vain did he remonstrate. In vain did he point out that he was persecuted by creditors who were simply creditors, because, on his security, they had advanced their funds to the Government of Pondichery. In vain did he write a memoir, setting forth in modest but graphic style, all he had done, the sums of money he had advanced. For seven years he urged and pressed his claims, supporting them by incontestable proofs. He received not even the shadow of redress. Nay, more. Many of those whom he had befriended in his prosperity, and who had advanced sums to the Pondichery Government, sued him for repayment. Even Bussy, who was to have become his stepson, deserted him in his extremity, broke off the marriage, and appeared in the list of claimants against him. To such a state of misery was he reduced that, three months before he died, his house was in

* "Sketch of Sir John Kaye," p. 156.

the occupation of bailiffs. Three days before that sad event he thus wrote in his memoir: 'I have sacrificed my youth, my fortune, my life, to enrich my nation in Asia. Unfortunate friends, too weak relations, devoted all their property to the success of my projects. They are now in misery and want. I have submitted to all the judiciary forms; I have demanded, as the last of the creditors, that which is due to me. My services are treated as fables; my demand is denounced as ridiculous; I am treated as the vilest of mankind. I am in the most deplorable indigence; the little property that remained to me has been seized. I am compelled to ask for decrees for delay, in order not to be dragged into prison.' Thus wrote, three days before he died, the man who had done for France more than all her kings, beside whose exploits the deeds of her Condé, her Villars, her Turenne sink into insignificance. The founder of an Empire treated as the vilest of mankind, his just claims unattended to then, unsettled even to this day; the man who acquired for France territories larger than France herself, treated as an importunate impostor! Not long could even his brave spirit endure such a contest. He died November 10, 1764.

"Not the less will he rank with posterity as one of the greatest of Frenchmen; not the less will even the descendants of his rivals in Hindustan place him on the same pedestal as the greatest of their own heroes—on the pedestal of Clive, of Warren Hastings, of Wellesley."—*French in India*, pp. 417–19.

It may not be deemed presumptuous to follow up such a graphic description by remarking that our first interest in Dupleix was awakened at Hyderabad in 1845–46. There the admirable General Fraser, the Resident, in his usual obliging way, granted the young aspirant to Anglo-Indian literary fame the loan of a very rare book, entitled "Mémoire pour le Sieur Dupleix," and some extracts from this valued work were inserted at the conclusion of a little "Tale of the War of Coromandel." *

Some remarks were also made regarding Labourdonnais,

* In the author's "Notes on Pondichery; or, The French in India," 1845–46.

the renowned French sailor of fortune, which will show how disgracefully he was treated by the great French nation on arrival in his native land. On arrival there he was well received, but had not been long in France before he became a victim to party rage: that great man who had left Mauritius in a flourishing state, and had done his best for the extension of French power in Asia, was now seized and dragged to prison, through the jealousy of an ambitious rival (Dupleix), although far away from the theatre of their jealousies. At length, after three years' imprisonment in the Bastille, a solemn decision proclaimed the innocence of Labourdonnais. They punished his accusers, and restored him to his family, but not to his country. He soon became unfit for the service of the State. A paralysis which he had obtained during his long confinement entirely undermined his constistution. Such was his reward for the distinguished services he had rendered his country. A short time after his liberation from the Bastille, sinking under the weight of premature infirmity, he died on the 9th day of September, 1753. A year after this Dupleix returned to France with a shattered fortune, and an almost broken heart. France lost in M. de la Bourdonnais one of the most illustrious men she had ever produced; posterity has done justice to his memory, and condemned his accusers. Had no rivalry existed between Dupleix and Bourdonnais, French power in the East might have existed a little longer; but the departure of these two great men tolled the death-note of French power in Asia. It is now time that we should return to Colonel Malleson's literary labours.

The next work in order of publication was "An Historical *Sketch* of the Native States of India in Subsidiary Alliance with the British Government;" and then came forth "Studies from Genoese History," in which heroes like Fiescho—in his own opinion Genoa's greatest man—were very different from the founders of our Indian Empire. He has also written "Final French Struggles in India and the Indian Seas," and, perhaps, his most celebrated and important work, the "History of the Indian Mutiny" of 1857–8, in three volumes, descriptive of the events during the great Rebellion, from the close of Sir John Kaye's second volume of "The History of the Sepoy War." This book is described as "very characteristic of Colonel Malleson's literary style, and of his impartial criticism; for, while crediting the deserving with their just due, he has not neglected those left out in the cold, but has brought to the light of day the exploits of many who have not, until the appearance of these volumes, received any meed of praise whatever." Modern history with him is certainly not what the great Napoleon considered all history—*a fable* agreed upon! The following is an extract, taken at random, from "The History of the Indian Mutiny" (vol. iii. p. 55):—

"How Bombay was served I have just told. The reader will have seen that the danger was real, the peril imminent; that but for the unlimited confidence placed by Lord Elphinstone in Mr. Forjett—a man of his own selection—it might have culminated in disaster. . . . In the presence of the massacres of Ránhpúr and of Jhánsi, of the defence of Lakhnao, and of the siege of Delhi, the attitude of Lord Elphinstone, less sensational though not less heroic, has been overlooked. Had there been an uprising attended with slaughter in Bombay, the story of its repression and the deeds of valour attending that repression would have circulated throughout the land. Instead of that we see only calm judgment and self-reliance meeting one danger and defying another, carefully selecting the most experienced instruments, and by their aid preventing a calamity so threatening that, if it had been met by men less tried, and less worthy of confidence, it must have culminated in disaster. It is an attitude which gains from being contemplated, which impresses the student of history in an ever-increasing degree with admiration of the noble character of the man, whose calm trust in himself made possible the success of the policy he alone inaugurated."

Then followed "The History of Afghanistan," "Herat, the Granary and Garden of Central Asia," "The Life of Lord Clive," and "The Decisive Battles of India." In the opinion of a high authority, the latter work is "the most complete history of the conquest of India by England that has ever been written," and it gained the rare distinction of producing "a leading article in the *Times* the day after publication."

His later works are "The Life of Field-Marshal Loudon;" the "Battlefields of Germany;" "Final French Struggles in India;" "Captain Musafir's Rambles in Alpine Lands;" and "Ambushes and Surprises," with a portrait of a nobleman who distinguished himself during the Indian Mutiny, General Lord Mark Ker, K.C.B. In addition to such useful works, he is ever a valuable contributor to some of our high-class periodicals, whose editors well know that the charm of Colonel Malleson's style consists in vividness of description, "dramatic power," and an unfailing accuracy of facts. From "The Decisive Battles of India"—which originally appeared in the "Army and Navy Magazine"—we shall now conclude our extracts with a passage from one of the least known, that of Úndwa Nálá ("Where is it?" of course English students, and even some Anglo-Indians, with no great knowledge of Indian geography, will be sure to ask):—

"One word more with respect to the hero of the campaign. In little more than four months Major Adams had begun and brought to conclusion a campaign which did more than confirm the advantages which Clive had gained for his countrymen by the victory at Plassey. Contending with a comparatively small force against a prince whose soldiers had been drilled after the European fashion, who was served for the most part by officers of tried ability, who was well furnished with cannon manned by Europeans, and with supplies; who, moreover, was supported by the sympathy and affections of his people—Adams . . . . . defeated him in three pitched battles, drove him from his dominions, virtually reconquered Bengal and Bihár, the capital of which he stormed, captured four hundred pieces of cannon, and carried the Company's arms to the banks of the Karamásá. Regarded as a military achievement it can compare with any in the history of the world. It was possible only on the condition of the display of military conduct of the highest order, of gallantry, devotion, and tenacity on the part of the troops. All these qualities were displayed to a degree which has never been surpassed. Whether we look at the genius of Adams, the tenacity of Glenn, the conduct of Knox . . . . . of Irving, of Moran, and the other officers, and of the men who served under them, we fail to find a flaw; we can see only that which is worthy of admiration."

Thus we have, through Colonel Malleson's historical research, another distinguished Anglo-Indian added to our *Valhalla,* in the person of Major Adams. We daresay that, before the account of this battle was so completely written, many excellent people rejoicing in the name of "Adams"—among them probably some of the gallant Major's descendants—never thought that Indian history possessed any such hero to adorn or immortalize it. But such is one of the uses of History; it makes deserving men live over again, causing us delight in their actions—often so different from events and deeds we hear of in our time;—and it ever gives a healthy tone to records of civil as well as military life. Sir John Kaye may be said to have fairly begun for the splendid dominion of the Queen-Empress this almost new mode of public instruction among us; and we assert, in conclusion, as we began, that in Colonel Malleson we have the fitting reply to the demand of Anglo-Indian Literature,—ANOTHER MAN TO TAKE THE COLOURS!

Colonel George Bruce Malleson was married, in 1856, to Marian, only daughter of G. N. Battye, Esq., Bengal Civil Service, and sister of the two devoted and brave officers, who, serving in the Corps of Guides, fell gloriously before Delhi and in Afghanistan. He has no children, but his nephew, Lieutenant Wilfrid Malleson, of the Royal Artillery, now serving in India, is believed to be the "child of his predilection."

SIR JOHN MORRIS, K.C.S.I.

—o—

THE following list of services of a distinguished Bengal civilian will give the British public a fair idea of how zealous and able servants of the Queen-Empress work in Her Majesty's splendid dominion, presenting also a synopsis of labour in a career remarkable for its utility and variety.

Sir John Henry Morris, K.C.S.I., eldest son of Henry Morris, Madras Civil Service, was born 9th April, 1828. Was educated privately, and entered Haileybury in July 1845, and after obtaining two medals and eight prizes, left College the head of his term. Was appointed to the Bengal Civil Service in 1847, and reached Calcutta on 8th January, 1848. Obtained in Calcutta a gold medal and three certificates of High Proficiency in Persian, Hindustanee, and Hindee, and was posted to the Punjab as Assistant to the Resident in December 1848. Served in the Punjab as Assistant Commissioner in the Kangra and Hoshyarpore Districts, and was transferred to the Settlement Department in March 1851. Served as Assistant Settlement Officer in the Jallundhur, Hoshyarpore, Umritsur, and Lahore Districts, and was promoted to Settlement Officer in December 1853. As Settlement Officer, entirely completed and reported the Settlements of the Gorgraunolah and Mooltan Districts, and proceeded on furlough in March 1859. Returned to India November 1861, and being attached to the N.W. Provinces, was appointed Magistrate and Collector of the Allahabad District, which post he held till September 1863, when he was promoted and transferred to the Central Provinces as Settlement Commissioner. In this appointment he supervised and reported on the revision of the Settlements of all the eighteen Districts of the Central Provinces, and in April 1867, was appointed to officiate as Chief Commissioner of the Central Provinces. He held this acting appointment for eight months, and was again appointed to officiate in April 1868, and was confirmed as Chief Commissioner in May 1870, which post he held continuously till May 1883, when he retired from the Service.

The Annual Administration Reports of the Central Provinces for fifteen years were prepared by him, and during his career as Chief Commissioner he drew up elaborate Minutes and State papers on the Nagpore and Chattisgarh Railway, the Warora Colliery, the Pandhree Assessment of the Central Provinces, Forest Conservancy, Trade Statistics, Excise Management, Municipal Administration, and Local Self-Government in the Central Provinces. Here is certainly a charming variety of occupations for the Bengal civilian.

The following Acts applicable to the Central Provinces, and specially designed to promote the welfare of the people of the Province, were, at his instance, passed by the Government of India, viz., the Land Revenue Act (XVIII. of 1881), the Local Self-Government Act (I. of 1883), the Tenancy Act (IX. of 1883), the Land Improvement Act and the Agricultural Loans' Act. Such labour, mental and physical, in a tropical climate, can only be duly appreciated by those who have themselves worked and seen others working for the welfare of India.

He also commenced and carried through with many others the following important public works, viz., the Great Northern Road, the North-Western Road, the Great Eastern Road, the Raepore and Sambalpore Road, and numerous smaller roads and railway feeders; the Wardha Coal State Railway, the Nagpore and Chattisgarh State Railway, the Warora Colliery, the Nagpore Water Works, and the Jabbulpore Water Works.

To have carried all these Acts and works through in England, we may wonder how many zealous M.P.'s, what number of committees, and how much of the "law's delay," would have been considered absolutely necessary?

Sir John Morris was created a C.S.I. in July 1877, and a K.C.S.I. in May 1883, on his retirement from the Bengal Civil Service. Having in this brief sketch of his career alluded to Sir John's multifarious duties, we are reminded of what was the just opinion, many years ago, of officers of the old East India Company's Army, that they possessed one great and incalculable advantage in the diversity of employments they were called upon to fill. They were by turns military, civil, and diplomatic; and their ideas became expanded. The Duke of Wellington was also quoted as an instance of the great advantages to be derived from diversity of employment; and the Munros and Malcolms, who were associated with him in India, were of the same sterling stuff. The really first-rate Indian civilian should be able to do nearly everything; to defend his house, like another Davis; to crush a famine, or start a force for service, like Sir Richard Temple, without a moment's delay; to strategize a railway, like the late Sir William Andrew; to assess and collect the revenue of a district; to give justice like a Mansfield; and to examine a school. With such qualifications he is nearly perfect.

The following, regarding the subject of our sketch, is a copy of a notification by the Home Department of the Government of India:—

SIMLA, *the 19th April*, 1883.

The Governor-General in Council desires to place upon public record his recognition of the services rendered in the Central Provinces by Mr. J. H. Morris, C.S., C.S.I., who is now about to take his departure from India.

Mr. Morris first joined the Central Provinces as Settlement Commissioner in September 1863. He was appointed to act as Chief Commissioner in April 1868, and confirmed in that office in May 1870. His intimate acquaintance with every part of his extensive charge has, during the long years of his administration, imparted a thoroughness to his work which the Government of India have frequently been glad to acknowledge. Mr. Morris has always had at heart the best interests of the population entrusted to his care. His excellent management of his province has shown him to be an administrator of the first rank, and he has in many important respects carried out with marked success a series of valuable reforms. The Governor-General in Council has great pleasure in tendering to Mr. Morris the best thanks of the Government of India.

The high appreciation of the Government displayed in this notification must be particularly gratifying to Sir John Morris; and it is this hearty and well-deserved approval of conduct which has cheered so many Anglo-Indians on in their difficult and often dangerous careers.

It may be well to follow up this tribute with an extract, paragraph 19, part i. of Report of the Administration of the Central Provinces for 1883-84; and paragraph 20, for 1884-85.

"The policy of this Administration has been to make the elementary education of the masses the chief object of expenditure, and the promotion of higher education was thus left to private effort. The spirit of self-help, which has been relied on in extending the privileges of Local Self-Government to the people of the Province, came to their aid in this matter. The meetings which were everywhere held at the close of Sir John Morris's administration, with the view of associating his memory with some work of public utility, resolved that higher education should be provided for by means of a 'Morris Memorial Fund.' The northern districts joined in an effort to have the collegiate course of the Jabbulpore High School made complete; and subscribed Rs.78,940 for this end. The southern districts (excepting Sambalpore) combined to provide a local college at Nagpore, and subscribed Rs.1,70,460. The people of the Sambalpore district collected Rs.18,000, and offered this sum in aid of a scheme for raising the Sambalpore Zillah School to the grade of a High School. The Chief Commissioner, in March 1884, sanctioned the Sambalpore scheme. Since the close of the official year the sanction of Government has been received to the addition of 3rd and 4th year classes to the Jabbulpore Collegiate course, and to the necessary increase in the staff of the College. The projected College at Nagpore (the

'Morris College') is to be managed by a private body, and not by Government. The members of this body have been chosen, and arrangements are in progress for giving the necessary legal basis to their corporate action."

"Large subscriptions have been raised for the purpose of establishing a College or Colleges to commemorate Sir John Morris' administration. It was decided that the Jabbulpore High School should be raised to the status of a College, remaining under the management of the Department, and not a College under independent management, but aided by Government, should be established at Nagpore. The subscribers of the Southern Districts, acting under the advice of the Chief Commissioner, registered themselves as a Society under Act XXI. of 1860, and have established a College at Nagpore, which is now working. The necessary classes were added to the Jabbulpore College. The Free Church Institution at Nagpore has established F.A. Classes, and is prepared to compete with the 'Morris College.' The wants of the Province have therefore been more than sufficiently supplied."* And thus Sir John Morris acted his part right well in the difficult drama of Indian administration and improvement.

We shall now present to our readers one of those valedictory addresses,† not unfrequent in India, teeming with gratitude to the departing officer, who had at length turned his footsteps homeward, after long wandering and toiling in a foreign land:—

Vale !—Never before, or hardly ever, has a subordinate ruler resigned the reins of Government in this country who could survey, retrospectively, the results of his administration with more legitimate pride and fitting complacency than the distinguished official who has just laid down his exalted office in the Central Provinces. Mr. Morris, although he has not yet been gazetted "out," is at any rate officially

* Paragraph 20, part i. of 1884-85 Report.

† *The Express*, Lucknow, April 7, 1883.

moribund: and, even though far removed from the area of his singularly successful administration, "we cannot permit" (we are driven, for want of a readier, to the expression of this droll official conventionality) that gentleman to quit the scene of his unwearied and congenial labours, without proffering him the expression of our regretful adieux.

Mr. Morris constitutes in his own person a remarkable illustration of the palpable profit derived from what we may phrase the retention of office indefinitely. As the Central Provinces know, to their lasting advantage, the distinguished Tetrarch on whom they have lately looked their last, possessed a marvellous capacity for work; and from the day, now several years ago, on which he assumed the duties of his highly responsible post, he has devoted himself, heart and soul, and with unflagging energy, to the interests of the millions confided to his care. And well and nobly has the State been served, and the conspicuous devotion of its able and conscientious servant signally manifested before all the world. For the prestige of Mr. Morris' administration has travelled far beyond the limits of the British Empire in India.

Some of the most distinguished contemporary journalists and litterateurs at home have not hesitated to point to the Central Provinces as affording a striking exemplar of good government, and their ruler as the embodiment or practical prosopopœia of a Model Administrator.

In noticing the termination of the Chief Commissioner's rule over the extensive Provinces so long under his immediate control, we are by no means minded to recapitulate the various and, not seldom, very striking phases of his administration: that pleasing task devolved on and received felicitous expression a little while ago at the hands of one of his genial and not undistinguished lieutenants in another place. But we have ourselves followed the whole circle of Mr. Morris' administration with exceeding interest and unqualified admiration.

It has been objected that Mr. Morris, from the outset of his administration to its terminal point, developed an overpowering penchant for those flowers of chaste literature which, when full-blown, assume the attractive though not always aromatic form of official reports.

Possibly so. But, for ourselves, we feel free to say that, for a long series of years, embracing the entire period of his government, Mr. Morris' are the only administrative reports—we make the observation in no invidious sense—that we have been betrayed into discussing or ever reading right through. And with an equally good conscience we make bold to aver that, utterly unlike some of those literary authors of officialdom in other places, Mr. Morris has never penned a line which may have met the public eye, that could fairly be voted irrelevant or out of place; nor did he suffer that sin on the part of his lieutenants to pass unrebuked. Were that eminent man (Mr. Cross classes him, worthily, amongst his "eminent Indian authorities"), Sir Richard Temple, to revisit the scene of his former success—for it may with truth be said Sir Richard initiated good government in the Central Provinces—that capable and accomplished administrator would not readily recognize the province he left behind him some years ago. So wholly changed, so robust and vigorous has it grown under the fostering care, the prescient tutelage of its essentially disinterested, self-denying, thoroughly practical Proconsul. Where can one look for such marvellous feats in the educational field? What system of land-tenure can rival that conceived, brought forth, and matured, it may be said, by the truly able Chief who now, to the unspeakable regret of his subjects universally, turns his back regretfully for evermore on that great Tetrarchy he has governed so long, so wisely, and surely so well! Mr. Morris' administration well merits—what is not invariably deserved elsewhere—the designation of thorough. No man among his contemporaries ever suffered less from sentiment.

Few of his compeers of this, or indeed of the past generation, could claim a truer appreciation of the vital value of what has come to be correctly expressed as practical politics. He has been the true, and honest, and undeviating exponent of local legislation.

No official hierarch amongst them all cherished more contempt for political claptrap or "patriotic" charlatans; was less imbued with a spirit of, let us call it, romantic ad ministration. Mr. Morris dealt essentially in solids. He never sacrificed a pen's point for an "idea;" above all things, he devoted himself—as we could wish those in higher places had, if only for their own weal, even unwittingly, devoted themselves—to the practical expression of substantial and tangible government; the ideal he cast to the winds.

Surely such a successful and capable career cannot have finally closed politically? Room might well be made, and with vast advantage, in another place across the water, for the sound judgment, administrative ability, and sagacious course of this distinguished official. At any rate, it cannot be needed for us to say that the knighthood which doubtless awaits the ex-Tetrarch at home could not well be—Her Majesty the Empress can scarcely fail to reflect—more deservedly bestowed; assuredly officialdom bristles with civil knights, not a few of whose escutcheons might derive lustre from the reflection of the feats emblazoned on that borne by the late Ruler of the Central Provinces. This unpretending, and indeed it is felt very inadequate, tribute to the worth of an official who has done so much politically, socially, and morally, for his subjects of yesterday, comes from a pen utterly unknown to the subject of it; whose holder has not the smallest ken of Mr. Morris personally, or in any possible way other than through his official acts, but who, still, may claim the privilege of tendering to that really "honest gentleman" and "strong" man a respectful farewell.*

* *See* also Appendix No. II.

SIR JOSEPH FAYRER, K.C.S.I., LL.D., F.R.S.

—o—

WE have always entertained the highest respect for the medical profession in India. Having seen much of its members, on service and in cantonment, or say in every variety of Anglo-Indian life, there can be no hesitation in affirming that, take them for all in all, a finer or more useful class of men never trod God's earth. From Boughton, the surgeon and diplomatist, curing the Mogul's beautiful daughter, and founding our trade in Bengal, to the eminent Bombay physician, Dr. James Burnes, curing an Ameer in Sindh, or down to more recent times, when the distinguished subject of the present sketch accompanied their Royal Highnesses the Prince of Wales and the Duke of Edinburgh, during their travels in India, there has ever been various excellence among Indian medical men, which has, doubtless, tended to uphold their high character at the present day, and will do so as long as we hold India, which must, in spite of every absurd *phobia*, be ours till the end of time! The admirable Dr. Burnes, whose career has been imperfectly sketched in the *First Series* of this work, must have possessed address, tact, and temper, in addition to great skill, to have been so successful in whatever he attempted. These are qualities as necessary to the physician as to the diplomatist; and we venture to think that they are to be found in Sir Joseph Fayrer to a very considerable extent, as will not only be seen from the following sketch,* but from a few extracts hereafter

* Chiefly from the *Biograph and Review*, September 1881; which sketch has been revised, with various additions, and brought down to a later date.

to be given from his diaries, while accompanying the Royal Princes on their visits to India.

The annals of the India Medical Service present no career so eventful and distinguished as that of Sir Joseph Fayrer. In military prowess he was, perhaps, excelled by Dr. Wyllie, of the Madras Army, who at Corrygaum, during the Mahratta war of 1816-17, defended a post, with two guns, against an overwhelming force of the enemy. He afterwards became Physician-General. Dr. Brydone also, the "last man" of the first Afghan war, was another distinguished member of the Indian Medical Service; and there are several others.

For upwards of a quarter of a century it fell to his lot to take a more or less prominent part in the principal events in the history of our Indian Empire, and in each, though greatly diversified in their character, he proved himself fully equal to the occasion, Whether it was as surgeon on the battle-fields of Burma, or as Residency-Surgeon and Honorary Assistant-Resident, at Lucknow, or subsequently as one of the noble band of defenders of that city, during its memorable siege (in which his duties partook as much of a military as professional character), or as Professor of Surgery in the Calcutta College, or as Physician to the Duke of Edinburgh and the Prince of Wales, during their respective tours in the East; or as President of the Indian Medical Board, and Physician to the Indian Council, the unanimous voice of the profession, as well as of the public, pronounced him to be the right man in the right place. It may be said of him, which can be said of few, that he has attained his present distinguished position without exciting a spark of feeling of envy or ill-will in the breasts of any of his professional brethren. It is admitted on all hands that his success has been a deserved one.

Sir Joseph Fayrer, K.C.S.I., M.D., LL.D. Edin., F.R.S. Lond. and Edin., F.R.C.P. Lond., F.R.C.S. Eng. Edin., Surgeon-General late H.M. Indian Army, President of the Indian Medical Board, Physician to the Secretary of State for India in Council, Member of Army Sanitary Commission, Member of Senate of Army Medical School at Netley, Honorary Physician to H.M. the Queen and the Prince of

Wales, Physician to the Duke of Edinburgh, &c., is second son of Commander R. J. Fayrer, R.N., of Haverbrack, Westmoreland, was born at Plymouth, December 6th, 1824. Having completed his early education at private schools, and on the continent, he commenced his medical studies at the Royal Naval Hospital at Bermuda; these were subsequently continued at the Charing Cross Hospital, at King's College, London, in Palermo and Rome, and at the University of Edinburgh, where he graduated M.D. in 1859.

In 1847 he entered the Royal Navy as Assistant-Surgeon on H.M.S. *Victory*, and, having volunteered for this service, when travelling in Sicily he served in the Military Hospitals of Palermo, during the siege of that city, from December 1847 to March 1848, during which period he performed many capital operations, and had the care of many wounded. He was also present at the siege of Rome by the French Army in 1848; and here had further opportunities of studying military surgery in all its branches.

In 1849 he took the degree of M.D., by examination, at the University of Rome, and returning to England he resigned the Navy, and was appointed Assistant-Surgeon, Royal Artillery, at Woolwich, where he remained till April 1850, when he received the appointment as Assistant-Surgeon, H.E.I. Company, on the Bengal establishment. Arriving in Calcutta in October 1850, he was posted first to the artillery at Dum-Dum, and subsequently to the Sylhet Light Infantry, with charge of the civil station at Cherra Poonjee.

In 1851 he was posted to the 74th B.N.I., at Dacca, the regiment being at the time prostrated with fever. He was sent in charge of this regiment, all sick, in a fleet of native boats on the river, during which expedition they were attacked by and suffered severely from cholera. He remained in charge of this regiment till March 24th, 1852, when he was appointed to the Field Hospital of the Burma Field Force. He served throughout the Burmese War; was present at the taking of the stockades at the river side, and was in charge of the Field Hospital for the greater part of the operations in the vicinity of, and at the capture of, Rangoon. During this campaign Dr. Fayrer greatly distinguished himself by the able manner in which he discharged his arduous duties. He won golden opinions from all, no less by his professional skill, especially as an operating surgeon, than by his kindness of heart, his unwearying zeal, and his exertions in the cause of humanity. In recognition of his services, he was appointed (Feb. 2nd, 1853) Civil Surgeon of Rangoon, which he held, together with the appointment of Medical Storekeeper of the Bengal Division of the Army of Burma, till the following August, when he received the appointment of Residency-Surgeon at Lucknow, from the Governor-General, whose letter on the occasion is a testimonial of the highest value. It ran as follows: "Sir,—The Residency-Surgeoncy at Lucknow has been vacant for some time. I have purposely reserved it that I might bestow it as the best medical appointment in the gift of the Governor-General upon the Assistant-Surgeon who should be found to have rendered the most approved services during the war with Burma. The testimony that has been borne to your professional skill, exertions, and character by the Superintending Surgeon under whom you have served, has determined me to select you for this office, and I have much satisfaction in thus bestowing upon you the reward which your merit has won.

"(Signed) DALHOUSIE.

"To Assistant-Surgeon Fayrer."

Previous to leaving Rangoon to take up this important post, he received a public letter of thanks from the merchants and residents of that city, accompanied by a testimonial in the shape of a valuable gold watch and chain, as "a permanent record of our esteem, and high sense of your services and goodness."

On his way from Rangoon, when in Calcutta for a short period, he passed the College in Hindostanee.

In accordance with orders, Dr. Fayrer now moved to Lucknow, and on August 19th, 1853, he took charge of the appointments of Residency-Surgeon and Postmaster, to which, in September 1854, was added the appointment of Honorary Assistant-Resident. On the annexation of Oudh he was appointed (March 20, 1856) Civil Surgeon and Superintendent of Charitable Institutions in Lucknow, and he continued in these offices until the Sepoy Mutiny of 1857, and until the siege of the Residency, throughout which he served, and was one of the Council of War convened by Brigadier-General Sir Henry Lawrence, to consider the question of holding or abandoning the Residency. His house in the Residency was one of the chief garrisons, and in it he lost many killed and wounded during the defence, which forms one of the most brilliant and glorious episodes in the annals of Indian warfare. That brave and good man, Sir Henry Lawrence, the man "who tried to do his duty," was one of those who died in Fayrer's "garrison." To attempt to enter into details of all Dr. Fayrer had to go through during that eventful and momentous period would exceed our limits; but for the attention, skill, and energy which he, in common with Superintending-Surgeon J. Scott, Drs. Boyd, Bird, Campbell, Bryden, Ogilvie, Partridge, Greenhow, Darby, and the apothecary, Thompson, displayed in the discharge of their onerous and most important duties, the Governor-General in Council tendered their cordial thanks (G. O., December 8th, 1857). High testimony is likewise borne to Dr. Fayrer's individual exertions by Sir J. Inglis and Sir J. Outram. Writing nineteen years subsequent to this date ("Journal," p. 88), Dr. Fayrer observes: "I little thought in 1857 that I should live to show the ruins of my house to the Prince of Wales! Much of it is still standing, but the roof and the floor are gone. I tried to find the old tally I kept on the wall of some fourteen killed and forty wounded, but the plaster had fallen away. The shot and shell marks still remain, showing how it was battered. * * * I lost all my property and many valued things, but I saved those dearest to me; thank God, no grave, there at least, holds any of my loved ones!"

For his services during the defence of the Lucknow Residency he was promoted to the brevet rank of Surgeon, received a medal and clasp, and was allowed to count a year's service towards retirement. Dr. Fayrer was subsequently present at the relief of Cawnpore by Lord Clyde, having for the purpose made a forced march of more than thirty miles to reach that city. The great bodily and mental exertions which he went through at this period proved too much for his strength, and he returned home on medical certificate in 1858.

During the year at home he studied hard in the University of Edinburgh, took the degree of M.D., and was also elected a Fellow of the Royal Society of Edinburgh, and Fellow of the Royal College of Surgeons, Edinburgh.

Returning to India in the following year, Dr. Fayrer was appointed, May 12th, 1859, Professor of Surgery and *ex-officio* First Surgeon of the Medical College Hospital, Calcutta, and in 1865 Consulting Surgeon to the Howrah General Hospital; in these important posts he greatly distinguished himself by his professional skill as a physician and as an operating surgeon. Portions of his experience in these hospitals and elsewhere he subsequently published in his "Clinical Surgery in India," 1866, and in his "Clinical and Pathological Observations in India," 1873.

In addition to the above, Dr. Fayrer held in Calcutta several other important posts. In 1860 he was appointed to the medical charge of the Mysore princes; in 1861 he was made a Fellow of the Calcutta University and a Member of the Senate; he served two years as President of the Medical Faculty, and received, on retiring, the public thanks of that body; he was likewise for many years Examiner in Surgery at the University. In 1867 he was made President of the Asiatic Society of Bengal, and in 1868 Government Trustee of the Indian Museum, and Justice of the Peace for the town of Calcutta. In the same year he was made Companion of the Star of India.

In the early part of 1870 his onerous and important duties at Calcutta were interrupted for a time by his being appointed to accompany the Duke of Edinburgh during his tour in Upper India. This lasted from the 7th of January to the 10th of March, and on parting he received an autograph letter from the Prince, thanking him for his services during the trip. In the following year (July 22nd, 1871) he was appointed Honorary Physician to the Queen.

Having presented to the Indian Government a splendidly illustrated work on the "Poisonous Snakes of India," he was thanked by the Government, who published it in August 1872.* A second edition was issued in the following year. He received the thanks of the Acting Governor-General and a piece of plate for his services on the occasion of the death of Lord Mayo in 1872. In the cold weather of that year he was obliged to seek rest in England, where, soon after his return, he was appointed a Fellow of the Royal College of Physicians, London, Croonian Lecturer in 1882, and Member of the Council of the College in 1886; also elected a Member of the Old College of Physicians' Club (21 members) in 1877, and a Member of the Indian Medical Board, of which he became President, with the rank of Surgeon-General and the very responsible post of Physician to the Secretary of State for India in Council in 1874. In July of that year he was appointed Physician to the Duke of Edinburgh. He resigned the service in that year, receiving a very handsome despatch from the Indian Government in acknowledgment of his services. He accompanied the Prince of Wales throughout his Indian tour in 1875–76. On his return he was appointed Honorary Physician to His Royal Highness. He was advanced to the rank of K.C.S.I. in India before his return with the Prince, and at the same time as Generals Probyn and Sam. Browne. He was elected F.R.S. in 1878. In the following year he received the degree of LL.D. from the University of Edinburgh, and, in accordance with one of their bye-laws, the College of Surgeons of England selected him as one of two members for the special grant of their fellowship. In 1886 he was elected Foreign Correspondant Étranger de l'Académie de Médicine, Paris, and Foreign Member of the Société d'Hygiène, Paris; in 1885, Foreign Member of the Royal Academy of Medicine, Rome; in 1886, Foreign Member of the Society of Public Health of Belgium, Brussels, Member of the Academy of Science, Philadelphia, and Honorary Fellow of the College of Physicians, Philadelphia. He is also

* *See* NOTE at end of Sketch.

Consulting Physician of Charing Cross Hospital, and Governor of Guy's and Charing Cross Hospitals.*

Besides the treatises already named, Sir Joseph Fayrer is the author of numerous important works, monographs and published addresses. Among these may especially be mentioned his work on "Tropical Disease," published by Churchill in 1881; on "Some of the Physical Conditions of the Country that affect Life in India"; a work on "The Tiger"; "Journal with the Princes" (for private circulation); on the "Physiological Action of the Poison of Naja Tripudians" (in conjunction with Dr. Brunton); three parts in the *Proceedings of the Royal Society of London;* a paper on the "Claws of the Felidæ"; "On the Anatomy of the Rattlesnake"; "Climate and Fevers of India," being the Croonian Lectures for 1882; The Lettsonian Lectures on Dysentery, 1881; Paper on Liver Abscess in the *Lancet,* 1883–84; on Tropical Diarrhœa, 1884; rewrote chapter in Murchison on Tropical Abscess of Liver, 1886; and he wrote numerous other memoirs on subjects in natural history, climate, tropical meteorology, &c.

At the General Election he was invited by the Conservative interest to stand for the University of Edinburgh. They submitted an application to the Law Officer of the Crown, asking if Sir Joseph Fayrer could retain his appointment at the India Office if he were elected. The decision was adverse—a curious finding, as the appointment is purely a military one, and other military officers, when serving, are not debarred thereby from sitting in Parliament. Sir Joseph Fayrer did not wish to give up either the appointment or his professional work for a seat in the House of Commons, much as he would have rejoiced to have had the opportunity of advocating the claims of medicine in the service, or of education generally.

Sir Joseph Fayrer married, in 1855, Bethia Mary, eldest

* He was President of the Epidemiological Society in 1879 and 1880; President of the Medical Society of London in 1883; represented India with T. R. Lewis at the International Sanitary Conference at Amsterdam, in 1883; and at Rome, Diplomatically and Medically, in 1885.

daughter of the late Major-General Andrew Spens, and has had six sons (one died in infancy at Allahabad after the siege of Lucknow) and two daughters.

NOTE.

With reference to Sir Joseph Fayrer's admirable work "On the Poisonous Snakes of India," the author of "Ashé Pyee"—the Eastern or Foremost Country—while (1881) recording the destruction of wild animals and snakes in India and Burma, was led to remark:—The study of snake-poison evidently requires another Sir Joseph Fayrer in India at present; while some engine of wholesale destruction, for wild animals in our Eastern dominions, remains to be invented. To think that, in Bengal alone, during 1880, there were 10,000 deaths from snake-bite, and 360 by tigers, and a total in eleven provinces of nearly 3,000 from wild beasts, and 19,150 from venomous snakes, is enough to make humanity shudder, showing that, with regard to populations in the East, still—

> "The trail of the serpent is over them all!"

All honour, then, to our distinguished Anglo-Indian for having, through his study of the deadly poison in snakes, done for humanity in India what M. Pasteur has endeavoured to do, and partly succeeded in doing, for the good of mankind by the cure of hydrophobia in Europe!

We shall now add to this Sketch some extracts from Sir Joseph's "Diaries" or "Notes" with the Princes in India, which exhibit just the style for such composition; here and there also evincing very considerable powers of description. We begin after the departure from Benares.*

The Prince and suite were received at Lucknow by Sir G. Couper, Chief Commissioner of Oudh, and several high civil and military officers. The station was tastefully decorated, and a sumptuous breakfast prepared. Here, among

* *See* end of Appendix No. I.

others, Sir Joseph met his old friend, Dr. Loch.—At this stage of the Prince of Wales's visit to India, we are led to note that all arrangements as to health, comfort, variety of amusement, and other important accessories, seem to have been truly admirable. The Physician-General throughout displays a will of his own, without which a man in high position is worse than useless, or a mere cypher. After two or three days' residence at Lucknow—where he played so distinguished a part during the Mutiny—we find the energetic diarist remarking:—"I danced, walked, and talked with old friends. How all is changed and changing since the siege! This house (Chutter Munzil) was full of dead sepoys when Outram relieved us in 1857." But what a far greater change in 1887—Her Majesty's Jubilee year—when India contributed to the Imperial pageant her grand procession of Indian Princes! *

REMINISCENCES OF LUCKNOW.

". . . . Hoc est
Vivere bis, vita posse priore fui."—MART.

"*Sunday, 9th January*, 1876.—After lunch the Prince, the Duke of Sutherland and some of the suite, with Sir G. Couper, drove to the Residency. We got out at my old house, and went over it. I pointed out my room, and the spot where Sir H. Lawrence lay, and where he died; where the ladies lived, and where many interesting events took place. The Prince was deeply interested. We then went all over the site of the old defences; each place was pointed out, and each garrison explained. The Prince ascended to the top of the Residency tower, from which he had a beautiful view of the country, and of the line of approach through the city of Outram and Havelock's force. He went into the Tye Khana, and, in short, saw all, from beginning to end. We visited the churchyard, and there saw Sir H. L.'s tomb with its simple inscription:

'Here lies Henry Lawrence,
Who tried to do his duty.'

The Prince asked many questions, which Sir G. Couper and I replied to; here also he seemed much interested! [Some particulars from this entry have already been given.] I gathered a few flowers to send to my wife from her old

* Appendix III.

home. The Residency is kept in beautiful order, and is a striking memorial, but the ruins look old—so old, one can hardly realize that they were once smiling and happy homes of some who are still quite young. The events of that evil time look so far back in the past that they hardly seem to belong to the present generation! And yet, as I stood at the door of my ruined house, the past seemed to come so near that I could have imagined myself once more in my old place, and that I was about to mount my horse or get into my carriage and drive to cantonments! I felt, as I have always felt on revisiting my house, how much cause I have to be thankful, and how many there are who still live, only to look back to the time and place as among the saddest of their recollections."

Cawnpore and Delhi possessed much of interest for the Prince and suite; and they will do so for all keen-eyed European travellers yet to come. The terrible Mutiny has made these places almost classic ground. On the 12th, the Prince entertained at dinner in the Delhi camp all the generals and other high officers who had been present at a grand review of 20,000 men (four divisions) in the morning. After dinner they went to a ball given to the Prince in the Dewan Khäs in the fort. "Perhaps," writes Sir Joseph Fayrer, "Hafiz's couplet * written on the wall never spoke more truly than on this occasion." And again—"The decorations of the ancient hall of audience were splendid, the lighting and all that could conduce to beauty and splendour were admirably arranged." As on the eve of Waterloo, it might be truly said at Delhi that 'bright,' at this ball, graced by the presence of the Prince,

"The lämps shone o'er fair women and brave men!"

On the 16th the party left Delhi by train for Lahore. Many people, including ladies, were at the station to see the Royal train start.

* "Agur firdous be rui zamin ust:
Hameen ust! hameen ust! O, hameen ust!"

which is thus translated:—

"If there is a paradise on earth
It is this! it is this! oh, it is this!"

This will remind the reader of Moore's beautiful adaptation in *Lalla Rookh*:—

"And, oh! if there be an elysium on earth,
It is this, it is this!"

VISIT TO LAHORE.

"*Tuesday, 18th January, Umritsur.*—We had chota-hazari, and put on full dress to enter Lahore, where we arrived at about 9.40 A.M. The station was decorated. The Lieut.-Governor, Sir H. Davies, with military and civil authorities and native chiefs were waiting to receive the Prince. We drove in procession to Government House, passing the encampments of the native chiefs, pitched along the roadside. They had elephants, troops and followers drawn up, and were all waiting the Prince's arrival. The road wound round the fort, and the sight was most interesting, with the elephants in their gay-coloured trappings, the camels, sowars and every variety of native troops; salutes were fired, and bands played as the Prince passed. There were great crowds of natives along the whole route. The forts, the mosques and minarets looked very picturesque, and the groups of elephants and attendants in front of each chief's camp were most imposing. Each chief was seated on his elephant, and rose and salaamed as the Prince passed.

"We had breakfast soon after arriving at Government House, where the Prince was received by Sir Henry and Lady Davies—then a numerously attended levée, and a reception of native chiefs. An address from the municipality was read, and presented in a rich casket. About thirteen native chiefs were presented with the usual ceremonies, a salute, according to his rank, being fired for each. There was the Nawab of Bhawalpore, the Rajahs of Fureedkote, of Chumba, of Mundi, of Sukeet, Sirdar of Kulsia, Nawabs of Patowdi, of Laharoo, of Dojarra, Rajah Shumshir Sing, of Goler; of Maler Kotta, of Kupurthulla, of Nabha, and, I think, some others, but I do not remember their names.

"After lunch we drove to the central jail and saw all the arrangements, and the manufactures—carpets, clothes, towels—of the prisoners. We also visited the Thuggie Department, and several noted old Thugs, whose lives had been spared on turning approvers—that is, who saved their lives on condition of betraying others—were brought before the Prince. They can hardly be considered prisoners now, and some of them are most venerable and respectable-looking old gentlemen. One or two of them told us how many lives they had taken with the Rumal (handkerchief), and one showed how the strangling process was effected, and exhibited it, with a handkerchief, on my arm—instead of a neck—giving it such a wrench that I felt it for days afterwards. Several prisoners—one or two Europeans or East Indians, whose conduct had been good during their confinement—were liberated at the Prince's request; about twenty-five men and twelve women (natives) were released.

"Some purchases of manufactures were made. We then drove to the fort, went over it and the citadel; Runjeet Sing's house and the Sheesh Mahul, where there is a beautiful view of the plain on the banks of the river, where Runjeet used to review his troops, and where, perhaps, Alexander's troops may have exercised. There was a glorious view of the distant snowy ranges from the roof. The sun setting over Runjeet's tomb and the Badshahi mosque, was very beautiful. We dined at Government House at 8 P.M. Lord S. is laid up with symptoms of dysentery. Put him regularly under treatment in bed. The day cold, but beautifully bright and clear—air dry. Met many old friends, Col. Williams, R.E., and others. There was a ball given at the Montgomery Hall; I met several old friends. Left pretty early, before supper, and went to bed at 11.30. The night was cold, but fine. I am in a large tent in the camp surrounding the Government House, which itself is an old tomb converted into a dwelling-house. The reception-rooms are large, but the accommodation is not very extensive; several of our party are in tents. It was so when I was here in 1870 with the Duke of Edinburgh."

On the 20th of January the party left what the Eastern poets style "the splendid city of Lahore," with its mausoleums and shrines, magnificent and numberless, and "where Death appeared to share equal honours with Heaven"—a rather different band of travellers from that to which Lalla Rookh—Rajahs and Omras in her train—belonged when leaving the same city for the beautiful and luxurious valley of Cashmere. They left by special train for Wuzeerabad! —enough of itself to break the spell of Poesy. Here they found breakfast prepared in tents by Mr. Kelner, the grand purveyor for this expedition, as he had been for that of the Duke of Edinburgh. Carriages and drags conveyed them to Jummoo—another breach of an Eastern poetic spell! On entering the Jummoo territory, they found that the

Maharajah of Cashmere had made a cutcha road all the way, beginning where our metalled road ended, and thus presenting no impediment. The city of Jummoo was entered in what is styled "great state," just as the sun was setting. The journey from Wuzeerabad had only occupied eight or nine hours, including a halt at Sealkote. The Maharajah, with his son and sirdars, and body-guard in helmets and cuirasses, made a splendid show to welcome England's Prince, which Sir Walter Scott would have loved to describe. The elephants crossing the river in procession, and the troops, made a most picturesque foreground to a lovely scene. "The hills, the river, the forts on the heights, and the city of Jummoo," were all before them.

BRILLIANT SCENE IN JUMMOO.

"There was the usual accompaniment of music, salutes, fireworks, and every sort of demonstration of joy and welcome as the procession moved up the hill and entered the gateway of the old city. The windows, the streets, the roofs of the houses and the balconies were occupied by picturesque groups of people in every variety of costume, from Cashmir, Tibet, and the plains. We entered in single file, passing under the arch of the gateway of the city, and very picturesque it was to see the line of gaily caparisoned elephants, each with its howdah occupied by a native chief or an English officer, winding through the narrow streets. On an elevated spot the Maharajah had built an enormous square building, with large reception rooms, with the special object of entertaining the Prince. It has only occupied three months in construction, and is really wonderful, considering the short time. The rooms were beautifully decorated, but so very damp they were not desirable sleeping places. A number of tents had been pitched on the surrounding plateau for the Prince; they were decorated and hung with shawls. We each had a very good tent, in which shawls formed part of the furniture and decoration.

"We went at once to the great hall of the new building, where a Durbar was held, and mutual presentations took place with the usual Oriental ceremony—attar-pan, &c. We then adjourned to the front terrace, commanding a fine view of the surrounding country. On the plain below there was a grand display of fireworks. The city was illuminated, and the effect, as darkness came on, was very beautiful. We then adjourned to our tents, and dressed for an immense dinner party, given by the Maharajah. All the officers and ladies from Sealkote, and many from other stations, were present. After dinner there was a nautch, which was as tame and stupid as those entertainments generally are."

On the 21st the party set off on elephants on a shooting expedition to the low jungle at the foot of the hills. They forded the river, where they crossed on the previous day; and, driving to a covert, a beat for deer and nilgye was speedily organized. But there was little sport—a few pigs and nilgye only being seen. They got back to their tents in the afternoon. There was now to be a grand entertainment at the Maharajah's palace, and a dinner party in European style, which, of course, as usual, must have cost a large sum. This grand repast was hardly a fitting close to "a tiring day."

AT THE MAHARAJAH'S PALACE.

"The approach to the palace through the city, on elephants, was very interesting; the streets were illuminated, decorated, and crowded with people of all sorts. On arriving at the palace there was a Durbar, at which the Sirdars were presented to the Prince, and offered their nuzzurs. We all sat in a semi-circle, as usual, and watched the ceremony, which was like that we have now so often seen in other parts of India. We then adjourned to dinner in another large room, which we reached after passing through several courtyards and galleries. It was draped with Cashmere shawls, and hung with pictures. The dinner was laid out in European style. The hall looked on to a courtyard with fountains, where there was a beautiful alcove inlaid with mosaic; all the windows and doors were draped with beautiful Cashmere shawls. The carpets, too, were of lovely Cashmere work with coloured embroidery on a white ground. After dinner we adjourned to the great Durbar hall, where we found not only the native chiefs, but the European officers and ladies from Sealkote and neighbouring stations.

"Then followed a grotesque dance of Ladak and Lassa Llamas in hideous masks, accompanied by the wildest and most barbaric music, part of it produced by long copper tubes, like Alpine horns, on which the performers blew the most dismal blasts of discordant sounds. There were cymbals and other instruments altogether, making wild and fantastic music, to which they contorted themselves in a grotesque sort of dance. It reminded me of the masks in a Christmas pantomime at home.

"After this there was a display of fireworks in the court-yard, so near that the smoke nearly suffocated us. Some animals were led into the hall and presented to the Prince, among others a fine Barasingha stag, which looked wild and frightened. He is to go home with us in the *Serapis*. There were crowds of European ladies and gentlemen, who seemed much interested with the entertainment. We then took leave of the Maharajah and his son, mounted our elephants and returned through the illuminated city to the camp; it was a clear night—not too cold, and the fresh air and bright starlight were very pleasant after the heat and smoke of the palace. Among other things presented to the Prince by the Maharajah was a magnificent sword, richly jewelled, said to be worth a lac of rupees, with a magnificent diamond in the belt. There was also a great collection of skins, horns, and heads of Himalayan and Cashmerian animals.

"The weather had been cloudy all day, a few drops of rain fell in the morning; the air quite mild. The distant mountain range generally hidden, but the nearer hills looking lovely."

THE PRINCE'S FIRST TIGER.

"*Saturday, 5th February, Jeypore.**—At 8 A.M. the Prince, Aylesford, Carrington, Rose, of 10th Hussars, Lord A. Paget, Bradford, Hall, with myself and one or two others, rode or drove out to some cover on the spurs of certain hills covered with low jungle, about four miles from the town, where there are some tigers—more or less preserved, I imagine. We had only two or three elephants, as the shooting is to be from a block-house, built on one of the ridges, and commanding the direction a tiger is likely to take when the beaters begin to move forward. Carrington and I remained at the foot of the hill on an elephant, on broken ground, cut up by ravines, masses of rock, mounds of earth, and low jungle of a scrubby character—just the place for hog, deer,

* On Friday, the 4th, the party left Agra for Jeypore.

pea-fowl, and other game. The Prince and attendants rode along a path which led up the hill, and soon we saw them on the top of the block-house, ready. The beat then advanced from the other side. Carrington and I, keeping an eye on the jungle below the Prince, were ready, if the tiger should come our way. I had a No. 12 rifle. We were both on the same elephant. After a time we saw movements on the block-house, and heard shouting and tom-tomming from the beaters. Soon after we heard a shot or two, and then I saw a tiger come over the brow of the hill slowly, as if wounded. As it crept along the side of the hill I saw it roll over and fall into a clump of bushes. I immediately got off the elephant, and sent it up for the Prince to mount and follow the tiger. We then moved slowly towards where it was lying wounded, about 200 yards ahead of us. The ground was very difficult here; we had mounted the other elephant. The Prince by this time was coming down the hill. We pointed out the place where the tiger appeared, and, just at this moment, he fired. The tiger had got up, and turned back round the shoulder of the hill.

"We followed with the Prince, but could not find it. Beaters came up, and threw in stones and anars (fireworks), but it made no sign. The Prince was standing in a spot where, if the tiger moved, it must be seen, and as we felt sure it had not passed, I expected a good charge, as I thought the animal was wounded and lying close, sulking, in the low thick jungle; the Prince waited very steady and cool! I went round a hillock to get at the spot where I thought the tiger might be lying, to try and make it move, when suddenly I heard some of the beaters shouting that it was there. I got off the elephant and scrambled up the side of the hill, and there we found it lying quite dead in a thick clump of grass. She was a fine tigress, 8 feet 2 inches in length. She had been hit twice, if not thrice. The Prince had hit her from the Oody (block-house), and again when she turned, after he came down the hill. The Maharajah was much pleased, as this was the Prince's first tiger. We then left the jungle, and had luncheon in an old palace. The shade of fine trees and some deliciously cool running water was very refreshing; here we drank to the Prince's first tiger."

Doubtless His Royal Highness has often since thought of this sporting incident in his life, so well related by Sir Joseph Fayrer.

The Maharajah of Jeypore is described as a very agreeable, clever little man, a Rajhput of ancient descent. After the tiger incident, a grand Durbar and dinner party took place. The Maharajah came in at dessert, and proposed the Queen's health. The Prince then proposed the Maharajah's. The Maharajah of Jodhpore's brother was with the party, acting as Aide-de-Camp to the Prince. He was with H.R.H. at Delhi. The Jodhpore potentate (Maharajah), it may be mentioned, in a splendid spirit of liberality, has, it is said (July 1887), given, through H.R.H. the Prince of Wales, £10,000 to the Imperial Institute.

This is a grand sign of the times ; and in taking leave of Sir Joseph Fayrer and his excellent Diaries—which we trust may one day see the light in their entirety—it may be remarked that we can have no sounder Indian policy than to keep well with, and secure the lasting friendship of, the great Princes of India !

HON. SIR ASHLEY EDEN, K.C.S.I., C.I.E.

(A MODEL LIEUTENANT-GOVERNOR OF BENGAL.)

—o—

GREAT power in India may be thought, not without some reason, to make its holders, or those who have held it, a little conceited. There is a characteristic anecdote of the late Sir Ashley Eden, exemplifying the self-confidence of a distinguished Anglo-Indian during a brilliant career.

His eventual successor in the Lieut.-Governorship of Bengal unveiled a statue of him in Calcutta, and expressed himself (as will afterwards be seen) in very laudatory terms of Sir Ashley, in the course of his speech on the occasion saying, he was the "most enlightened," "the best administrator," &c., &c., Bengal had ever been blessed with. On the report of this speech appearing in the papers, one of Sir A. Eden's colleagues in the India Council (London) remarked laughingly to him—"Eden, do you see what Bayley has been saying about you? You should be in one perpetual blush!" "No," replied Eden; "what has he been saying?" "Why, Bayley" (the present Lieut.-Governor), "says you are the most enlightened and the ablest administrator India, or rather Bengal, has ever had." "Is that all?" said Eden. "Why, I knew that before well. Can't he say anything more original than that?"

But there is simply a strong conviction of innate—even exceptional—excellence in this jocular reply—no conceit whatever. Having fully studied the failings and the best attributes of his predecessors, in his own mind, he determined to become, either the best Lieut.-Governor, or one of the best rulers the great Bengal Presidency ever had.

The story of such a life is told in the usual brief official way:—

Eden, Hon. Sir Ashley, K.C.S.I., C.I.E., late Bengal C.S. —Educated at Winchester and Haileybury, and appointed to the Bengal Civil Service in 1852; arrived in India April 1852; Assistant Magistrate and Collector of Rajshahye, 1854; Assistant Special Commissioner in the Sonthal insurrection, 1855; Deputy Commissioner of the Sonthal Pergunnahs, 1856; Magistrate and Collector of Baraset, 1856; Junior Secretary Board of Revenue, 1859; Special Envoy to Sikhim, 1861; Special Envoy to Bostan, 1864; Secretary to the Government of Bengal, 1862–71, and Member of Council of the Lieutenant-Governor for making laws and regulations, 1868; Chief Commissioner of British Burma, 1871 to 1877; Officiating Member of the Governor-General's Council, 1875; Lieutenant-Governor of Bengal, 1877–82; retired in 1882; Member of Council of Secretary of State, 1882.* And now we have the melancholy duty to add:—Died July 9, 1887, at his residence, 31, Sackville Street, London.

About the middle of June, the author, desirous of having an Anglo-Indian of such reputed eminence as Sir Ashley Eden in his Second Series of "Sketches," applied to him for any notes he might be inclined to furnish regarding his successful and important career. To be candid, hardly any reply was expected to such a request. But, from one possessing a kindly and courteous nature—generally to be found with great minds—came a speedy answer, couched in the following terms:—

"While I am much flattered by your request that I should furnish you with notes of my Indian career, I am afraid that it is not within my power to comply with your request, because I have not kept by me any materials for such a purpose, and could only give a brief memo. of my employment, such as in 'Men of the Day.' I have too little time for

* *The India Office List for* 1886: an excellent and useful little work, comp ed by a promising young civilian of the India Office.

writing such a paper, and it is difficult, under any circumstances, to write of one's self.

"I venture to enclose to you a report of what some of my friends said of me at a public meeting held at Calcutta when I was giving up Bengal.

"Yours truly,
"A. EDEN."

On the following day (16th June) came another packet, and another kind note:—

"In continuation of my note of yesterday, I now enclose a copy of the Calcutta *Englishman* of the 16th April, containing the speech of Sir S. Bayley on the unveiling of my statue in Calcutta, and a leading article on the same subject, which may help you if you still wish to write a notice of me in any future edition of your work."

The public meeting at first alluded to by Sir Ashley was held, in honour of the Lieutenant-Governor of Bengal, at the Town Hall, Calcutta, on the 21st April, 1882. It was a grand and in many respects wonderful assembly, such as no other Empire or nation in the world could produce. Such a largely-attended and influential meeting of the inhabitants of Calcutta and the interior of Bengal, a province with an area falling little short of France, or of Germany, and its population of 70 millions, enormously outnumbering that of either of them, was in every respect most creditable to British rule in India. It was to record their high appreciation of the successful administration of Sir Ashley Eden as Lieutenant-Governor of Bengal that the city of palaces and suburbs had sent forth to that famous hall English Judges and Councillors, merchants and gentlemen held in the highest estimation by the citizens, civilians of every class; while Hindus, Mahomedans, and Parsees of note were also there, the two great Oriental classes headed by wealthy and influential Hindu Maharajahs, Rajahs, and Mahomedan Princes. Among the Maharajahs was his Highness of Burdwan; and, writing in eventful 1887, while India flourishes under the Queen-Empress, reminds us of a little anecdote of one of his ancestors, from which it may easily be deduced that local or Indian faith in British Government is far greater now than it was sixty years ago. It will give some idea of how British tenure of India was valued by the Rajah of Burdwan in 1826, or towards the conclusion of the First Burmese War, if we remark that at this time Lord Amherst (Governor-General) asked the Rajah for a loan of a certain sum of money, promising to repay it at the end of twenty-five years. The Rajah declined, saying he did not know whether twenty-five years hence the East India Company would possess the country!

On the motion of Maharajah Narendra Krishna, the Honourable Sir Richard Garth was voted to the chair. Sir Richard gracefully introduced the object of the meeting, which was to do honour to Sir Ashley Eden, upon the eve of his departure from India; to express their admiration of "his wise, vigorous, and successful administration"; to present him with an address embodying their views and feelings, and to raise for him a lasting and substantial memorial of their appreciation of his high qualities, and the benefits which he had conferred upon the Province of Bengal.

Mr. Morrison, on being called on to propose the first resolution, in the course of a very able speech remarked:—"To be charged with the Government of so vast a country could not, under any circumstances, but inspire a deep sense of responsibility, and in Sir Ashley Eden such feelings must have been intensified by the knowledge that a large proportion of the subject multitude were sunk in ignorance and fatalism, and, in case of any serious variation in the march of the seasons, without resource except to die. The Lieutenant-Governor has, however, proved equal to his task. Familiar with the country and its wants, his opinions had been formed and ripened in course of a long period of good service and of close and accurate observation. Thus prepared for his high office, he has adorned it by the display of industry, patience, and foresight—quick appreciation of facts—calmness of judgment, courage for the truth, vigour in action, and the faculty of effective organization and command."

The decentralizing policy happily inaugurated by Lord Mayo had allowed Sir Ashley Eden full scope for skill in finance, with the results that, under his eye, the provincial revenue, during four years, increased by some 70 lakhs of rupees. But Mr. Morrison thought that such a statement alone proved little, rise of revenue being sometimes the cloak and consequence of oppression and misery; and not in Bengal could such a reproach be uttered. No fresh taxes had been imposed, but the larger income of the province was derived from her own investments, and from the increased use of taxed luxuries, by a people growing in wealth. It was, however, rather by that which he had wisely spent than by the money he had gathered in that thoughtful men would judge Sir Ashley Eden. They would not appreciate so highly the splendid balance which he made over to his successor as the 640 lakhs of rupees which, during his rule, had been laid out upon railways, upon irrigation, and upon other works of public utility. In a country like India it was impossible to exaggerate the value of railways, whether considered from the standpoint of the man of business or of the philanthropist. "They foster and even create trade—encourage agriculture, promote manufactures, diffuse wealth—diminish sickness, humanize, civilize, educate. They are at once the messengers of peace and the best allies in war; and, whilst rendering actual famine impossible, they take its place in the wondrous scheme of nature, not by destroying redundant population but by transporting it to districts where its labour can be usefully employed."

By his consistent and enlightened advocacy of roads and railroads to be made if possible by the State, but in any event to be made, Sir Ashley Eden would have amply earned the gratitude of Bengal, even had he done nothing else to deserve it. Education had found in him an earnest friend. The village school and the learned college had alike been aided and encouraged. It had been his merit to appreciate the value of technical training for native youths, and to perceive how, at the very root of all moral and intellectual growth for the people of India, is the education of native women. In legislation, Mr. Morrison took care to inform the meeting, Sir Ashley could claim that he had not forced upon an unwilling people superfluous enactments which nobody asked for, and which few could understand; and, in the Council Chamber, there had been many occasions on which he had rendered the public good service by his frank and cogent utterances. The speaker seemed to be painting an almost perfect Governor. His executive had been vigorous and efficient. Jails had been rebuilt and re-organized upon thoroughly philanthropic principles, and they had been kept moderately empty, not by inhuman treatment within their walls, but by the prevention of crime without. Sanitation, medical charity, and hospital management had been the Lieutenant-Governor's special study, and many who condemned his policy reversed their judgment in presence of the logic of facts. Merchants, tradesmen, ship-owners, seamen, had all much for which to thank Sir Ashley Eden. The poor had had his protection, and the wealthy had profited by his advice; whilst to every class, creed, and race he had been at all times freely accessible.

Judging by this concise recital of his excellences, Sir Ashley appears in some respects to resemble Sir Arthur Phayre—by far the greatest Chief Commissioner which Burma ever had—whose appointment he had successfully held in the rising land of the Golden Foot.

Mr. Morrison concluded his speech with the following excellent remarks:—

"To commit mistakes is the lot of all men, and to make some enemies the fate of every strong ruler. Hard things have been said of Sir Ashley Eden, and have been repented of; but this much may safely be asserted to-day—he has acted honestly. He has tried to do his duty, and we, assembled here, say that he has succeeded well. He has caused two blades of grass to spring where but one grew before, and he has increased the sum of the happiness of those amongst whom he has laboured. He leaves behind him as legacies, resulting largely from his own good work, the peace, not of exhaustions, but of content, security certain for person and for property, empty jails and full treasuries, taxation light, food and clothing cheap, trade advancing by leaps and bounds, wealth spread abroad, knowledge gradually covering the land, thousands rescued from preventible diseases, millions rendered safe from the horrors of famine.

"Gentlemen, may we not safely record our high appreciation of the successful administration of Sir Ashley Eden as Lieutenant-Governor of Bengal."

The resolution was seconded by the Maharajah of Hutwa, put, and carried unanimously.

Mr. Branson moved the second resolution, namely, "That a marble statue of Sir Ashley Eden be erected in this city as a memorial of his distinguished career in this country."

In the course of an eloquent speech it was remarked:—"There have been many Lieutenant-Governors who have reigned over us, but in the case of none has it been proposed that there should be such a recognition of his services as that which is proposed by the resolution which I move. And this is not due to the fact that there has been wanting talent or ability amongst Sir Ashley's predecessors, as many of them have been men of great talent and ability." But though these predecessors had been great and able, it appeared to him (Mr. Branson) that that which had above all things commended Sir Ashley Eden to the meeting had been his strong common sense. He had had the power of quickly seeing the true aspect of any schemes which were propounded to him, it mattered not by whom. Endowed with a clear perception, and a clear comprehension, he had been able, when an idea had been suggested to him, to, as it were, focus it before him, and to see and decide not only how it looked to him, but how it was likely to look to others; and thus he was able to grasp the true merits of a scheme, and to "decide quickly whether he would accept it or reject it." Nothing could have been better than alluding to this great merit in a ruler, a chief among the many which so distinguished the retiring Lieutenant-Governor. He had also had the courage of his opinions when he had once formed them. He had stretched his hand through the immediate present to reach the good in the future which he foresaw would be the result of his action.

A civilian of Bengal, he had endeared himself to the people of the province, and had even won the affectionate esteem and gratitude of the sturdier inhabitants of Behar. The Eurasians and Anglo-Indians, who formed a considerable class of the community, had been the subject of his anxious solicitude, as the establishment of the Seebpore Engineering College showed. The harmonious relations between the planters of Behar and the Zemindars and their ryots, to which Sir Ashley Eden himself had recently adverted, were due also to his wise interference. Last, but not least, were his efforts for the good of the silent millions who could not speak for themselves, and who could hardly think for themselves, and for whom he had, with the assistance of Mr. Justice Field and his colleagues of the Rent Law Commission, set on foot a scheme to regulate the relations of landlord and tenant—a scheme which bade fair to be beneficial equally to the ryot and the Zemindar.

All this pointed to the anxious care which Sir Ashley had had for the people entrusted to his administration. In conclusion, the speaker remarked:—"There is much to be said in review of the administration of Sir Ashley Eden, and words would not be lacking to speak of all the good he has done among us."

Maharajah Jotindra Mohun Tagore, in seconding the resolution, said he thought he could hardly add anything, after the eloquence he had heard, in favour of it. "If, therefore," he said, with a touch of humour and knowledge of Goldsmith, "you find my remarks to be 'wondrous short,' they have this recommendation, that 'they cannot hold you long.'" . . . Without further preface, then, he begged to second the resolution which had been moved by his learned friend, Mr. Branson.

Nawab Abdool Luteef, Khan Bahadoor, here asked permission to read a letter which he had received from Moung Hla Oung, a Burmese gentleman, and holding a responsible position in the Financial Department of Government. In this the writer begged to say that "the friends and admirers of Sir Ashley Eden in British Burma would like to contribute their quota towards perpetuating the memory of Sir

Ashley Eden in the metropolis of India, in case the memorial should take a form which would be appreciated by the natives of British Burma. We would be much gratified to see a statue put up in a visible place in Calcutta." In the event of the memorial taking the form of a statue, the writer requested his own name to be put down for a handsome donation, and intimated that other Burmese gentlemen would subscribe on their learning the result of the meeting.—The resolution was then put and carried unanimously.

The next resolution was moved by Dr. Goethalls, "That the necessary funds for the erection of the statue be raised by inviting subscriptions, and that some artist in England be entrusted with the work, for which Sir Ashley might give sittings, and so forth."—The Doctor felt sure that all those who knew Sir Ashley's good qualities would consider that his memory would be more durable than any material of iron or brass, but he still felt that they would not have done justice to the feeling which brought them together if a material memorial was not erected.

The Maharajah of Giddhore seconded the resolution, which was carried unanimously.

Mr. Zemin then moved that an address—suitable and admirable in every respect—be presented to Sir Ashley Eden, K.C.S.I., C.I.E. After reviewing his administration, it concludes with the striking passage:—"In now taking leave, we have the consolation of knowing that with your departure from this country your official connection with it will not cease. In your seat at the Council of the Secretary of State you will still have opportunities for the exercise of your knowledge, experience, and sympathies in promoting the cause of good government in India. We wish you a safe voyage home, and pray that the Author of All Good will bless you with long life, prosperity, and happiness."

Maharajah Narendra Krishna seconded the resolution, which, after an excellent speech from his Highness, was put and carried unanimously.

The Honourable Durga Churn Laha next moved a resolution that a deputation be formed, consisting of the Honourable Sir Richard Garth, H.H. the Maharajah of

Kuch-Behar, the Maharajah of Burdwan, numerous influential British merchants and citizens, and various wealthy Hindus, Mahomedans, and Parsees, Maharajahs and Rajahs, Princes, and gentlemen respectively, to present the address to Sir Ashley Eden.

Nawab Abdool Lutief, Khan Bahadur, in seconding the motion, said that the Mahomedan community of Bengal were under deep obligation to Sir Ashley Eden for the great interest he had evinced in their behalf, both in placing facilities in their way of acquiring higher English education, as well as in the distribution of patronage amongst Mahomedan gentlemen who were considered deserving high appointments.—When the last resolution had been put and carried, another, moved by Babu Joykissen Mookerjee, and seconded by Mr. Amir Ali, that, to save time, the deputation should sign the address, met with similar approval; and at length Mr. J. Keswick moved that a Committee be formed to receive subscriptions and carry out the resolutions passed at the meeting. A very influential Committee was appointed, and the resolution was seconded by Mr. Manickjee Rustomjee, and, of course, carried.

The report of this well-managed, business-like meeting, than which there had been few in Calcutta more interesting or enthusiastic since the famous day when Sir Charles Theophilus (afterwards Lord) Metcalfe was entertained for fighting the battle of the liberty of the Indian Press,* concludes with the following incidental and affecting remarks:

Rajah Rajendra Narain, Deb Bahadur, asked permission to have the following address read by Kumar Surendra Narain, which was done:—

"Chairman and Gentlemen,—Words, expressive of the sentiments and feelings which swell my heart on the present occasion, I have none. Stricken in years, borne down with infirmities of age, and unblessed with the powers of eloquence, if I at all attempt to open my lips, I do so from an irresistible impulse of duty, gratitude, and friendship.

* *See* "Distinguished Anglo-Indians"—*Anglo-Indian Periodical Literature*—pp. 324-25. The Free Press dinner took place on the 15th September, 1835.

"In testimony and just praise of the virtues of Sir Ashley Eden as the ruler of the most advanced Province of India, what has already been said I have little to add to.

"It is but natural that his views of statesmanship should find favour with some, and disfavour with others. But his deep-seated and solid regard for the interests of our country, his love of the people whom he has tried to study and to know as no Governor has ever done, and, above all, his unshaken allegiance to his convictions and fearless efforts to carry them out, none can, I trust, gainsay.

"I beg to be pardoned by this public audience if I allude to my personal friendship with Sir Ashley. I ought to say the friendship of the illustrious Eden family with mine, which commenced between my grandfather and the late Lord Auckland, was maintained in the days of my father, and has been continued to me by Sir Ashley, who has honoured me with it almost from the very time he set his foot in India. While, therefore, I join my countrymen in this valedictory demonstration for a retiring worthy Governor, I can scarcely give utterance to my feelings towards a parting noble friend, whom I esteem, and honour, and love with all my heart.

"While, again, I participate the hope and wish of my countrymen that in the new sphere of action in which, fortunately, he is about to be placed, he will lose no efforts to continue to benefit our country by his counsels, I have a personal longing that when he returns home beyond the oceans, he will not forget an humble friend he leaves on the shores of the Ganges, and who has but few short days to linger on this earth."

After such a kind effusion from a distinguished native gentleman it is not easy to deny—as is frequently the case—gratitude in the people of India towards their rulers. Many cases could be cited which, if not exhibiting in a strict sense our idea of gratitude, seem very like it.

This great meeting then came to a close, Rajah Narendra Krishna (the Hindu Apollo *) Bahadur moving thanks to the chair.

* To those unacquainted with Hindu mythology, it may be remarked

From the foregoing remarks it will be seen how much good was done by Sir Ashley Eden as a statesman. But he was also a most hospitable Englishman in every sense. No matter how great a Governor may be, as a general rule, he is nothing if not hospitable; for the simple reason—especially in India—that it is impossible to work with an inhospitable potentate. Sir Ashley's splendid hospitality, which made Belvidere so familiar to the citizens of Calcutta, and that at the more romantic retreat of the "Shrubbery," at Darjeeling ("the bright spot"), so favourite a resort of the dwellers in the Hill country, are well remembered by many who now lament the familiar face that is gone. This administering of a noble hospitality at both his homes was well alluded to by Mr. Branson, who thought that by so doing the Lieutenant-Governor had wisely carried out that shrewd but sound advice of a great general to his lieutenant. He had been attentive to the wants of the ladies, in catering for them in the way of public and semi-public amusements. And he had won the hearts of the men through their palates as well as their judgments. This, it is well said, "is a matter which it does not do to neglect; and the greatest statesmen cannot neglect it without the danger of becoming unpopular." These, and his other qualities combined, made Sir Ashley Eden respected and beloved among those over whom he ruled.

We now pass over five years from the date of the above meeting, and arrive at the day (April 15, 1887) when the ceremony of unveiling the statue of Sir Ashley Eden, placed at the north-west corner of Dalhousie Square, was performed by His Honour the Lieutenant-Governor of Bengal, in the presence of a large gathering of European and native gentlemen, both official and non-official. A large shamiana had been erected immediately in front of the statue, under which the ceremony took place. A raised daïs was erected in the centre, with chairs set around for those present. On the

that there are many points of similarity between it and the mythology of Greece and Rome. Krishna at Jagánnath, or in the worship of Vishnu (the Preserver), has a far greater number of votaries than the son of Jupiter ever had. Hence the introduction of the favourite in a name.

arrival of Sir Steuart and Lady Bayley, they were met by the members of the Eden Memorial Committee, and, after being seated, the Hon. Justice H. T. Prinsep opened the proceedings by speaking as follows :—

"Before asking you, Sir, to perform the ceremony for which we are here assembled, I propôse shortly to state the origin of the movement which we are now bringing to a conclusion. Five years ago, at the termination of Sir Ashley Eden's tenure of office as Lieutenant-Governor of Bengal, a public meeting was held at the Town Hall, at which all classes of the community in Calcutta and throughout Bengal were numerously represented, and it was there unanimously determined, in appreciation of his eminent services, to erect in this city some memorial of the high estimation in which his administration was held. To carry out this, a Committee was appointed, many members of which are no longer present among us, and of them I would only mention the Chairman, Sir Richard Garth, in whose absence I have been invited to preside on this memorable occasion. A marble statue of Sir Ashley Eden has been constructed by Mr. Boehm, an eminent sculptor of London, which is now before us. It is not for me at present to ask your criticism of that work, but I have no doubt that when it is exposed to your view, you will not fail to recognize its excellence, both as an accurate resemblance of its illustrious original and as a work of art. I am fortunately able to express my own opinion, as I had an opportunity, some eighteen months ago, in London, to accompany Sir A. Eden to his last sitting to Mr. Boehm. I was then able to compare the original with his representative and to appreciate the labour and talent of the artist.

"It seems almost unnecessary that I should attempt to remind you of the successful character of Sir A. Eden's administration as Lieutenant-Governor of Bengal, which we desire now to commemorate. Those who were present in Calcutta and in Bengal five years ago cannot have forgotten the enthusiastic meetings held everywhere to do honour to our departing Governor, or the overpowering outburst of feeling shown by assembled crowds at the place of embarkation to bid him a regretful farewell. You, Sir, as one who has long been intimately associated with him in the public service, are in a better position than I to expatiate on the distinguished character and services of Sir A. Eden, and I therefore feel that in your presence it is not fitting in me to undertake this duty. History will record, and future generations will admit, that, without any invidious comparison with his illustrious predecessors, he fairly surpassed them all in the brilliancy and soundness of his administration and in the lasting benefits that he conferred on all classes of the community. It may be said that he was fortunate in his opportunities, but I venture to assert that no one, not even the most captious critic, can fairly say that he failed to grasp the situation, and did not avail himself to the utmost of every one of those opportunities. It was on such an occasion that the force of his character as an administrator asserted itself to our admiration. The keenness of his perception; his incisive analysis of every scheme suggested to him; the vigour and resolution with which he carried through what he had become convinced was for the benefit of the country; the fertility of his resource to overcome obstruction; his long and varied experience; and, above all, the thorough honesty of purpose and the confidence he inspired among all, official and non-official, with whom he was placed in contact, combined to secure that brilliant and successful administration which will ensure for his reputation a monument more durable than it is in our power to erect.

"One word more. To the lasting honour of Sir A. Eden be it borne in mind that on more than one occasion, and with some risk to his own public career, he has courageously stood forth as the redresser of wrongs, the champion of the oppressed, and has been the means of securing liberty and freedom of action to the poorest classes of the community. We are justly proud of such a distinguished public servant, and rejoice at doing honour to his memory in India." (Applause.)

After these true and eloquent remarks by one bearing the distinguished name of Prinsep, it may be well, before coming to the great speech of the day, to notice the brilliant leading article* alluded to by Sir Ashley in his last note. "The devil is loose," said a certain gentleman to another, when the tidings were telegraphed from Delhi that Ashley Eden was to be Lieutenant-Governor of Bengal.

It was indeed to many an ominous message. But the article commences by alluding to the special fitness in the circumstance that it should have fallen to Sir Steuart Bayley to unveil the statue of Sir Ashley Eden. The present Lieutenant-Governor was not only the intimate friend, but also the trusted coadjutor, of his great predecessor in the Government of Bengal. Soon after his accession to the Lieutenant-Governorship, Mr. Eden summoned his old secretarial colleague from the Commissionership of Patna to be his Chief Secretary, and when, in the early, and perhaps the most critical, days of his administration, it became known that its watchword was to be "common sense," men generally felt that, if the watchword was given with the clearness of natural conviction by Mr. Eden, it was communicated with firmness and courtesy by Mr. Bayley. His administration was an eminent success. "Without crotchets, and without vanity, with broad views and much human sympathy, able, strong, just, and fearless, Ashley Eden would have been a successful Governor even if Fortune had not smiled so radiantly upon the finances of his time. He had always been known to be a man of masculine will and strong individuality, and there were those who, conscious of having sought to injure him, heard the news of his coming with terror and apprehension." Among them was the gentleman already mentioned; and his exclamation, "The devil is loose," was in every respect a sublimely natural one! But a very great quality in a successful ruler—MAGNANIMITY—was possessed by the model Lieutenant-Governor to a remarkable extent.†

Without further enlarging on his merits, let us now proceed to the

* Calcutta *Englishman*, April 16, 1887.

† *See* Appendix IV.

UNVEILING OF THE STATUE OF SIR ASHLEY EDEN.

His Honour the Lieutenant-Governor of Bengal spoke as follows :—

"Mr. Prinsep, Ladies, and Gentlemen,—

"It is with special pleasure that I respond to the call made on me by the Committee to preside at the unveiling of the statue of Sir Ashley Eden. This statue, as you have heard to-day, was subscribed for and voted five years ago by a very full and enthusiastic public meeting, representing all classes of the community, classes with very conflicting interests, and with very diverse views on many matters, but all determined to sink those differences and unite in the common object of doing honour to their departing ruler.

"But many members remain, and to them, as representing all the most distinguished elements of the Calcutta community, I return my thanks for the privilege of presiding on this occasion. I began by saying it gave me special pleasure to do so, because though I could well have desired that the occasion were graced by better oratory than I can boast, and I confess the making of speeches is to me always a difficult and painful duty, but inasmuch as I have for nearly thirty years been on terms of close intimacy, both personal and official, with Sir Ashley Eden, and it is so greatly due to his encouragement, guidance, and support, that I owe what measure of success I have achieved, I feel that there is a certain appropriateness in his former pupil and subordinate being called on to offer the crowning honour to his Indian career.

"It was when he was magistrate of Baraset that I took charge of my first sub-division, Halasor, in his district, and it was then I learned from him some of the most valuable lessons of my career, especially that of unrestrained intercourse with natives. Later cn, during almost all his career as Secretary to the Government of Bengal, I was his Junior Secretary, I was again his Secretary when he became Lieutenant-Governor of Bengal, and during his absence on the Army Commission I was selected to officiate for him.

"It is this intimate knowledge which emboldens me in undertaking a task, which in other circumstances I should gladly have transferred to more accomplished hands. I will not go at any length into the incidents of his career. He first distinguished himself by his bold and vigilant attitude during the Santhal outbreak, and the sound and practical advice he gave in regard to Santhal administration. Now going for his health to the Mauritius the oppressions practised on the Indian emigrants attracted his attention, and he succeeded in arousing the authorities here to vigorous and successful action on their behalf. His next fight was the great battle against the old system of indigo as then carried on. The interest opposed to him was enormously powerful, and he entered on the struggle, so far as he knew, almost singlehanded. It was not long, however, before he received the full support of Sir J. P. Grant, without whose determined aid and sympathy the battle would not perhaps have been won so soon; but to Sir A. Eden is due the initiation of the struggle, and on him was heaped the obloquy which those who enter on such a struggle must be content to accept as one of its accidents. From this he soon rose first to the Secretaryship on the Board of Revenue, and then, after a service of only ten years, to the Secretaryship of the Government of Bengal. From this period, with brief intervals of his mission to Bhutan, and his absence on leave, with the exception of the five years during which he administered Burma, his official history is to a great extent a history of Bengal; for as a strong and trusted Secretary he took an important part in shaping the measures of Sir C. Beadon and Sir William Grey, and from the beginning of 1877 till he left these shores the administration of the province was in his own hands. The address which was presented to him by the meeting, of which you have heard to-day, recapitulated briefly those points in his administration as Lieutenant-Governor which had specially attracted attention.

The address dwelt on his administration of Bengal finance, on the extension of internal communication, roads, railways, and canals; on the development of education, and especially the foundation of the Sibpur College, on the improvements of the courts, on improved judicial administration, on his encouragement of sanitation, his sound views in regard to legislation, and above all on that which came upon him daily—the smooth working of the administrative machinery. It is unnecessary that I should go over the same ground again. I would add a few points. The great care which he bestowed on the administration of the hospitals so as to combine economy with efficiency, the wise action he took in dealing with threatened indigo troubles in Behar, the interest he displayed in the foundation of industrial and art museums in Bengal, and the pains he took to maintain peace and harmony in the great historic families of Bengal. The greatest, perhaps, of all his labours, and the one which gave most evidence of his singular ability and mental vigour, was the work he did as President of the Army Commission. The work has hitherto been well-nigh fruitless owing to difficulties and obstructions which have their origin elsewhere than in India, but the day will come when men will wonder why such obvious reforms should have been delayed, and his work on the Commission will be properly appreciated. These were the acts of his administration which exacted general admiration, and which led them to vote to him the honour, unique as applied to a Lieutenant-Governor of Bengal, of erecting his statue in Calcutta. A very capable judge of these matters, who is well known as a keen critic and a cautious observer, said to me the other day that Sir A. Eden was the best Lieutenant-Governor Bengal had ever had. Without entering into comparisons of this nature it will perhaps be admitted that he was the most successful, and one great element of his success was, no doubt, as pointed out to you just now, the use he made of opportunities in managing to secure the approbation, not of this class or that class, but of almost all classes. Looking through the speeches made on the occasion of the Town Hall meeting five years ago, I find all the speakers alluding very much in the same terms as my hon. friend has done to-night to the qualities which specially characterized Sir A. Eden as a ruler. Thus Mr. Morrison spoke of his 'quick appreciation of facts, calmness of judgment, courage for the truth, vigour in action, and the faculty of effective organization and command.' Mr. Branson said that which above all commended Sir A. Eden to them was his 'strong common sense. He had the power of quickly seeing the true aspect of any schemes which were propounded to him.' The address itself says 'he evinced thorough knowledge of the country, strong common sense, zeal, vigour, firmness, and frankness, and above all a generous and enlightened sympathy with all classes of the people.' And lastly, his aged friend, Rajah Rajendro Narain Deb, dwelt on his knowledge of the people, his unshaken allegiance to his convictions, and his fearless efforts to carry them out.

"To this sketch of his character drawn by various hands (and I have intentionally preferred to place before you their words rather than my own), I can add little ; but, apart from the strength of his character and his sound common sense, which were obvious to all, I was always struck by the extraordinary quickness and acuteness of his mind. He had an intuitive faculty, which Lord Ripon in one of his speeches has also noticed, of getting at salient facts. He would grasp all the leading points of a complicated bundle of papers, while another man would be still fumbling over the top letter. He managed to be acquainted with all that was going on around him, and he had a genius for supplying the missing links in a chain of circumstances, which he applied to the facts of every-day life—a genius almost like that which enabled the great palæontologist, Professor Owen, to reconstruct an antediluvian monster from a single bone. But nothing served him better than the genuine and sympathetic friendship unrestrained by constant intercourse with the native friends who had gathered round him in the early part of his career and clung to him to its close, and in this respect he offered an example by which I hope the younger members of the service, anxious to walk in his footsteps and render their service of real use to the country, will not fail to profit. He was always ready to receive his native friends, and talked to them with the utmost fondness. He was never stiff or formal, nor did he shrink if necessary from saying unpleasant things. But he treated them as friends because he felt towards them as friends, and this was one of the many elements of his success. Of course there were faults on which his policy failed or stumbled. This, however, is not the time or place to speak of these, and I leave the ungracious task to others. Of course also he was extraordinarily fortunate in the two facts that the years of his Lieutenant-Governorship were blest with bountiful harvests, and that his promised contract was made in '77 rather than in '87. I look back upon the resources at his command with feelings of envy and amazement. He was able to spend out of strictly provincial resources no less than 103 lakhs in five years on original civil works, besides devoting 60 lakhs to capital expenditure on railways and canals. Those were halcyon days indeed. If I am able to devote one-fourth of this sum to the same purposes, I shall deem myself fortunate, and so far as I can see what he could afford to spend on material progress in one year must now last Bengal for five. I need not tell you, gentlemen, what this means. You know as well as I do that with an empty treasury neither administrative nor material progress is to be looked for. I do not complain of this. Of the two alternatives of increased taxation or diminished provincial resources, I for one do not hesitate to choose the latter. But be it well understood that the price we pay for this is a check on our administrative progress, and a policy of strict economy and niggardly public works, and I cannot help looking back with feelings of envy to the opportunities which Sir A. Eden had, and of which, be it added, he made such excellent use.

"One word more about Sir Ashley's administration before I sit down. He once said in public that he had no policy. This I take it, if analyzed, means the same thing as a remark which I once heard fall from Sir J. P. Grant, that good administration was like a good digestion. It did its work, and you heard nothing about it. Sir Ashley meant that he did the day's work as it came, and constructed political formulæ—large generalizations which require a great deal of piercing and cutting off of angles before you can square them with the facts to which they are to be applied. Of course this can be carried too far, but with him it merely meant 'take your stand on facts rather than on theories,' and as a matter of fact his well-known dislike of fads and theories was consistent with a very sound appreciation of political and economical science.

"I will not detain you longer, or I would have liked to say something about his faculty for getting the best work out of subordinates, while interfering very little with them or confining himself to the captain's duty of setting the ship's course without always laying hold of the helm. His Secretaries knew what he wanted done, and how he wanted it done, without constant reminding, and so thorough was his vigorous mental attitude impressed on them that their personal idiosyncrasies were wholly absorbed in it. I should like to have said something of his admirable hospitality, guided as it was by excellent taste on a strong sense of decorative art and beauty, of his personal qualities, which made him the best liked and most trusted of friends, while to many outsiders he seemed reserved and morose. But I have already detained you too long, and I can only in conclusion congratulate this city of statues, as Lord Lytton called it, on the addition of one more worthy endowment to those works of art which form one of its special claims to distinction."

His Honour's speech was greeted with frequent bursts of applause, and at its conclusion Sir Steuart Bayley unveiled the statue, and the ceremony was completed. The statue, it may be remarked, is an admirable one, and the sculptor has succeeded in chiselling the form and face of Sir Ashley Eden with remarkable fidelity.

Few sensible Englishmen will deny that the above is, in many respects, an admirable speech; and we should like to see it spread broadcast over this land to show what a great country India is, and what a great Anglo-Indian administrator has the power of doing. It has long been truly said of

India that the reality of soldier-life is there. In work like that accomplished by Sir Ashley Eden we have the reality of administrative capacity. No patching up, no delusive bringing to credit, no useless talk, no want of decision, no improvement neglected in that quarter of the world where he governed, and governed fearlessly and well, a population nearly fourteen times as large as that of Ireland! To do all the good in his power was evidently his only policy; and from his vigorous rule some wise lessons could be learned by our home statesmen and senators of the present day. What a blessing it would have been during a long period for Ireland if, as in Bengal, there had been really good and suitable administration, allowed to work freely, and little said about it! But words and theories have bred ruin; in common parlance, there have been "too many cooks," and there is no saying where the mischief will end.

In this age especially, when people live at such a railroad pace, a would-be-great statesman or administrator must take his stand on facts rather than theories; and this is applicable to the East as well as to the West. Knowing this so well made Sir Ashley Eden, what Sir Steuart Bayley so ably demonstrated, an eminently practical man—or, it may be said, practical statesman—in local government what James Watt was in science, when, in one of his great triumphs in improving the steam-engine, he shouted to his friend and fellow-labourer, Boulton, "Give me facts; I am sick of theories!" In the lives of distinguished Anglo-Indians the appreciation and exercise of political and economical science have by no means been neglected. The life of Sir Ashley Eden furnishes a splendid example of such knowledge. We have read, on the authority of one of our most pleasing writers and able journalists, that Lord Salisbury is reported to have said that "Indian civilians make good administrators, but poor statesmen."

We trust that his Lordship excepts, at least, such distinguished rulers as Lord Lawrence, Sir Arthur Phayre, and Sir Ashley Eden. The subject of our imperfect sketch must be looked upon in an entirely different light from that in which we are accustomed to view such able and distinguished statesmen as Sir Robert Peel, Lord Palmerston, Mr. Gladstone, and Lord Salisbury himself. A knowledge of statesmanship from the working of the British Constitution would have been of little use to great Anglo-Indian administrators in India: they could have done next to nothing with it, except promised; too frequently worse than nothing. Indian administrators—or call them what you will—have totally different lines to work upon. Let it be remembered, by all candid readers and observers, that Sir Ashley Eden managed to "spend, from provincial funds alone, sixty lakhs of rupees on railways and canals, while court-houses, jails, schools, water-works, drainage works, roads, and bridges, testify to his statesmanlike liberality in providing for the wants of the Province." If by pure statesmanship is meant a certain creative power in Government, which builds up in the face of another party ever ready to destroy, then India is poor in statesmen; for her distinguished civilians have not, never had, nor do they seek, any such opportunity. Vishnu (Preserver), the Conservative, and Siva (Destroyer), as some think the ultra-Liberal, work after their own fashion—no such very bad one after all! Sir Ashley Eden and other Indian civilians would have found themselves too much shackled in England to become great statesmen.—Our distinguished Anglo-Indian succeeded Sir Arthur Phayre as President of the Annual Burma Dinner; so another familiar face of that social and festive board has passed away.

Sir Ashley Eden was born in 1831, the third son of the third Lord Auckland, some time Bishop of Bath and Wells, by the daughter of Mr. F. E. Hurt, of Alderwasley, Derbyshire. He was educated at Rugby and, as already stated, at Winchester, and entered Haileybury before the time of competitive examinations, when that institution educated young men who had already obtained nominations for the India Civil Service, which he entered in 1852. He was created a C.S.I. in 1874, and gained his knighthood as Knight Commander of the Star of India in 1878, in which year he was also made a Companion of the Order of the Indian Empire. Sir Ashley married the daughter of the late Admiral Money, C.B., and was left a widower in 1877.

The funeral of the late Sir Ashley Eden took place at Armthorpe, near Doncaster, on July 14. Lord and Lady Auckland were at Kissengen, in Bavaria, on account of his lordship's health, and were unable to attend. The service was conducted by Canon Childers, rector, and among the mourners and friends who attended were the Honourables Henley Eden, Morton Eden, Geo. Eden, Sir William and Lady Eden, Mr. and the Hon. Mrs. Sutton-Nelthorpe, the Earl of Ilchester; General Blake, late commander of the troops in Burma; Sir R. A. Dalyell, who represented the Indian Council; Mr. Seton Karr, Bengal Civil Service; Mr. H. A. Cockerell, secretary to Sir Ashley in Bengal; Mr. P. Dickinson, nephew of deceased; Mr. Bacon Frank, Captain Ashton, Captain Childers-Thompson; Rev. W. Eardley, vicar of Cantley; Mr. E. Greaves, Mr. J. Roberts, &c. The coffin was of polished oak, and bore the following inscription:—"Ashley Eden, born 13th November, 1831, died 9th July, 1887." Wreaths and crosses were sent by Lord and Lady Auckland, the Earl and Countess of Ilchester, Lord and Lady Hothfield, Earl and Countess Lytton, Lady Beadon, Sir William and Lady Eden, Hons. Florence, Maria, Mary, and Ashley Eden, Mrs. H. W. Wood (late of Calcutta), Mrs. Sutton-Nelthorpe, Mrs. C. Childers, &c.—At the Northbrook Indian Club, on the 12th July, the Earl of Northbrook feelingly alluded to the recent losses sustained by the club and the society by the deaths of two such distinguished men as Sir Barrow Ellis and Sir Ashley Eden.*

It may be considered a fitting conclusion to this sketch if we venture to remark that honours to Viceroys, Governors, and Lieutenant-Governors, as well as to other distinguished men, who have done really good service in the welfare and improvement of our Indian Empire, form a very pleasing feature in our Indian annals. "Well done, thou good and faithful servant!" are words more applicable now than they were when first said nearly two thousand years ago.

On the 30th of March a statue of Lord Lawrence was unveiled at Lahore by Sir Charles Aitchison, Lieutenant-

* *See* Appendix IV.

Governor of the Punjab. Lord Lawrence is represented as holding a pen in one hand and a sword in the other; and at the base there is the inscription—"Will you be governed by the pen or the sword?" Standing by Mr. Boehm's excellent work, Sir Charles modestly remarked "it would be pure impertinence in him to eulogize Lord Lawrence, at whose feet he had the privilege of learning and working."

At Bombay, the Governor (Lord Reay, LL.D., C.I.E.) unveiled a statue of Sir Richard Temple on March 31. "He hoped that the Civil Service would in future boast many men equal to Sir R. Temple in personal energy, unfailing industry, and versatility." It was most gratifying to read this brief epitome of the Indian statesman's excellences, already endeavoured to be brought prominently forward in the Sketch presented to public notice.*

Such were the two statues whose unveiling so lately preceded that of Sir Ashley Eden, who, as before observed, was the only Lieutenant-Governor of Bengal who had ever received such an honour in "the city of statues." The good work Sir Ashley did in Burma now suggests a thought of the greatest of Burmese administrators, or Chief Commissioners, and an allusion to the Phayre Memorial. In May last, among the Committee, appeared the names of Lord Napier of Magdala, the Hon. Sir Ashley Eden, Sir C. E. Bernard, General H. W. Blake, and Sir Joseph Fayrer. An alternative scheme had been submitted, by which it was shown that for £1,200 they could obtain a bronze statue—with a handsome pedestal—the figure not less than seven feet high, executed by one of the most eminent sculptors of the day, an R.A. This would give to Rangoon a work of artistic merit, and a very suitable memorial of Sir Arthur Phayre.†

But, after all, what is a statue? It is only useful to make us think of the author of the good work accomplished, if books and prints and photos have not satisfied us already.

* *See* "Distinguished Anglo-Indians," *First Series*, p. 227.

† For this grand object, in honour of such a distinguished Anglo-Indian, donations were to be sent to the gallant and energetic Hon. Secretary, Major-General Barnett Ford, 31, Queensborough Terrace, Hyde Park, W.

And such little statue-talk reminds us of the saying of that fine old Roman orator, Cicero, whose words will be found on the title-page—particularly applicable in the cases of even greater Indian statesmen and administrators than Sir Ashley Eden—of which the following may be accepted as a translation :—

Ought we not, since many illustrious men have left behind them statues and images, representations, not of their minds, but of their bodies; ought we not, I say, to prefer to leave behind us an image of our counsels and our virtues shaped out and finished off by the highest intellect?

SIR AUCKLAND COLVIN, K.C.M.G., C.I.E.

(LIEUTENANT-GOVERNOR N.W. PROVINCES.)

—o—

IT is rare, in official life, for a worthy and distinguished son to succeed to the great post once held by a distinguished father, after an interval of thirty years. Sir Auckland Colvin, the fifth son of the late Hon. John Russell Colvin, Lieutenant-Governor of the North-West Provinces during the Indian Mutiny, was appointed to the Indian Civil Service from Haileybury College in 1857. He was born in 1838, and owes his Christian name to Lord Auckland—the Governor-General of India, with whom his father was then associated as Private Secretary—being his godfather.

The early years of Sir Auckland Colvin's Indian career, namely, from 1857 to 1864, were spent in the North-West Provinces as an Assistant Magistrate and Assistant Settlement Officer; and it was during these valuable years of experience that he laid the foundation of that thorough knowledge of the land revenue system of India which has, in his later official career, caused him to be regarded as perhaps the most trustworthy guide to Government in that important branch of administration. It was Sir Auckland who, on the occasion of some suggested raising of the land revenue to meet the financial requirements of Government, warned the authorities to stay their hand, with the pithy and piquant saying, "Take care that, in raising the land revenue, you do not also raise the people." The experiment was not carried into effect.

In 1864 Sir A. Colvin, whose abilities had already

attracted notice outside the sphere of his immediate surroundings in the North-West Provinces, was selected by the Government of India to act as Under Secretary, first in their Home, and latterly in their Foreign Department. In this last department he served under Sir Henry Durand, for whom he entertained the profoundest admiration, and of whom he consistently speaks as perhaps the greatest mind in all respects he was ever thrown into contact with. But Sir Auckland's special usefulness as a Revenue officer led to the North-West Provinces Government loudly calling for his return to those Provinces; and in 1870 he was appointed Secretary to the Board of Revenue at Allahabad. In this post he did excellent service, and his marked ability as a Revenue officer became so prominent that from that time he was evidently destined for high promotion. Between 1870 and 1879, besides holding office as Secretary to the Revenue Board, he was selected by Sir John Strachey, the then Lieutenant-Governor of the North-West Provinces, as his Secretary to Government; and he was also deputed, during those years, to place his valuable experience as a Revenue officer at the disposal of the Bombay Government, in connection with serious land disturbances which had occurred in that Presidency, at Poona and Ahmadnagar.

The present Sir Evelyn Baring, while serving in India as Private Secretary to his cousin the Viceroy, Lord Northbrook, had been thrown into contact with Mr. Colvin, and was much impressed, in addition to his intimate acquaintance with revenue questions, with his sound sense and general trustworthiness on all matters brought before him; and when, later, Sir Evelyn found himself in Egypt controlling financial matters, and sadly in need of a trustworthy, resolute lieutenant, he bethought him of Mr. Colvin, and induced the Indian Government to lend his services to Egypt for a time, in the capacity of a Land Revenue Officer. Mr. Colvin soon took up the tangled skein of Egyptian land administration, and was gradually but surely restoring order and method where before irregularity and corruption reigned; when, on Sir Evelyn Baring being called away to the post of Finance Minister of India, Mr. Colvin was, by general consent, both of those on the spot in Egypt and our Foreign Office in London, selected to succeed him as Joint Controller of Egyptian Finance, with a French colleague. M. de Blignieres was the French colleague; and it is to the rare sagacity and mutual wise forbearance of these two joint managers of Egyptian finance that that country owes much of its present prosperity and credit in the European money markets. The elements of international rivalry were rampant at that time in Cairo, and both Mr. Colvin and M. de Blignieres were being constantly urged by their respectively impetuous fellow-countrymen to adopt a so-called "patriotic" course of stealing marches on each other by pushing the interests of their own Governments at the expense of Egyptian interests. Cool and resolute, both the Joint Controllers kept their heads. They succeeded in working together in admirable harmony; and, by their judicious arrangements, managed to steer the Egyptian ship of finance through the troubled waters of this international Scylla and Charybdis, and landed it in the comparatively smooth waters in which it has since sailed. It was said at that time, by an acute and experienced looker-on of the intrigues then raging in Cairo—"There are some men in whose neighbourhood intrigues and small plots seem naturally to grow; there are others, though rarely to be found, in whose presence such mischief seems just as naturally to wither and die. Happily for England, at this critical juncture, Mr. Colvin is one of this last class of men." But difficulties other than international soon came upon the land of the Pharaohs, for, in 1881, the military pronunciamento, which was headed by Arabi Pascha, came to a head, and the Khedive was openly defied by Arabi and his followers in front of his palace at Cairo. Mr. Colvin happened at that time to be alone in Cairo, Her Majesty's representative, Mr. E. Malet (now Sir E. Malet), being absent on leave in England, and he acted with praiseworthy promptitude. He was by the Khedive's side when the standard of rebellion was practically raised by Arabi on that morning of September 9, 1881, and his fearless advice to the Khedive was at once to assert his sovereignty, and demand of Arabi, in the presence of all the troops, his sword and submission, before discussion of the so-called grievances. Had Mr. Colvin's advice been followed by Tewfik, there is no doubt that Arabi, who was more than half frightened at his own temerity, would have yielded, the troops would have acquiesced, and the Egyptian campaign of a few months later would have been averted. But, in spite of Mr. Colvin's earnest entreaty and offer to run all risks side by side with him, the Khedive's mind, Oriental-like, faltered at the critical moment, and, by temporizing and entering into parley with Arabi, the golden moment was lost, and there followed, as is known to all, the virtual submission of the sovereign to his subject, till Arabi and his following were conquered at Tel-el-Kebir, and Cairo recaptured for the Khedive by the British forces under General Wolseley. Mr. Colvin was present on the Admiral's fleet at the bombardment of Alexandria, and afforded Admiral Sir Beauchamp Seymour much valuable political advice at that time. On the restoration of order Mr. Colvin, who had in the interval been created a Knight Commander of the Order of St. Michael and St. George by Her Majesty's Government, in recognition of his valuable services, returned to Egypt by desire of our Foreign Office, and at the special desire of the Khedive, in the position of financial adviser to the Egyptian Government, and remained on in that capacity, again soon showing his rare skill and management of men and measures by his firm though gentle handling of the complicated state of Egyptian affairs till 1883, when he was summoned to India, to take up there the management of the finances of that country, then being relinquished by Sir E. Baring.

Sir A. Colvin's (exceptional) qualifications as a Finance Minister have been severely tried during the four years he has held office in India. A constantly falling rupee, large military expenditure on our North-West frontier, and the heavy outlay consequent on the annexation of Burma, have tried the resources of Indian revenues to the utmost; and it has required constant care and vigilance to enable the Indian Exchequer to meet the serious demands on its resources. That they have been met without any considerable addition to the taxation of the people is the one satisfaction which Sir A. Colvin must carry away with him on relinquishing office; though the looker-on, and those interested in Indian finance, cannot but wonder how long this constant piling up of liabilities on a structure whose supports are not proportionably strengthened is to last without the natural result of a serious financial catastrophe. Sir A. Colvin cannot be accused of leaving those about him and above him in ignorance of the serious state of affairs, for he has availed himself of every opportunity to point out the dangers of the financial position in India. Indeed, it is mainly owing to his persistent and often eloquent representations that the question of the depreciation of silver has been taken in hand by Her Majesty's Government, and a Royal Commission appointed to examine and report on the whole question. Much, very much to India, depends upon the outcome of the deliberations of this Committee.

Sir A. Colvin has recently been offered and accepted the important post of Lieutenant-Governor of the North-West Provinces, which office he was to take up in November, 1887.* As at first remarked, it is an unusual instance of a son following his father's footsteps exactly thirty years later, Mr. John Russell Colvin having died at his post at Agra as Lieutenant-Governor of the North-West Provinces in the midst of the great Indian Mutiny of 1857. Of Mr. J. R. Colvin's seven sons, four were in the Bengal Civil Service—James, Bazett, Elliot (who died in 1883, while Commissioner of Meerut), and Auckland (now Sir Auckland), the hero of our Sketch. Mr. Clement S. Colvin, who once held the important appointment of Private Secretary to his Grace the Duke of Argyll and the Right Hon. Sir Louis Mallet, in the India Office, is now Assistant Secretary in the Public Works Department, and Assistant Government Director of Indian Guaranteed Railways. He entered the India Office in 1863,

* After a brief furlough to England, Sir Auckland Colvin took over the Lieutenant-Governorship of the North-West Provinces from Sir Alfred Lyall on November 21, just six days after the latter, as Chancellor of the Allahabad University, had delivered an interesting address.

and is one of the most useful and prominent members of the Home Civil Service.

It is the serious question of finance which has recently turned men's eyes on Sir Auckland Colvin. The Indian Budget is, in many respects, a more extraordinary affair than the British one, so carefully exhibited to the public from year to year. The customary indifference to the Eastern one is vanishing; but it has not quite vanished yet. The finances of both countries are fortunately elastic to a very great degree; but the Chancellor of the Exchequer in England has advantages which it is impossible an Indian Finance Minister can possess. Public works, or works of utility, must be done at once; in England they can stand over for a more convenient season. And it is the same with various other contingencies, which can only arise in India. In the middle of 1886 the Indian finance position simply stood thus: Owing to depreciation in value of silver, which was worse than anticipated in Sir A. Colvin's budget, expenses in connection with Burma (also worse than anticipated), and large outlay in frontier railways and roads, the slight surplus budgeted for by the Indian Chancellor of the Exchequer would probably be converted into a deficit. Great economy was therefore called for on the part of India to pay its way during 1886–1887.

Having now sketched a distinguished Anglo-Indian's career, it may be remarked that Sir A. Colvin's success in Egypt is a strong instance—if such were required—of Anglo-Indians rendering useful and often brilliant service in whatever duties they are called upon to undertake.

Again, with reference to a Finance Minister, it will never (we think) be very difficult to pick out a good one from among the local distinguished civilians who must ever exist in India. In such a vast arena, men good at figures are always to be found. That is the first requisite; tact and judgment will generally follow; and thus in India, as in Europe, financiers have been created with powers almost equal to change two into four. Perhaps, on the whole, civilians are better finance handlers than military men; and yet we could mention a few of the latter who rose to eminence in the art.* We dare say, in times to come, the Indian Exchequer will be presided over by men hardly inferior in financial requirements to, and producing budgets with as much skill as Peel, Gladstone, Disraeli, and other familiar names imperishable in our history. Prudent taxation in itself is a theme requiring the study of half a lifetime; and it is now strange to think that what was at first thought by many judges to be imprudent—the Indian Income Tax—drove the very able Sir Charles Trevelyan from Madras, where he might have become a second Lord William Bentinck. Public men who, like Sir Auckland Colvin, have the wish and ability to do justice to a great and interesting nation, must ever be asking themselves the questions, What shall I take off? and, What shall I put on? It is a decided case of mystery or surprise in both countries that must be followed; and the want of money, as in India at present, is the prime mover of all financial success or failure. We recollect, some time before leaving for India, hearing the great Macaulay address the electors of Edinburgh in words which have never faded from our memory: "An urgent and important necessity has arisen of finding money some way or other for the service of the State. There are two ways of finding it, gentlemen; the one is to tax you, the other is to release you of the burden!" Then followed something about sugar, and Lord Sandon's speech in the House of Commons—all tending to have a man consider himself a Finance Minister ready made. We lately read in the "Life" of Lord Macaulay that on one occasion (Dec. 1853) Mr. Disraeli's plan for a budget was "nothing but taking money out of the pockets of the people in towns and putting it into the pockets of growers of malt." It was doubted whether he would carry it; but the famous critic said "the Chancellor had raised his reputation for practical ability."

We shall now turn very briefly to what the natives thought

* Sir William Mansfield (Lord Sandhurst) would have made a better Finance Minister than he did Commander-in-Chief. General Sir George Balfour, M.P., among the living, may also be honourably mentioned in Indian Finance.

of Sir Auckland Colvin's "practical ability" in the middle of April, 1877. It should be remarked that the intelligent members of the Indian community are, as a rule, wonderfully good critics, although the tendency to go to extremes—as in some of our London friends—is sometimes painfully manifest.

Regarding the Budget, it was affirmed in Calcutta and elsewhere, that from the pockets of the poor people of India a great deal of money had been spent on the annexation of Burma, for fear of the Czar, and for payment of the Amir of Afghanistan. The Government, they thought, should not have spent money in this manner. The License Tax, they said, was introduced to make a famine fund, but last year that fund was amalgamated with the general income. In this matter the native critics actually accused the Government—of course very foolishly—of betraying the people. Then the Government had become the guardian of the minor son of the late Maharajah Scindia. Of the money left by the late Maharajah, millions of rupees would be borrowed; while sixty-four lakhs of rupees would be taken from the Provincial Government, and reductions made in the Educational and Public Works Departments of Bengal. All this money would be spent on the Burmese War [this Burmese war, or rather expedition, would appear to be interminable] and in checking Russia by increasing troops and extending railways on the frontier. The *Dakka Prokash* then shakes his head and declares that in the Budget of the present year there is nothing on which India may be congratulated. Nothing is said, it will be seen, on the good prospects of the Afghan boundary question, our strenuous endeavours to put down dacoity in Burma, and our general desire to live peaceably with our Indian neighbours and with all men. But, according to the *Suravi and Pataka,* in the Budget there is one thing with which people may be pleased. No new taxation would be imposed. But what had become of the Finance Committee? Sir Auckland Colvin had not said anything on the subject. Then came the serious assertion that reduction would be made by dispensing with the services of some natives of India. And, again, no taxes would be reduced. An increase had been shown in the income by taking away the money from the famine fund. Lastly, according to the *Pratikar*, a very trifling surplus had been shown in the Budget of the current year. It was doubtful whether there would be any surplus at all; and many were of opinion that the Indian Empire would be ruined, as there was no equilibrium in the income and disbursement of the country. Then it is not known what notion the English entertain of the Indian Empire. But, on account of financial difficulties, the Government will gradually be placed in a difficult position. Then comes the only remedy: Unless the military expenditure and prevailing high salaries be curtailed, no good will be done. In short, it all amounts to this, that educated natives alone should govern India—notwithstanding the kind and generous latitude given by the Ilbert Bill. And so in years to come—perhaps contemporary with the New Zealander on the broken arch of St. Paul's—some ambitious Hindu, or Mahomedan, or Parsee gentlemen carrying out what they now only behold in the mind's eye, will be competing for the post of Finance Minister at Calcutta! From the above remarks it will be seen how difficult it is to frame a Budget to the satisfaction of the Indian public, whose intelligence and consequent ambition the light of education is beginning to make so palpable. And greater men than Sir Auckland Colvin might have equally despaired of pleasing them. Probably he, like some of his illustrious predecessors, is firmly of opinion that the game of self-financing for India would be as dangerous a one to play as that of "Home Rule," for then there would be neither head nor tail to any Budget!

In the East India Financial Statement* (1887–88)—Sir Auckland's last Budget—it is explained that the Government had before it, in connection both with the years 1886–87 and 1887–88, the alternatives of deficit, fresh taxation, or temporarily withholding of the grant from revenue to railways, and reduction of debt, under the head of famine insurance. For reasons given, the latter step having been determined upon, "the sum of £1,049,400, thereby made

* Ordered by the House of Commons to be printed, 2nd May, 1887.

available to meet other expenditure, has obviated deficit." On the 5th of September the annual Indian Financial Statement, soon to be made in London, in the course of public business, was looked forward to with a shade more of interest than usual. Even obstruction was baffled when there was nothing left to obstruct. In a deservedly popular London journal, in a very able leader, it was remarked:—"The Indian Budget has again to take its chance of exciting interest in the dying days of the Session. The little knot of Anglo-Indian experts will, no doubt, complain, with reason, of the disabilities under which they are placed; but they can solace themselves with the reflection that the monopoly of criticism they have long enjoyed is hardly likely to be infringed upon by outsiders."* It was truly considered, from every point of view, regrettable that the financial policy of the Indian Government, year after year, should be treated with what seemed akin to supercilious scorn, as if it were a third-rate instead of a first-rate subject of interest to the Parliament of the Empire. And the peculiar state of parties in the House at the time called forth the just remark from the writer above quoted:—"But the interests of India fare no worse at the hands of the Party of Obstruction than the domestic interests of England and of Scotland." No true Liberal Unionist, or respectable Conservative, and certainly no true friend of India, can think over such lamentable apathy without extreme regret. But, to proceed with Sir Auckland Colvin's Budget, before taking leave of him and his good work, it should now be remarked that, on the 9th of September—nearly five months after one had been published in Calcutta—Sir John Gorst made his annual statement in Committee with reference to the finances of India. Instead of a small surplus, as when the Budget estimate was framed in India, there was now an estimated deficit; but the Government had been so cautious in their estimate of the revenue that he believed in an increase to make it up. Regarding the disputed question of taxation in India, it was remarked that "the amount paid per head was only two shillings, against two pounds ten shillings per head in

* September 6, 1887.

this country." Sir J. Gorst believed the Government of India was the justest which history gave us any account of.

Mr. R. T. Reid, General Sir George Balfour, Mr. Hanbury, and Mr. Gourley criticized the statement; and Sir Richard Temple assured the House that the finances, on the whole, were satisfactory.* Such a remark from such a distinguished Anglo-Indian administrator must have been very welcome to Sir Auckland Colvin, who in Indian finance had at least tried to do his duty; and, although a deficit of two or three millions is hinted at in the next Budget, he may be said to have left his difficult post with strong hopes of an eventual surplus at a time when the Chinese are reported to have found out the cause of the depreciation of silver; and, the most important consideration of all- for that vast and wonderful territory, the North-West Provinces,† when the many millions he has now been called upon to rule are thinking over the past glories and triumphs of their Lieutenant-Governors, from the "big collector," Mr. Thomason, to Sir Alfred Lyall.

To the foregoing imperfect remarks on financial affairs in India, it is only doing Sir Auckland Colvin simple justice to add, on unquestionable authority:

It is now an open secret, and one greatly to Sir A. Colvin's credit, that when the large extra outlay of £2,000,000 a year was thrown on Indian revenues by the increase of 30,000 troops to the Indian army (a measure dictated by the Cabinet when Lord R. Churchill was Indian Secretary) he, Colvin, was alone in his protests against the step, as one in his opinion far beyond the needs of the moment, and likely seriously to embarrass Indian finance in the future. His predictions have been confirmed by lapse of time, for while the resources of India are at this moment being strained to meet the necessary outgoings, the voice of past Indian expe-

* The discussion was continued by that eminent authority, Sir G. Campbell, and others, when the formal resolution was adopted.

† *See* First Series—John Russell Colvin—p. 57.

rience, as expressed by Sir R. Temple in a recent debate in the House of Commons on Indian policy, points clearly to a reduction of military expenditure as a very proper and feasible mode of retrenchment.

The Viceroy, on his tour, arrived at Allahabad on the 13th of December, 1887, and was received by Sir Auckland Colvin and the local officers. There was an enthusiastic crowd to witness his Excellency's arrival, but no ceremonial during his stay as befitting a reign of sterling utility rather than of useless ostentation. Not long before, Lady Dufferin, when visiting the ladies in the palace at Kapurthala, received their thanks for the work she was doing for the women of India; so that, all things considered,—among them the boundary dispute supposed to be settled, the Amir safe for the present; Upper Burma gradually quieting down; a new able and energetic ruler (with financial experience) for the North-West—all in the Jubilee year of 1887,—there is room for hope that prosperity for India is nigh, and that a tranquil day is at length breaking out in the vast and splendid dominion.

At this stage, the following telegram of the Viceroy's tour is of interest:—

"BENARES, *Dec.* 16.

"The Earl of Dufferin to-day opened the Benares Railway Bridge over the Ganges. The bridge, which is named after his Excellency, connects the East Indian and Oudh Railways. In his speech at the opening ceremony the Viceroy expressed his appreciation of the compliment paid him by Sir John Pender, Director of the Oudh Railway, in naming the bridge after him. In reply to the toast of his health at the luncheon which followed the ceremony, Lord Dufferin said that the aim of the Government of India was to secure external and internal peace, and that it would devote its constant endeavours to the promotion of the prosperity of the country. He was glad to think that he could foresee no cloud likely to chequer the progress of such works as that which had just been completed."

HENRY WOODROW, M.A.,

THE "NESTOR OF EDUCATION IN BENGAL."

—o—

"The political reform is *external*, the moral is *intrinsic*, and, above all party spirit as it is, is necessary to the stability and efficiency of the political."—*Philosophy of Education*.

THAT the subject of Education, like the science of Geology, is progressive, few sensible men will venture to deny; and there are few subjects on which greater difference of opinion exists. But the "wretched differences"* which at the present day sometimes defeat the objects of genuine religion and sound education in England have not yet become quite so apparent in India; and it is earnestly to be hoped that such "noisome fogs"—as they have well been styled—will never retard progress and enlightenment in the splendid dominion of the Queen-Empress.

After all, BOOKS AND TEACHERS are the chief instruments necessary in the grand educational machinery of a country; and such must ever furnish leading topics in the arena of controversy and debate where no party spirit should exist. If the training of teachers is vital to a whole educational system at home, how much more vital must it be in India, containing seven or eight times as many millions as the British Isles! Among us, at the present day, it is in too many cases as it was just fifty years ago, the schoolmaster who professes to teach is *eo ipso* believed qualified; or it is the old story, When every

* Dr. Chalmers.—Simpson's "Philosophy of Education," p. 145.

other trade fails, one can always open a school! The qualifications of an efficient teacher are too often little known or even thought of; possessing knowledge is widely different from imparting it; and so in an age of school-boards, coaching or cramming for examinations, and female intellectual superiority and pretension, we still are occasionally apt to think of the good old anecdote of the crazy and ragged orator who applied at the Mansion House for a few shillings and a pair of shoes to take him back to Ireland, having found the pretensions of this island to learning exceedingly hollow. It will be remembered that in his harangue to the Lord Mayor—the orator must have been a Home Ruler!—he observed, with appropriate sarcasm, "that he had heard much of the schoolmaster being abroad in England, but that he had not had the good fortune to meet with him or find anybody who had!" And wiser men made, and still venture to make, the same complaint, not from the difficulty of meeting the schoolmaster, but from his occasional uselessness when met. He is too frequently not the right man in the right place. It was also said fifty years since, that, besides educating the schoolmaster, we must raise him in society to the rank and endowments he deserves. But neither in England nor in India is the teacher's, in general, considered a fourth learned profession, as it should surely be. Without well-trained and intellectual teachers it is simply impossible, however easy it may be to propound principles, to adopt any useful practical plan of education whatever. To remove such a grand obstacle, and other difficulties in the way of national enlightenment, is, of course, the desire of every zealous educationist; and, especially in India, the way to act too often puzzles the ever-thinking and hard-working Inspector of Schools, who beholds the high and coveted post of Director of Public Instruction looming in the distance. Most Englishmen are utterly ignorant of the various and difficult work assigned to these two useful functionaries in the East, on whose banner should ever be engraved *Excelsior*, while, among so many millions of an interesting and wonderful people, during a remarkable transition state of the Hindu and Mahomedan minds, denouncing ignorance as "the curse of God," and guiding while casting rays of light over what is still, in a great measure, a mystical and pagan land. Education in India is, therefore, a great thing, and will always be so; for in a country with one-sixth of the human race to people it, what the poet says of "Serene Philosophy" may be applied to education there with rare truth—

> "Without Thee, what were UNENLIGHTENED man!"

And in no other country in the world is there such a field for the exercise of versatile talent and constructive power among its Inspectors and Directors—qualities particularly remarkable in the career of the great Anglo-Indian educationist whose career is about to be presented to our readers.

Originality of conception is rarely to be found in would-be successful educationists; and the felt want of it often detracted from the usefulness of the present writer when employed in Burma and India.* During his educational experiences he can only take credit for two high aims—one being to enforce a knowledge of Indian geography in all schools, and the other to give subsidiary education by means of interesting and instructive lectures.

In the Sketch of Anglo-Indian Periodical Literature (*First Series*) allusion has been made to the various stages of education and enlightenment during the present century. The famous Serampore Baptist missionaries at the beginning of it are especially mentioned as forming a grand trio—Carey, Marshman, and Ward—almost matchless in its use to India at that time. It is interesting to look back to Carey translating the Scriptures; Ward printing the translations, the printer preaching in Bengali when time permitted; and Dr. and Mrs. Marshman with their schools. The popularity of these schools, we have remarked, was immediately proved by the occasional receipt of as much as 4,000 rupees (£400) a month for tuition; for everybody (Europeans, East Indians,

* First as Inspector of Schools, Rangoon, or British Burma (the first appointed by Lord Lawrence, on the recommendation of Sir Arthur Phayre) —and next as Superintendent of Army Schools, Madras Presideney, appointed by Lord Napier and Ettrick, when Governor.

and Natives) sent a son to Serampore.* Lord Hastings (1818) was also strenuous in his efforts to improve the native mind by education as well as by periodical literature; and some of our greatest statesmen in India, from the time of the venerated Lord William Bentinck down to the advent of the present versatile, energetic, and scholarly Viceroy, have done much to aid the cause of enlightening the natives. In Female Education, the honoured names of Mr. Drinkwater Bethune and Miss Carpenter are known to many Anglo-Indians, and that of the admirable American, Mrs. Mason, in Burma. Education in India and the East, therefore, cannot be said to have been neglected; and it is strange to think that the first solid impetus given to it in Bengal was not by members of our own Church of England, but by the Serampore Baptist missionaries just alluded to. This is a striking historical fact, and worthy of consideration, especially when we hear (October, 1887) a popular English statesman of the present day, while advocating the claims of a Baptist Sunday School, asserting, with great justice, that a man must be very ignorant of history who did not recognize the great part which the Baptists had played in the social, political, and religious history of this country." It was in October of the year 1799 that the first Protestant Missionary Establishment in Bengal was formed at Serampore. The missionaries published many works in Bengalee, and gave the first impulse to the cultivation of this language, more indebted to their exertions than to those of any other individuals. Such work, and what has already been stated, entirely warranted the remark of the late excellent John C. Marshman (C.S.I.), that "the first movements towards the civilization and improvement of this country may be said to have taken their rise at Serampore." Lord Wellesley, also, finding the Civil Servants imperfectly acquainted with the languages of the country, established, in 1800, the College of Fort William in Calcutta. So, of course, India, rather more than other parts of the British Empire, must be included in the liberal statesman's high eulogium. From Dr. Marshman to Henry Woodrow—there were neither Inspectors of Schools

* Page 341.

nor Directors of Public Instruction in the good old times—down to the present day, gives a space approaching ninety years, during which period there has been no more fit, accomplished, and zealous educationist in India than Henry Woodrow. The Memoir now presented is simply entitled—and we trust that every "faithful servant" going to India will read it—like the man, without ostentation—

AN INDIAN CAREER.

Henry Woodrow was born 31st July, 1823, at Norwich, of parents who held a good position in the county of Norfolk. On his mother's side he was descended from the ancient family of Temple of Stowe, John Temple, the purchaser of Stowe in 1590, being his ancestor. He was educated at Rugby, his first school years having been spent at Mr. Brewer's school, at Norwich, whence he was removed to Rugby. He was one of the "School House" boys at Rugby, and rose to the sixth form. He used to say in after years that he never had so much power and authority as when he was a præpostor at Rugby. He was an enthusiastic admirer of Dr. Arnold, and was one of the six boys who took supper with Dr. Arnold on the evening before his sudden death.

In "Tom Brown's School Days"* many incidents of Henry Woodrow's school-life are preserved, and will now be recognized by Rugbeians, but Mr. Hughes, in the exercise of the privileges of an author, has assigned these to different characters. At Rugby, among others valued in after life, Henry Woodrow made the friendship of the present (1876) Earl of Derby, Dr. Valpy French, the new Bishop of Lahore, Mr. Theodore Walrond, Mr. Thomas Hughes, Mr. Seton Karr, Mr. W. J. Evelyn, M.P., and of many others, which he maintained through life. From Rugby he went to Caius College, where he won a Scholarship; graduated in 1846 as Fourteenth Wrangler; was elected Fellow of his College; and resided a short time afterwards at the University and

* Early in October, 1887, we heard of the death, at Rugby, Tennessee (U.S.A.), of Mrs. Hughes, the mother of the genial and popular writer.

took pupils in mathematics. In November, 1848, he accepted the post of Principal of the Martinière College in Calcutta, which offered a salary of £1,000 a year, with a residence, and he arrived in Calcutta the 5th of January, 1849. He remained nearly six years at the Martinière. In 1854 Mr. Woodrow was appointed Secretary to the Council of Education, and thus entered the service of Government. With this appointment he received charge of the Government School Book Agency. The Government system of Education in Bengal was then administered by a Council of Education. This Council consisted of members all of whom had regular official duty of other kinds, and met from time to time for the despatch of business after the Government offices were closed. Under this system the whole details of administration were left to their Permanent Secretary, who was also a member of the Council of Education. At this time (1854) the whole number of schools connected with Government in Bengal (a province containing 60,000,000 people) was fifty-four. The only Vernacular Government Schools were the "Hardinge Schools," of which class Lord Hardinge, when Governor-General, had founded 101 in India. The immediate supervision of the schools scattered throughout the country was left to the Collector of Districts, gentlemen whose time was fully occupied with their Revenue, Judicial, Magisterial, and Administrative duties. Many of the Collectors, moreover, held the opinion that the introduction of education would give the people ideas beyond the sphere in which they would have to earn their bread, would make them dissatisfied, and render them more troublesome to manage. Part of the task of the Secretary to the Council of Education was the duty of stimulating these Collectors. The Council of Education conclude their Report for the year 1854 with the following sentence:—"Gradually, but surely, the Vernacular Schools, established by Lord Hardinge, have disappeared, until, at the beginning of the present year, there remained but twenty-six out of the original one hundred and one."

The Secretary of State (Sir Charles Wood) was so dissatisfied with this state of things that he determined to organize a separate department of Government, to be called "The Bengal Educational Service," whose sole duty should be the management of the Government education. A distinguished civilian, Mr. Gordon Young, was appointed the first Director of Public Instruction in Bengal in 1855, and Mr. Woodrow the first Inspector of Schools in Eastern Bengal.

The area thus assigned to Mr. Woodrow contained 15,000,000 inhabitants; and at that time he had only sixteen schools to inspect from Calcutta to Chittagong. This number had increased to eight hundred in 1861, and by the time he became himself Director of Public Instruction the number was more than five thousand. (It is difficult to state exactly, as the areas of inspection were from time to time altered.)

It is now to be explained how the gradual disappearance of the schools in Bengal was at once changed into so unexampled a development. Mr. Woodrow threw himself into his new work in 1855 with characteristic energy. He was not afraid of long marches in the sun of Bengal; he did not avoid tedious journeys in a small native boat or a country cart; he was possessed of great personal strength, and as a matchless swimmer ran little risk of sharing the fate which befell his coadjutor, Mr. Robinson, of Assam. He exerted himself, not merely to discharge his official duty, but to please the natives, and induce them to support a national education. He was always ready, whatever the personal hardship involved, to give them an experimental lecture on chemistry, electricity, or some subject in physical science. He spared no labour to make a solid lecture attractive; if he lectured on astronomy, he manufactured his hydrogen in Calcutta, and carrying it with him showed his magic lantern by the oxy-hydrogen light, far away in the interior of his district. In the earliest days of the electric telegraph Mr. Woodrow exhibited the machine to Calcutta audiences.

The natives presented many addresses of thanks to him for such lectures. Those who witnessed the splendid illuminations in Calcutta in honour of his Royal Highness the Prince of Wales on the evening of the 24th December, 1875, will not readily forget Mr. Woodrow's device of "The Star of India," composed of the electric light, emblem of the rays of knowledge to emanate from the Office of Public Instruction, over which the star shone brilliantly.* [Nothing could be better or more telling than this "bright particular Star."]

In 1855 Mr. Woodrow started the system of "Circular Schools." Under this plan one superior teacher visited, in turn, for one or two days' teaching each, among a cluster of village schools. This system, though nearly dropped now that good teachers are more plentiful, was very successful in raising the standard of the lowest class of schools in the early days of education in Bengal.

Mr. Woodrow was, above all things, anxious to make education attractive by showing the people that the Government teaching would give a boy an advantageous start in life. With this view he took up, among other subjects, surveying; he taught the teachers, he took the classes into the field, he set them the example of carrying his own chain, and he conducted the examinations himself. In many of the stations in East Bengal are still to be seen sun-dials, large brick buildings of the old Hindoo style, but corrected so as to give the time very accurately for the rest of the nineteenth century. These dials were all erected by Mr. Woodrow on the occasion of his visits to these places to inspect the schools. In those days there was no telegraph, and the finding the local time, even approximately, was a matter of importance to the business, both of the station and of its schools. In 1866, during the lamented Bishop Cotton's last tour in his diocese, in which Mr. Woodrow accompanied him, the Bishop used to say that in Assam four things usually considered as necessaries of life were wanting: there were "no clocks, no roads, no servants, no food."

In the technical business of his department; in all matters of form, of account, and of procedure in reporting, Mr. Woodrow's advice was always sought by Government, and almost always followed.

In the memorable Despatch of Lord Stanley in 1859,

* *See*, also, Appendix V.

when Sécretary of State for India, upon education in Bengal, Lord Stanley failed not to do justice to his former schoolfellow. In several paragraphs he quoted from his Reports, and showed his concurrence in the policy Mr. Woodrow had laid down for the promotion of popular education,—the improvement and far wider extension of education, both English and vernacular, having been the general objects of the Despatch of 1854 of Sir C. Wood.

In 1872 the system of Government Education was so widely spread and so firmly rooted in Bengal that the Lieutenant-Governor, Sir George Campbell, considered the time had arrived when a Special Department was no longer necessary to administer it. By a Government Resolution of 30th September, 1872, the administration of the schools was taken out of the hands of the Inspectors, and replaced in that of the Collectors of Districts, and the duty of the Educational Department was confined to teaching and reporting. In Mr. Woodrow's Report for the year 1872–73 he does not disguise his feeling that he had been robbed of his own bantling by the Resolution of 30th September, 1872, but he nevertheless accepted his position, and set himself manfully to do the work allotted to him by Government, and to induce the Collectors of Districts to cherish the schools thus handed over to them.

In 1873 Mr. Woodrow took eighteen months' leave to Europe, under the advice of the doctor, who considered that his heart showed signs of weakness. On this furlough his whole idea was not a holiday, but how to improve his own professional usefulness. He inspected the schools and colleges at Vienna; he studied the Swiss schools at Zurich; he spent his whole time at Brussels and Bonn in the schools. Whilst in England at this time he undertook the labour of Examiner in the Government Competitive Examinations under the Civil Service Commissioners. Having been, during his long experience, greatly impressed by the deficiency of the Bengal boys in stout physique, he warmly advocated in England that an examination in physical exercises should form a part of the Government Competitive Examinations.* It may be mentioned that, in March, 1879,

* *See* Appendix VI., *Critical Sketch.*

his pamphlet on the subject was forwarded to Viscount Sandon, Vice-President of the Council on Education, to the Right Hon. Lord Waveney, and also to the Right Hon. Lord Fortescue. The latter said he wished he had had it before making his speech in the House to advance Physical Training in the public services. Lord Waveney also spoke highly of the pamphlet. Mr. Woodrow showed that physical exercises could be satisfactorily made a test-subject in examination; he also pointed out that the education of not less than 50,000 boys in England is directed or influenced by the subjects appointed for the Government Competitive Examinations; and that the question involved is not merely whether bookworms make the most dashing Military, Naval, and Civil Servants of the Empire. It should here be related that Mr. Woodrow served as a volunteer during the Mutiny in 1857, and obtained a good-conduct stripe. He was so frequently absent from Calcutta on his long inspectional tours in Lower Bengal, that he was unable to be regular as a member of the corps, and, consequently, could not be promoted; so he remained "a full Private," and was very proud of his stripe!

Mr. Woodrow was Chairman of the Uncovenanted Civil Service Pension Fund in Bengal; and as competent actuaries are scarce in India, he had himself calculated fresh tables for that Society. In recognition of the excellence of this work he was admitted, about this time, an Associate of the British Actuaries.

Mr. Woodrow had previously (in 1869) gone through a complete course of practical instruction in Metallurgy, and had been fully qualified as an Assay Master for the Mint. In this year, finding that a large section of English Mathematicians thought that Euclid as our teacher in the elements of Geometry should now be superseded, Mr. Woodrow set to work to consider the question for himself, reading through, not merely the new English and French text-books, but spelling his way even through the German Elementary Geometrics, a work of great labour to him, as he knew no more of German than most other Cambridge men of his day.

On his return to Calcutta, in 1875, Mr. Woodrow addressed the University with the object of inducing the University to extend its curriculum in Physical Sciences by curtailing studies in Metaphysics. He also wished and advised that Geometric Drawing should be a subject of instruction in *all* schools. He was appointed Chairman of a University Committee, and succeeded in carrying out, in the main, his views regarding the extension of the teaching of Physical Science. He had also been a most laborious Chairman to the Committee on School Books, instituted by the Viceroy, Lord Northbrook.

In the year 1860, Mr. Woodrow obtained the permission of Mr. Gordon Young, and subsequently that of Mr. Atkinson, Director of Public Instruction, to extricate from the mass of volumes of records, the minutes of Lord Macaulay, when President of the Council of Education, and republished them himself; for which he received the thanks of the Governor-General, Lord Canning. These minutes are considered most interesting as the record of the conflicting opinions of the best and noblest Englishmen in Bengal on the subject of education between the years 1833 and 1835, when the battle raged as to Western or Oriental instruction. It is almost needless to mention that the "great minute,"* as it has been termed, decided this vexed question in favour of Western (or European) education.

In 1875 Mr. Woodrow was for a short time the Principal of the Presidency College in Calcutta. He did not here confine himself to the discharge merely of his official duties. He joined the Students' Society or Association, and became its President.

In September, 1875, Mr. Woodrow was appointed to officiate as Director of Public Instruction in Bengal; and he succeeded to the post on the death of Mr. Atkinson in the following January, 1876. Thus Mr. Woodrow became head of the Educational Department. There are letters extant, which appeared in the daily papers at that date, which evince the satisfaction experienced by the natives of Bengal on Mr. Woodrow's appointment to be Director. On his appointment as Inspector of Schools, in 1855, fears had been

* *See* end of Sketch.

expressed in some quarters that, being so friendly to missionaries, the Bengalees would suspect the Government of a desire to proselytize them, and that they would refuse Government education altogether when the agent who proffered it was so Christian a man. The result proved how groundless were those fears. Throughout his career, while faithful to his earthly masters, he could still remember he had a higher Lord to serve.

In the autumn of 1876 he was summoned to Darjeeling, where the Lieutenant-Governor wished to consult with him personally on various educational matters. He received the summons with pleasure, for he loved the mountains; his only drawback being, as he said, that his wife did not wish to go; although, of course, she accompanied him, as had been her custom on all his long official tours since 1855. There he stayed some weeks. On the 10th October, in the afternoon, he attended at the Shrubbery to have an interview with the Lieutenant-Governor, and whilst arranging several important appointments Mr. Woodrow was suddenly seized by a violent pain across the chest. Sir Richard Temple kindly advised him to go home and take care of himself, but he preferred to remain and finish their discussion, as Sir Richard intended to start the next morning for Sikhim, and would be absent a fortnight. On his return from the Lieutenant-Governor's that evening he felt great oppression in breathing, and the violent pain continued, and at 3 A.M. of the 11th October, 1876, he got out of his bed, and died in a few minutes. "Died?" says the original author of this Memoir, who introduces it with the beautiful lines:—

> "He is not dead, whose glorious life
> Leads thine on high;
> To live in hearts we leave behind
> Is not to die."

The leading feature in Mr. Woodrow's character was uprightness; no person ever approached him but was quickly and profoundly impressed with the integrity and absolute trustworthiness of the man. It may be said that IN HIS WHOLE LIFE he never attempted to deceive or mislead, in the slightest degree, any one person on any single occasion. This was the real secret of his great success, and it, in the end, though not at first, carried him over all obstacles to a position of which he was worthy. It is true that his abilities were of a high order, that he was gifted with great personal strength and could work very long hours, that he exhibited patient perseverance in all that he attempted. Still, had his mathematical and scientific acquirements been less brilliant, his personal strength and courage less remarkable, he would have been a marked man, and it may be long ere we shall look on his like again. The work of his life was the establishment of a system of National Education in Bengal, and, diverse as may be the opinions of diverse persons on the subject of education, none can say that his work was not thoroughly well done. The Collector of the District of Midnapore, in an article in the *Calcutta Review*, for July, 1876, written with the object of depreciating the work of the Bengal Educational Service, yet refers to Mr. Woodrow as "the Nestor of Education in Bengal."

The European and the Native Press of India alike testified to this work.

The Natives of India are sometimes accused of want of gratitude towards the English; however, the people of Bengal raised a sum of £700 to erect a memorial bust in marble of Mr. Woodrow,* and to found a Scholarship to preserve his name. The Government of Bengal acknowledged the value of his services in the two notifications appended.†

To these we have added a few tributes of affection, showing the high esteem in which Mr. Woodrow was held, both in England and India, including the translation of a Sanskrit elegy. Such tributes are never brought forth unless there be some undeniable or intrinsic excellence about a public man. And we say, without fear of contradiction,

* His bust is in Caius College, Cambridge, as well as in the University of Calcutta.

† Appendix V.

that no man ever deserved them better—no man ever did more useful work in his vocation—than the "Nestor of Education in Bengal"!

THE DIRECTOR AND HIS WORK.

We now turn briefly to the European and Native Press of India, and to those who knew him well, for some opinions on Mr. Woodrow and his work, and cull the chief portion of the following matter from sixteen long columns of extracts from among many of the notices which appeared in the Calcutta journals, and other sources, chiefly published in October and November, 1876.

The *Calcutta Review* received the news of Mr. Woodrow's death with deep regret, styling him "THE NESTOR OF EDUCATION IN BENGAL."

With reference to his education at Rugby, and his being a staunch disciple of Dr. Arnold, "It has been said that he was one of those from whom Tom Hughes drew his characters for 'Tom Brown's School Days.' If so, it was none other than a manly and upright one that could be drawn from him."

As to "Circle Schools," in the Educational Department, "Mr. Woodrow's name is closely connected with the introduction of the 'Circle System'—a system intended to develop education among the masses at a cheap rate, and which has proved fully successful." Again, says the same authority—"It is not only in Calcutta that the loss of this most kind-hearted, good man will be deplored; and his widow has the consolation—such as it is—of a very general and sincere sympathy." On the 20th of October a meeting of "the friends and admirers of the late Mr. Woodrow was held at the Library of the Sanskrit College. There were present, headed by his trusty friend, Rajah Sourendra Mohun Tagore, several Sanskrit Professors, and many distinguished and learned native gentlemen. The Rajah alluded in glowing terms to 'the high character of the deceased gentleman, and his well-known services in the cause of native education and advancement, extending over a period of twenty-seven years.' Excellent speeches were delivered, and the best means of perpetuating his memory duly considered. It was also resolved to vote 'a letter of condolence to his bereaved widow, expressive of their heartfelt sympathy.'"

Such allusions to Mrs. Woodrow are frequent among the notices; and it was pleasingly natural for the good people of Calcutta to turn at such a time to one who had been the life-companion of the great Champion of Education in India; the "honoured and high-minded lady," as it is said, "and his almost invariable companion in difficult inspectional journeys." Such devotion on the part of a wife is apt to remind us of that displayed by the helpmates of some of our greatest Indian missionaries; and it especially causes the present writer to think of the admirable American Judsons in the First, and the Masons in the Second Burmese War. When, early in 1853, the Martaban land-column arrived to capture what was once the "ancient city" of Tonghoo, after a long and weary march through a difficult country, on taking a peaceable possession of the town and fort, the first pioneers we met, out of the column, were Dr. and Mrs. Mason, when the learned author of the "Fauna, Flora, and Minerals of Burma" began to talk to us about the roses and other flowers of the new Golden Land; while his amiable and accomplished wife was busy aiding him in his great work for the education and enlightenment of the Karens and other tribes, on which the entire pacification and civilization of our new conquest in no small measure depends. To return to the acknowledgment of the educational efforts, and the valuable labours of Mr. Woodrow.

A public meeting was held at Belvidere—so well known to the residents of the City of Palaces—on the 23rd of November, with a view to perpetuate his memory. The gathering was a large one, representing all sections of the community—European, Eurasian, Hindu, and Mahomedan—"demonstrating unmistakably the high respect in which the deceased was held by all classes." The Lieutenant-Governor of Bengal—Sir Richard Temple—ever alive to the importance of such meetings, and to doing good wherever it could possibly be achieved, presided;* and, in opening the proceedings, alluded to "the family ties which connected him with the lamented deceased, and an acquaintance which commenced when His Honour and Mr. Woodrow were studying in the same school [Rugby], at the age of twelve years." Sir Richard feelingly mentioned the circumstance "that it had fallen to his lot to have the last business transactions with Mr. Woodrow at his own house at Darjeeling, when he was attacked with the illness which in a few hours carried him off." Mr. Radika Prasanna Mukhorji, a member, was appointed "Secretary Memorial Committee." It was proposed to have a personal memorial of the deceased in the form of a bust, and also one of public utility, such as a graduate scholarship in connection with the University. The President of the Memorial Committee was, of course, Sir Richard Temple, Bart., K.C.S.I., with a long list of influential members.

In Calcutta, January, 1877, the business of the meeting, in which it was resolved to honour the memory of the deceased, was announced to Mrs. Woodrow, when, after alluding to his lady in the touching words already given, it was moved by Prince Mahamud Ferokh Shah, and seconded by Rajah Hurrendra Krishna, Bahadur, "That with a view to preserve, for the benefit of succeeding generations, some recollections of the versatile talents for public usefulness exhibited in the late Mr. Woodrow's life," a Committee be appointed "to decide upon a suitable form of memorial to perpetuate his name." It consisted of Princes, wealthy Babus, and Professors—all anxious to do him honour. Before this a meeting of the Syndicate of the Calcutta University, (of which he was Senior Member) had taken place, when it was recorded that the value of Mr. Woodrow's official labours had been recognized by the Government whom he served; and the Syndicate and the University had to deplore, by his death, the removal from their number of a scholar of distinguished attainments, a judicious and energetic colleague, and "a strenuous supporter of all

* On the motion of Mr. R. B. Chapman, seconded by Moulvi Abdul Latiff Khan Bahadoor.

measures calculated to assist academic progress and educational improvement."

Koylas Chunder Bose, Hon. Secretary Bethune Society, wrote, "that the high esteem in which Mr. Woodrow was held by all sections of the Society, for the noble qualities, both of mind and heart, with which he was gifted by nature," and which he brought to bear so admirably upon his relations with the members, will ever endear his memory to all. In a resolution particular mention is made of the valuable lectures he himself delivered at the Society's meetings, and of "his kind exertions to get others to come forward and promote its usefulness."

Prosad Doss Mullick, Hon. Secretary Family Literary Club (Burra Bazar), also announced that the Club desired to place on record "the deep sense of the loss which it had sustained in the death of Mr. Woodrow, its late President." The Governors of the Calcutta Free School also desired to record the deep concern with which they heard of Mr. Woodrow's death. To the Free School he had been something more than an official adviser:—"The proceedings of the Governors for the last fifteen years abound in proofs of his affectionate interest in the well-being of the poor children educated by this Charity. In educational matters the School Committee have long been guided by his practical judgment; and his minutes, the result of much thought and careful consultation with the Government and the Bishop of the Diocese, have been, and probably will be, accepted for many years to come as the principles on which the discipline and instruction of the school must be based."

Mrs. Woodrow is likewise thanked for her services on the Ladies' Committee.

The Directors of the Uncovenanted Service Family Pension Fund (through their Secretary *) also expressed their deep sorrow on the occasion of losing their Chairman, and the ladies of the Native Ladies' Normal School offered their "sincerest sympathy." The Secretary to the Calcutta Missionary Conference (Mr. J. Hector) wrote that for a quarter of a century Mr. Woodrow had attended and highly

* Mr. W. H. Ryland.

benefited the meetings of the Conference by his "striking excellences," and that his character exhibited "a rare combination of power and tenderness, of decision and gentleness, of conscious dignity and unfeigned humility, of breadth of view and attention to minute details, of practical wisdom and guileless sincerity." In fact, he was a true friend and benefactor to the people of Bengal; as great and successful, perhaps, in the science of its education as Sir Richard Temple and Sir Ashley Eden (rulers under different circumstances) had been in its government.

In an able letter to the Editor of the *Indian Daily News*, the writer expatiated on the merits of "the great and good man who had just passed away." The *Bengallee* had a warm and touching tribute to his memory, "avoiding the common Oriental vice of over-rating the good qualities of a man." It spoke of the man *as it found him;* and in much the same spirit the correspondent of the *Indian Daily News* desired to recall two occasions on which Mr. Woodrow's "genuine good nature and kindliness of heart shone to peculiar advantage." The first was on the occasion of the landing of the Prince of Wales, when each of the various schools in Calcutta and its neighbourhood sent its quota of happy faces and strong lungs to welcome, and at the same time have a good look at, the Heir Apparent.* The genial Director of Public Instruction, we read, "could then be seen in his academicals, flitting from group to group, cordially grasping by the hand the masters and mistresses, who had come up with the young folks, and exchanging a few pleasant words with them as he went along." There was no icy officialism with him—no thrusting of his own importance as the great Director. He was the "big brother" for the nonce, and only intent on seeing order maintained and a good demonstration made by the younger people.

The next was when the gentlemen who had degrees conferred on them at the last Convocation of the Calcutta University retired with their friends, after the ceremony, to the Hindu School, for a few hours of pleasant social intercourse. Here, again, we see the good Director, the sole

* *See* Appendix V.

Englishman, we believe, in the room, his honest face reflecting how genuinely he rejoiced with the graduates in their success, and recollecting, doubtless, his own gladness of heart when, in 1846, the class lists proclaimed him Fourteenth Wrangler of his year.

Short as was the term allotted for his life's work; it was yet long enough for the doing of deeds which this generation, at least of Bengal, will not willingly let die. Like the highly-esteemed Bishop Cotton, Mr. Woodrow had come under the direct influence of that best of schoolmasters—Dr. Arnold of Rugby; and both exhibited in their lives how deep and abiding could be the teaching of one man if only he aim with single eye for the mental and moral elevation of those placed under his care, or coming within the range of his influence. The following pleasing anecdote is worthy of insertion :—During his career as Inspector of Schools Mr. Woodrow rendered exemplary services to the people of the country. Once he chanced to be at a place (name not remembered) several miles to the south of Calcutta, and, finding it populated by indigent as well as uneducated men who had no means to know the time, he, almost unassisted, raised a sun-dial in the midst of the locality, thus impressing the inhabitants with his unusual fondness for the welfare of the people. The cleverness of the natives of India at telling the time by the sun's shadow on the ground is well known to Anglo-Indians; but the amiable Inspector had now given them a *boná-fide* sun-dial, on which he might have written the inscription, with regard to himself—*Non numero horas nisi serenas!* *

In January, 1877, the *Journal of the National Indian Association* gave a prominent place to a notice in the *Bengallee,* in which it was stated that "Mr. Woodrow's ripe experience, profound scholarship, and varied attainments, made his premature death a public calamity in Bengal." No man ever did more for scientific instruction in Bengal than he; and his simplicity was as remarkable as his learning. "He would often correct his first impressions if his error was duly pointed out"—far from a common feature in

* I number not the hours unless sunny.

the character of great educationists, and so well alluded to by the *Bengallee*. Again, he brings another of the many "old familiar faces" before us when he remarks:—"The bluff, honest English face, the tone of earnestness which pervaded his speech and manner, the sincere desire to benefit those with whom his lot was cast, endeared him to many persons in Bengal." He was a staunch supporter of right; and his life was pure as that of a child, although his aims were high. It was also remarked, with a degree of sorrow, that, during the short time he worked as Director of Public Instruction, he laid the germ of many improvements "not destined to take root." Mr. Woodrow left behind him no children, but, we read, was ever a father to his nephews and nieces. His widow, as will have been seen, gathered consolation from the sympathy she received everywhere in Bengal and other quarters.* It should be noted that, though a sincere believer in Christianity, he would never wound the religious feelings of others; and he used to say to his native friends that there are excellent and pious men among Hindu Pundits and Mahomedan Moulavies as well as Christian missionaries. What particularly fitted the popular Director for his great work was, that he never made any race distinctions; and when he discovered that he had unjustly wronged a man, he did all in his power to compensate the injured party. Such, then, were, and probably still are, a few of the Bengal opinions on Henry Woodrow and his work.

LORD MACAULAY'S MINUTES.

Either to the Inspector of Schools, or Director of Public Instruction in India, who, like the subject of this sketch, does his work thoroughly, little time can be spared for general literary composition. But Mr. Woodrow appears to have been moulded from that rare die which gives men to the world who find time for everything. Mr. Woodrow prefaces his valuable little work entitled "Macaulay's Minutes

* Mrs. Woodrow left India in April, 1877, after some twenty-five years in the country.

on Education in India" with the following remarks, dated Calcutta, 20th May, 1862 :—

When valuable and forgotten writings of distinguished authors are discovered, and presented to the public, it is customary for the publisher to state where and how the manuscripts were found.

In the office of the Department of Public Instruction in Calcutta are hundreds of manuscript volumes and bundles, containing minutes, reports, and correspondence, accumulated during the last forty years by the several authorities who have exercised control over the course of Public Instruction in Bengal. The records of the Committee of Public Instruction extend from 1823 to 1842, when the Committee was superseded by the Council of Education, which, in its turn, in January, 1855, was displaced by the appointment of a Director of Public Instruction. In April, 1854, the offer of the appointment of Secretary to the Council of Education was accepted by me, and in this capacity I received charge of all the records, and became acquainted with the valuable minutes which lay buried in a vast mass of official correspondence. In January, 1855, the system prescribed in Sir Charles Wood's great Educational Despatch was carried out in Bengal, the Council of Education was abolished, and a member of the Bengal Civil Service was appointed to discharge its functions under the title of Director of Public Instruction. To the first Director, Mr. W. Gordon Young, my grateful acknowledgments are due for his unvarying courtesy, and for his permission to continue my researches among the old records of his office. I also received from him permission to use, in a public lecture, the educational minutes of Lord Macaulay. The permission accorded by Mr. Young was continued by his successor, Mr. W. S. Atkinson, the present Director of Public Instruction, to whom also my thanks are due.

A selection from Macaulay's minutes was read before the Bethune Society, which was established in Calcutta in 1851, for "the consideration and discussion of questions connected with Literature and Science;" and the following pages were published as part of the proceedings of this Society. Among the minutes will be found many which are of no general interest; but, apart from the desire to publish every scrap of Macaulay's writings, several of these minutes have still a local value in Bengal, though they are unimportant in other parts of the world.

The clear and concise style of the Director is also strongly apparent in a sketch (1862) of—

"Macaulay's Labours in India."

The Indian career of Lord Macaulay extends from the close of 1834 to the beginning of 1838. During these years he was the means of reforming the education, and simplifying the law of the land. Few men have set their stamp so broadly and deeply on the history of a nation's progress. By his educational reforms, the whole course of instruction was directed into new channels, which more or less it still occupies. His Penal Code, after lying under consideration for nearly twenty-four years, has recently become the law of India. Seldom does it fall to one man to be at once the chief Educator and the chief Lawgiver of a vast nation. Besides all this, his latest efforts in establishing the Civil Service Competitive Examination for India have contributed powerfully to stimulate native industry and ability by opening to young men of ambition a prospect of sharing in the government of their country. True it is, that no native student has yet gained a footing in the Civil Service, but the feeling that such a position is possible, and can be attained by merit, has exercised much influence, and will exercise more. Already two young Hindoos of high connections have started for England, and others are eager to follow them. The restrictions which caste lays on travelling are felt by Hindoos of education with intense and increasing bitterness. It is highly probable that the Competitive Examination will bring to a head in Bengal some grand social outburst against caste, and thus Macaulay's name may become connected with one of the greatest benefits this country can receive—the overthrow of caste.

The latest statistics from all India, those for 1859, show

thirteen Government colleges containing 1,909 students, and four aided colleges with 878 students; seventy-four superior Government schools containing 10,989 scholars, and 209 aided schools, of the same or somewhat lower grade, with 16,956 scholars; twenty-five normal schools containing 2,241 students; and sixteen colleges for special subjects containing 1,154 students. Besides this, there are 5,454 vernacular schools with 127,507 pupils under Government management, and 380 aided vernacular schools with 20,744 scholars. This gives the whole of the educational institutions as 5,582 under Government management, and 593 aided, of which the former contain 143,700 pupils, and the latter 38,578. The whole cost has been for direction and inspection £68,400, for direct instruction £189,200, for aided institutions £18,700; forming in all a total of £276,300. In the Lower Provinces of Bengal there are about 10,000 students learning English in missionary and private institutions unaided by Government. Such are the results in a quarter of a century of Macaulay's labours in India.

To the above educational statistics of 1859, it may be useful to add, briefly, some information from the Report on the Progress and Condition of India, 1884–85. For those unacquainted with the subject, it should be stated that educational organization in India is a continuous system, from the primary school to the university, the maximum standard of one grade of school reaching the minimum one of that immediately above it. There are still local differences conspicuous in the various Provinces; but, since 1855 (the year, it will be recollected, of Mr. Woodrow's appointment), a greater degree of uniformity has been gradually introduced. "Broadly speaking," it is said, "the main object of educational policy in India of late years has been the improvement and extension of elementary education. It was this point to which the attention of the Education Commission of 1882–83 was especially directed." From the top of the educational organization (the universities), working downwards, it is easy to see how the different parts of the system are linked together. The Universities of Calcutta, Madras, Bombay, and the Punjab, it should be kept in mind, are purely examining bodies on the model of the University of London,—exercising a general control over the colleges which prepare students for degrees, and through them over the higher secondary schools with a view to successful candidates for matriculation. Of course, degrees are conferred by the universities in Arts, Law, Medicine, and even in Engineering. The colleges have now been affiliated to the universities, and may practically be regarded as their teaching branches. Admission to them is confined to those who have matriculated at the university, the curriculum being adapted thereto. Next come secondary schools in two classes, the second or middle schools being subdivided again into middle-English, in which English is compulsory, and middle-vernacular, in which it is voluntary; and below these come primary schools, in which the standard varies from preparatory requirements down to the most elementary instruction. Supplementary to these are the technical schools attached to primary and secondary education. The majority of these are normal schools for training masters and mistresses; but, in addition to these, there are "industrial and engineering schools." There are also Oriental colleges, independent of the general system, in which the main object is the study of the Oriental classics according to Oriental methods. With such stupendous machinery, surely education in India is a great thing.* As usual, schools and scholars in Bengal had increased in 1884–85.

In 1883–84, there were 372 Departmental institutions, with 35,080 pupils; those aided and inspected, 67,310, with 1,332,301 pupils; and Extra-Departmental, 2,575, with 25,228 pupils; giving totals of 70,257, and 1,392,609 respectively. In 1884–85, the totals were 72,641 institutions, and 1,470,180 pupils. These figures include schools and pupils of both sexes. It is pleasing to read that the girls' schools in Bengal had risen in number from 1,785 to 2,309, and the

* In all India the number of schools, in 1884–85, was 141,137, with 3,437,552 scholars, the receipts and expenditure being nearly equal, or over twenty-three millions of rupees. By the new Report, for 1885–86, issued in 1887, the number of schools in the former year was 122,516, and scholars 3,332,851, with over 24 millions of rupees, receipts and expenditure.

girls under instruction from 64,883 to 75,770, and also that (in 1884–85) the interest felt in female education was illustrated by the munificent donation of Rs. 150,000, given by the Maharani (Great Queen) Surnamayi of Cossimbazar, towards founding "a hostel for female medical students." During the present memorable year of the Queen-Empress Victoria's Jubilee, the interest in bettering the condition of Indian women may be said to have been at its climax; and the noble and philanthropic exertions of Lady Dufferin, and others in high position, will never be forgotten by the people of India.

Had Mr. Woodrow lived twelve years longer, he would have beheld good work going on everywhere in India to aid the cause of education and enlightenment. He would have seen that the natives are gradually becoming impressed with the idea that we govern them, in a great measure, for their good. He would have seen the great country passing through a phase which had never been reached before, when intelligent and well-educated natives were freely allowed to occupy posts of honour under the Government; and such an acute and practical mind as his might have ventured a suggestion or two on the faults and beauties of the great and, to some people, terrible Ilbert Bill. He would have been pleased to look with pride on a field in which he had won so many triumphs, boasting such favourable educational statistics; and it might have tickled his fancy to find—in a Blue-book of 1886—that, among the Marathi books of the Bombay Presidency, was an adaptation of Lord Tennyson's "Princess," which, it was considered, should help to render the Eastern mind familiar with Western ideas upon the actual liberty of women.

It is almost needless to say that Mr. Woodrow ever took a lively interest in the Native Press of India. With reference to "Literature and the Press," in the North-Western Provinces and Oudh, during 1885–86 (Report published June, 1887), occasionally, municipal affairs were usefully and intelligently reviewed. Articles on the Central Asian Question showed a decided preference for English to Russian rule, advocating an alliance with Turkey. The war with Burma —or rather the Third Expedition to the land of the Golden

Foot, for it hardly comes up to the dignity of a war—except at the outset, and the Copyright Bill, and the administration of the license tax, were generally condemned.

As to the so-called war with Burma, it is a wonder that our Indian friends did not see that it was totally UNAVOIDABLE. King Theebau would have been a thorn in our side to the last, and was growing bolder, more cruel, and more wicked every day. We do not say that his actions would have culminated in taking Bengal, or marching Lord Dufferin—as Bundoola, in the first Burmese War, threatened to do with Lord Amherst—in golden fetters to Mandalay; but there is no saying what a vast amount of trouble he might have given us on our Eastern frontier, besides keeping Lower, or British Burma, in continual hot water, and encouraging evil-disposed tribes—even leading to serious complications with China—had not the mandate gone forth from the Secretary of State (Lord Randolph Churchill) and the Viceroy, that the whole of Northern Burma must be annexed, and become British for the present and all future generations of men.

There is much in Burma which would have interested the subject of this Sketch; and the Buddhist system of education, through the priesthood—first recognized by the great Sir Arthur Phayre—would certainly have engaged the attention of Mr. Woodrow's vigorous and liberal mind; while the old creed of the Karens, with a history of the fall of man not unlike our own, might have caused him to wonder, if not to admire.

It may now be useful and interesting to give, as supplemental to what has already been remarked in this rather discursive, but, we trust, faithful sketch of the Nestor of Education in Bengal, some of his facts regarding early Education in India, which have not yet been generally published. Lord Macaulay's "Great Minute," also—which will be new to very many English and Indian readers—alluded to in the Memoir, and at the conclusion of the following paper—is valuable, if it be only as the brilliant and exhaustive, though rather caustic, production of the mighty wielder of the English tongue.

ENLIGHTENMENT OF THE NATIVES OF INDIA.

CONTROVERSIES IN THE COMMITTEE OF PUBLIC INSTRUCTION.

The first attempt for the enlightenment of the natives of India in the science and literature of Europe was the establishment in 1816 of the Hindu College. This celebrated institution owes its origin to the exertions of Sir Edward Hyde East, David Hare, and Raja Rammohun Roy. When the native community of Calcutta were roused to consider the plan for the establishment of a Maha Bidyálaya (*i.e.*, great seat of learning) as the Hindu College was originally termed, it was found that many of the orthodox Hindus held aloof from the plan, and refused to co-operate in any movement with Raja Rammohun Roy. Rammohun Roy accordingly, with a magnanimity worthy of his noble character, retired from the management of the proposed institution. Self-denial such as this is almost unknown in Calcutta, for he was the earliest advocate of the establishment of the College, and was eminently fitted by the gifts of nature, by his high position, wise discretion, deep learning, and earnest patriotism, to develop and carry out his own project. He was willing nevertheless to be laid aside, if by suffering rather than by acting he could benefit his country.

The Hindu College was for many years under native management. In 1823, the funds were so low that application was made to Government for aid, which was liberally conceded. The capital of the College, moreover, was reduced to Rs. 21,000, by the failure in 1827 of Baretto's house, in which it was deposited. The income accordingly fell to less than Rs. 100 a month. Government supplemented the rest with ever-increasing liberality, but till 1841, when its contribution was Rs. 30,000 a year, took but little share in the management. The Hindu College, therefore, is seldom mentioned in the controversies which raged in the Committee of Public Instruction concerning the management of Govern ment schools. This Committee was established in 1823 by the Governor-General in Council, and in the instructions addressed to its members, the object of their appointment is stated to be the "considering, and from time to time submitting to Government, the suggestion of such measures as it may appear expedient to adopt with a view to the better instruction of the people, to the introduction of useful knowledge, including the sciences and arts of Europe, and to the improvement of their moral character." The institutions placed under its charge were the Arabic College at Calcutta, and the Sanscrit College at Benares. The Calcutta College was established in 1781 by Warren Hastings, who at his own expense supplied a school-house. Government gave lands yielding about Rs. 30,000 a year, and designed the college for instruction in the principles and practice of Mahomedan law. The Benares College was projected by Mr. Jonathan Duncan, the Resident of that city, in 1791, with a view to "endear our Government to the native Hindus, by our exceeding in our attention to them and their systems the care ever shown by their own native princes." Lord Cornwallis, in 1791, assigned for the support of the College Rs. 14,000 a year, afterwards increased to Rs. 20,000.

On their foundation the Colleges at Calcutta and Benares were placed under native management, and abuses of the grossest kind soon became universal. Mr. Lushington says, in his work on the Charities of Calcutta, that "The Madrussa was almost useless for the purposes of education;" and that "its ample resources were dissipated among the superior and subordinate drones of the establishment." In 1820 Dr. Lumsden was appointed Secretary, and, under his charge, abuses were checked and many reforms in discipline and study were introduced. After the departure of Mr. Duncan, the early years of the Benares College were remarkable only for an utter absence of instruction and order. Gigantic misappropriations of funds were made by the first Rector, styled by the wonderful name of Sero Shastri Gooroo Tarkalankar Cashinath Pundit Juder Bedea Behadur Mr. Brooke, the Governor-General's Agent, suggested improvements, which were with some amendments carried out by Mr. W. W. Bird in 1812. In 1820 Captain Fell was appointed Secretary and Superintendent, and under him the college attained the reputation for Sanscrit learning that it has since maintained.

With these two institutions the General Committee of Public Instruction commenced its labours. The Sanscrit College at Calcutta was opened by it in 1824; the Delhi College was opened in 1825, for instruction in Arabic, Persian, and Sanscrit. The Allahabad school was opened in 1834, and encouragement was given to private schools at Bhagulpore, Sagar, Midnapore, &c.

In 1834 the operations of the Committee were brought to a stand by an irreconcilable difference of opinion as to the principles on which Government support to education should be administered. Half of the Committee, called the "Orientalists," were for the continuation of the old system of stipends, tenable for twelve or fifteen years to students of Arabic and Sanscrit, and for liberal expenditure on the publication of works in those languages. The other half, called the "Anglicists," desired to reduce the expenditure on stipends held by "lazy and stupid school-boys of thirty and thirty-five years of age," and to cut down the sums lavished on Sanscrit and Arabic printing. At this juncture, Government requested the Committee to prepare a scheme of instruction for a College at Agra. The Committee were utterly unable to agree on any plan. Five members were in favour of Arabic, Persian, and Sanscrit learning, and five in favour of English and the Vernacular, with just so much of the Oriental learned languages as would be necessary to satisfy local prejudices.

The Orientalist party consisted of the Hon. H. Shakespear, Messrs. H. Thoby Prinsep, James Prinsep, W. H. Macnaghten, and T. C. C. Sutherland, the Secretary of the Committee.

The Anglicists were Messrs. Bird, Saunders, Bushby, Trevelyan, and J. R. Colvin.*

* Afterwards Lieut.-Governor of the N.W. Provinces, and father of the present Sir Auckland Colvin.

Of this Committee, Sir W. H. Macnaghten became Envoy in Afghanistan and was assassinated there, and the Hon. J. R. Colvin died during the mutinies at Agra. James Prinsep is immortalized by his Sanscrit discoveries, and Sir Charles Trevelyan still remains alive,* beloved and honoured. He deserved, though he did not obtain, for his zealous educational labours in Bengal, the love he has won for his Government at Madras.

Over this Committee, Macaulay, on his arrival in India, was appointed President; but he declined to take an active part in its proceedings till the decision of the Supreme Government should be given on the question at issue. The letters of the two parties in the Committee, setting forth at great length their opinions, and bearing date the 21st and 22nd January, 1835, came before Macaulay in his capacity of Legislative Member of the Supreme Council, and on them he wrote his minute of the 2nd February, which was followed on the 7th March by Lord Bentinck's decision of the case in favour of the English language.

Soon after this decision many new members were added to the Committee, among whom may be mentioned Sir Edward Ryan, Mr. Ross D. Mangles, Mr. C. H. Cameron, Colonel James Young, Baboo, now Raja Radha Kant Deb, Baboo Russomoy Dutt, Mr. C. W. Smith, Captain, now (1862) General Sir J. R. H. Birch, and Dr. Grant. Sir Benjamin Malkin was added at a later time. The business of the Committee was chiefly conducted by minute books. The minutes of Sir Charles Trevelyan are very elaborate. He was indefatigable in the cause of education, and had something to say on every subject. Macaulay's minutes are neither so numerous nor so long as Trevelyan's. Three-fourths of his opinions on the proposals submitted by Mr. Sutherland, the Secretary, are conveyed in the concise expressions "I approve," "I do not object," "I would decline the offer," &c.

Should some of the opinions of Macaulay concerning expenditure appear unnecessarily harsh and niggardly, it must be remembered that the sum available for English

* This distinguished Anglo-Indian died 19th of June, 1886.

education was but the pittance that could be saved by reductions in the Oriental assignments, and that it was right for him to spend with strict frugality what was gained at the cost of many painful struggles.

It is often said that if a person cannot write five lines of English without blots and corrections he must be a very poor scholar indeed. Now, there is no doubt that neatness and accuracy are highly desirable, and that the clear and beautiful writing and the finished style of Lord Dalhousie and of Lord Canning indicate a wonderful power in the use of language. Yet it is a great mistake to imagine that the absence of a habit of writing without corrections is a sure mark of inferiority.

Scarcely five consecutive lines in any of Macaulay's minutes will be found unmarked by blots or corrections. He himself, in a minute dated 3rd November, 1835, says, "After blotting a good deal of paper, I can recommend nothing but a reference to the Governor-General in Council." No member of the Committee of Public Instruction in 1835 wrote so large and uneven a hand as he, and my copyist was always able instantly to single out his writing by the multiplicity of corrections and blots which mark the page. These corrections are now exceedingly valuable, more valuable than the minutes to which they belong. They are themselves a study, and well deserve a diligent examination. When the first master of the English language corrects his own composition, which appeared faultless before, the correction must be based on the highest rules of criticism.

The great minute of the 2nd February combines in a small compass the opinions which are expressed in nearly the same words through a score or two of detached remarks in the records. This minute was published in England in 1838, but is difficult to obtain in India. I could not find it in any one of the four great libraries of Calcutta, in the Public Library, nor in the Libraries of St. Paul's Cathedral, of the Asiatic Society, and of the Presidency College. Mr. Arbuthnot, the Director of Public Instruction in Madras, has conferred an obligation on all interested in the preservation of valuable papers by including it in one of his Reports.

To rescue it from the oblivion into which it has fallen in Bengal, I add it to these unpublished minutes.

Macaulay's unpublished educational minutes are scattered among some twenty volumes of the records of the General Committee. Four of these volumes are now lost. Some of the books were circulated among the fourteen or fifteen members of the Committee, others were sent only to Sub-Committees, containing five or six members. There were Sub-Committees on finance, on books, on the selection of schoolmasters, on the Medical College, and on the Hooghly College. Of the books which went the round of the whole Committee, two were reserved for particular subjects; one marked G. was for the selection and printing of books, and another marked I. for Medical College questions. The other books were kept in constant circulation, and, as they came back to the Secretary, were started afresh with précis of new topics for discussion. The same matter is consequently discussed at its different stages in different books. The General Committee seldom met. All business was transacted by the books. Several of the members urged their opinions with greater warmth and earnestness than is now customary in official correspondence.

Lord Auckland, in his elaborate educational minute of the 24th November, 1839, remarks, concerning their discussions, "Unhappily I have found violent differences existing upon the subject of education, and it was for a time (now I trust past, or fast passing away) a watchword for violent dissension, and, in some measure, of personal feelings. I judged it best, under these circumstances, to abstain from what might have led me into unprofitable controversy, and to allow time and experience to act with their usual healing and enlightening influence upon general opinion." *

* Some extracts, illustrating the warmth of feeling with which the controversy was conducted, were here introduced, but Mr. Woodrow felt it undesirable to publish them.

THE "GREAT MINUTE."

Again, as regards the "Great Minute" on Education in India, the following information (for the first time published) will be curious and interesting to many readers, as to the why or the wherefore of publication *versus* non-publication of one of the finest efforts of Lord Macaulay's unequalled pen.

Soon after Mr. Woodrow's "Macaulay's Minutes" had been collected and printed for *private circulation* in Calcutta, there appeared in one of the London magazines of the day, believed to be sent by Mr. G. O. Trevelyan (now Sir George, and the well-known statesman), his nephew, "Lord Macaulay's Great Minute"; and it was thought rather singular that Mr. Trevelyan had not mentioned the Minute having been in print before. But, although Mr. Woodrow had sent two copies of his "Minutes," in which the "Great Minute" appeared, to Sir Charles Trevelyan, it was considered just possible that, during Mr. G. O. Trevelyan's visit to Calcutta in 1862, he might have taken the opportunity to copy the Minute from the Records of the Bengal Government. Mr. Woodrow possessed a copy of the "Great Minute" (of 2nd of February, 1835), and appended it to his little book, as completing Lord Macaulay's Minutes on Education. As Mr. Woodrow's Preface—already given—was not in the copy first sent to the present writer, it was afterwards kindly forwarded to him in the Calcutta edition of 1862. Mrs. Woodrow helped her husband to copy the Minutes, and to supervise Mr. Woodrow's copyist in 1862. Mr. Woodrow was advised by influential friends in Calcutta to print and publish these Minutes by Lord Macaulay when he visited England in the same year; but he would not do so without the permission of Lord Macaulay's literary executor, who was Sir Charles Trevelyan, his brother-in-law. As Sir Charles thought fit to withhold his sanction, Mr. Woodrow took no steps to publish the Minutes in England. It may be added that the little volume was registered in the office of the

Government of Bengal in May or June, 1862—Mr. Woodrow having been advised to do so by kind and influential friends in India, for the little book was much thought of as the educational monument of Lord Macaulay's versatile genius. If he had done nothing else in the way of literary work, our "Nestor" deserved the approbation of the enlightened portions of mankind for having first collected and given, in a concise form, such admirable Minutes—and especially the "Great Minute," rescued by him from the white ants—to the world.

MR. (LORD) MACAULAY'S GREAT MINUTE.

(ENGLISH *versus* SANSCRIT AND ARABIC.)

2nd February, 1835.

As it seems to be the opinion of some of the gentlemen who compose the Committee of Public Instruction that the course which they have hitherto pursued was strictly prescribed by the British Parliament in 1813, and as, if that opinion be correct, a legislative act will be necessary to warrant a change, I have thought it right to refrain from taking any part in the preparation of the adverse statements which are now before us, and to reserve what I had to say on the subject till it should come before me as a member of the Council of India. It does not appear to me that the Act of Parliament can, by any act of construction, be made to bear the meaning which has been assigned to it. It contains nothing about the particular languages or sciences which are to be studied. A sum is set apart "for the revival and promotion of literature and the encouragement of the learned natives of India, and for the introduction and promotion of a knowledge of the sciences among the inhabitants of the British territories." It is argued, or rather taken for granted, that by literature the Parliament can have meant only Arabic and Sanscrit literature, that they never would have given the honourable appellation of "a learned native" to a native who was familiar with the poetry of Milton, the Metaphysics of Locke, and the Physics of Newton; but that they meant to designate by that name only such persons as might have studied in the sacred books of the Hindoos all the uses of cusa-grass, and all the mysteries of absorption into the Deity. This does not appear to be a very satisfactory interpretation. To take a parallel case: suppose that the Pacha of Egypt, a country once superior in knowledge to the nations of Europe, but now sunk far below them, were to appropriate a sum for the purpose of "reviving and promoting literature, and encouraging learned natives of Egypt," would anybody infer that he meant the youth of his pachalic to give years to the study of hieroglyphics, to search into all the doctrines disguised under the fable of Osiris, and to ascertain with all possible accuracy the ritual with which cats and onions were anciently adored? Would he be justly charged with inconsistency if, instead of employing his young subjects in deciphering obelisks, he were to order them to be instructed in the English and French languages, and in all the sciences to which those languages are the chief keys?

The words on which the supporters of the old system rely do not bear them out, and other words follow which seem to be quite decisive on the other side. This lac of rupees is set apart, not only for "reviving literature in India," the phrase on which their whole interpretation is founded, but also for "the introduction and promotion of a knowledge of the sciences among the inhabitants of the British territories"—words which are alone sufficient to authorize all the changes for which I contend.

If the Council agree in my construction, no legislative act will be necessary. If they differ from me, I will prepare a short act rescinding that clause of the Charter of 1813 from which the difficulty arises.

The argument which I have been considering affects only the form of proceeding. But the admirers of the Oriental system of education have used another argument, which, if we admit it to be valid, is decisive against all change. They conceive that the public faith is pledged to the present system, and that to alter the appropriation of any of the funds which have hitherto been spent in encouraging the study of Arabic and Sanscrit would be downright spoliation.

It is not easy to understand by what process of reasoning they can have arrived at this conclusion. The grants which are made from the public purse for the encouragement of literature differed in no respect from the grants which are made from the same purse for other objects of real or supposed utility. We found a sanitarium on a spot which we suppose to be healthy. Do we thereby pledge ourselves to keep a sanitarium there if the result should not answer our expectation? We commence the erection of a pier. Is it a violation of the public faith to stop the works, if we afterwards see reason to believe that the building will be useless? The rights of property are undoubtedly sacred. But nothing endangers those rights so much as the practice, now unhappily too common, of attributing them to things to which they do not belong. Those who would impart to abuses the sanctity of property are in truth imparting to the institution of property the unpopularity and the fragility of abuses. If the Government has given to any person a formal assurance—nay, if the Government has excited in any person's mind a reasonable expectation that he shall receive a certain income as a teacher or a learner of Sanscrit or Arabic, I would respect that person's pecuniary interests—I would rather err on the side of liberality to individuals than suffer the public faith to be called in question. But to talk of a Government pledging itself to teach certain languages and certain sciences, though those languages may become useless, though those sciences may be exploded, seems to me quite unmeaning. There is not a single word in any public instructions from which it can be inferred that the Indian Government ever intended to give any pledge on this subject, or ever considered the destination of these funds as unalterably fixed. But, had it been otherwise, I should have denied the competence of our predecessors to bind us by any pledge on such a subject. Suppose that a Government had in the last century enacted in the most solemn manner that all its subjects should, to the end of time, be inoculated for small-pox, would that Government be bound to persist in the practice after Jenner's discovery? These promises, of which nobody claims the performance, and from which nobody can grant a release; these vested rights, which vest in nobody; this property without proprietors; this robbery, which makes nobody poorer, may be comprehended by persons of higher faculties than mine. I consider this plea merely as a set form of words, regularly used both in England and in India, in defence of every abuse for which no other plea can be set up.

I hold this lac of rupees to be quite at the disposal of the Governor-General in Council, for the purpose of promoting learning in India, in any way which may be thought most advisable. I hold his Lordship to be quite as free to direct that it shall no longer be employed in encouraging Arabic and Sanscrit, as he is to direct that the reward for killing tigers in Mysore shall be diminished, or that no more public money shall be expended on the chanting at the cathedral. We now come to the gist of the matter. We have a fund to be employed as Government shall direct for the intellectual improvement of the people of this country. The simple question is, what is the most useful way of employing it? All parties seem to be agreed on one point, that the dialects commonly spoken among the natives of this part of India contain neither literary nor scientific information, and are, moreover, so poor and rude that, until they are enriched from some other quarter, it will not be easy to translate any valuable work into them. It seems to be admitted on all sides, that the intellectual improvement of those classes of the people who have the means of pursuing higher studies can at present be effected only by means of some language not vernacular amongst them.

What, then, shall that language be? One-half of the Committee maintain that it should be the English. The other half strongly recommend the Arabic and Sanscrit. The whole question seems to me to be, which language is the best worth knowing? I have no knowledge of either Sanscrit or Arabic. But I have done what I could to form a correct estimate of their value. I have read translations of the most celebrated Arabic and Sanscrit works. I have conversed both here and at home with men distinguished by their proficiency in the Eastern tongues. I am quite ready to take the Oriental learning at the valuation of the Orientalists themselves. I have never found one among them who could deny that a single shelf of a good European library was worth the whole native literature of India and Arabia. The intrinsic superiority of the Western literature is, indeed, fully admitted by those members of the Committee who support the Oriental plan of education.

It will hardly be disputed, I suppose, that the department of literature in which the Eastern writers stand highest is poetry. And I certainly never met with any Orientalist who ventured to maintain that the Arabic and Sanscrit poetry could be compared to that of the great European nations. But when we pass from works of imagination to works in which facts are recorded, and general principles investigated, the superiority of the Europeans becomes absolutely immeasurable. It is, I believe, no exaggeration to say, that all the historical information which has been collected from all the books written in the Sanscrit language is less valuable than what may be found in the most paltry abridgments used at preparatory schools in England. In every branch of physical or moral philosophy, the relative position of the two nations is nearly the same.

How, then, stands the case? We have to educate a people who cannot at present be educated by means of their mother tongue. We must teach them some foreign language. The claims of our own language it is hardly necessary to recapitulate. It stands pre-eminent even among the languages of the West. It abounds with works of imagination not inferior to the noblest which Greece has bequeathed to us; with models of every species of eloquence; with historical compositions, which, considered merely as narratives, have seldom been surpassed, and which, considered as vehicles of ethical and political instruction, have never been equalled; with just and lively representations of human life and human nature, with the most profound speculations on metaphysics, morals, government, jurisprudence, and trade; with full and correct information respecting every experimental science which tends to preserve the health, to increase the comfort, or to expand the intellect of man. Whoever knows that language has ready access to all the vast intellectual wealth which all the wisest nations of the earth have created and hoarded in the course of ninety generations. It may safely be said, that the literature now extant in that language is of far greater value than all the literature which, three hundred years ago, was extant in all the languages of the world together. Nor is this all. In India English is the language spoken by the ruling class. It is spoken by the higher class of natives at the seats of Government. It is likely to become the language of commerce throughout the seas of the East. It is the language of two great European communities which are rising, the one in the south of Africa, the other in Australasia; communities which are every year becoming more important, and more closely connected with our Indian Empire. Whether we look at the intrinsic value of our literature, or at the particular situation of this country, we shall see the strongest reason to think that, of all foreign tongues the English tongue is that which would be the most useful to our native subjects. The question now before us is simply whether, when it is in our power to teach this language, we shall teach languages in which, by universal confession, there are no books on any subject which deserve to be compared to our own; whether, when we can teach European science, we shall teach systems which, by universal confession, whenever they differ from those of Europe, differ for the worse, and whether, when we can patronize sound Philosophy and true History we shall countenance, at the public expense, medical doctrines, which would disgrace an English farrier; Astronomy, which would move laughter in girls at an English boarding-school; History, abounding with kings thirty feet high, and reigns thirty thousand years long; and Geography, made up of seas of treacle and seas of butter. We are not without experience to guide us. History furnishes several analogous cases, and they all teach the same lesson. There are in modern times, to go no further, two memorable instances of a great impulse given to the mind of a whole society, of prejudices overthrown, of knowledge diffused, of taste purified, of arts and sciences planted in countries which had recently been ignorant and barbarous.

The first instance to which I refer, is the great revival of letters among the Western nations at the close of the fifteenth and the beginning of the sixteenth century. At that time almost everything that was worth reading was contained in the writings of the ancient Greeks and Romans. Had our ancestors, as the Committee of Public Instruction has hitherto acted; had they neglected the language of Cicero and Tacitus; had they confined their attention to the old dialects of our own island; had they printed nothing and taught nothing at the universities but Chronicles in Anglo-Saxon, and romances in Norman-French, would England have been what she now is? What the Greek and Latin were to the contemporaries of More and Ascham, our tongue is to the people of India. The literature of England is now more valuable than that of classical antiquity. I doubt whether the Sanscrit literature be as valuable as that of our Saxon and Norman progenitors. In some departments, in History, for example, I am certain that it is much less so.

Another instance may be said to be still before our eyes. Within the last hundred and twenty years, a nation which had previously been in a state as barbarous as that in which our ancestors were before the crusades, has gradually emerged from the ignorance in which it was sunk, and has taken its place among civilized communities. I speak of Russia. There is now in that country a large educated class, abounding with persons fit to serve the State in the highest functions, and in no wise inferior to the most accomplished men who adorn the best circles of Paris and London. There is reason to hope that this vast empire, which in the time of our grandfathers was probably behind the Punjab, may, in the time of our grandchildren, be pressing close on France and Britain in the career of improvement. And how was this change effected? Not by flattering national prejudices; not by feeding the mind of the young Muscovite with the old woman's stories which his rude fathers had believed; not by filling his head with lying legends about St. Nicholas; not by encouraging him to study the great question, whether the world was or was not created on the 13th of September; not by calling him "a learned native," when he has mastered all these points of knowledge, but by teaching him those foreign languages in which the greatest mass of information had been laid up, and thus putting all that information within his reach. The languages of Western Europe civilized Russia. I cannot doubt that they will do for the Hindoo what they have done for the Tartar.

And what are the arguments against that course which seems to be alike recommended by theory and by experience? It is said that we ought to secure the co-operation of the native public, and that we can do this only by teaching Sanscrit and Arabic.

I can by no means admit that when a nation of high intellectual attainments undertakes to superintend the education of a nation comparatively ignorant, the learners are absolutely to prescribe the course which is to be taken by the teachers. It is not necessary, however, to say anything on this subject. For it is proved by unanswerable evidence that we are not at present securing the co-operation of the natives. It would be bad enough to consult their intellectual taste at the expense of their intellectual health. But we are consulting neither—we are withholding from them the learning for which they are craving, we are forcing on them the mock-learning which they nauseate.

This is proved by the fact that we are forced to pay our Arabic and Sanscrit students, while those who learn English are willing to pay us. All the declamations in the world about the love and reverence of the natives for their sacred dialects will never, in the mind of any impartial person, outweigh the undisputed fact, that we cannot find, in all our vast empire, a single student who will let us teach him those dialects unless we will pay him.

I have now before me the accounts of the Madrussa for one month—the month of December, 1833. The Arabic students appear to have been seventy-seven in number. All receive stipends from the public. The whole amount paid to them is above 500 rupees a month. On the other side of the account stands the following item: Deduct amount realized from the out-students of English for the months of May, June, and July last, 103 rupees.

I have been told that it is merely from want of local experience that I am surprised at these phenomena, and that it is not the fashion for students in India to study at their own charges. This only confirms me in my opinion. Nothing is more certain than that it never can in any part of the world be necessary to pay men for doing what they think pleasant and profitable. India is no exception to this rule. The people of India do not require to be paid for eating rice when they are hungry, or for wearing woollen cloth in the cold season. To come nearer to the case before us, the children who learn their letters and a little elementary arithmetic from the village schoolmaster are not paid by him. He is paid for teaching them. Why, then, is it necessary to pay people to learn Sanscrit and Arabic? Evidently because it is universally felt that the Sanscrit and Arabic are languages the knowledge of which does not compensate for the trouble of acquiring them. On all such subjects the state of the market is the decisive test. Other evidence is not wanting, if other evidence were required. A petition was presented last year to the Committee by several ex-students of the Sanscrit College. The petitioners stated that they had studied in the college ten or twelve years; that they had made themselves acquainted with Hindoo literature and science; that they had received certificates of proficiency: and what is the fruit of all this? "Notwithstanding such testimonials," they say, "we have but little prospect of bettering our condition without the kind assistance of your Honourable Committee, the indifference with which we are generally looked upon by our countrymen leaving no hope of encouragement and assistance from them." They therefore beg that they may be recommended to the Governor-General for places under the Government, not places of high dignity or emolument, but such as may just enable them to exist. "We want means," they say, "for a decent living, and for our progressive improvement, which, however, we cannot obtain without the assistance of Government, by whom we have been educated and maintained from childhood." They conclude by representing, very pathetically, that they are sure that it was never the intention of Government, after behaving so liberally to them during their education, to abandon them to destitution and neglect.

I have been used to see petitions to Government for compensation. All these petitions, even the most unreasonable of them, proceeded on the supposition that some loss had been sustained—that some wrong had been inflicted. These are surely the first petitioners who ever demanded compensation for having been educated gratis—for having been supported by the public during twelve years, and then sent forth into the world well furnished with literature and science. They represent their education as an injury which gives them a claim on the Government for redress, an injury for which the stipends paid to them during the infliction were a very inadequate compensation. And I doubt not that they are in the right. They have wasted the best years of life in learning what procures for them neither bread nor respect. Surely we might, with advantage, have saved the cost of making these persons useless and miserable; surely, men may be brought up to be burdens to the public and objects of contempt to their neighbours at a somewhat smaller charge to the State. But such is our policy. We do not even stand neuter in the contest between truth and falsehood. We are not content to leave the natives to the influence of their own hereditary prejudices. To the natural difficulties which obstruct the progress of sound science in the East, we add fresh difficulties of our own making. Bounties and premiums, such as ought not to be given even for the propagation of truth, we lavish on false taste and false philosophy.

By acting thus we create the very evil which we fear. We are making that opposition which we do not find. What we spend on the Arabic and Sanscrit Colleges is not merely a dead loss to the cause of truth; it is bounty money paid to raise up champions of error. It goes to form a nest, not merely of helpless place-hunters, but of bigots prompted alike by passion and by interest to raise a cry against every useful scheme of education. If there should be any opposition among the natives to the change which I recommend, that opposition will be the effect of our own system. It will be headed by persons supported by our stipends and trained in our colleges. The longer we persevere in our present course, the more formidable will that opposition be. It will be every year re-inforced by recruits whom we are paying. From the native society left to itself, we have no difficulties to apprehend; all the murmuring will come from that Oriental interest which we have, by artificial means, called into being, and nursed into strength.

There is yet another fact, which is alone sufficient to prove that the feeling of the native public, when left to itself, is not such as the supporters of the old system represent it to be. The Committee have thought fit to lay out above a lac of rupees in printing Arabic and Sanscrit books. Those books find no purchasers. It is very rarely that a single copy is disposed of. Twenty-three thousand volumes, most of them folios and quartos, fill the libraries, or rather the lumber-rooms, of this body. The Committee contrive to get rid of some portion of their vast stock of Oriental literature by giving books away. But they cannot give so fast as they print. About twenty thousand rupees a year are spent in adding fresh masses of waste paper to a hoard which, I should think, is already sufficiently ample. During the last three years, about sixty thousand rupees have been expended in this manner. The sale of Arabic and Sanscrit books, during those three years, has not yielded quite one thousand rupees. In the meantime the School Book Society is selling seven or eight thousand English volumes every year, and not only pays the expenses of printing, but realizes a profit of twenty per cent on its outlay.

The fact that the Hindoo law is to be learned chiefly from Sanscrit books, and the Mahomedan law from Arabic books, has been much insisted on, but seems not to bear at all on the question. We are commanded by Parliament to ascertain and digest the laws of India. The assistance of a Law Commission has been given to us for that purpose. As soon as the code is promulgated, the Shasters and the Hedaya will be useless to a Moonsiff or Sudder Ameen. I hope and trust that before the boys who are now entering at the Madrassa and the Sanscrit College have completed their studies, this great work will be finished. It would be manifestly absurd to educate the rising generation with a view to a state of things which we mean to alter before they reach manhood.

But there is yet another argument which seems even more untenable. It is said that the Sanscrit and Arabic are the languages in which the sacred books of a hundred millions of people are written, and that they are, on that account, entitled to peculiar encouragement. Assuredly it is the duty of the British Government in India to be not only tolerant, but neutral on all religious questions. But to encourage the study of a literature admitted to be of small intrinsic value, only because that literature inculcates the most serious errors on the most important subjects, is a course hardly reconcilable with reason, with morality, or even with that very neutrality which ought, as we all agree, to be sacredly preserved. It is confessed that a language is barren of useful knowledge. We are to teach it because it is fruitful of monstrous superstitions. We are to teach false History, false Astronomy, false Medicine, because we find them in company with a false religion. We abstain, and I trust shall always abstain, from giving any public encouragement to those who are engaged in the work of converting natives to Christianity. And while we act thus, can we reasonably and decently bribe men out of the revenues of the State to waste their youth in learning how they are to purify themselves after touching an ass, or what text of the Vedas they are to repeat to expiate the crime of killing a goat? It is taken for granted by the advocates of Oriental learning that no native of this country can possibly attain more than a mere smattering of English. They do not attempt to prove this; but they perpetually insinuate it. They designate the education which their opponents recommend as a mere spelling-book education. They assume it as undeniable that the question is between a profound knowledge of Hindoo and Arabian literature and science on the one side, and a superficial knowledge of the rudiments of English on the other. This is not merely an assumption, but an assumption contrary to all reason and experience.

We know that foreigners of all nations do learn our language sufficiently to have access to all the most abstruse knowledge which it contains, sufficiently to relish even the more delicate graces of our most idiomatic writers.

There are in this very town natives who are quite competent to discuss political or scientific questions with fluency and precision in the English language. I have heard the very question on which I am now writing discussed by native gentlemen with a liberality and an intelligence which would do credit to any member of the Committee of Public Instruction. Indeed, it is unusual to find, even in the literary circles of the Continent, any foreigner who can express himself in English with so much facility and correctness as we find in many Hindoos. Nobody, I suppose, will contend that English is so difficult to a Hindoo as Greek to an Englishman. Yet an intelligent English youth, in a much smaller number of years than our unfortunate pupils pass at the Sanscrit College, becomes able to read, to enjoy, and even to imitate, not unhappily, the compositions of the best Greek authors.

Less than half the time which enables an English youth to read Herodotus and Sophocles, ought to enable a Hindoo to read Hume and Milton.

To sum up what I have said, I think it clear that we are not fettered by the Act of Parliament of 1813; that we are not fettered by any pledge, expressed or implied; that we are free to employ our funds as we choose; that we ought to employ them in teaching what is best worth knowing; that English is better worth knowing than Sanscrit or Arabic; that the natives are desirous to be taught English, and are not desirous to be taught Sanscrit or Arabic; that neither as the languages of law, nor as the languages of religion, have the Sanscrit and Arabic any peculiar claim to our engagement; that it is possible to make natives of this country thoroughly good English scholars, and that to this end our efforts ought to be directed.

In one point I fully agree with the gentlemen to whose general views I am opposed. I feel with them, that it is impossible for us, with our limited means, to attempt to educate the body of the people. We must at present do our best to form a class who may be interpreters between us and the millions whom we govern—a class of persons, Indian in blood and colour, but English in taste, in opinions, in morals, and in intellect. To that class we may leave it to refine the vernacular dialects of the country, to enrich those dialects with terms of science borrowed from the Western nomencla-ture, and to render them by degrees fit vehicles for convey-ing knowledge to the great mass of the population.

I would strictly respect all existing interests. I would deal even generously with all individuals who have had fair reason to expect a pecuniary provision. But I would strike at the root of the bad system which has hitherto been fostered by us. I would at once stop the printing of Arabic and Sanscrit books, I would abolish the Madrassa and the Sanscrit College at Calcutta. Benares is the great seat of Brahmanical learning; Delhi, of Arabic learning. If we retain the Sanscrit College at Benares, and the Mahomedan College at Delhi, we do enough, and much more than enough, in my opinion, for the Eastern languages. If the Benares and Delhi colleges should be retained, I would at least re-commend that no stipends shall be given to any students who may hereafter repair thither, but that the people shall be left to make their own choice between the rival systems of education without being bribed by us to learn what they have no desire to know. The funds which would thus be placed at our disposal would enable us to give larger encouragement to the Hindoo College at Calcutta, and to establish in the principal cities throughout the Presidencies of Fort William and Agra schools in which the English language might be well and thoroughly taught.

If the decision of his Lordship in Council should be such as I anticipate, I shall enter on the performance of my duties with the greatest zeal and alacrity. If, on the other hand, it be the opinion of the Government that the present system ought to remain unchanged, I beg that I may be permitted to retire from the chair of the Committee. I feel that I could not be of the smallest use there—I feel, also, that I should be lending my countenance to what I firmly believe to be a mere delusion. I believe that the present system tends, not to accelerate the progress of truth, but to delay the natural death of expiring errors. I conceive that we have at present no right to the respectable name of a Board of Public Instruction. We are a Board for wasting public money, for printing books which are of less value than the paper on which they are printed was while it was blank; for giving artificial encouragement to absurd history, absurd metaphysics, absurd physics, absurd theology; for raising up a breed of scholars who find their scholarship an encumbrance and a blemish, who live on the public while they are receiving their education, and whose education is so utterly useless to them that when they have received it they must either starve or live on the public all the rest of their lives. Entertaining these opinions, I am naturally desirous to decline all share in the responsibility of a body, which, unless it alters its whole mode of proceeding, I must consider not merely as useless, but as positively noxious.

Thus, to the extreme satisfaction of the model Governor-General, Lord William Bentinck, the English section in the Committee received a defence of their views which, in force and elegance, no other writer of the time could have conceived or penned. It was a clear case of Eclipse first, and the rest nowhere! And this leads to the remark that, after having entirely concluded our Sketch, with its rather numerous accessories to ensure completeness, and having copied out the Great Minute in full, it suddenly struck the present writer that it would be well and proper to see what Sir G. O. Trevelyan had to say on the subject of the "Minutes" in his most interesting and admirable "Life and Letters of Lord Macaulay."* Before introducing his readers to the "Great Minute,"† Sir George says, what is beyond all

* By his nephew, the Right Hon. Sir George Otto Trevelyan, Bart. New Edition, London 1886.

† Of which he gives some two pages, followed up by interesting extracts from the "Unpublished Minutes."

question, that "it is fortunate for India that a man with the tastes, and the training, of Macaulay came to her shores as one vested with authority, and that he came at the moment when he did; for that moment was the very turning point of her intellectual progress." The distinguished uncle himself could not have expressed this fact in more elegant language. Of the Minutes, the author of the biography writes in a note, that "the extracts are taken from a volume of Macaulay's Minutes, 'now first collected from Records in the Department of Public Instruction, by H. Woodrow, Esq., M.A., Inspector of Schools at Calcutta, and formerly Fellow of Caius College, Cambridge.'" We are also informed that "the collection was published in India." But there is nothing about the magazine publication in London of the Great Minute, already attributed to the learned and versatile "Mr. G. O. Trevelyan."

(For a few extracts from "Unpublished Minutes," *see* Appendix VIII.

BRIEF NOTICES OF DISTINGUISHED ANGLO-INDIANS.

—o—

"*Sans peur et sans reproche.*"

—o—

SIR FREDERICK HALLIDAY, K.C.B.

THE first worthy subject of our "Brief Notices" being an octogenarian, at the end of another year, naturally leads to a reflection on the wonderful vital powers displayed by English civilians and politicians, as well as by those who have had a purely Anglo-Indian career, during the second quarter and the latter half of the nineteenth century. Longfellow, as we all know, begins his famous "Psalm" by causing "the young man" to deny "that life is but an empty dream." But one is almost tempted to think that were the sweet Psalmist of Israel to appear among us just now, some surprise might be occasioned by meeting so many men, who have played their parts well in life's wide theatre, of whom it can hardly be affirmed, at or near, or past eighty, in physical as well as in intellectual activity, that their days are those of "labour and sorrow." It is much the same with military men, of whom a goodly array of octogenarians have lived, and are still living, in our time. In both Services it is easy to call at once to mind three of the past and one of the living among Anglo-Indians—distinguished men such as Sir Robert Hamilton (Central India*), Sir George Pollock

* Sir Robert North Collie Hamilton, K.C.B., died on May 30, 1887, at Avoncliffe, Stratford-on-Avon, in the eighty-sixth year of his age, having held several high offices in India. He was also eminently useful at home, and was succeeded by his eldest son, Major Frederick Harding Hamilton, of Baraset, Stratford-on-Avon.

(Afghanistan), Sir Robert Hussey Vivian (Madras Army, and Turkish Contingent), and Sir George Clerk (Bombay), which are familiar names associated even with some half-dozen years past the venerable age of eighty

This remarkable *vis vitæ*, in the opinion of some thinkers, loses much of its significance when placed beside what the poet styles the "godlike and undying intellect" of younger men; but it is quite natural, in many cases, to give it a fair share of our admiration, especially after much good work done by those who have found Life *real* and *earnest*, and who do not like to think of parting with it, even in the sunset, except in the spirit of some exquisite lines, much admired by Wordsworth and Rogers, written by the well-known, accomplished Mrs. Barbauld, when she was very old:—

"Life! we've been long together,
Through pleasant and through cloudy weather:
'Tis hard to part when friends are dear;
Perhaps 'twill cost a sigh, a tear;'
Then steal away, give little warning,
Choose thine own time,
Say not Good Night, but in some brighter clime
Bid me Good Morning."

From the excellent Record of Services (in the India Office), already quoted, we extract the following summary—well pleased to think that the Lieutenant-Governor of Bengal in 1857 is still well and hearty at the end of 1887:—"Appointed to the Bengal Civil Service in 1824; arrived in India, 8th June, 1825; served in Bengal as Assistant to the Agent in the Saugur Division, and Assistant Registrar of the Sudder Court; Joint Magistrate and Deputy Collector in Bundelcund, and afterwards in Noacolly and Bullooah, 1831–35; Magistrate and Collector of the Zillah Court at Dacca, February, 1835; Magistrate, Collector, and Salt Agent, Cuttack, February, 1836; Secretary to the Sudder Board of Revenue, April, 1836; Secretary to the Government of Bengal, Judicial and Revenue Departments, May, 1838; Member of the General Committee of Public Instruction, June, 1838; Junior Secretary to the Government of India, Revenue,

Judicial and Legislative Departments, in addition to his other duties, March, 1840 to 1843; Secretary to the Government of India, Home Department, 1849; Member of Governor-General's Council, December, 1853; Lieutenant-Governor of Bengal, 1st May, 1854, retired in 1859; Member of Council of Secretary of State for India, 30th September, 1868.

In the India List for January, 1887, the familiar name of Sir Frederick Halliday ceases to appear on the first page.

After these few remarks, we proceed to record that, at the end of 1886, it became of importance to notice, in a popular Anglo-Indian journal, in something like the following plain, straightforward manner, the retirement of Sir Frederick Halliday; the reason assigned being the very natural one of eighty years of age:—

We are informed that Sir Frederick J. Halliday, K.C.B., intends at the close of the year to retire from the Council of the Secretary of State for India. Thus another old familiar name will be removed from the distinguished circle of able and experienced Anglo-Indians by whose advice the policy o the Secretary of State is moulded in no small degree. Sir Frederick Halliday's long and valuable services hardly need to be recapitulated. Entering the Bengal Civil Service so far back as 1824, he became an annuitant of the Civil Fund in 1859, having served with distinction through some of the most stormy times of Anglo-Indian history. In the day of severest trial he occupied the critical post of Lieutenant-Governor of Bengal.* He was created a Civil K.C.B. for his varied services to the State, in May 1860, and for a long period he has been constantly at work in the India Office. Many good wishes will accompany the veteran administrator into his retirement. As Sir George Pollock was a fine type of the old military Anglo-Indian, Sir Frederick James Halliday, still enjoying a vigorous old age, may be taken as a worthy representative of the higher class of Indian civilians.

* During his tenure of office, Sir Frederick being an excellent musician—a rare performer on the violoncello—Belvidere was celebrated for its concerts,—the Lieutenant-Governor thus doing good to society while ably serving the State.

SIR WALTER ELLIOT, K.C.S.I., LL.D., F.R.S.

The death of this distinguished Madras civilian took place at Wolfelee, his seat at Roxburghshire, on March 1, 1887, in his eighty-fifth year. Sir Walter Elliot was one of the distinguished civil servants under the *régime* of the old East India Company, having received an appointment to the Madras Presidency in 1818, and held various offices in the Revenue and Political Departments till 1836. In 1838 he became a member of the Madras Board of Revenue, Secretary to Government in 1841, and Member of the Council in 1854. In 1858, when the government of India was assumed by the Crown, he was acting Governor of Madras, and retired from the Madras Civil Service in 1860. In 1866 he was nominated a Knight Commander of the Order of the Star of India, in recognition of his long official services. On his return to England he published various papers in scientific journals on the antiquities and natural history of India, and was elected a fellow of the Royal Society. Sir Walter Elliot married, in 1839, Maria Dorothea, eldest daughter of Sir David Hunter Blair, the third baronet, of Blairquhan, in Ayrshire. Since 1862 he had been a magistrate for Roxburghshire. Sir Walter's was indeed one of the "old familiar faces" of Madras.

GENERAL SIR JAMES ALEXANDER, K.C.B.

Entering the Bengal Artillery in 1820, this veteran Anglo-Indian has had a long and distinguished career. The recital of his war services is not a long one, but they cover a vast deal of important ground:—

Sir James Alexander served at the siege and capture of Bhurtpore in 1825–26 (medal with clasp); commanded the Artillery in the Afghanistan campaign of 1842, under Sir George Pollock, including the forcing of the Khyber Pass.

action of Tezeen, and re-capture of Cabool (Brevet of Major and medal); Gwalior campaign, including battle of Maharajpore, 29th December, 1843 (Brevet of Lieut.-Colonel, and bronze star); Sutlej campaign of 1845–46, including the affair of Buddiwal, and battles of Aliwal and Sobraon (medal and clasp, and C.B.) Appointed a Military Knight Commander of the Bath, 20th of May, 1871; and attained the rank of General in 1872. Sir James Alexander retired in 1877, and appears as a retired officer in the India List for 1887.

Among distinguished Royal (formerly Indian) Artillery General Officers, who retired under the Royal Warrants of August 1877, May 1878, and June 1881, appear also (1877) Sir G. Balfour (Madras), K.C.B., J. Abbott, C.B., and Sir F. Turner, K.C.B. (Bengal); and of later dates, among the retired and "Unemployed" Generals, such distinguished names as Sir H. E. L. Thuillier, C.S.I. (Bengal), Sir A. B. Kemball, K.C.B., K.C.S.I. (Bombay), Sir W. Olpherts, K.C.B., V.C. (Bengal), and R. Cadell, C.B. (Madras).

GENERAL GEORGE CAMPBELL, C.B.

General George Campbell, C.B., late of the Bengal Horse Artillery, died on Tuesday, 2nd August, 1887, at his residence in Byng Place, Gordon Square, in his 79th year. Entering the Army in 1823, he served in the Burmese War of 1825–26, including the siege of Donabew, and the actions of Prome, Maloon, and Pagammew. He obtained a lieutenancy in 1826, was promoted to captain in 1838, and in 1843 took part in the Gwalior campaign and the battle of Punniar. For this service he obtained the Brevet rank of Major. He was engaged in the Sutlej campaign, including the battles of Ferozeshah and Sobraon, commanded the Artillery Division at Lahore during the Punjab campaign of 1848–49, and served through the Indian Mutiny in 1857–58. He became major-general in 1858, lieutenant-general in 1868, and full general in 1875. Truly, a varied and distinguished career.

GENERAL JOHN COLPOYS HAUGHTON. C.S.I.

(A HERO OF THE FIRST AFGHAN WAR.)

Few now living took in the full significance of the announcement that Lieutenant-General John Colpoys Haughton, C.S.I., died on the 17th September,* but we cannot pass over in silence the departure from among us of one who, had his services been performed now, would have filled the papers with his achievements and been handsomely rewarded. General Haughton's services were performed in days when there were no special correspondents and no telegraph to India. Men quietly and nobly did their duty and died, or, if they survived, were not sought out with feverish haste to receive well-earned rewards; and so it is that as brave and noble-minded an officer as ever lived goes to his grave after performing eminent services in a past generation with nothing more than a modest C.S.I.

The events of his early career and his remarkable defence of Charakar are well known among military Anglo-Indians. After his return from Afghanistan, General Haughton held many important appointments. Among others, those of Superintendent of the Andaman Islands and Commissioner of Assam, and afterwards of Cooch Behar, in all of which he distinguished himself by great ability, firmness and justice, combined with a high-minded gentleness which won the hearts of all, native and European. One of those who served under him records how, years after General Haughton left Assam, in passing through the province he heard natives talking with pleasure and reverence of the "Hâth Katta Sahib" as he was called, from the loss of his hand. In the neighbouring province of Cooch Behar he did excellent work, and endeared himself to all, and during the Garrow campaign his military talent enabled him to give valuable advice.

General Haughton retired in 1873, after nearly forty years' active service. To say that his services were not adequately

* *Homeward Mail*, 24th September, 1887.

recognized is saying what may be said of many an old officer who lived and fought in the times when duty and not decoration was the order of the day; his life was a great example to those around him, and it may be said of him, in a wide sense, that he was "*sans peur et sans reproche.*" This is surely a pleasant retrospect of the career of a distinguished Anglo-Indian.

GENERAL H. LAWRENCE—COLONEL WILLIAM PRICE.

(THE OLDEST EAST INDIA COMPANY'S OFFICERS.)

GENERAL H. LAWRENCE.—One of the oldest, if not indeed the oldest, of the old East India Company's officers died on Nov. 23, 1887, at his residence, Camden Gardens, Chiselhurst Road, Richmond Hill, in the person of General Henry Lawrence, who had reached the age of ninety-seven. Entering the East India Company's service at an early age, he served on board the *Astell*, East Indiaman, in command of two guns on her quarter-deck in a severe action fought in the Mozambique Channel, in 1810, between his own vessel and two other Indiamen and three French vessels—two frigates and a corvette—and subsequently received a commission in the 19th Bengal Native Infantry. Promoted to a lieutenancy in 1814, he took part in the operations against and the attack on the Fortress of Malown in the Nepaul War of 1814–15, for his services in which he received the medal with clasp, and from 1817 till 1819 served with the Reserve of the Grand Army during the Mahratta campaign. Transferred to the 67th Bengal Native Infantry in 1823, he received the brevet rank of captain in 1826, and in 1835 took part in the operations against the Coles tribes, and in the two following years was in command of a brigade of all arms employed against the same tribes. He became general in 1874, and was placed on the retired list in 1877.—"J. C. C. S." writes from Richmond in reference to the death of General Lawrence:—Notwithstanding his great age, General Lawrence was not the oldest of the old East India Company's officers, inasmuch as there still lives (at a distance of a quarter of a mile from this late officer's residence) Lieutenant-Colonel William Price, whose first commission was dated 1803, and who is now in his hundredth year (Nov. 1887).* [Eventually the London journals announced the death, at Egerton House, Richmond, Surrey, of Lieutenant-Colonel William Price, late Bengal Army, in his hundredth year.]

CONDUCTOR JAMES.

FROM a General to a Conductor of Ordnance must seem a vast step in the march of these "Brief Notices"; but knowing the true value of many such warrant officers, and having had charge of them while the Indian Mutiny was at its height, and at other times, it cannot be wrong, before leaving the olden time, to notice what in the journal of one of the best writers and ablest editors of the day is styled—

AN AGED PENSIONER.—Mr. James, an old pensioner, who had long resided in Bangalore, died on March 3. A local paper, in the course of a notice of the deceased's career, says that Mr. James was born on Dec. 10, 1792, and was therefore in his ninety-fifth year. He went out to India in the year the battle of Waterloo was fought—viz., 1815, having then been a soldier—one of the old 22nd Light Dragoons—for four years, he having enlisted in 1811. The 22nd was then quartered in Bangalore, and Mr. James arrived in a draft of recruits. On the return of the 22nd to England, Mr. James volunteered into the relieving regiment, the 13th Light Dragoons, now the 13th Hussars. Shortly afterwards he was appointed to the Ordnance Department, in which he rose to the rank of Conductor. He served in the Mahratta War, and was present at Goomsoor in 1837. In December of that year he resigned the military service, and was appointed by Sir Frederick Adam, Governor of Madras, to

* *Overland Mail*, December 2, 1887.

be Postmaster of Bangalore. Mr. James remained in the Postal Department until 1865, when he retired on pension, at the age of seventy-two, and with a total service of fifty-four years. On the reorganization of the Postal Department, Mr. James was appointed Inspecting Postmaster of the Bangalore Division. On two occasions he acted as Presidency Postmaster. He and his family became well known and respected throughout all Mysore. For years his family owned the *Bangalore Herald* newspaper, which, after a long and brilliant career, became incorporated with the *Bangalore Spectator*. For several years past Mr. James had been confined to his house by feebleness of age, but last Christmas Day he attended Divine service in St. Andrew's Kirk. It is stated that from the time Mr. James first arrived in India—in 1815—down to his death he never left the country. A continuous residence of seventy-two years, fifty-four being spent on duty, does not speak badly for the climate.*

LIEUT.-GENERAL RICHARD STRACHEY, R.E.

In our *First Series*† we remarked that the brothers Strachey are great names, and have served India well. The services of the elder brother are thus simply recorded:—Strachey, Richard, Lieutenant-General, R.E. (Bengal), C.S.I., F.R.S.; 2nd Lieutenant, Bengal Engineers, June, 1836; was employed on irrigation works in the N.W. Provinces from 1840, and appointed Executive Engineer, Ganges Canal, July, 1843; Under-Secretary to Government of India, Public Works Department, 1857; Secretary to Government, Central Provinces, 1857; Consulting Engineer, Railway Department, Sept., 1858; Secretary to Government of India, Public Works Department, 1862; Inspector-General of Irrigation, and Chief Engineer, 1st Class, Dec., 1866; Additional Member of Governor-General's Council, 1869;

* *Homeward Mail*, April 4, 1887. On March 4, another man named James, a pensioned Conductor, died, aged ninety-two, at Bangalore.

† Page 185—"Sketch of Sir Henry Rawlinson, K.C.B."

Inspecting Engineer of Machinery and Stores for State Railways, India Office, 1871; Member of Council of India, 1875; Special Duty in India, 1878; Officiating Financial Member of Council of Governor-General, 1879; Officiating Member of Council of Governor-General, 1880; President of the Famine Commission, 1880; reappointed Member of Council of India, 1880.—This ought to give the British public some idea of an Engineer officer's useful and varied career in India, of the scientific arm still associated in England with such great names as Pasley and Burgoyne, the study of Vauban and Carnot, or blowing up, and sapping and mining operations. About the middle of 1887, Sir Richard Strachey was appointed to the highly-distinguished scientific post of President of the Royal Geographical Society, shortly after which we read*:—

The appointment of General Richard Strachey, R.E., to be President of the Royal Geographical Society in London, says the *Englishman*, must be recognized, in some measure, as a compliment to the Indian Services. It may be that General Strachey, during the time that he was employed in the Public Works Department in India, was neither conciliatory nor popular. But that is a long time ago now. In the snug harbour which he has found for himself in the Council of India, although he still clings to some of his old crotchets, much of his former asperity has been smoothed down. If he wishes for controversy, he can find it from day to day in the Government Meteorological Office, of which he is the chief. It is a happy incident, in connection with his nomination as President, that it should have devolved upon him to present the Founder's Medal to Colonel Holdich, R.E., for his services to geography in connection with the surveys of Afghanistan.

* *Homeward Mail*, July 25, 1887.

SIR JOHN STRACHEY, G.C.S.I.

This distinguished Bengal civilian's services are thus recorded :—Strachey, Sir John, G.C.S.I., C.I.E., late Bengal C.S. Appointed to the Bengal Civil Service fom Haileybury College in 1842; served in the N.W. Provinces in the grades of Assistant Commissioner and Assistant Magistrate and Collector; Senior Assistant, Kumaon, 1848; Magistrate and Collector, Moradabad, 1854; Officiating Commissioner of Kumaon, 1861; President of Commission to inquire into Cholera Epidemic of 1861; Judicial Commissioner, Central Provinces, 1862; President of the Sanitary Commission with Government of India, 1864; Chief Commissioner, Oudh, 1866; Member of Governor-General's Council, 7th March, 1868; Acting Viceroy and Governor-General, on death of Earl of Mayo, 1872; Lieutenant-Governor, N.W. Provinces, 1874; retired from the Civil Service, 1876; Financial Member of the Governor-General's Council, 23rd Dec., 1876 to 1880; left India, Dec., 1880; Member of Council of Secretary of State for India, 1885; joint author with Lieutenant-General R. Strachey of "The Finances and Public Works of India," 1882. [The brothers are still Members of the Secretary of State's Council.]

SIR ALEXANDER J. ARBUTHNOT, K.C.S.I., C.I.E.

Towards the end of October, 1887, it was announced that the Queen had been pleased to approve the appointment of the above-named well-known Madras civilian to be a Member of the Council of India, on the expiration of the term of office of Sir Robert Dalyell, K.C.I.E., C.S.I. Referring to the appointment of Sir A. Arbuthnot to the India Council, the *Times of India* (Bombay) remarked :

Sir Alexander Arbuthnot, K.C.S.I., was for several years a member of the Council of Fort St. George. He had previously had a varied experience in various posts in the Madras Civil

Service. On first joining in June, 1843, he was appointed Acting Assistant to the Collector of Chingleput, and became Assistant to the Principal Collector and Magistrate of Nellore in February, 1844. In March of the following year he was entrusted with the duties of Head Assistant to the Registrar to the Court of Sudder and Foujdaree Adawlut; in a little over eighteen months—namely, in October, 1846—he was Officiating Secretary to the College Board and Madras University; in January, 1848, he was gazetted Acting Head Assistant to the Collector of Cuddapah, an office which he filled for only a few months, being entrusted with the duties of Acting Malayalam Translator to Government in July of the same year; and in March, 1849, he was substantively appointed to the latter post. Two years later he was ordered to act as Secretary to the College and University Boards, an office which he was subsequently confirmed in. In March, 1852, he again became connected with the Sudder and Foujdaree Adawlut, first in the capacity of Acting Deputy Registrar, and afterwards as Deputy Registrar and Acting Registrar. In July, 1854, he was removed to a fresh sphere as Member and Secretary of the Board of Examiners. In March of the succeeding year he was Director of Public Instruction—a post which he filled with ability. In 1861 he was entrusted with the duties of a Commissioner for the Uncovenanted Civil Service Examination, and was Acting Chief Secretary to Government from May 1, 1862. He was elected a Fellow of the University of Madras in the same month, and was promoted to be Chief Secretary to Government in the October following. His next function was that of an Additional Member of the Council of Fort St. George, the duties of which he entered upon in November 1864. Three years later he was a Member of Council. His present appointment, the Bombay writer thought, was likely to be popular in Madras. But, we may add, doubtless it was well received in Calcutta, where Sir Alexander did some useful work, and to whom, as Chancellor of the Calcutta University, allusion has been made in our Sketch of Mr. Henry Woodrow. As stated in our *First Series,* he is the author of a work on Sir Thomas Munro, the famous Governor and Commander-in-Chief of Madras, whose excellence drew forth the intense admiration of that unrivalled judge of men —George Canning.

Sir Alexander Arbuthnot was appointed a Knight Commander of the Star of India on the 24th of May, 1873; and, on the date of the institution of the New Order (1st January, 1878), an *ex-officio* Companion of the Indian Empire.

SIR THOMAS DOUGLAS FORSYTH, K.C.S.I., C.B.

(LATE BENGAL C.S.)

IN some respects, Sir Douglas Forsyth may be considered as having been one of the most remarkable among our distinguished Anglo-Indians; and it is to be regretted that, from want of original materials, we have been unable to give a fair sketch of his career. In our original preface (March, 1875) to the *First Series* we have endeavoured to do Sir Douglas brief justice, chiefly with reference to his famous visit to Yarkand five years before; and it was with regret that, at the end of 1886, we received the announcement of his death at Eastbourne, on December 17, after a very short and sudden illness. Sir Douglas Forsyth, as he was generally called, was, wrote the *Times,* one of those Anglo-Indians who, trained in a great school, hovered during their careers on the verge of greatness itself, and, if they did not quite attain the highest distinction, became associated at least with one or two important passages in the modern history of British India. "Among these men of the second rank, second rather in their opportunities than their abilities, Sir Douglas Forsyth must be allowed a high place, and there were one or two incidents in his life that seemed to presage a more distinguished future, because in them he evinced some of the best qualities of the English character. That this statement may not seem to be made at random, we may at once specify his promptitude during the Mutiny in warning his official superior, and the vigour with which he acted during the Kooka outbreak, when the promptitude of his measures prevented the spread of a serious religious movement.

"Sir Douglas Forsyth was the younger son—the elder being Mr. William Forsyth, Q.C.,—of the late Mr. Thomas Forsyth, of Liverpool, and he was born in 1827. He was first educated at Rugby, and then went through the usual course at Haileybury before entering the Bengal Civil Service, which he did in 1848. He entered the service at an exciting moment, when the final conquest of the Punjab was in progress, and on the eve of the formation of the junior division of the Civil Service, which has now appropriated so much of the fame and position that formerly belonged to the three Presidencies. At a very early stage of his career he was sent to this new province, the organization of which Lord Dalhousie entrusted to the very ablest men at his disposal, and when the Mutiny broke out, nine years after his arrival, he was acting as Deputy Commissioner in the Cis-Sutlej States—his superior, or the full Commissioner, being Mr. George Barnes. The principal duty that devolved upon these officials was to provide means of transport for the troops ordered from the Punjab to Delhi, but on their tact and firmness also depended to a great extent the attitude of the protected Sikh States. Mr. Forsyth took a bold initiative in calling upon the Maharajah of Puttiala for assistance, and the appeal, being promptly responded to by that loyal chieftain, awakened a responsive echo in the other Sikh chiefs of Jheend and Nabha. His measures for the defence of Umballa were prompt and sufficient. He raised a police force of Sikhs for the purpose, and, under the direction of the Commissioner, Mr. George Barnes, it was he who provided for the security of the road from Umballa to Kurnaul up to the siege and capture of Delhi. The reputation he gained during the Mutiny (and for his services he received the C.B.) ensured his rapid promotion, until he became in due course Commissioner of the very important district of Umballa. But in 1869 a still more important subject than the management of the Sikhs had come to the front, and that was our future relations with

Russia. Lord Mayo had just received the Ameer Shere Ali in durbar at Umballa, and as it was considered desirable to bring the views of the Indian Government on the Central Asian question in a clear and unmistakable form before that of St. Petersburg, Mr. Forsyth was considered the most competent person to be entrusted with the responsible duty of Indian Envoy to the Russian Court. There can be no doubt he fully justified the confidence thus reposed in him, as he established the very basis of the arrangement which, despite the rapid progress of Russian arms in the interval, was carried out in the agreement two years ago to delimit the Afghan frontier by a joint commission. The main point which he then established was that Russia consented to respect the territory then in the possession of Shere Ali; and it will be found during the negotiations with Russia that we have not advanced much beyond this stage at the present moment.

"Immediately after his return to India Mr. Forsyth was entrusted with a second mission, more interesting in its surroundings if less important in its consequences than his visit to St. Petersburg. The travels of Mr. Shaw had introduced to us the little-known country of Chinese or Eastern Turkestan and its famous ruler, the Atalik Ghazi, or Yakoob Beg. An envoy from this potentate visited India, and Mr. Forsyth was sent on a return mission to Yarkand. Unfortunately, Yakoob Beg was engaged in a distant campaign, and Mr. Forsyth, whose instructions required his return to India before the commencement of winter, had to return without accomplishing the main object of his journey. The only satisfactory result of the mission was that he learnt something definite about a State which at the time was neither Russian nor Chinese. Three years later Mr. Forsyth was sent on a second mission to Kashgar, not merely that he might complete his observations of the earlier date, but also that he might acquire a precise knowledge of what the future relations of Russia with this State would be, for at that moment Kashgar, not less than Khiva, stood under the menace of Russian invasion. At all events, he was successful in seeing the Atalik Ghazi on this occasion, and he visited both Yarkand and Kashgar. His report on the mission forms a most useful guide to the politics, natural history, and physical condition of Eastern Turkestan. For this mission he was rewarded with the K.C.S.I. His diplomatic work did not end here, for in 1875 he went to Burma, chiefly to obtain an explanation of the King's reception of Lisitai, and to effect a settlement of the Karennee question. This mission was denounced as a failure, and Sir Douglas Forsyth came in for some unfriendly criticism; but Sir Douglas printed for private circulation a succinct and really unanswerable account of his conduct during his journey to Burma, and of the proper execution of his mission. Shortly after this he retired from the service, and since his return to England he has taken a prominent and active part as director of several of the larger Indian railways. He married, in 1850, Alice, daughter of the late Mr. Thomas Plumer, of Canons, Middlesex, by whom he leaves three daughters, and the late Sir Harry Parkes married the younger daughter of the same gentleman. If Sir Douglas Forsyth's character had to be summed up in a line it would be accurate to say that he was a plain, straight-dealing, truth-telling English gentleman, who on critical occasions exhibited the qualities of a hero."

The *St. James's Gazette*, referring to the statement in the above notice that Sir Douglas "established the very basis of the arrangement carried out in the agreement to delimit the Afghan frontier by a joint commission," said: "True. But Sir Douglas Forsyth was most justly indignant at the way in which that arrangement was executed. In a letter to us, published on Feb. 26, 1885, he wrote of his mission to St. Petersburg in 1869:—'A map was produced, and a line was indicated, commencing from Khoja Saleh to the Oxus, across desert, in the direction of Sarakhs, as the probable boundary of Afghanistan. The towns of Andakhoi, Maimena, and Penjdeh were distinctly recognized as within Afghan territory.'"

The following is the brief official summary recording the services of this distinguished Anglo-Indian:—He served in the N.W. Provinces and Punjab in the grades of Assistant

Magistrate and Collector, and Assistant Commissioner; Deputy-Commissioner, Umballa, 1857; Secretary to Chief Commissioner, Oudh, 1858; Officiating Commissioner in Punjab, 1860; C.B. for services in Mutiny; Commissioner of Lahore, 1863, and subsequently of Jullundur, 1865; deputed on Special Mission to Yarkand, 1870; Commissioner of Umballa, 1871; transferred to Oudh, 1872; Envoy on mission to Kashgar, 1873; K.C.S.I., 1874; Additional Member of Governor-General's Council, 1874; Envoy on Special Mission to Burma, 1875; retired 1878.

Of Sir Douglas Forsyth, and other Anglo-Indians possessing similar natural activity, it may be truly said that he had what gives our lives the *swing*, which, according to a famous writer, "men see and admire, and by which we accomplish our successes." Such is well styled "the intrinsic joyousness of natural activity." Again, "We live in the midst of inward shouts and cheers and huzzaing, until we seem all fortitude, and learn to disbelieve in the impossible. We do various work, and variety always multiplies the amount of work, at least by ten. Our results are visible, and the vision of them is a grand attraction. There is nothing dry about results." * We also read that results make a noise, and that noise is an endless battle-cry to an active spirit. A fair number of such spirits have now been brought forward; and a few more are yet to come in these various sketches.

About the middle of 1887, it was interesting to learn that Miss Forsyth, the daughter of Sir Douglas, had opened a technical training school for women in Ebury Street. This institution—the first of its kind—supplied a want which had long been felt, doing the benevolent lady aspirant to fair fame infinite credit. Regarding the scheme, it was considered one which deserved to succeed, and Miss Forsyth had all the qualities to make it do so. Like her illustrious father, she appeared eminently practical; for she actually set herself the task—no very easy one—of "developing the practical side of woman's nature."

* Dr. Faber's *Spiritual Conferences*, pp. 362–63.

And, towards the end of the same year, an advertisement appeared in the London journals, to the following effect:—

From this interesting work may now be learned all that is required to be known of the active and acute Anglo-Indian traveller and diplomatist.

EDWARD FRANCIS HARRISON, C.S.I.

Here Indian Finance lays claim to a distinguished son.

Mr. Harrison was educated at Rugby, under Dr. Tait, and, passing through Haileybury, entered the Bengal Civil Service in 1849. He was soon employed in the Financial Department, in which he much distinguished himself. Among other services, he was mainly responsible for the introduction of the paper currency in India. In 1865, at Rangoon, he reorganized the Financial Department of Burma. He was President of the Bank of Bengal, and held the appointment of Comptroller-General of India for twelve years. In 1878 he was sent by the English Government to inquire into the state of the finances of Turkey, and acted as Vice-President of the Commission of Inquiry. He was made a C.S.I. in 1882, and received from the Sultan the Order of the Osmanli (second class). He was a Director of several well-known City Companies. He died on June 5, 1887, at his residence, Thornley, Upper Norwood.

SIR AUGUSTUS RIVERS THOMPSON, K.C.S.I., C.I.E.

This distinguished Anglo-Indian, whose name of late years has been so much before the public of India and England, has filled some of the highest posts in the Empire, and was, according to the India Office Record, appointed from Haileybury College, June, 1850; arrived in India, 28th December, 1850; served in the Revenue and Judicial Departments, as Assistant Magistrate and Collector and Joint Magistrate and Deputy-Collector; Junior Assistant to the Governor-General's Agent, South-West Frontier, September, 1853; Superintendent of Survey, January, 1859; Officiating Junior Secretary, Board of Revenue, April, 1859; Officiating Junior Secretary, Government of Bengal, July, 1859; Magistrate and Collector (first grade), April, 1861; Officiating Secretary, Board of Revenue, April, 1861; Officiating Collector of Customs, November, 1861; Civil and Sessions Judge, August, 1865; Officiating Superintendent and Remembrancer of Legal Affairs, February, 1868; Officiating Commissioner of Revenue and Circuit, Presidency Division, January, 1869; Officiating Secretary to the Government of Bengal in the Revenue and General Departments, September, 1869, and in the Judicial and Political Departments, November, 1871; Secretary to the Government of Bengal, December, 1873; Chief Commissioner of British Burma, 1st May, 1877; Governor-General's Council, 18th April, 1878; Lieutenant-Governor of Bengal, 24th April, 1882.

March, 1887, is a month which will long be remembered by Sir A. R. Thompson, for it was during this month his rule in Bengal was rapidly drawing to a close; and on March 24th he was waited on by a number of influential Mahomedan noblemen and gentlemen, who presented the Lieutenant-Governor of Bengal with an address, thanking him for his successful endeavours to improve Mahomedan education, and restore that community—one of such vast importance—to the place which it should never have lost.* Sir Augustus said emphatically that he hoped a new era

* In March, 1887, throughout India, it may be said that greater or lesser events were apparently taking place, and on the gale. In the Bori Valley, Sirdars and leading chiefs of the Zob and Bori tribes (25th) were paying their respects to the son of the Queen-Empress, the Duke of Connaught; the Governor of Madras met the Central Jubilee Committee about the same time, saying that 156 local Committees in that Presidency had joined in the Jubilee address, and that the celebrations of the Jubilee in Southern India were a good example to the governed as well as to the Government, and a proof that the people were most loyal and devoted to their sovereign; Sir Lepel Griffin was to take a year's furlough, thus temporarily abandoning the important post of Governor-General's Agent at Indore; Mr. J. B. Lyall was soon to arrive at Lahore, and at once take over the charge of the province; General Sir Hugh Gough, V.C., K.C.B., had succeeded to the temporary command of the Lahore division on General Murray's departure; a well-known and very able and scientific General Officer, H. F. Hancock, R.E., died in Calcutta, of liver complaint, and was deeply regretted in Bombay, where he was widely known and highly respected; also, early in March, His Highness Raghbir Singh Bahadur, G.C.S.I., Rajah of Jhind, had gone the way of all flesh, attended in his last moments by Drs. Bennett and Doyle, who, of course, were aware that the father of their illustrious patient was the only chief present with the English forces before Delhi, and rendered signal service; Miss Edith Pechey and Miss Charlotte Ellaby had been appointed respectively first and second physicians of the Cama Hospital for Women and Children; the Maharajah Holkar was about to visit England, probably accompanied by Sir Lepel Griffin, which would be the first occasion of one of the greater chiefs visiting British shores; intelligence had been received in Bombay that authentic news had arrived from the Governor of Herat that the Governor of Turkestan had ordered Iskander Khan, with 12,000 men, to take Herat by surprise, and that the Ameer had ordered 10,000 men to be in readiness to reinforce the Herat garrison; Sir William Hunter, late Director of the Statistical Department of the Indian Government, and famous by his admirable "Imperial Gazetteer," was to leave Bombay for England on April 1st; a Silk Conference was to be held in Calcutta, with a view to practical work; Sir Dimshaw Manockjee Petit, Sheriff of Bombay, was said to be the largest cotton-mill proprietor in the country, employing no less than 9,500 hands. A St. Petersburg telegram of March 27 said that the surrender of Port Hamilton had given rise to various comments in the Russian Press. It was regarded by one party as a triumph of Russian diplomacy, and by another as only one more instance of British astuteness, in first seizing what did not belong to them, and "then restoring the stolen goods for a material consideration in the shape of a guarantee against annexation of any part of Corea by Russia."—And thus a very fair amount of real and speculative work in India was done in March, 1887.

was opening in the cause of Mahomedan progress and fitness for public service.*

On the very same day, in another quarter of the Empire, Sir Charles Aitchison, the retiring Lieutenant-Governor of the Punjab, said to Europeans and Natives, who had gathered to present farewell addresses, that they were living in a time of transition. The old order was changing and giving place to the new. It was a distinct sign of life and growth that the direction which things might take could not fail to be influenced by the views of the educated native community. Sir Charles had already alluded to the spread of education—which subject his Honour might have styled the Grand Master of Peace—and concluded his farewell address by saying that he left the province in profound peace, "even on its remotest borders." Thus did two mighty wielders of power in India, the one at Calcutta and the other at Lahore, gracefully adjust their mantles before yielding up their posts, during the holding of which the people committed to their charge had found the yoke of foreign masters to be far lighter than that of any native dynasty; for they had been governed by Indian administrators belonging to that noble body of functionaries, so well described by the most brilliant historical essayist, "not more highly distinguished by ability and diligence than by integrity, disinterestedness, and public spirit."

On the 2nd of April Sir A. R. Thompson handed over the Lieutenant-Governorship of Bengal to Sir S. Bayley; and his departure from India (3rd) was final.† The *Times* correspondent at Calcutta wrote:—

> It has been Sir A. R. Thompson's fate to rule the largest, richest, and most populous of the Indian provinces through five eventful and difficult years, and during that time he has so borne himself as to win the affection and respect of all classes, except a small section of noisy Bengalee agitators who have never forgiven his opposition to the unhappy Ilbert Bill. For weeks past the organs of those agitators have been attacking him with increasing bitterness. It seems clear, however, that they do not represent the views of

* The Mahomedan Literary Society of Calcutta boasts men of high intellect among its members.

† Sir C. Aitchison was to return to India in six months to take his seat at the Supreme Council.

the great mass of the Hindu community, while there can be no doubt of Sir A. R. Thompson's great popularity among the Europeans and Mahomedans. The leading characteristics of the departing Lieutenant-Governor have been well summed up by an Anglo-Indian journal as balance of mind, practical wisdom, common sense, sobriety of judgment, and moderation.*

A public man, in any country, could hardly expect greater praise than the above on retiring from high office. The difficulties which such a Lieutenant-Governor had to surmount can only be fairly known to those who understand India; and, no doubt, the conflicting interests of Hindu and Mahomedan, aided by the vast difference between the Vedas and the Koran, formed, and will continue to form, for many generations of men, the chief obstacle to national harmony. Friends of India must ever look well to the fact, which is becoming more apparent every year, that the Brahman has, through our benevolent presence, lost his social, and the Mahomedan his military, sway in the vast country which the munificent old East India Company gave to England. Generally speaking, there is a far greater gulf fixed between Hindus and Mahomedans than there is between the Unionists and Separatists who, on the interminable Irish question, are so distracting our executive British statesmen at the present time. The Hindu and Mahomedan may not inaptly be compared to two mighty and rapid rivers, running parallel and near to each other, rolling along with a sort of competitive vengeance, with, like parallel lines, the utter impossibility of their ever meeting so as to form one grand force which, if by a miracle obtained, would raise India to be far more than the first of Oriental nations. But as such mutual working for the best apparently can never be, the only way for our Governors, or Proconsuls, is to wisely conciliate the governed of every creed, keeping in mind the

* Comparing the two careers, the discerning critic continues, in a fairly liberal spirit:—Regarding Sir C. Aitchison's career in the Punjab there are greater differences of opinion. His great ability, experience, and strong sense of duty are universally admitted, but he does not appear to have succeeded in making himself generally popular, and his administration has been somewhat of a disappointment, a fact which is, perhaps, largely due to circumstances for which he is not to blame.—*See also* remarks on Lieutenant-Governors as failures.—*First Series*, p. 237.

famous saying of Archbishop Fenélon, that as God tolerates all religions, man should tolerate all. Of course, in such a large and popúlous province as Bengal, where the Hindus so vastly outnumber the Mahomedans, it would be absurd to suppose for an instant that any rational Anglo-Indian statesman of note could be prejudiced in favour of either race or creed; but it is this fancied prejudice which is the boundless Upas, the all-blasting tree which Governors have to contend against, as, most probably, Sir A. R. Thompson well knew during his five years of progressive and benignant rule. Every Lieutenant-Governor cannot be a Munro, an Elphinstone, a Malcolm, or a Metcalfe; and such eminent statesmen, so much admired and respected in their day, would have received the same amount of vituperation as many of our Indian rulers have been treated to, had they, if by any means possible, fought, consolidated, or governed vast provinces in ours. The tendency of this somewhat brazen age, East and West, is to abuse everything and everybody, too often without thought or reason. We shall now enrich this notice with interesting and suitable matter from a comprehensive and discriminating paper on "Sir Rivers Thompson and his Critics."

The writer commences the defence in a noble spirit—the defence of a worthy civilian who had thirty-six years' experience of Native character:—

During his tenure of office Sir Rivers Thompson has learnt much of the advantages which the system of education under British auspices has ensured in order to establish loyalty and good understanding between the ruler and the ruled. Bengal has in this respect been the most favoured of all the provinces of India, and what has been the result? A continual attack on, and misrepresentation of, the policy of Government in the vernacular Press, to which we have given the widest license. In the April number of the *Asiatic Quarterly Review*, Sir Lepel Griffin, in his paper on "The Public Service of India," wrote:—

Sir Rivers Thompson will have vacated his post and returned to England before this article appears in India. I may, therefore, without impropriety, refer to him as one of the most upright, equitable, modest and kindly officials who have ever directed the fortunes of Bengal. Yet Sir Rivers chanced to take the opposite from the popular view with regard to the ill-conceived and misshapen bantling that is passing down to posterity under the name of the Ilbert Bill. The consequence has been that he has been persistently attacked in the most savage and mendacious manner. Not only his policy, but his character and private life, have been the subject of the most venomed abuse. This is the fate of every Lieutenant-Governor of Bengal. I have seen a long series, extending from Sir John Peter Grant, and I do not know one who has not been the subject of the most persistent and libellous attack.

Sir Rivers Thompson, so far as his own countrymen and the Mahomedans of Bengal are concerned, has laid down the reins of office after gaining their confidence and esteem, and he carries with him into his retirement their best wishes and warmest sympathies. It is the Bengali Babú—that educational monstrosity which our own folly has shaped—who continues to throw mud at the departing Governor. "He has," says one of the organs of this class, "no sympathies with the people. Whether in connection with the Ilbert Bill or with the Local Self-Government Scheme, or with the Calcutta Municipal Corporation, or with the Native Press, he showed a positive antipathy to the people of the country." Another journal says, "Sir Rivers Thompson could not dissociate British power from the idea of brute force, and it naturally happened that never, except in the times of the Mutiny, was race hatred at such a height as during the five years of his rule over us." We have quoted from only the mildest of his native critics, but there could scarcely be brought against a Governor of an Indian Province a more serious charge than that he stirred up race antagonism and alienated the affections of the people from their rulers. Yet this wicked, lying accusation is what Sir Rivers has had to put up with. Against such may be put his own noble words in his reply to the farewell address presented to him by the community of Calcutta:—

In the presence of people divided among themselves by every form of creed and religion, and yet all of whom are in enjoyment of equal rights, the power of England is a bulwark against all the forces of commotion and anarchy; but none the less, as the sons whom England has sent forth to assert the pre-eminence of her laws and liberties and literature, there will always be, I trust, between the people of this country and Englishmen, that mutual forbearance and friendship and generosity of sentiment on the growth and permanence of which alone the highest welfare of India depends.

But it is this very reference to British power which always stirs up the ire of the Bengali Babú. He declares that Sir Rivers Thompson "belongs to the old class of rulers to which brute force, power, supremacy, and general good are all synonymous terms. Bengal is struggling for a higher ideal." What that ideal is all Englishmen who have any experience of the Babú know. Sycophant and self-seeking as he is, he has no more sympathy with the poor and suffering of his fellow-countrymen than he has with the tortured and goaded bullocks that he meets in his daily walks. But he revels in the license, which he has acquired under British rule, to vituperate that rule and the English officials who are striving to carry it out for the well-being and happiness of India. Of such officials no man has had a higher claim to the respect and esteem of those over whom he has ruled than Sir Rivers Thompson; and yet, as he leaves the scene of his hard and honourable work, his lips seem to have been "tuned to such grief that they say bright words sadly":—

I trust that the remembrance of me as Lieutenant-Governor of Bengal will be at any rate the thought of one who strove with very great imperfection to do his duty in the state of life to which he was called.

With this modest hope he has bidden Bengal farewell. If at last he reaches his Ithaca of repose it has been over no "summer seas," but his honest labours and his good name will survive all calumny and misrepresentation at evil hands. In the meantime rest will doubtless be as grateful to him as the breath of the evening to one who has borne the heat and burden of a trying day.*

It should also be noticed that, on the eve of departure, the Rivers Thompson Memorial Fund amounted to more than Rs. 25,000; also that the Viceroy had directed, as a mark of respect due to Sir Rivers Thompson's character and services, that all the honours and distinctions to which he was entitled as Lieutenant-Governor of Bengal should be continued to him from April 2, the day on which he resigned his high office, until his departure for Europe. But, perhaps, the chief honour conferred on the retiring Lieutenant-Governor was his being entertained at dinner at the United Service Club (Calcutta, March 26) by the members of the Bengal Civil Service. The chair was filled by the father of the Civil Service, Mr. Skipworth Tayler, the Judge of Burdwan, on whose right sat Sir Rivers Thompson, and on his left Sir Steuart Bayley. The Chairman happily remarked that the splendid successes of their distinguished guest's official career had been foreshadowed by those on the river and the cricketing-fields at Haileybury. This tends to remind one of the famous saying of the great Duke, with reference to the sister Service, that Waterloo was won on the playing-fields of Eton.

We now pass on to one of the most able and distinguished actors in the great drama of Indian Government, prefacing a few remarks with the record of Indian service:—

SIR ALFRED COMYNS LYALL, K.C.B., C.I.E.

(LATE LIEUTENANT-GOVERNOR NORTH-WESTERN PROVINCES.)

APPOINTED to the Bengal Civil Service from Haileybury College, 1855; arrived in India, 2nd January, 1856; served in the North-West Provinces as Assistant Magistrate and Collector, and Joint Magistrate and Deputy-Collector; transferred to Central Provinces, April, 1864, and served

* See *Allen's Indian Mail*, April 18, 1887.

as Deputy-Commissioner, Officiating Secretary to Chief Commissioner, and Officiating Commissioner of the Nagpur Division; transferred to Hyderabad Assigned Districts, July, 1867, and appointed Commissioner, West Berar, August, 1867; Secretary to the Government of India, Home Department, March, 1873; from November, 1874, served in the Foreign Department of the Government of India, and was appointed Resident, 1st Class, and Agent to the Governor-General in Rajputana, and Chief Commissioner of Ajmere; on Special Duty in England, August, 1876; Secretary to Government of India, Foreign Department, April, 1878; on Special Political Duty in Kabul, March, 1880, and again in September, 1880; Lieutenant-Governor, North-West Provinces, and Chief Commissioner of Oudh, 17th April, 1882.

Early in December, 1887, it was announced to the British public that the general desire among the Natives of the North-West Provinces to found some memorial of administration of Sir Alfred Lyall was taking organized shape, and that a considerable sum had been already subscribed. Also in a *Gazette Extraordinary*, the new Lieutenant-Governor, Sir Auckland Colvin, had directed that, as a mark of respect due to the character and services of Sir A. Lyall, all the honours and distinctions to which he was entitled as Lieutenant-Governor should be continued to him as long as he remained in the Provinces. Thus both Natives and Europeans sought to do honour to the retiring chief of the famous Provinces, to which he was so well entitled. Shortly after, Sir Alfred left India for good. Bombay gave the most graphic and eloquent description of the occasion:—

To-day Sir Alfred Lyall leaves for England, after a long and distinguished career which adds lustre to the history of British administrators in India. Coming to this country in 1856, the year before the Mutiny, he has given thirty-one years of valuable and varied services to the Government and the community. During the troublous times of the Mutiny he showed a discretion and a tact which were, perhaps, more remarkable in a youth fresh from Eton and Haileybury than the gallantry which prompted him, a civilian, to join in a charge across a nullah upon guns firing grape. As Sir John Edge, the Chief Justice of the North-West Provinces has so well said, a few days since, had his profession been that of arms, he would have proved himself a valiant and a gallant soldier. As it was, his career has been that of an able administrator, who has brought to his work the elevated aims and principles of a statesman. He has found recreation in literature, prose and verse coming with equal facility from his vigorous and graceful pen. His best known poems, the Old Pindari and the Fakir, evidence his sympathy for the people and the ideas of the country in which his busy life was passed. The Foreign Office found in him a capable secretary during the Afghan War, his services in that capacity earning for him the Knight Commandership of the Bath. For five years and a half he has been Lieutenant-Governor of the North-West Provinces, where he has been so successful in developing railway communications that there is no village which has not a railway within forty miles of it. Private enterprise helped in the extension of the railway system in the Provinces—a fact which is rather to the credit of the head of the local administration, for without encouragement and co-operation, such undertakings are usually left to Government resources. He has favoured the growth of local self-government, giving a large measure of power to popular bodies while seeing that it was turned to good use. His latest work is the inauguration of the Allahabad University, to release the North-West, Oudh, and the Central Provinces from the leading-strings of the Calcutta University, which has sufficient scope for its energies in teaching Bengal with its vast population. It was time that the very different people of the North-West should have a system of education suited to their special needs and aptitudes. The interests of the agricultural population have been consulted in a revision of the system of assessment which lightens their burdens, and in Oudh gives to the occupiers some fixity of tenure while recognizing the rights of the zemindars.

There is something very touching and very characteristic in the regretful and pathetic tone of Sir Alfred Lyall's farewell to the North-West Provinces. The change which he has witnessed since the time when he first set foot in those Provinces, the nearest railway being eight hundred miles distant, must be difficult to realize. But as Sir Alfred well says, the epoch of the Mutiny, which upset everything, was really that from which everything was set on the right course. Out of the nettle, danger, men like Sir Alfred Lyall have plucked the flower, safety. The pregnant sentences in which he condenses the three periods of an Indian career deserve to be set in verse by his own hand or by Edwin Arnold's: "We who come to India pass the first few years of our service in looking back rather eagerly to our English homes: we suffer from what is called nostalgia. That is the first period, when we call India the land of regrets, and wish for the cool, grey skies of England. Then comes a middle period, when we harden to our work, and subside into contented exile. And, afterwards, if we stay long enough, comes the last period, when the regrets revive, but their object and direction are changed; and the country that we are sorry to leave, and to which we look back, is India."*

Thus, to the Anglo-Indian statesman, as well as to many others, come three periods, bringing to memory the fairly well-known remark of one of the most famous novelists and statesmen of our time, that youth is a blunder, manhood a struggle, and old age a regret. But there is certainly little or no blunder in the early part of Sir Alfred Lyall's career; and there can be no doubt whatever that, had he been a soldier, he would have served a gun or led a charge with the ready bravery of a Roberts or a Wolseley. These are the men, civil and military, for India, to the manner born, which manner defies all competitive examination, and which only Nature can fashion. As an Indian administrator it will be seen how well he served his country through a most trying period of India's history, and what a vast amount of good he effected before, in almost the prime of life, like a well-graced actor, he left the stage.† Among "the green spots

* *Bombay Gazette*, December 2, 1887.

† After making over charge (21st) to Sir Auckland Colvin, a farewell ball was given at Allahabad to Sir Alfred and Lady Lyall on November 18; and

in memory's waste," to which Sir Alfred Lyall can look back, not the least remarkable was his being asked by one of his intelligent subjects of the North-West for permission to commit suicide! If such a strange request from those entertaining views of "self-slaughter" were put forward in London, it would save the learned magistrates a vast deal of trouble Towards the end of December, in London, the following announcement regarding a well-known literary Anglo-Indian and Sir A. Lyall appeared:—

Sir W. W. Hunter having definitely retired from the Bengal Civil Service, after more than twenty-five years' service, it is understood that he will now devote his leisure to literary pursuits. Almost the whole period of his service in India has been devoted to literary and statistical work. Besides several important statistical works, Sir William Hunter has published a book on rural Bengal, a dictionary of the non-Aryan languages of India, a life of Lord Mayo, and several other works on modern British India.

Another well-known Anglo-Indian, Sir A. Lyall, is expected to take up his permanent residence in London, and it is to be hoped that he will be able to resume his long-interrupted Asiatic studies, which appeared at intervals some years ago in the *Fortnightly Review*.

And so, in addition to his other qualifications, Sir Alfred Lyall was a distinguished contributor to Periodical Literature. A grand career is yet in store for him at home; but, of course, like other most able Anglo-Indians, it will be simply impossible for him to gather as much fame in England as he did in India—the glorious land of his adoption. Still, beyond a doubt, his sound judgment and discretion will be frequently brought into action; and so, for the second time, he may achieve greatness, if he has not a new phase of greatness thrust upon him. It may be well to conclude this notice with the following brief remarks of the leading Bombay journal, which savour of impartiality

the period between November 21 and December 2 was devoted to visiting Poona and Mahableshwar, as the guest of Lord and Lady Reay (the popular Governor of Bombay seeming determined to honour Sir Alfred Lyall), accompanied by Mr. Miller, his private secretary.

and knowledge of the subject:—"The first five years of his career were spent in the North-West Provinces, the heart, as he said on parting, of the Empire, and a sound and well-regulated heart." Again, "No one can read," as Sir John Edge said, "the 'Old Pindar,' or the 'Fakir of Delhi,' or the 'Asiatic Studies,' without seeing, not only that the author was a poet and a scholar, but a man who had studied and understood the people amongst whom he had lived." His work during the most important five years of his life included the Oudh Rent Bill, the establishment of the Allahabad University, the Councils' Act, the extension of the High Court to Oudh, and the construction of 1,300 miles of railway. It can now be said that there is scarcely a village in the Provinces that is forty miles from a railway. In short, Sir Alfred Lyall's whole career tells us of "sound work honestly performed by a man of the highest capacity."* It must candidly be confessed that very few of our public men in England come near such a standard of excellence and good work as the subject of this notice, and some of our most distinguished Anglo-Indians. True enough, they have not the field or opportunity, and, as before hinted, they have not the independence of action so requisite to effect unlimited work, and achieve vast distinction.

SIR STEUART COLVIN BAYLEY, K.C.S.I., C.I.E.

(LIEUTENANT-GOVERNOR OF BENGAL.)

APPOINTED from Haileybury; arrived in India 4th March, 1856; Assistant Magistrate and Collector, 24 Pergunnahs, November, 1856; Junior Secretary to Government of Bengal, February, 1863; officiated as Secretary to the Government of Bengal in 1865, 1867, and 1871; Magistrate and Collector, First Grade, Monghyr, February, 1867; Officiating Civil and Sessions Judge, May, 1867; Commissioner, Dacca Division, July, 1873, and subsequently of the Patna Division, Septem-

* *Times of India*, December 9, 1887.

ber, 1873; Secretary, Government of Bengal, May, 1877; Additional Secretary, Government of India, Financial Department, August, 1877; Personal Assistant to H.E. the Viceroy, for Famine Affairs, September, 1877; Additional Secretary, Government of India, Public Works Department, Famine Branch, December, 1877; Secretary, Government of India, Home Department, June, 1878; Officiating Chief Commissioner, Assam, June, 1878, also Officiating Lieutenant-Governor of Bengal, July–November, 1879; Chief Commissioner of Assam, June, 1880; Resident, First Class, Hyderabad, March, 1881; Governor-General's Council, 9th May, 1882. To this record may be added—April 2, 1887, Lieutenant-Governor of Bengal. He was, it may also be remarked, towards the end of 1886, deputed to Hyderabad,—the chief question engaging his attention being the Council of State.* In the sketch of Sir Ashley Eden, our readers will have made some slight acquaintance with Sir Steuart Bayley, who evidently, on his gaining the same high post, firmly resolved to do his duty as well as his very able and zealous master had done it. Succeeding a Lieutenant-Governor like Sir Rivers Thompson rendered the task less easy than it would otherwise have been. And the same remark may be applied to the successor of Sir Alfred Lyall. But, on the whole, it seems fairly certain that two better men could not have been chosen for their high posts than Sir Steuart Bayley in Bengal, and the present ruler in the North-West Provinces. All that is required now is simply to give them time to complete the great work they have commenced, and leave criticism to a more convenient season, which cannot be for two or three years to come. We, like Hindus and other Asiatics, are too often impatient in such matters. It is no use to judge the merits of your driver while he sits, arrayed in his best, on the box. You must wait till the gallant greys, or whites, or browns, are set in motion, when we shall be able to see how the sturdy coachman handles the ribbons and keeps the team in hand.

* Lord Dufferin, during his visit to Hyderabad (1886), did much to smooth matters between Sir Salar Jung, the 2nd, and the Nizam (*lit.* putter in order) of Hyderabad.

During a long and useful career, in high and difficult situations, it is something for Sir Steuart Bayley to have pleased such Viceroys as Lords Northbrook and Lytton (afterwards Earls), the Marquis of Ripon, and Earl Dufferin.

Having thus casually mentioned the names of our energetic and brilliant Viceroy and his predecessor, it may be remarked that an Anglo-Indian politician of Sir Steuart's knowledge of Indian affairs must have read with pleasure and interest what Lord Dufferin said at Rawul Pindi (November 30) during his tour. The local chronicler writes:—

"Lord Dufferin arrived here to-day from Peshawur. In reply to an address from the Municipality, his Excellency reminded his hearers that the city was, two years ago, the scene of the memorable interview between the Ameer of Afghanistan and himself. That interview had contributed in a powerful degree to the accomplishment of a difficult task, namely, the settlement of the Afghan Boundary. It was right for him to state that the negotiations with that object were commenced under the auspices of his distinguished predecessor, the Marquis of Ripon, who had also been the first to strongly urge the despatch of an invitation to the Ameer to visit India. The Viceroy added that to the moderation and good sense of the Ameer the success of the negotiations was largely due." *

* *Standard*, 1st December, 1887. His Lordship arrived in Calcutta from Benares, 17th December, 1887. Shortly before going to press, the announcement came upon the public (February 9, 1888), producing surprise and deep regret, that Lord Dufferin, from private reasons, intended to resign the Viceroyship at the end of the year, to be succeeded by the Marquis of Lansdowne. His chief acts are thus summed up by a very able authority:—The annexation of Burma; the settlement of the Afghan Boundary dispute; the increase and improved organization of the army; the extension of railways on the frontier; the creation of a line of frontier defence. "These are events which would distinguish any Viceroyalty; their consequences are not temporary; they will cause his reign to stand out hereafter as a marked, and even a brilliant, epoch in the history of India." A distinguished Anglo-Indian editor in London also wrote that the feeling of all classes in India to-day is possibly best expressed in the well-known lines:—

> "As in a theatre, the eyes of men,
> After a well-graced actor leaves the stage,
> Are idly bent on him that enters next."

And now it may be said that peace reigned—as far as in India and the East it is possible to reign—from Peshawur to Bengal.

As his first year is not yet up, Sir Steuart Bayley must still be designated—and we must all wish his government to be a great success—

THE NEW LIEUTENANT-GOVERNOR.

It is amusing, if not instructive, to read some of the local notices of the new Lieutenant-Governor and his predecessor. "Bengal is now (middle of April, 1887) in a critical condition. No one will be able to govern it, unless he is clever, impartial, and possessed of good character. The Anglo-Indians will feel offended if he is favourably inclined to natives. If he sides with the Anglo-Indians he will lose the respect of the natives. Now what is to be done? He ought to act considerately, impartially, and fearlessly, without leaning to either side. He will not then be to blame if any party feels offended." Such is the candid opinion of the *Shome Probash*.—Again, in a spirit of warning, a rather more personal critic appears on the stage; but no one can deny his intelligence. "There cannot be any doubt as regards Sir Steuart Bayley's abilities. But, without disrespect to him, it may be doubted whether he will be able to please the Bengalis in every way. Sir Rivers Thompson at the time of his departure said that it was difficult to satisfy all classes of people in this vast Empire. How can all classes be satisfied? The English, as a rule, are lovers of their own nationality. But Sir Rivers Thompson proceeded too far in this respect, and became unpopular. His example may serve as a lesson to Sir Steuart." Well might Sir Rivers have said, on seeing this, "Is it not delightful?" following up the remark with Canning's famous line—as regards the able writer in the *Nababibhakar and Sadharani*—

"Save me, O save me from my candid friend!"

But yet a third appears—the most severe of all: "When Sir Rivers Thompson became Lieutenant-Governor of Bengal many hoped that the Bengalis would be benefited. After five years the Bengalis found that they never had such a mischievous and worthless ruler. Whether our new Lieutenant-Governor will do us good or harm is in the womb of the future. If he does us no good, we may ascribe it either to the ill-luck of the Bengalis or to the soil of Belvidere." * Comment on this judge is unnecessary. Truly, in Bengal, as elsewhere,—

"Uneasy lies the head that wears a crown!"

SIR LEPEL HENRY GRIFFIN, K.C.S.I.

THE following record of the services of this distinguished Anglo-Indian is a very brief one; and we are not the less pleased to repeat it because it is that of a brilliant "Competition-wallah":—

Appointed to the Bengal Civil Service after open competitive examination of 1859; served in the Punjab as Assistant Commissioner; Under-Secretary to Government of Punjab, 1871; Superintendent of Kapurthala State, 1877; Deputy Commissioner, Lahore, 1878; Secretary to Government of Punjab, Civil Department, 1879; Agent to Governor-General, Central India, 1882. He must indeed have been a careless observer of Indian affairs during the last few years who will not be ready to confess that Sir Lepel Griffin is, in many respects, one of the most extraordinary Indian men of the time. His physical energy, as well as his powers of writing and expounding, appear to be unlimited. He is a man of very strong convictions, and has the courage of his opinions far above the majority of his fellow-men. We can easily imagine such a gifted official's views not always being palatable to the higher authorities; but "It is just like Lepel Griffin," answers every objection to the forward march of the man's ever-working intellect. So far back as October, 1886—a long time in the life of such a public man—when it was fully thought that he would succeed Sir Charles

* The residence of the Lieutenant-Governor of Bengal.

Aitcheson as Lieutenant-Governor of the Punjab, it was remarked by a shrewd and experienced authority—"Lepel Griffin is a man of brains and energy, who would have found opportunities to bring himself to the front, even had Fortune been adverse to him, which she has not been. As Lieutenant-Governor of the Punjab he will be the strong man in the right place, especially at this time, when dangers threaten our North-West Frontier of India." The dangers, like everything Eastern, of course were magnified; Sir Lepel Griffin did not become the ruler of the Punjab, but was with the mighty chief, the Maharajah Holkar, on the visit to the Abbey on the great Jubilee day instead, and in England as in India, doing everything, and being everywhere. He may have employed some of his leisure during a short furlough—although on a high duty, and not strictly on furlough—in translating a verse or two of one of the pleasing skits of the day into idiomatic Hindustani or Persian.* It has been said that Sir Lepel Griffin has frequently been misunderstood; he has even been thought by some foolish people to be an arrant coxcomb or an idler, "simply because he thoughtit wise to laugh at fools, and to answer them, as King Solomon advised, according to their folly." It is impossible to contemplate such an Anglo-Indian without wondering at his ubiquity and constant usefulness. He opens libraries or institutes, settles disputes, and writes Minutes with equal ease.

Although you may greatly differ from his opinions—which cannot be always sound—on men and things, Oriental and otherwise, you cannot help admiring him for his courage and so firmly standing on the pedestal of purpose. This latter attitude has recently been strongly brought out in his famous speech at Gwalior in December, 1887. We venture

* Such a verse, for instance, as the following, which loyal Englishmen as well as Eastern princes (especially Mahomedan) were sure to admire:—

> "The Princesses rode seven by seven;
> And they looked like angels out of Heaven,
> As they rode to the Abbey on the great Jubilee day!"

From the amusing "Jubilee Guide" of a popular London evening journal, June, 1887.

to think that such a speech would not have been possible by a Civil servant under the old East India Company. It is in some respects one of the boldest and cleverest, though most imprudent, speeches in Indian annals. There is a wonderful flow of language, all meaning something; and it is better than a great many of the speeches we hear from public men at home. The occasion was an important one, being the ceremony of laying the foundation-stone of the New Free Library and Museum which the Council of Regency had resolved to build at Lashkar, the capital of the Gwalior State, when Sir Lepel Griffin was asked to preside. He was received in the Durbar tent with the usual pomp and ceremony. Rajah Sir Ganpat Rao Khattney, K.C.S.I., President of the Council of Regency, addressed a few words to Sir Lepel Griffin and the company present. In reply Sir Lepel read a speech in English, which was afterwards read in Mahratti by Ramchunder Vithal, Secretary to the Council. It is necessary to give the speech in full, as it would be simply ruined by curtailment. He said :—

MAHARAJAH SAHEB, NOBLES AND GENTLEMEN,—The building of which the first stone is laid to-day, in presence of your Highness and so many of the principal citizens of Lashkar, will, I trust, form in future the focus and centre of the active intellectual life of this large, flourishing, and rapidly increasing city. I understand that this ceremony is not held on the real site of the proposed library; but in these days of change, when the foundations of so many things that we hold sacred are shaken and removed, we must not be surprised if foundation-stones share the general mutability. I remember seeing the late Viceroy, Lord Ripon, lay the foundation-stone of Municipal Hall at Bombay some years ago; but after the ceremony, the stone was removed and has never yet found a peaceful and final resting-place. But we have good assurance that the stone we provisionally lay to-day will be more fortunate, and that you will ere long see arise in the heart of the city a beautiful and stately building, combining within its walls a public library, reading-rooms, and museums, free to all the respectable citizens of Lashkar. No object can be more worthy, or more certain, to increase the happiness and enlightenment of all; and there is no ceremony in which I can with more confidence invite our beloved young prince to take part than one which will teach him to take pleasure in the happiness of his subjects. I hope that the public library which is now to be formed will be worthy of the Gwalior State and the Maharajah. You should have a collection of all famous Sanskrit books and manuscripts, so that your pandits may be able to study and expound their ancient religion, and teach to the

Brahmin youths the beautiful and interesting Sanskrit language with which all the great languages of Europe and India are connected, and from which many have directly descended. You must have a complete collection of Mahratta books, as is fitting in a Mahratta capital; and I hope that learned men will be encouraged, by suitable endowments and rewards, to write new original Mahratta works, and to translate English books into their native language. You must have a Persian library, the most cultivated of the modern languages of the East; and a careful selection of English books, both in science and literature, as it is from the West for many years to come that the people of India must take new ideas, and learn to make their own the wonderful discoveries in art and science which have given European countries their strength and civilization. The public libraries and reading-rooms which we found to-day are but a supplement to the Victoria College, named in honour of the Empress of India, which is now being built, which will accommodate five hundred pupils, and which will be one of the most beautiful and commodious buildings ever erected in India. The Gwalior State has not hitherto borne a high reputation for learning; but it rests with the Council of Regency and the able men associated with the administration to remove this reproach. The English language has been especially neglected, and, although at Indore almost all the high officials speak English fluently, it is the exception in Gwalior to find an official who is acquainted with English. I have been accused by some enthusiastic supporters of high education with being opposed to the teaching of English to natives of India; but, in reality, there is no warmer advocate of English education than myself. All that I urge is that English ideas and English education should be imparted with discretion; and that, when they are imbibed unwisely, they are apt to have the effect of too much wine in intoxication, and a bad headache the following day. It is foolish, in my opinion, to teach English to peasants and artisans, who have to work with their hands for a living, like their fathers before them, and whom an education above their station only renders bad workmen and discontented subjects. In England, every gentleman is expected to know the French language; but we do not teach French to our ploughmen and grooms. So English should in India be confined to the higher castes, who are accustomed to office and literary work, and who may have to take their share in the administration of the country. In India all classes have their assigned place, and only foolish people hope to see the triumph of what is called in Europe democracy, and what would signify in India confusion, anarchy, and the ruin of society. I especially desire to see you, Mahratta gentlemen and your sons, studying English; because I have a great affection for the Mahrattas, and great admiration for their intelligence and spirit. No race is more highly gifted than the Mahrattas; and for intellectual capacity I place them first among the people of India. In the Deccan they have distinguished themselves by their acquirements in Oriental and English learning, and they are not only apt to learn, but they have the more valuable qualities of moderation and sobriety of judgment. This is what makes them loyal subjects of the Queen, as well as useful critics of Government measures, and what the Mahrattas of the Deccan are doing I want you, Mahrattas of Gwalior, to do. Come to the front, remember your past national history, try again to show yourselves a nation, worthy to take an honourable and honoured place in the annals of India. This is well within your power, if you accept the education of the West with its system of enlightenment and just government. We do not desire to extinguish your national sentiment, but to encourage and strengthen it. It is not much more than a year ago that, under the orders of his Excellency the Viceroy, I placed the Council of Regency in power, and organized the entire administration of this State. But you all know well that we have done nothing to impair the strength and national character of Gwalior. We have left all authority in Mahratta hands: the few officers whom I have brought here, at the request of the Council, have been Mahrattas; the old system of administration has been preserved. All that we have done has been to insist on a removal of abuses, and that progress shall be real and substantial. The Government has no fear of a national spirit in the people: on the contrary, nothing could be a greater source of strength to it than this worthy pride of race and country in Mahrattas, Sikhs, and Rajpoots. We know that all of you, who can see with your eyes and hear with your ears, know that we are your true and disinterested friends, and the Government consequently rejoices that you should love your own country and take pride in its history. One of the reasons for which I urge you, Mahrattas, to utilize the educational advantages which we offer you, is, that you may take your rightful intellectual place in India and keep the Bengalis, who are now everywhere very active, in their proper place. You are their superiors in ability, in strength, and in courage. They are only your superiors in noise and volubility. If they should be your leaders, it would be an army of lions commanded by grasshoppers. If you look at the history of the world you will find that strong nations, like the English, Mahrattas, Rajpoots, and Sikhs, were never ruled by weak and unwarlike races like the Bengalis. Courage is the quality which governs the world, and the bravest people are everywhere and justly triumphant. Do not, then, allow the Bengalis to deceive you with their talk about national congresses and representative institutions. Be content with your own Mahratta nationality, and believe me that representative institutions are as much suited to India as they are to the moon. India is composed of many different nations, with very little in common, and it is as foolish to hope to unite them as to join in one nation Russians, Frenchmen, and Englishmen, who are more closely connected by civilization and descent than the various peoples of India. The so-called National Congress is a sham, and the delegates are only appointed by themselves and their friends. Hindus of position and authority will not join it; and the only Mahomedans who attend are a few obscure and notoriety-seeking persons. How do you believe that anything national can come out of a meeting where the chief promoters have lost their own nationality, and have adopted the dress and food and ways of foreigners? My advice to you, Mahrattas, is to distrust natives of

India who have given up their caste and their national dress. Cherish and observe your ancient and noble religion. Cherish and observe strictly your rules of caste, which missionaries and philanthropists tell you is a bad thing, but which is in reality the mortar which holds together the building of Indian society. If you take it away, nothing will be left but ruins. There are many bad and inconvenient things in caste, but its advantages are greater than its evils. We cannot have perfection; and if we destroyed everything that was not perfect we should have to get rid of all our friends, and possibly make away with ourselves. Maharajah Saheb, I have only one word more to say. This public library, now to be built, is only one among many buildings designed to beautify your capital of Lashkar. Colleges, hospitals, serais, guest-houses, and other public buildings, all beautiful in design, and adorned by the wonderful stone carving which is the pride of Gwalior, are rising everywhere around. Public gardens, for the comfort and delight of the citizens, are being laid out, and I prophesy that when you, Maharajah, come to the gaddi, Lashkar will be one of the most beautiful cities of India, far more beautiful than Jeypore, and a place which all travellers will come to visit. I shall not see these things, for I am leaving India very shortly; but I hope that you, Maharajah, and my Mahratta friends present, will not forget me, and will sometimes associate my name and memory with these important works, as well as with the restoration of the famous fortress of Gwalior to Mahratta hands. I thank Rajah Sir Ganpat Rao and the Council of Regency publicly before the Maharajah and the Resident of Gwalior, and this great assembly, for the patriotic, loyal, intelligent, and liberal spirit in which they have carried on the administration, and have been anxious and eager to further and encourage every scheme for the good of the people. When I recommended their appointments to his Excellency the Viceroy, I had confidence in their goodwill and success; but the results they have achieved have surpassed my expectations, and I wish publicly to acknowledge their services.

It may be noticed that in his speech Sir Lepel Griffin, for the first time, publicly announces his intention to leave India shortly, which was understood to mean during the cold weather of 1887–88.

About a fortnight before the above remarkable speech (November 17), Sir Lepel Griffin had formally opened the new Victoria Library at Indore, whence he had reached Gwalior *viâ* Ajmere and Agra.

Criticism had now to follow Sir Lepel's great oratorical effort, powerful enough, one might think, to cause a war among the races. It was clearly impolitic to bring forward such a forcible comparison between two so intensely different as the Bengali and the Mahratta. The talented speaker had expressed "some very strong political convictions in very trenchant and bitter language." For this he could hardly be blamed; for bitter language everywhere is the order of the day, especially with men of strong convictions. And we must look to what we hear at home if we would learn to out-venom all the worms of Nile. About the so-called "National Congress" being "a sham," at the end of December, it was declared by a leading authority in Calcutta, regarding the forthcoming Native Congress at Madras,* that the so-called native public opinion in India is "in many instances, and in nearly all political matters, simulated, insincere, and fictitious."

It was probably this feeling which made the Bengal Mahomedans decline to be represented. Sir L. Griffin's "Counterblast" is partly accounted for by his having been for some time bitterly and scandalously assailed by a portion of the Bengali Press. "Fortunately for him," says the writer already quoted, "his Indian career is practically closed, otherwise it would be doubtful whether, though equipped as he is with unbounded audacity, he would have dared to affront the hyper-sensitive vanity of the political spoilt infant of the Indian Government."

Gwalior was also signalized in December by the exceptional honour of a salute of nine guns, in British territory, being granted to Rajah Sir Ganpat Rao Khattney, K.C.S.I., President of the Gwalior Council of Regency, in recognition of his wise and energetic administration of the Gwalior State. With the exception of ruling chiefs, no native gentleman since the late highly-distinguished Sir Salar Jung of Hyderabad had been the recipient of such an honour.

A special meeting of the Council of Regency was held at the Council Chamber, Lashkar, on December 21, which was attended by Sir Lepel Griffin, K.C.S.I., Agent to the Governor-General for Central India, Colonel Bannerman, the Resident, and Mr. Ramsay, Political Assistant. After thanking the members of the Council individually for the able manner

* The Native Congress was to meet at Madras on December 27 (1887), when it was expected that 600 delegates would be present.

in which they had assisted the efforts being made for the improvement of the administration of the State, Sir Lepel Griffin informed the President of the great honour which had been conferred upon him by the Queen on the recommendation of his Excellency the Viceroy. A salute was shortly after fired in honour of the occasion.

It is sad to think that while the Gwalior State was winning so much real glory, in this same month of December a last scene took place near its close. The promising young Maharajah Scindia had passed away, and, on December 28, his remains were formally consigned to the Ganges.

No grand chief of the famous old House, young or old, ever had a more able or more faithful servant than Sir Lepel Griffin; and there can be no doubt that there are points about him which even Sevajee, the founder of the Hindu warlike race, and Scindia, our immortal Wellington's enemy at Assaye, would have greatly admired.

Let us now turn for a moment to Burma. A few years before, when affairs looked by no means satisfactory in Afghanistan, Sir Lepel Griffin was considered a political necessity. At the end of 1886, people began to write and talk about him and Burma, just previous to the grandest stroke of policy in Lord Dufferin's administration. As we have said elsewhere, Lord Dalhousie knew it would come; and, doubtless, he believed that the only wise stroke possible would fall long before it did come. A plan was announced for the permanent administration of Burma, after the termination of General Sir F. Roberts's campaign, which was to include Sir Lepel Griffin at Mandalay as Lieutenant-Governor; and Brigadier-General White—a distinguished officer—was to be left in military command. In opposition to this plan, however, which would have placed him over a new country of which he had little knowledge, Anglo-Indian opinion seemed unanimous in agreeing that Sir Lepel Griffin's claims to the Lieutenant-Governorship of the Punjab were superior to those of any other official; so it was thought that the Viceroy would decide on making the appointment, and leaving Sir Charles Bernard to finish the work *in esse* on the Upper Irawadi. It was even said in

London, a year before this, that had either Sir Richard Temple or Sir Lepel Griffin been sent to Mandalay, most of our early difficulties in the new conquest might have been obviated. Notwithstanding the mention of such distinguished Anglo-Indians—especially Sir Richard Temple—we are not quite sure that such an issue would have, although it might have, been. Ever taking an interest in *Ashé Pyee*, the Eastern, or foremost country, it is impossible to refrain from giving the following notes from a great authority, already quoted:—"Burma has a magnificent future. The obvious way to mitigate the burden imposed upon the Indian finances by the heavy expenditure involved in its pacification would be to raise a Burma loan, guaranteed by the Indian Government. In this way Burma would cease to be an incubus upon Indian revenues, and by 'temporarily discounting her brilliant future,' would be enabled easily to pay her way in the present, and thus to remove 'the only ground of reproach' associated with the annexation." But let us return to Sir Lepel Griffin, in order to bid him "Good-bye"; and we humbly think our readers will now have formed a tolerably correct idea of him. There has been, and is still, a strong combination of energy and universality about the man. It will have been seen how he has been called to the front on emergent occasions; and when he reaches the happy shores of Old England, notwithstanding a few Oriental vagaries, into which the culprit, Over-zeal, may have led him, he may yet be sent, not, of course, to treat with the Pope or to pacify Ireland, but to St. Petersburg, to tell Russia not yet to think of taking India, as Albion's star or power there is very far from being on the decline!

GENERAL SIR ARTHUR MITFORD BECHER, K.C.B.

This experienced and highly meritorious officer, brother of the distinguished and lamented General John Becher, already sketched, died on October 5, at St. Faith's Mede, Winchester, aged seventy-one. He was the sixth son of the late Colonel G. Becher, of the Bengal Light Cavalry. He was born in India in 1816, and married, in 1841, Frances Anne, the third daughter of the late Captain M. W. Ford. He was educated at the Military College, Addiscombe, and entered the army as ensign in 1833. He afterwards served throughout the campaign in Afghanistan in 1839, and was present at the storm and capture of Ghuznee, for which he received a medal. Serving throughout the Sutlej campaign of 1845 and 1846, including the battles of Moodkee, Ferozeshah, and Sobraon, he was appointed brevet-major and aide-de-camp to the Governor-General of India, receiving for his services a medal with two clasps. He also served during the Punjab campaign in 1848 and 1849, including the siege and surrender of Mooltan and the battle of Goojerat. General Becher received, in 1849, the brevet of lieutenant-colonel and a medal with two clasps for his services at Mooltan and Goojerat. He was quartermaster-general of the army from 1852 to 1863, and in that capacity was present with the army headquarters at the siege of Delhi in 1857, when he was severely wounded. He received for his services a medal with clasp, and in 1858 was created a Commander of the Bath. He also commanded the Sirhind Division, from 1865 to 1869, and was made major-general in April 1861, lieutenant-general in June 1870, and general in June 1877.*

Sir Arthur Becher was created a K.C.B. on the 24th of May, 1873; and ere fifteen more years had elapsed another ornament to the distinguished Becher family quietly passed away.

COL. SIR J. U. BATEMAN-CHAMPAIN, K.C.M.G.

An old Cheltonian sent the following particulars in reference to the death† of Colonel Sir John Underwood Bateman-Champain, K.C.M.G., F.R.G.S., of the Royal (late Bengal) Engineers, late Director-in-Chief of the Indo-European Telegraph Department, London.

* *Overland Mail*, October 14, 1887.

† *Overland Mail*, February 11, 1887.

"Sir John Bateman-Champain was the son of the late Lieutenant-Colonel Agnew Champain, of the 9th Regiment, and was born June 22, 1835. He was educated at Cheltenham College, whence he proceeded to the East India Company's Military Seminary, Addiscombe, and passed out first engineer in June, 1853, gaining the Pollock Medal, in addition to the first prizes in fortification, military drawing, civil drawing, and Hindustani. He was gazetted second lieutenant in the Bengal Engineers July 11, 1853, and became first lieutenant July 13, 1857; captain, September 1, 1863; major, July 5, 1872; lieutenant-colonel, December 31, 1878; and brevet-colonel, December 31, 1882. Lieutenant Champain served in the Indian Mutiny campaign, as adjutant of the Bengal Sappers, at the actions on the Hindun, the battle of Budleekeserai, and throughout the siege and capture of Delhi, where he was wounded; he commanded the headquarters' detachment at the taking of Futtehpore Sikree, and in the Agra district, under Colonel Cotton; he served as adjutant at the siege and capture of Lucknow, and was specially employed under Brigadier Douglas in the Gazeepore and Shahabad districts, and was present at the final capture of Jugdespore, and at the pursuit of the rebels to the Kymore Hills, for which he received a medal with two clasps. In 1862 Lieutenant Champain was transferred to the Royal Engineers, and in the same year he accompanied the late Lieutenant-Colonel P. Stewart, R.E., to Teheran on special service, under the British Minister, and later on was employed in Persia on special duty in connection with the telegraphs. In 1870 he assumed the additional name of Bateman, in compliance with the will of his uncle, Thomas Bateman Esq., of Halton Park, Lancaster, to whose property he succeeded. In the following year Captain Bateman-Champain was appointed Director-in-Chief of the Indo-European Telegraph Department, London; and for his services in connection with this department her Majesty conferred on him the K.C.M.G. in December, 1885. In the previous June he had received a sword of honour from the Shah of Persia in recognition of his labours in the establishment of the telegraph in that country. In October, 1882, he was Delegate for British India at the Submarine Cables Protection Conference at Paris. Of late Sir John Bateman-Champain had been suffering from asthma, and to alleviate this he had gone to San Remo, where he passed away on February 1, 1887, in his fifty-second year. He leaves two sons, the eldest of whom is Lieutenant Arthur P. Bateman-Champain, of the Norfolk Regiment."

COL. SIR CHARLES MACGREGOR, K.C.B., C.S.I.

THE death was announced from Cairo, on February 5, 1887, of Sir Charles Metcalfe MacGregor, of the Bengal Staff Corps. This distinguished officer came of a military family, his father having been a major in the Bengal Artillery, and his grandfather, James MacGregor, of the MacGregors of Glengyle, a major-general in the Bengal Cavalry. The late Sir Charles MacGregor was born at Agra on August 12, 1840, and, having been educated at Marlborough College, entered the Bengal Staff Corps when he had attained his sixteenth year. He was promoted to a lieutenancy in 1857, became captain and brevet-major in 1868, major in 1868, brevet lieutenant-colonel in 1869, and brevet-colonel eight years afterwards. He served throughout the whole of the Indian Mutiny, the campaign in China in 1860, and the Bhootan campaign 1864–65, having acted in the latter as brigade-major and deputy assistant quartermaster-general. He also took part in the Abyssinian campaign and was present at the capture of Magdala. He served in 1874 as director of military transport in the Tirhat famine, and in the second Afghan campaign as deputy quartermaster-general on the line of communication in the Khyber, and in the third Afghan war was chief of the staff to Sir F. Roberts and Sir Donald Stewart. He was present in all the actions, and commanded the 3rd Brigade of the Cabul-Candahar field force at the relief of Candahar. In the East Indies he acted as quartermaster-general from 1880 to 1885. During his lengthened career he was several times wounded—once at the action of Bhurmoreghat, in India; twice at the action of Sinho, during the campaign in China; and once again during the Bhootan Expedition. Sir Charles was created a K.C.B. in 1881, and was also a Companion of the Star of India, and a Companion of the Order of the Indian Empire. He was the author of some military works, including "Our Native Cavalry" and "Mountain Warfare." He was twice married—first in 1869, to a daughter of Sir Henry Durand, Lieutenant-Governor of the Punjab; and secondly, in 1883, to the daughter of Mr. Frederick W. Jardine.

This is, we may add, certainly one of the most important military careers it has fallen to our duty to record. Towards the end of 1887, the MacGregor Medal, designed by Mr. Archer, displayed on the obverse a group of Sepoys and a Highlander, and on the reverse a profile head of Sir Charles MacGregor. The members of the illustrious Clan MacGregor may well be proud of the undying fame of their distinguished, chivalrous, and ever-active Anglo-Indian brother, Sir Charles.

SIR J. WEST RIDGEWAY, K.C.S.I.

This is one of the most ubiquitous of our distinguished Anglo-Indians; roaming, as he has done, through all latitudes as easily as a Kalmuc. His fame will rest on his services as the Chief of the Boundary Commission in Afghanistan, to which allusion has already been made by the Viceroy, in his brief speech at Rawul Pindi, during his tour.

Lumsden, Ridgeway, and Yate are names which will live in Indian history; and, probably, that of the clever and versatile opponent to Sir Joseph's work will live also. The different views entertained by Mr. Charles Marvin, and the subject of this notice, will produce their good effect in helping us to view all sides of the question.

Looking back to the days of Peter the Great and Catherine, the idea of a *Boundary* Commission at all seems, at first acquaintance, rather ludicrous. Aggression, or justifiable extension of territory, has always been, and will ever be, the policy of Russia; and we might as well try to keep back the tide of the mighty ocean as endeavour to prevent it.

Early in August, 1887, it was well remarked by a popular London "Society" journal:—"After a lengthy absence at St. Petersburg, Sir Joseph West Ridgeway has returned to London, no doubt in that pleasant state of mind which springs from the consciousness of work satisfactorily accomplished."

Colonel Sir Joseph West Ridgeway, K.C.S.I., C.B., was appointed to succeed Sir Redvers Buller as Under-Secretary for Ireland, and was to take over the duties about October 15, 1887. It was then written that Sir West Ridgeway is the son of the late Rev. Joseph Ridgeway, of Tunbridge Wells (a descendant of Sir Thomas Ridgeway, of Torre Abbey, Torquay, who was created Earl of Londonderry in 1622), and was born in 1844. He entered the Bengal Army in 1861, became captain 1869, major 1880, lieutenant-colonel 1881, and colonel 1885; and he was successively attached to the 20th Regiment, the 98th Regiment, the Rifle Brigade, the 25th Bengal N.I., and the 3rd Goorkhas. Colonel Ridgeway was appointed by the Earl of Mayo to the political service in 1869, and he has been employed in various political posts under successive Viceroys. He served in the Afghan war of 1879-80, being twice mentioned in despatches and receiving the medal and bronze star, after which he was appointed Under-Secretary to the Government of India (Foreign Department). In 1884 he commanded the Indian Contingent of the Afghan Frontier Commission, consisting of 1,100 men, 1,276 camels, and 774 horses, which he conducted to Penjdeh (a distance of 1,052 miles) at the average rate of sixteen miles a day, without loss of life or property, and was thanked for this service by the Viceroy of India and by her Majesty's Government. Colonel Ridgeway was in charge of the Afghan Frontier Commission which was formed in 1885, when he was appointed Commissioner for the Delimitation of the Afghan Frontier. The *Gazette* of September 9 contains the following notice:—"Brevet.—Lieutenant-

Colonel Sir Joseph West Ridgeway, K.C.S.I., Bengal Infantry, to be colonel, in recognition of distinguished service rendered by him while head of the Afghan Boundary Commission, and subsequently as her Majesty's Commissioner at St. Petersburg." Sir J. West Ridgeway married, in 1881, Caroline, daughter of Mr. Calverly Bewicke, J.P., D.L., of Coulby Manor, Yorkshire. He was created K.C.S.I. in 1885.

It may be added, that, at first sight, an energetic Anglo-Indian, fresh from Afghanistan and Russia, acting the part of a Secretary in Ireland, does give the idea of a fish out of water; but this notion vanishes when we think that Erin may have boundary disputes, as well as the country of the Amir, and that *effective boundaries* in the matters of lands and speeches would do much to bring about what is so difficult to great statesmen like Mr. Gladstone and Lord Salisbury, pacification; and thus the gallant Colonel may yet help to obviate the necessity of his ever being required to play the part of a second Oliver Cromwell!

DAVID THOMAS ROBERTS, B.C.S.*

DAVID THOMAS ROBERTS, Magistrate and Deputy Commissioner of Jhansi, entered the Civil Service in 1868, and by the ardour with which he has identified himself with his work, and has laboured to advance the prosperity of the districts to which he has been appointed, he has won the devoted gratitude of the Indian people, as well as the respect and confidence of the Government.

In the year 1879 Baliyâ was made into a separate district and placed under the charge of Mr. Roberts; and the character of this extraordinary man is best illustrated by

* For this Sketch we are indebted to a learned friend—a distinguished Orientalist—who writes:—"I have received several private letters from natives of the N.W. Provinces, who speak of Mr. Roberts in the highest terms of praise. He is one of the good men who hold the natives faithful to the British Râj."

the following translation from a Hindî book, written by Pandit Ravidatta Sukla, for the information of his own countrymen:—"The ancient town of Baliyâ was swept away by the Ganges, and the present town is a new creation, of which Mr. Roberts may be styled the architect. In a place where there were only a few cottages, he has called into existence a noble city, with roads, a market-place, a hospital, an ornamental square, a school, a bridge, public offices, &c. He has ever had a kindly regard for the spread of knowledge, and has converted the village-school of Baliyâ (where formerly only two teachers gave elementary instruction) into a large institution, in which English is taught to 400 pupils, some of whom now compete in the Entrance Examination of the University of Calcutta. Such rapid development as this is not the work of an ordinary man; it is the achievement of one who has secured the cordial support of the native population."

The inhabitants have themselves founded a public library and a charitable dispensary, both of which institutions have been called by Mr. Roberts's name; and, at the ceremony of opening, a native gentleman said, "If her Majesty would send to India such men as Mr. Roberts, native loyalty and attachment to the Imperial Throne of England would be stimulated and strengthened day by day." A man who has called forth such feelings among the people whom he has been appointed to govern, deserves a place among "Distinguished Anglo-Indians."

SUPPLEMENTARY SKETCHES.

—o—

I.

FIELD-MARSHAL SIR WILLIAM MAYNARD GOMM, G.C.B.*

"How youngly he began to serve his country—
How long continued."—CORIOLANUS.

THIS distinguished officer was born in 1784, and died in 1875; thus covering a life over ninety years, and including one of the most interesting and remarkable careers in the whole history of Englishmen who have made their names famous. From the simple fact of Sir William Gomm's having been a steady and useful, rather than a fitful and brilliant, life, we at once learn the cause of his being far from sufficiently well known to British readers of our time; and, again, until the appearance of the goodly volume, edited by Mr. Francis Culling Carr-Gomm, in 1881,† there was no attempt to chronicle the actions of one of the most devoted officers in the Peninsula—a noble and conscientious captain, destined to become Commander-in-Chief of India, a Field-Marshal, and Constable of the Tower of London.

Strange enough, Mr. Carr-Gomm has on his title-page the same motto (which heads this notice) as that we find on the pedestal of Sir John Burgoyne's statue in club-land—another Field-Marshal who stands forth as more useful than

* Contributed by the author of this work to the *Cosmopolitan* (December, 1887)—a new candidate for public favour in British Periodical Literature.

† London : John Murray, Albemarle Street.

brilliant in his long and scientific career. By his excellent work—only a volume of which has as yet appeared, but which evidently contains the cream of the "long eventful history"—the author (for he is more than editor) has proved himself to be an ornament in the literary ranks of the Madras Civil Service. In placing Sir William Gomm, however, in our list of eminent Anglo-Indians, it should be distinctly understood that the admirable Field-Marshal is hardly, strictly speaking, an Anglo-Indian. The term, as a rule, would seem correctly to imply an officer—civil or military—who rose in the munificent old East India Company's service—who, from long residence in the country, the "nursery of captains," was wont to return home too often with a bad liver, though blessed with a good heart!—Seven years in the Mauritius and five in India, then, scarcely constitute an Anglo-Indian, though, in exceptional cases, as has been done by the present writer, some latitude must begiven to the title.

The immense range of such a biography as the present will at once be admitted, when we state that the "Letters and Journals" of the venerable Field-Marshal only reach from 1799 to Waterloo, 1815. It was Mr. Carr-Gomm's intention to leave to some future opportunity "the project of preparing for the public the later voluminous and more general papers." What have been published were arranged by Sir William Gomm himself; but his wife prepared them in some measure for publication. Lady Gomm survived her husband two years, but in that little time did much to celebrate his memory; while the editor has described Sir William's letters as displaying "the well-read scholar, and man of refined feelings and high character." The soldier-boy first comes out on the canvas, in his baptism of fire, or under fire, a few weeks after joining the 9th Regiment, in a bloody engagement with the French among the "Sand dunes of Holland." The same coolness and courage carried him well through every campaign, and almost every battle, from the Helder, Walcheren, and Corunna, to the Lines of Torres Vedras, Bayonne, and Waterloo, which secured the peace of Europe—all of which are more or less fully described in Mr.

Carr-Gomm's pages. Sir William's biography is therefore not only a chapter of his life, but of public history. Of course, in a brief sketch it will not be possible to say much; but we shall endeavour to bring forward some facts and remarks which may please our readers.

Sir William Gomm's life is divided into four distinct periods,—

1. From 1799 to 1816, a purely *active military life.*

2. From 1817 to 1839, *home military life,* when he was promoted from the rank of Lieutenant-Colonel in the Coldstream Guards to that of Major-General. It was during this period that he married his first wife, Sophia Penn, granddaughter of William Penn, the founder of Pennsylvania, who died in 1827.

3. From 1839 to 1856, *colonial administrative life.* From 1839 to 1842 he held the chief command, and was Member of Council at Jamaica during Sir Charles Metcalfe's administration; and he did much for the health of European troops at the time, by establishing in the island the mountain barrack of Newcastle. For nearly a quarter of a century British troops there enjoyed "absolute immunity from yellow fever." On his return, in 1842, Sir William Gomm was gazetted to the command of the Northern District; but in November of the same year he became Governor and Commander-in-Chief in Mauritius, in place of Sir Lionel Smith. Here he remained till 1849. He did much for the famed island,—so well known to us from La Bourdonnais and *Paul and Virginia,*—receiving the thanks of the Treasury at home. From Mauritius he proceeded to Calcutta, having received information from the Horse Guards that he had been appointed Commander-in-Chief in India. He just arrived in time to hear (June 2) that another of the Peninsula captains, and eventually the hero of Meanee, had arrived before him; and that Sir Charles Napier had at once proceeded to the Punjab. Here was an extraordinary state of things, the like of which had probably never happened before.

But Sir William found at Calcutta ample explanations from the Duke of Wellington and Lord Fitzroy Somerset (afterwards Lord Raglan of Crimean celebrity). Such a bitter disappointment had rarely befallen any man; but it had fallen on a mind ever prepared to take life at its true value. He met the blow heroically, as is seen by a memo of July 1849. It should be mentioned that the disastrous battle of Chillianwallah, before it was followed up by the crowning artillery success at Gújerat, enabled the powerful Court of Directors to do battle with the direct patronage of the Crown. They wanted an opportunity; "and," writes Sir William Gomm, "such an opportunity presented itself most prominently in the person of Sir Charles Napier, and India had been the very scene of his successes."

Like a true military philosopher, he found consolation in the fact of his supersessor being considerably his senior in the army, and as such entitled to the preference *in limine*. "It was notorious that a quarrel which Sir Charles Napier had with the Court of Directors had been the only bar to his appointment, in the ordinary course, in succession to the gallant Tipperary Commander-in-Chief, Lord Gough," an obstruction which the panic of the hour at once swept away.

The Duke's famous remark to Napier—"If *you* do not go, sir, *I* must!" will be remembered through *Punch's* famous cartoon, which attracted great attention at the time. The Duke was not frightened by Chillianwallah, nor for India. On this point Mr. Carr-Gomm remarks admirably: "Had he been left to himself he would not have superseded Sir William Gomm in the command to which he had been named; but he was overruled. *Æquam memento rebus in arduis servare mentem* is an old piece of advice, but it is few who can follow it. The Duke did when the news of Chillianwallah staggered England. Sir William Gomm did when the news of his supersession was his welcome to Calcutta." Sir William returned to England in January, 1850; and, in the following August, he was appointed Commander-in-Chief of Bombay. On the eve of starting, however, he was appointed to the chief command in India, Sir Charles Napier having suddenly resigned in consequence of differences with "the boy political," as the irascible warrior, Sir Charles, contemptuously styled the great Proconsul who gave us the Punjab and Pegu.

Sir William Gomm arrived in Calcutta in December; and the five years of his military command in India were comparatively uneventful. Between the second Sikh War and "India's severest trial," the great Mutiny of 1857, there was a decided calm, only to give way to a more decided rebellion, which taxed all our energies. During his Indian career, of course, it was considered probable that, in the event of success in the Crimean War, Russia would cast an eye on India; so, during two years at least, there was ample to occupy the mind of the Commander-in-Chief. At this stage it should be noted regarding the "Calcutta disappointment;" which had now been fully compensated, that one who had shown such a fine instance of patriotic devotion was just the right man in the right place. In December, 1881, a British poet,* alluding to the "disappointment," or "incomparable" sacrifice, wrote two sonnets on Sir William Gomm, the latter concluding with the following lines:—

> O nursling of the sea winds and the sea,
> Immortal England, goddess ocean-born,
> What shall thy children fear, what strengths not scorn,
> While children of such mould are born to thee?

We are now informed that to the wise kind-heartedness of the Commander-in-Chief, as well as to his intimate personal friendship with Lord Dalhousie, were due the cordial relations which existed between the civil and military authorities of that tranquil period. Commenting on this in 1875, a leading London journal commenced its eulogium with the remark: "Sir William Gomm's work was always thoroughly and smoothly done, and he had no enemies." At Simla, Anglo-Indian society could hardly have had a better head than Lady Gomm. With her personal influence and example she indeed worked wonders; and it was truly said that "never was the society of the capital of India in so healthy a state" as when she presided over it.

4. From 1856 to 1875, *dignified and honoured old age.* In 1863 he succeeded Lord Clyde as Colonel of the Coldstream Guards, "the regiment," as Mr. Carr-Gomm says,

* Algernon Charles Swinburne

"to which he had been transferred from the 9th, half a century before, for distinguished services through the Peninsular War." He passed his time either at his cottage in Hampshire, or at Brighton, or at his house in Spring Gardens; in the latter position being near an occasional display of troops, which may have stirred the old fire within him, and produced the wish to march through life again. On January 1, 1868, he received his bâton as Field-Marshal; and on the death of Sir John Burgoyne, in 1871, he became Constable of the Tower of London, on which occasion he was highly complimented by Mr. Gladstone. He rested from his long and arduous labour in the service of his country on March 15, 1875, in the ninety-first year of his age, closing an extraordinary soldier's career of eighty years.

In appearance, Sir William Gomm is described as short and slight; "but though slight he was wiry, and preserved his bodily and mental activity to the last." His passion for music was extreme, and his love of books and reading was great. Sir William also had a good deal of the poetical about him, and, judging from the examples given, he wrote graceful verses. His love of Homer was life-long; and Pope's "Homer" was also one of his father's favourite volumes. "His love of Homer," writes Mr. Carr-Gomm, "was all-pervading, and creeps out in his early letters from the battle-fields of Spain, and in his writings and diaries all through his life." A great love of animals in both Sir William and Lady Gomm is most fully commented on by the able biographer, who spares no pains in bringing out all the amiable as well as the sterner qualities of his hero. In India there is a splendid field for the exercise of this benignant qua ity—perhaps no better on earth.

With reference to his early military inclinations, it should be mentioned that Sir William Gomm's father entered the army, and served with distinction through the American and West Indian Wars from 1776 to 1794. Sir William was born in Barbadoes. To our mind one of the most interesting episodes in his long military career was that when, only twenty-four years of age, he was employed with the undaunted Sir John Moore at Corunna (1808). After the defeat of the whole army of Soult, 20,000 strong, in which victory the brave warrior lost his life, we read that to the 9th Regiment (Gomm's) was consigned "the sad though honourable duty of burying him on that fatal evening. It was they who

> 'Slowly and sadly laid him down,
> From the field of his fame fresh and gory;'

and it was they who were the last of the British force to embark in the darkness of the night. Captain Gomm himself commanded the very last picket." In the gallant Captain's own words: "The last fragment of rear-guard withdrawn from the heights consisted of my own company of the 9th Regiment; the regiment which had just

> 'Buried him darkly at dead of night,
> With his martial cloak around him.'

We were thus the last British remnants (I believe I was the last English fighting man) embarking, and were forced in consequence to thread the whole fleet in the turbid dark in quest of a berth. 'No room, three in a bed all round,' was all the answer we got." At length they got hold of the headquarters store-ship, which had been canonaded by the French from the heights, and which had been carried out of harm's way by a mate and boat's crew from the Admiral's ship. "Oh yes; plenty of room," was now the reply to the delighted captain and his soldiers. The crew had deserted with the compass; but the stout mate and his men were staunch to the last. They arrived in the chops of the Channel. Then came a storm; there was no way of telling their whereabouts. At length, through a miracle, they arrived at Spithead; and the worthy mate was soon after promoted by the Admiralty. Sir William then wrote to his dear sister Sophia—and it must be confessed with some reason—"I lose not a moment in letting you hear of my arrival at Spithead this morning (January 26, 1809) in a very crazy ship."

Sir William's last visit to the field of Waterloo (though

as late as 1871 he drove past Quatre Bras) was in his eighty-fifth year, in the summer of 1868, in company with Lady Gomm, Miss Howard Vyse, and his niece (afterwards Mrs. Carr-Gomm).

The two portraits, given in Mr. Carr-Gomm's work,* may be considered striking and suggestive likenesses,—the youth in the honoured decorated uniform, which we see in the old miniatures, at the age of thirty, the knowledge that he had achieved "the bubble reputation" beaming on his manly face; and the veteran Field-Marshal of eighty-four, with his numerous decorations, and a visage belonging to one every inch a soldier, which had been in many a hard-fought field long before entering on an unusally protracted spell of gentler work, with which Sir William Gomm closed a most useful and well-spent life.

* Reproduced in the *Cosmopolitan.*

II.

SIR ROPER LETHBRIDGE, C.I.E., M.P. FOR NORTH KENSINGTON.

WE have much pleasure in being able to present a brief sketch of a distinguished retired Uncovenanted Civil servant —a well-known literary, able, and hard-working Anglo-Indian—to our readers.

Mr. Lethbridge was born at Plymouth in 1840. He won a Scholarship at Exeter College, Oxford, and graduated from that College in Double (Classical and Mathematical) Honours, having been First Class in Moderations in Mathematics. He entered as a student of the Inner Temple in 1864; but before he was called, he was selected by Sir Stafford Northcote for a Professorship in the Presidency College of the Calcutta University, in 1868. In the autumn of that year he was appointed Professor of Mathematics, and also Professor of History and Political Economy, in the Kishnaghur College, Bengal; and was elected Examiner in History for the Premchand Roychand Studentship of the Calcutta University. Early in 1870 he was transferred to the Professorship of English Literature, to which was also attached the Professorship of History and Political Economy in the Hugli College; and contributed to the proceedings of the Bengal Asiatic Society an account of the ancient Dutch records of Chinsurah. In 1871 he became Editor of the *Calcutta Quarterly Review*, a post which he held till 1878, a longer period than that of any other Editorship—a post in which he followed Sir John Kaye and Sir Richard Temple. During the years 1869 to 1877 he was every year elected to an Examinership in the University of Calcutta—he was Examiner for the Staff Corps and for the Financial Department—and was Professor of English Literature, Professor of History and Political Economy, Professor of Mathematics, and Professor of Mental and Moral Philosophy in the Kishnaghur, Hugli, and Presidency Colleges of the Calcutta University; and in 1874 he became Principal of the Kishnaghur College. In the beginning of 1877 he was selected to prepare the articles on the Native States for the "Imperial Gazetteer," and was also appointed Secretary of the Simla Educational Commission, and Fellow of the University of Calcutta; and soon afterwards was transferred from the Educational to the Political Department, appointed a Political Agent of the First Class, and nominated to the newly-created office of Press Commissioner of India by Lord Lytton. In 1881 the Press Bureau was abolished by Lord Ripon, and Mr. Lethbridge was offered an equivalent appointment elsewhere; but he elected to retire on pension. The subject of our sketch, after much good service, had been created a C.I.E. on the first institution of that Order in January, 1878; and in 1885 he was knighted, on the recommendation of Lord Salisbury, for his "distinguished services in India."

Sir Roper Lethbridge married, in 1865, Eliza, daughter of W. Finlay, Esq., and a grand-niece and one of the coheiresses of the late Right Hon. John, Thirteenth Baron Teynham, of Lynsted Lodge, near Sittingbourne, Kent. Their eldest son, Mr. F. W. Lethbridge, of the Buffs (East Kent Regiment), has lately been appointed to the Bengal Staff Corps.

As M.P. for North Kensington (Middlesex—New Borough) Sir Roper is now afforded many opportunities of doing good service to the electors and his country. From his knowledge of mankind, his zeal and industry, he is beyond doubt a good and faithful servant; and even those who do not go entirely along with him in his political views, cannot withhold a fair share of admiration. In the year 1886 Sir Roper Lethbridge is recorded (C.) 3,394, against Mr. E. Routledge (L.) 2,443; giving a Conservative majority of 951. The population of his constituency is 82,517; the electorate being 8,297. In 1885, the poll stood thus: Lethbridge (C.), 3,619; Firth (L.), 3,011; Conservative majority, 608. As might be expected, Sir Roper is considered a "Progressive Conservative"—the meaning of which is neither more nor less than a Moderate Liberal—not a bad designation in an age in which the law is Progress.

Sir Roper is nearly forty-eight years old, and a member of the Jockey Club.

Towards the end of 1886 we again behold the now energetic M.P. in the Indian land. It was said he was going to make arrangements for the production of an Anglo-Indian journal at home. And it was asked by a popular Anglo-Indian journalist of high authority in this country, "Do none of the papers already published come up to his requirements?" He continued, "If, however, with Sir Roper's gifts of literary skill and official experience, he can produce a paper which will make English readers take a more abiding interest in Indian subjects, we shall not be the last in bidding the new birth a welcome." *A more abiding interest*—"aye, there's the rub!" The majority not taking any interest whatever, would be nearer the truth; and, although a slight improvement is dawning upon us, such wretched apathy or indifference is a shame and a reproach to the general intelligence of Great Britain. As we have remarked again and again, if England were to lose India, with its one-sixth of the human race, to-morrow, the calamity would produce less sensation or regret among a certain educated class than the destruction of the Crystal Palace by an earthquake, or the Alhambra being again destroyed by fire! We boast of the spread of education; but how many of those worthies who seek to shine, and too often seem to delight in sending listeners to sleep, in our great assemblies, if tested by examination, even towards the end of the nineteenth century, could answer, Which is the Malabar Coast, and which the Coromandel? Doubtless, a man of Sir Roper Lethbridge's experience and intelligence is well aware of much geographical and other ignorance regarding our greatest dependency—India, which Clive, and the admirable generals coming after him, conquered; and which Warren Hastings, and the glorious band of hard-working civilians following in his train, duly consolidated. On the 16th of November, 1886, Sir Roper and Lady Lethbridge were entertained at an afternoon party in Bombay, by Khan Bahadur Byramjee Dadabhoy.

Here it was necessary to speak on the popular subject of the day, the celebration of the Queen's Jubilee; and the speaker was quite equal to the august occasion. Sir Roper, in returning thanks for the toast of his health and that of Lady Lethbridge, said:—

Khan Bahadur Byramjee Dadabhoy, Sir Jamsetjee Jeejeebhoy, Mr. Justice Nanabhai Haridas, Ladies and Gentlemen,—I can assure you I am unable to find words adequately to express the gratification of Lady Lethbridge and myself at the exceedingly kind way in which my friend the Khan Bahadur has proposed our health, and the magnificent reception accorded to us this evening. When Mr. and Mrs. Byramjee did us the honour to invite us to this gathering I had no idea that we should find assembled here such a large and distinguished representation of the intellect, the enterprise, and all that is most enlightened and most progressive in Bombay and in India. We are deeply touched at the kindly feelings and the generous impulses which have brought together, to welcome us back to India, the acknowledged and popular head of the Indian community of Bombay—(applause)—and such a notable assemblage of the leaders and chiefs of thought and activity in every section of that community. (Cheers.) The Khan Bahadur has spoken in the kindest terms of some friendly services we were able to render his son Mr. Manickji in England, but this I can say, that the eminently successful career of Mr. Manickji in London—and I am delighted to be able to say so in the presence of parents who may justly be proud of him—has been such as to render quite unnecessary any help and any introductions that his friends could give him. I think it might encourage those young gentlemen here (and I hope there are many) who may be contemplating a visit to Eng-and, to know that Mr. Manickji's marked ability and eloquence, his high and independent character, and his amiable disposition have not only obtained for him the friendship of eminent politicians like Lord Harris and Sir John Gorst, but have also placed him in the honourable position of an elected member of the Council of the East India Association, and in other ways singled him out as a man of mark. Now that he has triumphantly passed his final examination for the Bar, and is about to return to India, I feel perfectly sure that a high and useful career awaits him in this country, and I am confident that you, gentlemen, will watch that career with interest and sympathy. (Cheers.) This Indian tour of my wife and myself, which has opened so agreeably to-day, has been undertaken with a twofold object. In the first place, we have come out to revisit old and beloved scenes, to awaken cherished memories, and to renew communion with old and dear friends. Of these latter, most are of course natives of the other side of India, where my own service and Lady Lethbridge's residence mainly lay, and I need not tell you we are looking forward to our visit to Bengal, where we received so many kindnesses of old; but after your reception this evening, I am sure we may be permitted to feel that, if it should please God to spare us again to revisit India, it will not be only in Bengal that we shall look up old and true friends. Then, too, we have come to enable me profitably to take part in the Parliamentary discussions on Indian affairs that are to take place in the House of Commons next session. In a friendly social gathering like this it would ill become me to enter into politics; but this I may say, that my great desire in Parliament—and it is a desire heartily approved of by my constituents in North Kensington and by the great heart of the British nation—is to render some real and true service to India, and to the peoples of India to whom I owe so much. I desire, if you will permit me—and I say this with all frankness and sincerity—to present your views and your wishes, the intelligent opinions and the just aspirations of the most enlightened communities of India, honestly and fearlessly to the impartial arbitrament of the British Parliament. (Loud cheers.) Pending the return to Parliament of capable representatives actually born in this country—a result which I ardently desire to see, and which such a gathering of able citizens as the present leads me to hope for in the not distant future—I venture to ask you to look upon me as a loyal spokesman of yours in the House of Commons. And let us not forget that the year on which we are about to enter will be one of especial interest to all those subjects of her Most Gracious Majesty who are imbued with that ardent spirit of loyalty for which you gentlemen of Bombay are so renowned. It will be the happy and glorious Jubilee of her Majesty's reign (cheers); and before I sit down I should like to advert to two movements in connection with that Jubilee, which I know will obtain your heartiest sympathy, and which I believe will have the happiest results for the future well-being of India. One of those movements, originated by the far-seeing and warm-hearted benevolence of her Excellency the Countess of Dufferin, aims at a celebration of the Queen's Jubilee in a way most pleasing to her Majesty's true womanly heart, by providing sorely needed medical help for the women of India. That movement has already taken deep root among us, both here and in England, and it eminently deserves your warmest interest. (Cheers.) And the other Jubilee celebration of which I would speak is a movement of similar national importance, and one from which I venture to predict a great increase of commercial prosperity for India, as well as a considerable enhancement of the prestige and dignity of India, her princes and her peoples, among the great civilized communities of the world. I need not say I refer to the proposal graciously made by his Royal Highness the Prince of Wales, and already enthusiastically taken up and adopted in London and in the colonies, for the celebration of the Jubilee of her Majesty by the establishment in the heart of the empire of a permanent Imperial Indian and Colonial Institution, to be the focus and centre of the industries, the arts, the learning, and, indeed, generally of the commercial, industrial, and scientific enterprise of the whole of the vast dominions of our beloved sovereign. The way has been admirably smoothed for such an institution by the very successful Exhibition of the past year. The ephemeral attractions of the Exhibition as a place of entertainment have brought together millions of Europeans and Americans of all classes, and interested them in the products and resources of our Empire; and now that those attractions have served their purposes, they will, of course, cease with the closing of the Exhibition. But if, by the fostering care of our patriotic Prince of Wales, and by the spontaneous loyalty to her Majesty of the princes and peoples of the empire, the instructive commercial and ethnographical elements of the Exhibition should be rendered permanent, and developed into a vast Imperial Institution, I am sure you will agree with me in believing that its establishment will mark a new era in the economic and scientific progress of the empire. And now, ladies and gentlemen, while heartily thanking you for the kindness with which you have listened to these few remarks of mine, I will end where I began, and beg to assure you, on behalf of Lady Lethbridge as well as myself, that this afternoon will ever remain a very bright spot in our memories, and that we shall cherish the remembrance of the great honour you have done us to the last day of our lives. (Cheers.)

A few days before this interesting and appropriate speech was made, His Excellency the Viceroy, being on his tour, had landed at Bombay, and was received by a distinguished company.

Lord Dufferin, on November 17th, received the visits of the Maharajah Holkar of Indore, and the Maharajah of Rutlam, at Government House, Malabar Point. His Excellency paid return visits to the two Maharajahs in the afternoon; and on the same evening distributed the prizes to the successful students of the Bombay School of Art. After an admirable speech, in which His Excellency praised the drawings and other works of the students, as displaying great talents and abilities, His Lordship concluded in his usual masterly way: "I can only express my regret that the director of this establishment should have been flattered by the presence of the Retrenchment Commission; but I can assure the authorities of the Bombay School of Art that, at all events in my person, they will always have some one to plead for them, and I am in hopes it will eventually be found that the bark of these excellent gentlemen who have been examining the financial condition of our Indian establishments will be worse than their bite." (Applause.)

Thus was Bombay honoured at the same time with the presence of a brilliant Viceroy and that of an Anglo-Indian, an able and zealous member of the all-powerful House of Commons. Such visits cannot be without good effect. Simple "globe-trotters" spend money wherever they go, true enough; but the visits of men of mark, however brief, especially in India, cause new views of things to be brought before a craving and ingenious people, with the chance of more money being spent as well.

On the 3rd of December, 1886, the Duke and Duchess of Manchester and Lady Alice Montague arrived at Hyderabad, as the guests of the Resident (John Graham Cordery, M.A.); Sir Roper and Lady Lethbridge arrived on the 4th, and the Earl of Fife was expected on the following day. In the old Company's time, flying trips to India would have been considered almost miraculous. But there is now every chance of such visits to the Eastern dominions of the Queen-Empress becoming popular among us, which must come to good.

Sir Roper Lethbridge must have taken back with him to England pleasant recollections of his visit to India. We should mention that, in 1886, we find him on a tour in the auriferous districts of Southern India*—ever with the name of action; and so it is with pleasure we look upon him as the educationist, the literary man, the traveller, and the M.P. In the latter capacity there is yet much good work to be done; but there is little or no fear about his doing it faithfully and well. Twenty, instead of half-a-dozen, earnest and able Anglo-Indians are required in the House of Commons. The two well-known distinguished veteran Sir Georges (Balfour and Campbell) cannot last for ever. The ubiquitous, shrewd, and versatile Baronet, Sir Richard Temple, must eventually retire from the public stage. Eng-

* *See* note..

land may then be forced to ask the question, regarding India: We want more, and, if possible, better actors; but where are the men?

NOTE.

THE GOLD-FIELDS OF SOUTHERN INDIA.

Under the auspices of the East India Association a meeting of gentlemen interested in the commercial affairs of the British Empire in the East was held at Exeter Hall on January 19, Lord Harris presiding, for the purpose of considering the recent new departure in the development of Indian gold-mining. The principal address was given by Sir Roper Lethbridge, C.I.E., M.P., late Press Commissioner in India, who furnished elaborate particulars of his recent tour in the auriferous districts of Southern India. He pointed out that the great and all-important difference between the Australian gold-fields and those of India is to be found in the fact that when the former were discovered they had hardly been trodden by human foot, whereas the latter have been the seat of a dense population and of a high civilization from time immemorial. In Australia the English and Californian diggers found the gold much as Nature had left it, not only in the rocky matrix, but cast up and expressed in the form of nuggets, and permeating great alluvial deposits or "placers." In India centuries of industrious toil and minute research have long ago removed all surface gold; wherever the old miners could get out the auriferous quartz by quarrying they have done so, and the only limits imposed on them have been due to their ignorance of those engineering appliances by which mines are drained, ventilated, &c., as well as of those chemical means by which the ores are treated. On the other hand, the gold-bearing rocks of India seem to be, on an average, far richer than those of Australia or America; and it is now fully established on official evidence, and from innumerable private investigations, that many of the auriferous reefs of Mysore, even at shallow depths, can yield one, two, and even three ounces per ton on an average of large quantities of crushings. Gross mismanagement, ignorance, and criminal extravagance ruined the credit of the enterprise in its early days, and Sir Roper Lethbridge expressed his conviction that, with honest work and good management, a period of great prosperity and profits await the miners in at least thirty of the gold-fields of Southern India. A discussion followed, in which the views of the opener were generally supported, and the proceedings closed with the customary votes of thanks.—*Overland Mail*, January 20, 1888.

In our *First Series*, at the beginning, were given a few slight sketches from the old East India House; in our *Second*, at the end, the writer begs leave to present his readers with a sketch of, not an Anglo-Indian, but a remarkable messenger of the new palatial India Office—

LORD BYRON'S "TITA":

A SKETCH FROM THE INDIA OFFICE.*

Soon after *Tita's* death, which happened some years ago, it was well remarked in London that the minutest associations connected with Byron should be precious to his countrymen; they should be especially so to our senior Anglo-Indians, who owed so much of their mental recreation in the East to the great poet; and in Tita Falcieri there disappeared a most interesting relic of the Byronic legends.

At the same time it was asked, What was there so very remarkable about the ancient Italian employé (messenger) of the India Office? The reply was simply this, that Tita Falcieri was "Lord Byron's Tita;" and he was with the great poet when he died at Missolonghi, at seven o'clock in the evening, on the 19th April, 1824. To many readers who, unlike one who is supposed to be a well-informed authority on the subject, I am sure are not inclined to look down upon "Lord Byron's servant," as knowing little of the famous poet, while he actually knew more of him than most of his higher-born contemporaries, it has struck the writer that it may be interesting to offer the following remarks, culled from what "Tita" himself related, and from information afforded by one who knew him well in his later years. When first employed at the India Office—some sixteen years ago—my attention was speedily directed to a tall, handsome old man, sitting at his work in the vestibule, more like a comfortably retired Anglo-Indian General than an assistant to the esteemed Head Office Keeper. He was then a hale old man, of about seventy-four years of age, his head adorned

* This Sketch, now revised and enlarged, originally appeared in the author's small volume of "Sketches" of the noble army of Anglo-Indians in 1875.

with an Albanian cap, wore a snowy white beard; and, whenever opportunity offered, spoke with the highest respect of the noble master he had served so well. In fact, any one who dared speak against the great poet might have excited his indignation to a dangerous extent.

In the course of conversation I learned that Giovanni Battista Falcieri used to swim with Lord Byron; but he was not with him till long after the famous feat of swimming the Hellespont, 3rd of May, 1810. The old chasseur told with infinite pride that, while wearing a costume (uniform?) similar to that of his master, he would be occasionally saluted for his lordship. "Tita," he said, was the Italian abbreviation of his name. On the difference of climate between England and Italy being remarked on, Tita replied that he had not been in his own country for forty years. He originally came over with the corpse of Lord Byron (1824)—afterwards returned to Italy—and, on his re-visiting England, was eventually appointed to service in the Board of Control Office, from which, on the Indian Government passing entirely to the Crown, through the influence of Sir John Cam Hobhouse (Lord Broughton), Falcieri was appointed to the India Office, where he was to be found daily, with every promise of reaching "a green old age,"—one of the few connecting links between the times of Byron and our own. On one occasion I penned a brief sketch of this faithful servant, and great was the delight of Falcieri when he read it in a popular journal; but greater still was his satisfaction when he received a letter from America quoting the same as a record of interest—the paragraph had been copied into an English illustrated weekly paper, which had a circulation in America—and requesting more information about the famous "Tita" of Lord Byron. At length he was called to follow his kind and world-renowned master into "the silent land;" or, to use the words applied to a distinguished Anglo-Indian soldier of the olden time,* the spirit of the single-minded and brave old chasseur passed

"From life across the sea of death—home."

* Lieut.-Colonel Dalton.

He died on Tuesday, the 23rd of December, 1874, aged seventy-six, at 60, Seymour Street, Portman Square. A *Times* correspondent was in error when remarking that Falcieri died at Ramsgate. For upwards of a year the old man had been absent from his duties in the India Office, in the vestibule of which (close to St. James's Park) he sat, under his friend Mr. Badrick (the obliging and intelligent Head Office Keeper), arranging and stamping letters, selling stamps, answering in broken English the questions of distinguished and ordinary Anglo-Indians, and, in spite of his reticence, lighting up at the very mention of the names of Shelley and Lord Byron. His habits were strictly abstemious; but, like poor humanity in general, Falcieri could not long carry on "conflict with the frosts of age." A stroke of paralysis was the first monitor; and then, towards the close of 1874, congestion of the lungs set in, to which he rapidly succumbed, and "Tita" was no more. During what seemed his convalescence, Falcieri occasionally hobbled down to the India Office, where I had a conversation with him a month before he died. The old fire seemed to be hovering about his eye; and I could not help thinking of "Tita" as one of the few men in London who connected the past romantic and poetical age with the distracting, too-fast, and ever busy present.

He was born in the year 1798, just ten years after Lord Byron, making him (as already stated) at his decease seventy-six years of age. He was buried at Kensal Green on the 29th of December 1874; Mr. Badrick, and one of the senior messengers of the India Office (Mr. Girard), following their respected old friend to the grave. Surely, such a distinguished member of the useful corps of messengers had never died before; distinguished, not on account of himself, but of him who admired the good and faithful "Tita," and died on his shoulder; the mighty genius whose chief characteristic, like that of the ocean he so loved to describe, was restlessness.

The following authentic sketch is given, with but few alterations; and, on perusing it, perhaps the readers of Rogers' "Table-Talk" will bring to memory what Mrs. Barbauld said to the "banker-poet," that she thought Byron wrote best "when he wrote about the sea or swimming." Giovanni Battista Falcieri (better known to the friends of Lord Byron as "Tita") entered the poet's service in 1818, being then twenty years of age, as gondolier. Rogers, in some beautiful lines, exactly describes the faithful character of the man. While writing of the author of "Childe Harold" he says:—

> "His motley household came—not last, nor least,
> Battista, who, upon the moonlit sea
> Of Venice, had so ably, zealously,
> Served, and, at parting, thrown his oar away
> To follow through the world; who, without stain,
> Had worn so long that honourable badge,
> The Gondolier's, in a Patrician House
> Arguing unlimited trust."

The poet of "Italy" also, in a note, remarks:—"The principal gondolier (*il fante di poppa*) was almost always in the confidence of his master, and employed on occasions that required judgment and address." He was afterwards his personal attendant and chasseur, attending his lordship in his equestrian and swimming exercises, and also with the carriage. Falcieri was accustomed to speak with pride on the richness of his uniform—a cocked hat with a plume of feathers; scarlet coat, richly embroidered with gold lace; pantaloons, also similarly embroidered; Hessian boots, with tassels; sword and sash completed his equipment when out on special occasions in attendance on his lordship. He appeared to enjoy the reminiscences of their swimming excursions very much, when his lordship and he would go out at night-time, each with a light in one hand, elevated over their heads, while they swam with the other; and he also mentioned an occasion when two gentlemen, swimming with his lordship and himself, one after the other gave in, but Lord Byron and Falcieri kept on. They had swam some two or three miles when his lordship turned to "Tita" to ask him if he felt disposed to go farther, which he was quite willing to do. On another occasion they lunched in the water. The table and provisions were tied together, and carried by Falcieri on his head; when they swam for some distance they then placed the board to form a table, drew the cork of the bottle, arranged the viands, and having partaken of lunch as much as they required, his lordship threw himself on his back, and with his foot kicked over the remains into the water.

Falcieri went with Lord Byron to Greece, and, as before stated, was with him when he died at Missolonghi. He then came to England with the body. The coffin was brought over in a cask of spirits, and Falcieri never left it; indeed, he said that if he had done so, the sailors would have pierced the cask to obtain the spirits; and when the body was placed in a house in Great George Street, Westminster, he slept on the coffin. He attended the funeral at Hucknall. Those among the more curious endeavoured to elicit something from him concerning Lord Byron, but to no purpose. His answer invariably was, "Me not know," or "I can't tell." He was unacquainted with English at that time. Such was his fidelity during his long stay in England, that nothing would ever induce him to betray any secret with regard to his late master. Among those desirous of hearing something important from him were distinguished persons of the higher classes; but their requests were of no avail. "Tita" had in his possession the passports of the gentlemen who were with Mr. Shelley when he was drowned off Leghorn. He started with the party in the boat, but an English vessel was "laying-to," and the party stopped to converse with the captain. Soon after Lord Byron had sent Falcieri in the boat he required his services, and sent another boat to recall him; otherwise, he would have been with Shelley when he was capsized, and the "strong swimmer" might have saved the poet of the "starry verse."

After the burial of Lord Byron, Falcieri went out in the service of Sir John Cam Hobhouse and Mr. James Clay, as courier. On his return to England he was engaged as valet to Mr. Isaac D'Israeli—the celebrated author of the "Curiosities of Literature," and father of the future Lord Beaconsfield. Sir John Cam Hobhouse then gave him, at the solicitation of Mr. Benjamin Disraeli, an appointment as messenger to the Board of Control, whence he came to the old India House in Leadenhall Street, and eventually to the India Office in Westminster. It should be mentioned that during his service with Mr. D'Israeli, Count D'Orsay produced a portrait of the late Lord Byron, which was shown to the personal friends of his lordship, and by them was pronounced a perfect likeness; but it was afterwards thought advisable that "Tita" should see it, to give his opinion. He was, therefore, sent from Bradenham, in Buckinghamshire, and he considered it an excellent likeness, with the exception of the hair, which was not quite the shade. As he had a piece of his lordship's hair, he sent it to Count D'Orsay; and it was found, as Falcieri had said, of a different hue. The alteration was made, and it was thought by "Tita" to be the best portrait he had seen of his illustrious master. As a compliment for this, Count D'Orsay presented him with a valuable ring, set with emeralds. This ring he valued very much; and, although too small for his finger, he would not have it altered. Falcieri, at my request, brought this ring one day to the India Office, along with Shelley's passports, which appeared to have been entrusted to his care. The ring was really a beautiful one, and the old man took it carefully from the box, and handled the treasure with a genuine pride. Even after the poet's death, "Tita" had done something for Lord Byron, correcting the mistake of a brilliant and highly-gifted Count—one of the social stars of the day—and clever artist. On another occasion, Falcieri brought an admirable photographic likeness of himself to the Office, which did him full justice; he being represented wearing his Albanian cap, and, with his amiable visage and superb white beard, looking as no Government messenger had ever looked before—which portrait he kindly gave me as a keepsake. Falci (as he was sometimes called) seemed to know a good deal about Shelley; and he would relate, with some graphic power, the story of the poet having set sail from Leghorn for Lerici, "in that treacherous boat which (some fifty-two years before) sank, with all on board, to the bottom of the Mediterranean." "Tita" had also a characteristic anecdote of Shelley, which had not yet been given to the world.

While the poet of the "Sensitive Plant" was living by a lake, he went to an adjacent hill, where the nurse appeared with the baby, which he took, and quietly laid down, and, sending the nurse away, became so much absorbed in the book which he was reading, that at length he went home, forgetting all about the child. On being asked where it was, he remarked that he had laid it down by the hill. Falcieri was immediately despatched to the hill, and found the morsel of humanity, with eyes wide open, quite happy and safe. The place was much infested with snakes, and "Tita" expressed his surprise that the child had not been bitten. Whatever may be said of Anglo-Indians, some judges may think them more careful of their young children in India than Mr. and Mrs. Shelley appear to have been of theirs in Italy!

Falcieri being asked if he were a better swimmer than his lordship, replied, he did not know; for they "never out-ran each other,"—a truly respectful answer. "Tita," in his early days, appears to have been of rather a pugnacious character. On one occasion, in Venice, when some police came to take him up for some offence, he looked at them and smiled, telling them they had better not venture. They attempted to take him, and he threw three of them into the street, while the other four took to their heels. The Commandant of Police went to Byron, and Byron went to the Grand Duke. His Highness remarked that it would be "all right," as the men "were being attended to in hospital!"

If all the mad pranks played by Lord Byron and his "Tita" in the "glorious city in the sea" were known, what amusing incidents would, doubtless, be found amongst them! and yet time and circumstances so alter us, that the old man generally seemed as if he had never played a prank in his life. "Childe Harold," before he awoke one morning, and found himself "famous," had played many strange games—"fantastic tricks before high heaven;" and had he lived to the age of seventy, he might have almost been as demure-looking at times as his servant, Falcieri. Regarding the two notices of him which appeared in leading London journals (January, 1875), full justice was attempted to be done to the departed India Office messenger, and a few interesting incidents were brought forward; there were also some mistakes, of no very great importance—Falcieri's first meeting with his dead master's friend, Mr. John Cam Hobhouse (afterwards Sir John and Lord Broughton), appears to have taken place when that gentleman took him into his service in London, as a courier, preparatory to again setting out on his travels. According to the "Chronology of Lord Byron's Life and Works," the poet left London "on his travels, accompanied by Mr. Hobhouse," on June 11th, 1809; so we find Falcieri with the latter gentlemen fifteen years, or more, after that memorable setting out of the two friends in the morning of life. In one of the journals it was said that "subsequently he officiated as *valet* to old Mr. Isaac D'Israeli, the author of the 'Curiosities of Literature,' and father of the then Prime Minister of England." As has been already noticed, he did serve under Mr. D'Israeli, in whose household he received much kindness. Falcieri well recollected the celebration of the occasion of the Prime Minister's first entering Parliament (M.P. for Maidstone, 1837), when he drank his health. It is quite correct that Falcieri, in 1852, obtained, through Lord Broughton's influence, a situation as messenger in the Board of Control Office, where his lordship was President. In the "East India Register" for the above year, he appears as John Falcieri, the second among three. India was transferred to the Crown in September, 1858. In the first half of 1859, however, we still find "G. B. Falcieri" as "office messenger" at Cannon Row, where a portion of the India Office Secretariat Department were employed, under the Assistant to the Secretaries, and Keeper of the Records, Mr. T. Nelson Waterfield, father of the present Henry Waterfield, Esq., C.B., the very able and energetic India Office Financial Secretary. Falcieri served the Crown, but not the East India Company (as messenger to the distinguished Anglo-Indian, Sir George Clerk) for a short time at the old India House in Leadenhall Street, which was vacated in September, 1860, on the occupation of the Victoria Hotel, Westminster, as a temporary India Office.—The present stately building, or palatial residence, in St. James's Park, was first occupied in September, 1867.

In addition to clearing away some doubts expressed by the journalist, these facts may be of use for reference hereafter. In the leading journal, Mr. Richard Edgcumbe wrote :—"To the admirers of Shelley, 'Tita' will also have some interest, since he is the gondolier who rowed 'Julian and Maddalo' past the madhouse at sunset." He also gives an interesting account of the death of Lord Byron, and the description (from Count Gamba's Narrative) would seem to be strictly correct. Falcieri told the present writer that Lord Byron died on his shoulder; and the truth of Tita's assertion at once became apparent from the following "last scene of all" in a brief, though strange, and "eventful history:"—

"It was after a consultation of the physicians," says Gamba, "that, as it appeared to me, Lord Byron was, for the first time, aware of his approaching end. Mr. Millingen, Fletcher, and Tita had been standing round his bed; but the first two, unable to restrain their tears, left the room. Tita also wept, but, as Byron held his hand, could not retire. He, however, turned away his face; Byron meanwhile looked steadily at him, and said, half smiling, '*Oh! questa è una bella scena!*' He seemed to reflect a moment, and having released the hand of Tita, with orders that Captain Parry might be summoned, a fit of delirium ensued." In the hour of death "Tita" stood beside the poet, "and finally forsook his country to follow his master to the grave."

It is impossible not to feel a respect for Falcieri, so prominent an actor in this touching scene. Here was Lord Byron, while dying, holding the hand of his faithful servant, whose presence probably suggested that "image of eternity," the sea—in which they had so often swam together; and the fact of his lordship in his last moments placing his head on the shoulder of his faithful servant to die, showed that the poet, in his noble, generous nature, esteemed at least *one* man, of the city which "Childe Harold" so loved from his boyhood—the gondolier of Venice—Giovanni Battista Falcieri!

In the graphic and sad account of Lord Byron's last moments collected from the mouth of Mr. Fletcher, who had been for more than twenty years his faithful and confidential attendant—latterly more of a butler or housekeeper it would seem, the functions of personal attendant being shared with "Tita"—the subject of this sketch is only twice mentioned. Of course it was only natural that the older servant—to whom the poet's dying and affecting instructions regarding his daughter Ada, his sister Augusta, and Lady Byron, were given—should wish posterity to consider that, through life and death, he was the chief attendant on such a master as Lord Byron. But Fletcher did not forget the more chivalrous and not less faithful "Tita." He stated, regarding his lordship's illness, just after relating that Byron had said he feared the doctors—Bruno and Millingen—knew nothing about his disorder, or he was sure they had mistaken his disease:—"My master on this day (17th April) said to me twice—'I cannot sleep, and you well know that I have not been able to sleep for more than a week; I know,' added his lordship, 'that a man can only be a certain time without sleep, and then he must go mad without any one being able to save him, and I would ten times sooner shoot myself than be mad, for I am not afraid of dying; I am more fit to die than people think.' I do not believe, however, that his lordship had any apprehension of his fate till the day after (the 18th), when he said—'I fear you and Tita will be ill by sitting up constantly night and day.' I answered, 'We shall never leave your lordship until you are better.'"

Again, Fletcher narrates: "The last words I heard my master utter were at six o'clock on the evening of the 18th, when he said—'I must sleep now;' upon which he laid down never to rise again! for he did not move hand or foot during the following twenty-four hours. His lordship appeared, however, to be in a state of suffocation at intervals, and had frequent rattling in the throat; on these occasions, I called Tita to assist me in raising his head, and I thought he seemed to get quite stiff. The rattling and choking in the throat took place every half-hour; and we continued to raise his head whenever the fit came on, till six o'clock in the evening of the 19th, when I saw my master open his eyes, and then shut them, but without showing any symptom of pain, or moving hand or foot. 'Oh, my God!' I exclaimed, 'I fear his lordship is gone!' The doctors then felt his pulse, and said—'You are right—he is gone.'" And so died, to the inexpressible grief of Fletcher, and the poet's "Tita," one of whom our most brilliant essayist writes, in his famous essay on Lord Clive: "Two men have died within our recollection, who, at a time of life at which many people have hardly completed their education, had raised themselves, each in his own department, to the height of glory. One of them died at Longwood, the other at Missolonghi."

Reverting for a moment or two, in conclusion, to "Tita," it may be stated that his pension was two-thirds of his pay, or about £93, and not £140 (the full amount), as asserted. An amusing anecdote was brought forward at his death, among the incidents in the life of "Tita" Falcieri; and I can vouch for the correctness of the concluding remark, having seen his writing (a fair enough hand for a foreigner) in the India Office:—Mr. Moore, the poet, in his reminiscence of a visit to Lord Byron at Venice, in the year 1819, alludes to Tita as the *segretario* in whose charge he was placed by his noble host. "So you keep a secretary?" exclaimed Moore, when he heard the title of his protector. "Yes," replied Byron, laughing, "a fellow who can't write." It is but an act of justice to the memory of Tita to inform the reader that this apparent deficiency in his education had been made up long before his death, "for" (says the writer) "I have in my possession some remarks made by Tita, written in a fairly legible hand." His pronunciation of English was his chief drawback. One able and shrewd India Office functionary, who knew him well, told me that it was occasionally almost impossible to understand him. He would say "Yes" or "No" continually, in answer to the querist, thinking it was sufficient; and by this means—not a bad lesson for some of the orators of this wordy age!—he would cover a multitude of sins. I was more fortunate, however, with the worthy "Tita," for I generally quite understood him.

One of Mr. Disraeli's most gracious acts, as Prime Minister, was that of recommending the widow of Falcieri to her Majesty for a pension from the Civil List, which she at once obtained, but did not live long to enjoy. Lord Beaconsfield must have long taken an interest in "Tita;" for, in addition to what has already been said on the subject, it was remarked by good authority that his father took the faithful *cassiatore* into his service, where he remained till the death of his benefactor in 1848. He had also well served the famous son, through whose influence Falcieri became a messenger in the India Office—one who was known to, and well appreciated by not a few, distinguished Anglo-Indians.

NOTE.

LORD BYRON AND INDIA.

Lord Byron has not much to say about India in his poems; so we cannot give him the place of even a *literary* connection. To a poet so fond of the "gorgeous East," there is much in the Indian land that might have been adorned by his pen. When he does allude to India it is in no very inviting colours. In "Don Juan," he mentions Nadir Shah, who built up "monuments defiled with gore," leaving "Hindustan a wild;"* and, again, in the "Curse of Minerva," he has some remarkable lines, written as if prophetic of the great mutiny of 1857! Minerva, with tears bedimming "her large blue eye," while

"Round the rent casque, her owlet circled slow,
And mourn'd his mistress with a shriek of woe!"

says, after making us feel pity for poor "lost Albion":—

"Look to the East, where Ganges' swarthy race
Shall shake your tyrant empire to its base;
Lo! there Rebellion rears her ghastly head,
And glares the Nemesis of native dead;
Till Indus rolls a deep purpureal flood,
And claims his long arrear of northern blood."†

* "And scarce to the Mogul a cup of coffee."—"Don Juan," Canto ix.

† "Curse of Minerva."

On this attack from the pen of genius it may be said in defence, that whatever may have been our faults in wielding the sovereignty of India, we certainly do not deserve the reproach of "tyrant empire." To aid the weak and restrain the strong have been marked features in our policy. As to the Indus, with its prophetic bloody torrent, such a calamity might have been, had the Punjab, during the mutiny, not remained staunch to us under its able and energetic Governor. It may also be remarked that, as we had little or nothing to do with the Indus (called by the natives *Sind*, and by the Mahomedan writers *Hind*) in Lord Byron's time, he also prophesied the annexation of the country of the five rivers; for the "purpureal flood" alluded to could hardly have been possible without the annexation of the Punjab. Something of the same kind may be said of Sind. To muse over Lord Byron in the light of a *seer* regarding India, increases the interest we all feel in the great poet; and it may furnish an argument in favour of having brought forward his name (coupled with his faithful "Tita") in this work, as one who thought highly of a devoted servant who afterwards beheld and conversed with some distinguished Anglo-Indians. Even the scholarly Duke of Argyll, when at the head of the India Office, would address a few kind words, in Italian, to Lord Byron's "Tita."

ANGLO-INDIAN ANECDOTES AND INCIDENTS.

—o—

LORD WILLIAM BENTINCK—1828 to 1835—was one of the greatest administrative successes that ever blessed India; and Lord Macaulay concludes his famous essay on Lord Clive, after remarking on the greatness of his hero as a conqueror :—"Nor will she [History] deny to the reformer a share of that veneration . . . . with which the latest generations of Hindoos will contemplate the statue of Lord William Bentinck." The work accomplished in the reign of this distinguished Governor-General was immense. His economical measures—abolition of the rite of Suttee—changes in the Civil and Criminal Courts—encouragement given to education and the study of English—the new Medical College—the Savings' Bank—Preparations for abolishing Transit Duties —introduction of Steam Navigation—are all remarkable events. Strange to say, no war with external enemies disturbed his administration, which closed in March, 1835. "It was passed," writes Marshman,* "in peace and tranquillity, and was devoted to the improvement of the people."

1.

ANECDOTES OF LORD WILLIAM BENTINCK.†

Lord Bentinck was accustomed to go about Calcutta, as Alraschid did about the streets of Bagdad, in disguise, and frequently assumed the garb and manners of a military pensioner. On these occasions he would accost any one he

* "History of Bengal."

† *Calcutta Review*, No. XXVIII., December, 1850: "Recent Military Memoirs."

happened to meet, whom he deemed suitable for his purpose, get into conversation, gradually introduce the subject of Government, and endeavour to elicit the opinion of his companion on his Lordship's own character and policy. He would also, under an assumed character, sometimes visit the public offices, seeking thus to discover abuses; and, where finding such, suspending or removing the parties implicated, and introducing a reform. On one of these occasions he entered the office of the Commissary-General in the tattered garb of a poor old soldier, and requested an interview with that personage on important public business. This the head clerk very haughtily denied him, demanded to know what he wanted, and, on his declining to communicate this, told him that his wishes could not be complied with, as the Commissary-General was out, and turned away without even offering him a chair, which, however, a more courteous understrapper brought, and requested him to be seated. After sitting some time unheeded, the supposed soldier solicited the clerk to favour him with pen, ink, and paper, as he wanted to step out, and would make his business known in writing to the Commissary-General, so that, in the event of that gentleman returning to the office and again quitting it ere he came back, he might receive the communication and leave a written reply to it. With much difficulty he obtained writing materials, the same being pushed towards him in a most supercilious manner. The old soldier scribbled a few lines, intimating his wish to see the Commissary-General, and concluded by subscribing himself "Bentinck." This done, he departed. Shortly after, the note was delivered by the clerk to his master (who had all this time been within).

No sooner had the Commissary-General glanced over it, and seen the signature attached to it, than he sprang from his chair, and hastened into the office, but seeing no one there, inquired what had become of his Lordship.

"Lordship, sir!" exclaimed the clerk, "we have had no one here but a ragged old soldier, who wanted to see you, and, when I told him he couldn't, because I knew you were busy, he asked leave to write the note which I just now gave you."

"Confusion! The old soldier, as you call him, was the Governor-General. Ho, Buxoo; buggy lao, jilda! jilda!"* (Bring the buggy, quick, quick!) shouted the officer, and in a moment sprang into his carriage, and drove off to Government House, leaving the astonished clerk panic-stricken and aghast.

In about half an hour the Commissary-General returned, bringing with him an order for the immediate dismissal of the head clerk for inattention to public business, and the appointment of the polite understrapper (should he be qualified for the situation) to the vacancy.

2.

"That was pretty well," said Captain C., when the major had finished his story. "But though an enemy to the neglect of public business, his Lordship was fond of a joke, and could laugh as heartily as any other, even when it was directed against himself. You remember the sensation produced by his Lordship's introduction of the half-batta measure. He was abused most awfully for it, and held up in every possible way to ignominy and contempt. Among other effusions of the day, a song was composed about this concern, in which his Lordship, of course, figured prominently, and was capitally lampooned. This song Lord Bentinck saw. Shortly after its publication, the Governor-General happened to pass through the station in which the officer, who had the credit of its authorship, was quartered. There his Lordship remained a day or two, and, the evening before leaving it, invited the officers of the different regiments to an entertainment. The Poet was of course asked, and of course attended. Supper being over, his Lordship called upon an officer near him for a song. This was given, and another was then called on, and so it went round, till it came to the turn of the author of the lyric on the half-batta question. He tried hard to excuse himself, when asked to sing: but the Governor-General would take no excuse.

* *Juldee, juldee!*

"'Pray, Mr. ——,' said his Lordship, 'at least oblige us with one of your own songs!'

"'My Lord?'

"'We shall be happy to hear one of your own compositions. Come, now, what say you to the song on the half-batta question?'

"Pocr ——! I shall never forget the consternation he evinced at that last question, or the almost suffocating attempts made to repress the mirth which his awkward situation excited on all sides. However, he could not help himself, and so at last he sang it; and really it was capital fun to see the good humour with which his Lordship bore each successive hit, while the poor vocalist sweated like an ox under the infliction, and seemed to tremble, lest his Lordship should get sore at the thwacks with which he was obliged, most involuntarily, to belabour him. The song at last ended, Lord Bentinck burst into a hearty laugh, in which the rest of the company joined, and the whole house seemed to shake with our united cachinnations. His Lordship soon after retired, and the Poet jumped into his palki unobserved, and was off like a shot."

3.

"I can readily credit the story, Captain," said our Colonel, when our merriment at this anecdote had a little subsided, "from a circumstance which came to my own knowledge, while on a visit to Calcutta some years ago. A most abusive letter was written to Lord Bentinck by some one in the metropolis, who, as he did not belong to the Service, and was, moreover, just about to return to England, cared not a straw for his Lordship, and had the impudence, accordingly, to sign it with his own name, and to send it to the Government House by one of his own messengers. It was delivered to the Governor-General, who, being at leisure, at once perused it, and ordered that the person who had brought it should be called in. When the messenger made his appearance, his Lordship presented him with five rupees, and requested him to give his salaam to his master."

AN ADVENTURER'S STORY.

A remarkable series of alliances, *à la* Hymen, took place at Cawnpore in the year 1842. H.M. — regiment had, on the formation of the North-Western Expedition, marched into Afghanistan, leaving, as usual, its depôt, which consisted of about two dozen sick soldiers, half a dozen non-commissioned, and two or three commissioned officers, and about 300 women behind it. Some time after its departure, another regiment, composed almost entirely of young and unmarried men, arrived. This corps had been but a short time there when tidings of the disastrous retreat of our troops from Cabul were received. It was found that the regiment first alluded to had been cut up nearly to a man. This was sad news for all, but more especially for the families of the deceased soldiers, whose wives were thus, all at once, left widows, and their children orphans. Tears, crape, and lamentations became with "the ladies" the order of the day, but not, as in England, of the year! They were too wise to think of prolonging their grief for such a period. On the second Sunday after the receipt of the "black despatches," the banns of some fifteen or twenty couples were read in our hearing at church. This was followed up week after week for a considerable time, with a continual increase in the number, so that at the expiration of a quarter of a year, out of the 300 "bereaved ones," only a few remained in a state of widowhood.

This, the *Calcutta* reviewer thinks, could hardly have been written by an officer in the Queen's Service, as the only Queen's regiment cut to pieces on the retreat from Cabul was the 44th, and that regiment, we need scarcely say, did not form part of the original "Expedition to the North-West." Of anecdotes, "good, bad, and indifferent," furnished by Anglo-Indian writers for home consumption, and of stories like the above in particular, the reviewer wisely laments how frequently they have astounded "the commonplace understandings of residents" in the City of Palaces! How much more must they have done so in the great modern Babylon of London!

SIR THOMAS MUNRO'S STATUE.

"But mentioning Sir Thomas Munro's statue," writes Captain Hervey, "reminds me of a little anecdote in relation to it. I was one day driving by the monument when I saw an old man in a red coat, with three chevrons on his right arm, standing leaning on his staff, and gazing silently on the exalted statue. He was evidently an old pensioner, not only from his dress, but from a certain degree of military carriage in his *tout ensemble* which there was no mistaking. Out of curiosity I stopped my buggy, got out, and addressed the veteran. 'What are you looking at, my fine old fellow?' inquired I. 'Do you know who that is intended to represent?' 'Who can have known the great Sir Thomas Munro,' replied the old man, 'without remembering him? And who can have known him without loving him? And how can I, who have served under him for many years, ever forget him?' 'Then you think that is a good likeness of our Governor—you recognize the face?' asked I. 'Yes, sir,' said he, 'it is a good likeness, but we shall never again see any like him. He was indeed the friend of the Indian, whether a sepoy or a ryot at the plough. Madras will never again have a Governor like him.' And raising his right hand to his head, he gave the old-fashioned salute, lifted up his bundle, and walked off, mumbling to himself about the impropriety of crows being allowed to build their nests on the top, and to dirt over the greatest man of his age."

The above is from Captain Hervey's interesting "Ten Years in India" (1850); and it is a good anecdote, one which illustrates the reverence and affection with which Munro was regarded in Madras, "which," adds the *Calcutta* reviewer, "may stand instead of any remarks of our own on this most attractive subject." * The natives equally admired Sir Thomas; and his name will be cherished with affection and respect so long as Southern India remains under British rule.

* For Munro, Maj.-Gen. Sir Thomas, Bart., see *First Series* of "Distinguished Anglo-Indians," pp. 135, 138, 237, 297, 305.

DUELLING IN THE OLD INDIAN ARMY.

General Albert Fytche, C.S.I., writes in his interesting and valuable work, " Burma, Past and Present" :—

"There was one feature of social life in those days which has now utterly passed away. I allude to the practice of duelling. In my early days a duel sometimes came off, but always under great risk; as principals, seconds, and all concerned, were liable to be cashiered. One of the officers who tried to save poor Captain Lumsden was afterwards cashiered on account of a duel. Wine was generally at the bottom of the mischief. There was more so-called conviviality in those days than in the present sober generation.* Men flushed with wine were too ready to give or take offence, and when they became sober they shrank from retracting their words, or offering an apology, lest they should be suspected of showing the white feather.

"The most remarkable duel that ever came under my immediate notice is a case in point. The Commandant of our battalion was a man of great social qualities, but a hot-tempered Irishman. He has been dead some thirty years, so there is no harm in telling a story about him. One night during a game at billiards a dispute arose between the Commandant and a civilian. Unfortunately the civilian was an Irishman likewise, and his temperament was equally fiery. A challenge passed between the two. It was in the small hours, but the disputants were so angry that they refused to wait till daylight. They insisted on fighting the duel at once by torchlight. I shall never forget the absurd uproar of the scene—the rage of the principals, the gravity of the seconds, the excitement of the lookers-on. Lighted torches were procured. The principals were posted in the

* "The good old times of 'no heel taps,' when the door of the mess-room was often locked after dinner, and the key placed in the President's pocket, so as to allow no officer to leave the table and 'shirk his liquor,' have now happily passed away."

compound * which surrounded the mess-house. The signal was given; both fired a shot; as good luck would have it, no one was hurt. The seconds promptly interfered; they refused to allow another shot to be fired; they declared that the honour of both was satisfied, and that the duel must not go on.

"The indignation of the principals was beyond all bounds. The Commandant especially was in such a towering passion that he called his second a coward. The matter was allowed to stand over till the morning. By this time all parties had cooled down. The expression was withdrawn; the word was explained away. The Commandant declared that he charged his second with moral cowardice only, not with physical! The apology was accepted under the circumstances, and nothing further was said of the matter.

"In the last century duelling was an established institution in India. Almost every man in society, military or civil, had, at one time or other, fought, or been concerned in, a duel. The late East India Company strove in vain to stop the practice. They were actuated partly by a laudable desire to prevent their servants from slaughtering each other, and partly from the loss which a killed or disabled officer brought on the public treasury.

"A brigade was stationed in Oude. There was constant rivalry between the cavalry and the infantry. The quarrels were frequent, and so were the duels. Whenever an officer was killed, another officer had to be sent up country, at a vast expense, to fill his place, whilst another one was sent out from England.

"The Court of Directors grew irritated and alarmed. At last they issued the most peremptory orders that any officer convicted of fighting a duel should be cashiered. These orders were duly forwarded to the brigade. The officers

* "An East Indian term; it means a yard or enclosure round a building, and is a corruption of the Portuguese word *campania*. Yule, however, thinks—and he is probably right—that compound is derived from the Malay word *Kampong*, and was introduced by the Portuguese from the Straits of Malacca, together with other words in common use in India, such as *Paddy*, Malay, *Padi*, unhusked rice."

were filled with consternation. There was no mistaking the order. No one wanted to be cashiered; yet it was obvious to all that the rivalry between the two arms of the service would still continue. At last, after much cogitation, they determined to settle all questions, present and future, by one great duel between the commandant of the cavalry and the senior officer of the infantry. That duel was to be final. There was no privacy about the matter. The duel came off one fine morning, in the presence of a large portion of the brigade. The signal was given, and the commandant of the cavalry was shot dead on the spot.

"A more sensational event had rarely occurred in the Indian Army. The Bengal Government was exasperated in the highest degree. A court-martial was ordered. Fears were entertained that Bengal officers would hesitate to convict a brother officer. Other officers were brought up at a great expense from Madras and Bombay. The court-martial was held; there was no denying the facts. The feeling in favour of duelling was so strong, that it overpowered all other considerations. The result was that the prisoner was acquitted." *

ADVENTURE WITH A TIGER.

The same author gives a sporting reminiscence, enough to satisfy the writer of "Wild Sports in India," † whose earnest wish and aim are, "that a thirst for adventure, and love of excitement and danger, may be engendered in the hearts of the rising generation of Englishmen":—

"I have shot tigers in various parts of Burma, but I never killed one, perhaps, that gave me more sport than the fol-

* "This anecdote regarding the duel between the two Commandants has never, to the best of my belief, been published. My authority for it is a distinguished officer of the Bengal Artillery, lately deceased. I tell it as it was told to me, and those who doubt it may perhaps admit what a certain cardinal is reported to have said of the New Testament—'Se non è vero, e ben trovato.'"

† Captain Henry Shakespear, Commandant Nagpore Irregular Force. London, 1860. (Smith, Elder & Co.)

lowing. I should explain that all post letters that were not sent by sea were carried through the jungle between Akyab and Chittagong by men known as dâk wallahs or post-runners. These post-runners were sometimes exposed to great perils from wild beasts. One evening, whilst dining at mess, news arrived that a post-runner had been carried off by a tiger near a village not very far from Akyab. Accordingly a brother officer and myself mounted our horses and rode off to the village. At daybreak we set the villagers at work to beat the jungle. At first they were very unwilling to go. They said that the tiger was a man-eater; that some of them would certainly be killed. We promised plenty of rupees; and at last the all-powerful prospect of buckshеesh induced them to encounter the danger. The haunts of this tiger were thoroughly well known to these men. Several of the villagers had already been carried away, and the seizure of the post-runner was a crowning exploit.

"There was a large open plain near the village, scattered as usual with patches of thick jungle. The tiger's lair was in one of these patches. Accordingly the villagers moved off towards it, whilst my companion and myself ensconced ourselves in two trees just outside the patch, and prepared to fire on the man-eater. My companion had never fired at a tiger before. He was most anxious to have the first shot, and, therefore, posted himself on the tree nearest the spot where the tiger was most likely to break.

"Scarcely had the beaters entered the jungle when we knew that they had come upon the tiger. They filled the air with their shouts. They made a still more horrible din with the so-called musical instruments, which they invariably carry with them on such occasions. Presently the brute appeared in the open. It seemed to take no heed of the deafening noise behind; it moved in a most majestic manner towards the tree where my friend was posted. My friend fired his two barrels. The tiger dashed off with his bristles up and his tail erect in the air, towards another patch of jungle. It was evidently wounded, but only slightly. The beaters saw this; they knew that its savageness would be increased by the wound, and they objected to having anything further to do with the business. We made light of it. There were no trees near this jungle, and we undertook to face the tiger in the open if the beaters would only drive it out. We would then make an end of the matter, kill the man-eater, and deliver the village from all further alarm.

"At last they consented to beat again. My companion, as before, wanted the first shot. We both knelt down upon the plain; but my friend was about fifteen paces in front of me. After firing he was to run behind me. The tiger suddenly appeared with a magnificent bound. He gave himself a shake, and then, with all his bristles up, he bore down straight upon us. My companion fired when the tiger was at a considerable distance, missed it, and then ran past me as was agreed upon. When the tiger was within twenty paces of me I fired my first barrel; when he was making his last bound I fired the second. He fell dead upon his head, with his body over me. Fortunately he fell upon his back, or he would have torn me to pieces in his dying agonies.

"It is strange that in a moment of excitement like this, every trifling incident is impressed upon the memory for ever. To this day I can see, in my mind's eye, the same things that I saw then. My friend was somewhat vain of his brown hair. He wore it very long, after a fashion in those days which used to be called 'a flow.' Charles Dickens used to wear his hair in the same fashion; he did so when Maclise painted his portrait for the first edition of 'Nicholas Nickleby.' My friend lost his hat in running away from the tiger, and, as he passed me, I could see, through the corners of my eyes, his long brown hair floating in the wind. When I got from under the brute, I saw my friend disappearing over some rising ground, with his hair streaming out in the bright sunshine. I turned round in the opposite direction, and saw the beaters coming out of the jungle. They were stretching out their arms in the air, evidently imagining that I had been destroyed by the tiger. They were undeceived when they saw that I was alive, whilst the brute was lying dead on the ground; and presently my friend reappeared upon the scene. We then examined the tiger. My friend's first shot from the tree had grazed its side. My first bullet had entered the chest, and was found near the stern. My second shot had struck between the eyes, and gone through the centre of the brain."

Having alluded to the great Battle of Ferozeshah, and the General and Governor-General, Lord Hardinge, in our "Sketches," * it is most pleasing to be able to illustrate the kindness of the Duke of Wellington's courteous and brave lieutenant in the Peninsula, as displayed in an

INTERESTING INCIDENT.

Denis Delany, who was to be found thirty-five years ago (August, 1852) in Dublin, served in the 31st Regiment as private in India, and had a pension of *9d.* a day for wounds. On the night of the first attack upon the Sikhs at Ferozeshah (1846), when lying on the ground, two officers with cloaks on came to the spot where he (Delany) was. One of them sat down, and the other went away. After a short time the officer sitting down asked him (Delany) if he would let him rest his head upon his body by way of pillow, that he might try to sleep. Delany willingly assented. After sleeping about an hour, the other officer came back and addressed the one who had been sleeping, calling him "your Excellency." Delany then felt sure that it was Lord Hardinge, the Governor-General, who had been sleeping; the other officer, he thought, was Colonel Bar, who, on returning, said, "I have brought your Excellency a small jumbo of water." Lord Hardinge drank some of the water, and then gave the pitcher to Delany, saying, "Here, my good fellow, I have made a pillow of your body; it is only fair that you should have some of the water." The troops were at this time suffering dreadfully from want of water, all the wells being in possession of the enemy. After some further conversation about a gun which was annoying the troops,

* That of General John Reid Becher, C.B.

the two officers went away to another part of the field, and Delany saw nothing more of them. With reference to the above—Denis Delany was appointed to the constabulary many years ago, by Colonel Browne, then Commissioner of the Dublin Metropolitan Police; resigning from that establishment, he enlisted in the 31st, and saw some severe service in India, and was severely wounded. Calling to see his old friend, Colonel Browne, he was questioned as to his services, and, in the course of conversation, recounted his having met with Lord Hardinge at Ferozeshah, as above related. The colonel communicated with Lord Hardinge, then Master-General of the Ordnance, recommending Delany at the same time for any humble situation he might be qualified to fill. A very kind answer was received by the colonel, stating the anecdote to be true, and the Secretary of the Ordnance wrote to the officers of Ordnance in Dublin directing Delany to be appointed to any small situation which might become vacant, and for which he would be found suited. This little narrative requires no comment. Could the most enthusiastic democrat have behaved better than this to his fellow-man? England may pause for a reply!

ENGLISH INTEREST IN INDIA FIFTY YEARS AGO.

Sir John Kaye wrote in the first number of the *Calcutta Review* (May, 1844) on the subject of "The English in India," and was of opinion that much of the interest, which had lately been attached to the news from India, owed its birth to the important and exciting character of the events, which had been enacted in the romantic countries beyond the Sutlej and the Indus. The history of the English in India, he thought, during the last six years—from 1838 to 1844—one of extraordinary interest. The founder of the *Calcutta* proceeds in the following graphic and eloquent strain:—

"The chronicles of the whole world do not furnish a series

of more vivid and exciting scenes of picturesque warfare. Contemplating the whole, it is difficult to believe that we are not poring over some highly-wrought narrative of fictitious adventure. 'Truth is strange; stranger than fiction.' The siege of Herat—Herat, wrested from the grasp of the Persian by the wondrous energy of a young British officer,* who, chance-guided to the 'gate of India,' threw himself into the beleaguered city to revive the failing energies of the besieged, and sustain them unvanquished, until diplomacy had done the rest; the assemblage of the 'Army of the Indus;' the magnificent gathering at Ferozepore; the march of the Bengal and Bombay columns of the grand force through an unknown and dangerous country; the triumphant entry of Shah Soojah into Candahar; the capture of the stronghold of Ghuznee; the preparations made for our reception at Urghundee, where Dost Mahomed, having drawn up his guns in position, was basely deserted by his followers; the flight of the Dost; the pursuit of the chivalrous Outram; the progress to Caubul; the mummeries enacted there; the march to Bameean; the passage of the Hindoo Khoosh; the return of the Bombay troops; the capture of Khelat, and the death of Mehrab Khan; the lull, the deceitful calm, and the reappearance of the Dost, the assemblage of the Oosbegs, and the rising of the Kohisthanees; the victory of Bameean; the defeat of Purwundurrah; the last gallant charge of the Ameer, and the surrender of the single horseman in his dress of goatskin at a moment when the pale face of panic was watching despairingly the progress of events. Have we not here the first volume of an exciting romance? It awoke the slumbering interest of the people of England. Peace had girt us around for many a long day; there was a 'pin-drop silence;' and the trumpet of war was heard from afar—heard for a time even above the din of sonorous faction.

"Country gentlemen were soon looking at the maps; and

* Eldred Pottinger, the sad tidings of whose death reached Calcutta in 1843–44.—Strange enough, he was the first actor in the Afghan War, and the last in the China War.

the works of Elphinstone and Burnes were diligently sought after by all the oracles of the town.

"Diners-out crammed themselves with forced-meat balls of Afghan history and geography; and members of Parliament learnt just enough to enable them to expose their ignorance to the world."

Sir John Kaye has thus given us a most striking chain of events or incidents, which, on the whole, have been quite equalled in importance and interest—especially during the great Sikh Wars and the Indian Mutiny—in the last forty-two years. The remarks of the historian of Afghanistan and the Sepoy Mutiny on the cramming with "forced-meat balls" of Indian affairs by highly worthy and educated men of an age passed away, are, we are sorry to think, in some measure, almost as applicable now. Russia and the Indian Budget, by turns, compel a sleepy interest in business men and the intelligent public; but it is far from being the right interest. There was hardly any enthusiasm caused in England by the righteous annexation of Upper Burma, simply because the country was not known, and the expediency of the act was not understood. And so it is, and for long will be, the acts or intentions of Government—Imperial and local—and distinguished Anglo-Indians entrusted with high authority, will not receive the earnest attention they deserve. Of course, people are far more excited by events nearer home. But we must get out of this selfish feeling if England is to hold her great Empire in the manner assigned to her. At the same time as the occurrence of the above first-mentioned events of so many years ago, Sir John Kaye thought it well to bring forward the fact that another great drama was being enacted in the far East. The war with China excited even more interest than the great Central-Asian tragedy. And why? People laid down their breakfast cup, read in the morning paper how Commissioner Linn had out-manœuvred Captain Elliott; and they sighed at the thought of losing their cup of tea! They cared little about England marching an army across the Indus. They knew nothing of Afghanistan, but they knew that China yielded Hyson and Bohea;

and the "cup that cheers" will long be dear to the English people. In the long and glorious reign of Her Majesty the Queen-Empress—which covers all the great events alluded to in these remarks—Indian tea is beginning to find great favour in the London market; so we are not now dependent on China. That cannot in these days take away our interest in India. Education in our Eastern Empire is becoming more and more "a burning question," which should excite a corresponding interest at home, without which, and an interest in every great Indian matter so much concerning England, India socially, morally, and politically—notwithstanding such a brilliant array of distinguished Anglo-Indians—will not be much in advance of fifty years ago, which will furnish sad materials for the future historian of the long and glorious reign of the Queen-Empress over her splendid Eastern dominion.

HENRY WOODROW AND THE STUDY OF TRIGONOMETRY.

Mr. Woodrow once told his wife that he believed his success in Mathematics at Cambridge, whereby he obtained his degree as Fourteenth Wrangler, was greatly due to his old grandfather giving him "a book to puzzle over" on the then to him unknown subject of Trigonometry, when confined to the sofa for three months in his mother's house from a displacement of the knee-cap whilst skating. Mr. Woodrow was then about sixteen, and at the end of the three months he had conquered the book, without a tutor, or any assistance from any one, and in spite of the severe pain in his knee. This anecdote greatly interested many of his friends; and to the rising youth of this generation, who are always wanting a "coach," when in many cases they might so easily walk alone, or become thorough in their study, if they only had the will to do so, we would say,—Think of young Henry Woodrow, and the book his grandfather gave him "to puzzle over" on the by-no-means-easy subject of

Trigonometry! Self-reliance can hardly be considered a general attribute among students and workers in the present age, which, by the way, the Hindus call the *Kali Yûg*, or evil one. Before this they have have had three Yûgs (ages) —the Satya, the Treta, and the Dwapar—all corresponding in their natures with the golden, silver, brazen, and iron ages of the Greeks. With a little more self-reliance among the youth of England or Bengal—keeping the great Director's early study of Trigonometry in view—we may yet have even a greater than Euclid, or than the immortal Napier of the Logarithms!

INCIDENT IN THE LIFE OF LORD MACAULAY.

(TAKEN FOR A COMMERCIAL TRAVELLER.)

We shall conclude this what is intended to be diverting, if not very instructive, portion of our work with a slight incident in the life of the illustrious Lord Macaulay, whose "great" contribution to our pages must so materially add to their interest and value. Most Englishmen are fond of a good anecdote; and we humbly think that here is not a bad one. Going on this way, it will not do to be displeased if our kind readers say that we have fairly arrived at, or got far into, what Samuel Rogers so aptly termed our "anecdotage." *

A gentleman in London related to the writer that he was on a business-tour in the rather severe winter of 1849. At the railway station, where he had just arrived, he met a "short, manly figure," with, as usual, according to his Lordship's biographer, a badly-tied neckcloth, who inquired if he knew how he could get to Olney, a distance of some nine miles. The London gentleman discovered that there was a rickety old omnibus about to start; but the stranger desired a private carriage in preference, at once. This could not be procured, and as it was raining or snowing, the obliging gentleman

* "Far gone in our anecdotage."—*See* a capital article on this subject in a late number of *Household Words* (edited by Charles Dickens).

suggested the stranger's being content with the omnibus, even kindly saying he would go outside and smoke. The stranger, like King James, was not partial to smokers. The conveyance at length started on its journey with a few passengers. The weather, however, became so severe that the outside gentleman ventured in, having put aside his pipe or cigar. He was at once beside the great unknown, who enlightened him for some miles on a variety of subjects. On arrival at Olney, the question of the best inn was now put, and at once answered by our friend, who was well acquainted with the landlord. Believing the new arrival—although carrying a mark of real distinction about him—to be a great commercial traveller, it was now proposed to conduct him to the commercial room, till the private rooms required were ready. After some pressing he entered, "the observed of all observers," but soon left on being informed by his landlord that the rooms were at his disposal. It was thought strange that samples of locks, books, cloths, and such like, did not accompany the illustrious stranger.

Our London friend then left the scene of action for a time; but, on return to Olney, the polite landlord (who, with the frequent intelligence of his class, had taken kindly to the stranger) informed him that the mysterious gentleman took a great interest in the neighbourhood so loved by Cowper, and that he had been requested to accompany his lodger to the poet's house, where the famous hares were engraved over the door, and where he wrote his hymns—at which juncture he heard an emphatic recital of the first verse of the beautiful hymn commencing, "God moves in a mysterious way." Before departure for Wolverhampton, from which place he had said that he intended starting at once for the House of Commons, the curious in the Olney inn looked into the hat, and found the honoured name, "T. B. Macaulay." The riddle was now solved. Every one had at least heard of the distinguished man. There was only one Macaulay; and probably there will never be another. Our London friend never forgot "the stranger" who had so entertained him on his journey to Olney; and twenty-eight years after Lord Macaulay's death (he died 28th December, 1859), we were now indebted to him for the recital of this little incident, carefully given in the street. Thus had the great Essayist of Lord Clive and Warren Hastings been taken for a commercial traveller; he had once before been mistaken for a ballad-singer, while collecting ballads at Whitechapel for his brilliant history. It would appear to be one of the penalties of greatness to be taken for some one else; and, not long ago, the London public were amused by reading that Earl Redesdale, who once led the House of Lords, and had a paper war on a sacred subject with no less distinguished an opponent than Cardinal Manning, on settling his own wine-bill, was taken for his own *butler!*

APPENDICES.

—o—

I.

BENARES.

THE district in which Benares is situated was ceded by the subsidiary treaty of 1775 to the British Power by the Nawaub of Oude, Asoph ul Dowlah, in compensation (as was alleged at the time) of the aid which he had received in reducing to subjection one of his tributary chiefs.* The city is built on the north or left bank of the Ganges, as that great river flows eastward, and presents a fine appearance when viewed from the water. The eye rests on a variety of noble buildings, some of them highly ornamented, and with terraces on their summits; while the view is improved by the numerous flights of stone steps which lead from the banks of the river to Hindoo temples, or serve the crowds of devotees in performance of their frequent ablutions. Sir John Davis, in his vivid "Chapter," writes:—"Mr. Macaulay has given the following graphic description of 'Benares, a city which in wealth, population, dignity, and sanctity, was among the foremost of Asia. It was commonly believed that half a million of human beings was crowded into that labyrinth of lofty alleys, rich with shrines, and minarets, and balconies, and carved oriels, to which the sacred apes clung by hundreds. The traveller could scarcely make his way through the press of holy mendicants, and not less holy bulls. The broad and stately flights of steps, which descended from these swarming haunts to the bathing-places along the Ganges, were worn every day by the footsteps of an innumerable multitude of wor-

* The compact in question was in reality a general treaty for furnishing a force to protect him against all enemies.

shippers. The schools and temples drew crowds of pious Hindoos from every province where the Brahminical faith was known. Hundreds of devotees came thither every month to die; for it was believed that a peculiarly happy fate awaited the man who should pass from the sacred city into the sacred river. Nor was superstition the only motive which allured strangers to that great metropolis. Commerce had as many pilgrims as religion. All along the shores of the venerable stream lay great fleets of vessels laden with rich merchandise. From the looms of Benares went forth the most delicate silks that adorned the balls of St. James's and of the Petit Trianon; and in the bazaars the muslins of Bengal and the sabres of Oude were mingled with the jewels of Golconda and the shawls of Cashmere. This rich capital, and the surrounding tract, had long been under the immediate rule of a Hindoo prince (the Rajah of Benares) who rendered homage to the Mogul Emperors. During the great anarchy of India the lords of Benares became independent of the court of Delhi, but were compelled to submit to the authority of the Nabob of Oude. Oppressed by this formidable neighbour, they invoked the protection of the English. The English protection was given; and at length the Nabob Vizier, by a solemn treaty, ceded all the rights over Benares to the Company. From that time the Rajah was the vassal of the Government of Bengal, acknowledged its supremacy, and engaged to send an annual tribute to Fort William.'" Benares was of old renowned as the principal seat of Brahminical learning. Robertson, in his "History of India," speaks of it as the Athens of the East, the residence of the most learned Brahmins, and the centre of their science and literature; and Sir Robert Barker, an early visitor, has described an observatory there, said to have been erected by the Emperor Akhbar,* in which were astronomical instruments of large dimensions, constructed with great skill and ingenuity. Mr. Davis, who was judge and magistrate of the district about the period of this narrative, and who will be found to perform a conspicuous part towards the conclusion of it, profited by his residence there to investigate the astronomical science of the Brahmins. He was the first Englishman who applied a knowledge of their sacred language to an examination of their books. The results of his researches were discussed by Mr. Cavendish, in the "Philosophical Transactions," and are known to

* The observatory was really built by Jysingh, Rajah of Jypore, about the year 1700. *See* "Asiatic Researches," vol. v. p. 177.

all who feel interested in the early history of the science to which they relate.* A Hindoo Sanscrit College, established in the year 1791, and supported by the British Government, has continued to prosper to the present day.—*Massacre of Benarès*, pp. 10, 11, 12, 13.

BENARES AND WARREN HASTINGS.

BENARES was the scene of one of the most remarkable adventures of Warren Hastings, the first Governor-General, whose life was so fertile in adventures—one in which he rashly exposed himself to great personal peril, but extricated himself with his accustomed resolution and skill. The transaction, it is said, from its "dubious character," formed one of the principal charges against the British Proconsul on his return home. A brilliant account of this affair will be found in the greatest Eastern historical essay ever written, Lord Macaulay's on Warren Hastings; so there is no use in dwelling on it here. Suffice it to say that, in the words of Sir John Davis, "the Governor-General had instituted a claim against the Rajah Cheyte Singh of some hundred thousands of pounds sterling, and he followed up the excuses and evasions of the Rajah by force. He visited Benares, and there, notwithstanding the personal submissions and protestations of the unfortunate Cheyte Singh, had him arrested by two companies of troops in his own capital. This extreme measure, accompanied as Hastings was by a mere handful of troops, soon led to an insurrection among the subjects of the outraged prince."—(*The Massacre*, p. 15.) Here is an interesting study for the student of Indian history.

The great importance of Benares as a military position will be seen in our sketch of General Neill (*First Series*, p. 81), the avenging angel of the Sepoy Rebellion. The latest, and by far the most agreeable, writer on Benares as a military station is Dr. James C. Dickinson, retired Staff-Surgeon, whose admirable topographical series of "Our Indian Military Stations," is now in progress. These sketches of the pen and the pencil form a most useful and inter-

* Cited by Robertson in his "History of India," Note lxviii.

esting feature in the *Illustrated Naval and Military Magazine* —quite a gem in the periodical literature of the day. Commencing with Allahabad, the learned Staff-Surgeon has now (November, 1887) arrived at Meerut, the great cantonment, and one of the most extensive stations in India (five miles in circumference) at the time of the Mutiny, and the headquarters of the Bengal Artillery; the station, unfortunately, immortalized in our Indian annals as the scene of action (or rather inaction) on the part of the General commanding the Meerut Division, and the brigadier in command of the Meerut Station, "unparalleled in military history as an instance of hesitancy and incapacity for command in times when promptitude and decision should be the characteristic attributes of a general."

THE PRINCE OF WALES IN BENARES.

It will now surely interest our loyal British readers if we pass over the greater part of a century, from the date of Mr. Davis's gallant defence—even going further back and putting Warren Hastings and Cheyte Singh from our minds—down to Tuesday, 4th January, 1876, and a special railway journey from Calcutta.—"We* arrived at Bankipore Station at 8.30. Here the Prince was met by Mr. C. J. Metcalf, the Commissioner, and other civil officers of the district, Sir R. Temple and his staff, and a guard of honour. The Railway Volunteers and the Volunteer Cavalry were drawn up at the station. Breakfast was prepared here. We then set off in carriages for the station. The road to the camp, where Durbar tents were pitched, was about a mile in length, and it was decorated with flags all the way. 320 elephants of all sizes, some of them magnificent tuskers, belonging, I believe, chiefly to the Zemindars and planters, were drawn up in a row near the Durbar tent and made an imposing sight. There was a great crowd of enthusiastic natives, and all the European officers and planters for miles distant were here to see the Prince. Among them I saw my old friend C. Shillingford, from Purneah, and several other friends.

"The approach to the Durbar tent was lined with native

* His Royal Highness the Prince of Wales, Sir Joseph Fayrer, the indefatigable diarist, and party.—"With the Princes in India," p. 50.

troops, whilst the Volunteer Cavalry escorted the Royal carriage. A daïs was erected in the large Durbar Shamiana, and here the Prince held a levée, the Lieutenant-Governor, the Commissioner, and the suite standing by his side. Sir R. Temple presented the officers who had done good service during the last famine, and other European and native gentlemen. After the levée there was a déjeuner, most sumptuously prepared, and attended by 420 persons, at which Sir R. Temple proposed the Queen's health. Then came a review of nearly 400 elephants—some beauties—they were marched past, some plainly and some handsomely caparisoned, four deep. Some addresses (one from the Freemasons) were presented, and the Prince gave his consent to a new college being called by his name. Some presents were made: elephant tusks, silver ornaments, and Gainie bullocks. The sergeants of the 109th Regiment presented the Prince with a tame leopard, brought up by themselves, which will be sent down to Calcutta to be embarked in one of the ships. One little elephant caused great amusement; he was made to dance, and do a variety of tricks. After this the Prince and party returned to the train, and at about noon left for Benares. The weather is delightful, rather hot in the day, but very cool at night. We stopped for a short time for lunch at Buxar. We hear rumours that Lord Northbrook is going to England, and that another Viceroy is coming out.

"At Benares carriages were waiting and the usual guard of honour and escort. There were crowds of natives, and on the platform the high civil and military officers and native chiefs. Salutes were fired, and all the pomp and ceremony attendant on the presence of Royalty were observed.

"We are now in the râj of Sir J. Strachey, and about five miles from the city we found a magnificent camp—such a camp as India only can produce—a long street of large double-poled tents for the suite and staff, each having a tent to himself, with his name on it, all most carefully prepared, with every attention to comfort. At the end of the street the Lieutenant-Governor and the Prince's tents, with a magnificent suite of reception rooms, a flag-staff in front for the Royal Standard, and round it plants in tubs or earthen jars, looked green and refreshing, whilst the short grass was kept green and fresh by frequent watering. On each side, and in the rear, were numbers of smaller tents for the servants and others; in the vicinity were the camps of such troops as have been kept there; others, owing to rumours of cholera, have been sent away to reduce numbers as much as possible. The greatest care is taken in reference to all sanitary arrangements, and regular reports are sent to me of the state of health wherever we go, especially as to cholera. A medical officer, Dr. Deane, is attached to the camp, with whom I shall constantly communicate. The Sanitary Commissioner, Civil Surgeon, and Deputy Surgeon-General are to keep me informed.

"When in Calcutta I had several interviews with Lord Northbrook, who was most kind, and gave directions that all my wishes on these matters should be attended to, and that a special medical officer should be attached to our camp when we get to Delhi. This, I had pointed out, would be necessary, as I could not undertake the executive medical charge of a large camp, such as we shall then have. Dr. Kellett, of the Artillery, is nominated for this duty.

"We dined with the Lieutenant-Governor in camp. Lady Strachey, Mrs. Halsey, and many other ladies were there.

"The weather is beautiful, quite cool and clear, with a bright sky, and heavy dews at night. Thermometer at night down to 50°, probably lower; up to 70° in the shade during the day. We are all well. Our double-poled tents are magnificent; each has a fireplace, so adjusted as not to incur any risk of setting fire to the tent, a brick fireplace and flue being attached. I slept soundly, as it had been rather a tiring day, and the night before on the railway was not quite so satisfactory as if in bed. The constant changing of dress is rather irksome, but it is inevitable.

"*Wednesday, 5th January*, 1876, Camp, Benares.—Quite cold this morning, and during the night thermometer down to 52°. Wrote letters for the mail. After breakfast the Prince held a levée. There was an address from the municipality, read first in Sanscrit by a very infirm old native gentleman—Baboo Futteh Narayan Singha—who nearly fainted in the effort, and had to be seated. H.R.H. spoke most kindly to the old man. After the levée the Prince inspected specimens of Benares workmanship and various breeds of cattle, including the little Gainies, brought, I believe, by Mr. Halsey.

"After this, lunch at 2 P.M. Here I met many old friends Sir J. and Lady Strachey, Messrs. Batten, De Bourbel, FitzJames, Dr. Walker and others. We hear that Lord Northbrook has resigned, and that Lord Lytton is to be Viceroy."

On the morning of the 6th January the party left Benares

by the Oude and Rohilkund Railway for Lucknow *viâ* Fyzabad.*

* It may also be mentioned that the Prince and Lieutenant-Governor drove to Benares in state, stopping to look at the exterior of the college, and then went on to lay the foundation-stone of a new hospital, when the Prince made a good speech. In passing the Mission Homes, the young native converts sang "God Save the Queen," and "God Bless the Prince of Wales"; and some Christian girls presented a sandal-wood box containing lace, for the Princess. Sir Joseph Fayrer observed at Benares the large picture of the Duke of Edinburgh and his suite, painted from photographs taken in 1870 at Chukiah, the Maharajah's country seat. He tells us that he recognized himself, "represented with red hair and whiskers!" For H.R.H. the Duke of Edinburgh in India, *see* Appendix VII.

II.

SIR JOHN MORRIS, K.C.S.I.

Mr. J. H. Morris, C.S.I., who has just retired from the Chief Commissionership of the Central Provinces, has had an exceptionally long tenure of that office, during a very critical period in its history. The Government of India have placed on public record their very cordial recognition of the services rendered by Mr. Morris. They have declared him to have proved himself "an administrator of the first rank." When such a man rules a province so long, at such a period, good work must be done, and real progress made; and a brief review of the salient points of his career cannot be without interest. The early part of Mr. Morris' Indian career may be briefly sketched. He left Haileybury in June 1847, first of his year and bearer of several honours. Within two months after his arrival in Calcutta he had passed in both languages; and six months later he had obtained certificates of high proficiency in Persian, Urdu, and Hindi. This taste for, and acquaintance with, Oriental languages has been of the greatest service to Mr. Morris. His intercourse with the people has been very free and intimate. He has been able to converse intelligibly with natives of all classes; and very few European officers in India could more intelligibly and easily expound Government measures, or address kind and friendly advice to assemblies of natives.

Mr. Morris joined the Punjab in 1849, and was engaged in District work for two years, and then in Settlement work for eight years. Here, under the able administrators of those days, he received the training for what has been undoubtedly the greatest work of his Indian career, the settlement of the Central Provinces.

In 1859 he took furlough; and on his return in 1861 he was posted to the North-West Provinces as Magistrate and Collector of Allahabad. Two years later he was called to the Central Provinces as Settlement Commissioner by Sir Richard Temple (then Mr.), whose skill in selecting his subordinates is subject of common fame. When Mr. Morris joined the Province, not a single district was settled, but within five years the settlement of the whole district was very nearly completed. When, in 1868, Mr. Morris was appointed to act as Chief Commissioner, he carried to his new position an intimate acquaintance with the people, their circumstances, and their home life, which has been of inestimable advantage to his administration. The Central Provinces had been formed in 1861 by the union of the "Saugor and Nerbudda Territories" with the "Nagpur Province," and had been committed to the charge of Mr. Temple, whose first report, in 1862, formed the first full and trustworthy information laid before the Government and the public regarding this unknown land. This borderland between Hindostan and the Deccan had suffered from centuries of misrule and turbulence. It was known as the battlefield of the conflict of races, the hunting-ground of the Pindaris, the scenes of the ravages of thugs, wild beasts, and pestilence. When Mr. Morris went there, about twenty years ago, there was no railway; communications were only being planned; and not many had any idea of how to get to Nagpur. Soon after the railway was pushed on from Bombay to Nagpur, the capital of the Provinces. A few years later the line from Bhosawal to Jubbulpore was opened, so that the great highway through India ran through the Central Provinces.

Later, the Wardha Valley line gave to the world's markets the cotton of the Hingwaghat Valley and the coal of Warora, where the success of the mines is fairly established; and now the Chattisgarh railway has opened up the great granaries of the East. Excellent roads now intersect the Province, feed the railways, and produce free circulation.

The trade of the Province is now important. It exports grain largely to other provinces and to England, and its cotton has an excellent name. It boasts several mills, and local capital is freely invested. The education and civilization of its people have advanced with tremendous strides. Some of its districts will stand favourable comparison with the most prosperous of the provinces of British India. And its administration in several departments has been frequently held up by the Government of India even as a model to "less backward" provinces. This era of rapid but persistent progress was inaugurated indeed by Sir

Richard Temple; but he did no more than inaugurate it; and when he bequeathed his work to his able and energetic lieutenant, he could not, as he says himself, have left it in better hands.

The prosperity of the Province is not only seen in the rapid development of trade and the free circulation of capital, but also in the general air of comfort which characterizes the people everywhere. It is admitted on all sides that this is due to the nature of the settlement.

That the detailed arrangements of the settlement should be excellent was only to be expected from the fact that it was carried out by a man of Mr. Morris' settlement experience, aided by officers like Elliott, Bernard, Grant, Chisholm, and Forsyth. The great danger lay in the fixing of its general principles. At a time when an era of progress had clearly set in; when railways and communications were about to be pushed on throughout the Province; when it was manifest that great development of trade and great changes in prices must result, there was grave danger that sanguine men might yield to a very natural tendency to base the assessments on too favourable forecasts. Against this tendency Mr. Morris strongly and determinately set his face. It is possible that more land revenue might have been squeezed out of the agricultural classes; but there can be no doubt that a heavy assessment would have hindered progress, and been simply disastrous. The moderate and statesmanlike policy pursued by Mr. Morris has had its natural result in years of prosperity to the people, in the easy collection of the land revenue, in the most friendly relations between the people and the officers of Government, and in the increase of revenue under every head of taxation. The efforts that have been made to develop the resources of the country have had their natural effect on the agricultural community: the area under cultivation has been enormously extended; the prices of agricultural produce have been permanently raised, in some districts to a marvellous degree; and there can be no doubt that the next assessment will yield a great increase of revenue. But this increase itself will be mainly due to the wisdom shown in fixing a moderate assessment for the new Province, and leaving it to time to develop.

The exclusion from settlement, as the property of the State, of an area of some 20,000 square miles of waste, largely covered with forest, was a very important feature of the settlement arrangements. This has become an important source of revenue, yielding yearly increasing receipts. In 1866-67, when Mr. Morris first assumed charge as Chief Commissioner, the gross income from forests was Rs. 3,70,719, with a net revenue of Rs. 1,69,852. The average annual gross revenue for the three years 1879–82 was Rs. 6,51,827, and the net revenue was Rs. 3,35,641. This surplus revenue is almost entirely due to the District or Second Class Reserves, which have been managed by district officers under Mr. Morris' close and constant supervision. But not only do these forests form a steadily increasing form of revenue; they are also fuel and grazing reserves. The want of these has been felt in many parts of India, and the necessity for creating them has been strongly insisted on in a recent Resolution of the Revenue and Agricultural Department of the Government of India. They are there, ready to hand, in the Central Provinces. The marked success of excise arrangements in the Central Provinces has been frequently noticed with approval by the Government of India. It is not only that the net revenue has risen from Rs. 9,75,543, when Mr. Morris assumed charge of the Province, to Rs. 19,92,041 in 1881–82; but also that illicit distillation and smuggling of liquor, and the untaxed consumption of drugs, have been practically suppressed, and that, while reasonable facilities for supply exist, immoderate consumption of liquor and drugs is systematically checked. The Excise Department was inaugurated, and all the principal excise reforms were introduced, under Mr. Morris' administration. The educational system of the Central Provinces has been brought very prominently to notice in connection with the labours of the Education Commission. It has been most favourably criticized. The attention given to primary education may be seen from the fact that of the money spent by Government on schools, over Rs. 44 per cent. are spent directly on primary schools; and if their estimated share of the expenditure on scholarships, inspection, school buildings, &c., be added, this amount is raised to over Rs. 61 per cent. of the whole expenditure. Yet higher education has its due place. There is at least one good zillah school in each district; and there is a most successful college in Jubbulpore, teaching up to the F.A. standard. When the Education Commission visited Jubbulpore, some of the people represented their wish to have this college raised to the B.A. standard. Mr. Morris had already recommended this to Government, but want of funds had prevented Government from sanctioning the proposal. Dr. Hunter, the President of the Commission, accordingly advised the people to make an effort to help themselves in the matter. They have acted on his advice, and gone even further. The Jubbulpore people have determined to have their college, and the Nagpur people have determined to have theirs also. Subscriptions have been freely given, and both schemes seem likely to succeed. The people have shown their appreciation of Mr. Morris' rule, and especially of his educational policy, by resolving that these colleges should bear his name. While education has been thus wisely fostered, other schemes for the improvement and comfort of the people have been prudently but steadily pressed. Dispensaries have increased in number and popularity; vaccination has been successfully carried out, and some municipalities have even lately made it compulsory; sanitary arrangements have been systematically made; and the water supply of all towns, and of many villages, has been greatly improved. Nagpur has long boasted an excellent water supply, but it is now surpassed by the Jubbulpore water-works, which it was one of Mr. Morris' last official acts to open, and which take rank among the finest in India. These schemes have been carried out by Mr. Morris largely through the agency of the people themselves, whose co-operation he has been singularly successful in securing.

The development of municipal institutions in the Central Provinces has been very remarkable, and Mr. Morris has been able to inaugurate without difficulty a very full application of the policy of local self-government. The scheme as applied to the Central Provinces disproves the truth of the attacks made on the Government policy by private critics and the home press. The control and supervision to be exercised by Government through its officers are full and efficient. The generally prosperous and peaceful character of Mr. Morris' administration received a shock in the Khond rising in the feudatory state of Kalahandi. But this only served to bring out the energy and vigour of his administration. The rising was promptly suppressed, but all excessive or vindictive measures of punishment were checked, and attention was at once directed to the settlement and improvement of the country. The measures adopted for this end seem likely to be crowned with great success. The rising may be noted as bringing out another feature of Mr. Morris' administration, viz., his excellent relations with the officers serving under him. The clamour raised in some of the Madras papers against the vigorous measures necessarily taken for the repression of this bloody and ruthless rising by the officer in charge of affairs at Kalahandi, cannot yet be forgotten. The cry raised was one which was calculated to make a great impression on Government, but the Government of India wisely awaited Mr. Morris' report. He stood by his subordinates, and manfully and successfully vindicated their policy. It was the certainty that Mr. Morris would not throw over an officer who really tried to do his duty, but would give him all possible support, that did much to render Mr. Morris' administration as successful as it was. He was loyally served by men who knew that they could rely on his grateful and honourable support. Mr. Morris is an excellent type of our Indian administrators. A man determined to push progress and leave his mark, but prudent and sagacious in his administration, deeply imbued with a desire to advance the interests of the people, able to trust and to use subordinates who showed that they deserved his confidence, he leaves the province he has ruled so long, with the cordial goodwill both of his officers and of the people, with the hearty expression of the approval of the Supreme Government, and with the assurance that his life-long labour in India has not been in vain.*

If the above little narrative does not show a vast amount of good and useful work in a limited time, we should like to know where, on the part of an Anglo-Indian, or of any one else, good work is to be found ?—The Central Provinces lie between N. latitude 18°–24°, and E. longitude 77°–83°. They stretch from Bundelkund in the north, to the Madras Presidency in the south ; from the frontier of Bengal in the east, to independent Malwa and the Deccan in the west. Their extreme length from north to south may be computed at 510, and their extreme breadth from east to west at 550 miles. Their area amounts to about 150,000 square miles. "The Provinces," writes Mr. George Duncan (1865), "are vast in geographical area, infinitely varied in local and topographical details, sometimes flat and fertile, but generally wild and rugged ; abounding in hills, forest, and brushwood, sparsely populated, and scantily cultivated for the most part, but occasionally opening out into long and broad tracts covered with harvests, and thickly inhabited ; on the

* *Bombay Gazette*, May 1, 1883.

whole, poor and unproductive at present, but rich in natural resources, and capable of indefinite development in the future." And such all-important development early began under Sir Richard Temple and Sir John Morris. Here, as in other parts of India, it may fairly be said—

> "Toil builds on toil, and age on age improves."

III.

THE PROCESSION OF INDIAN PRINCES.

THE following record of the Great Jubilee Day (21st June) is well worthy of preservation; displaying, as it really does, considerable graphic power:—

People who imagine that it is an Oriental trait to take things easy and never keep to time had a chance of discovering their error from the exemplary punctuality with which the carriages conveying the Indian potentates and delegates started on their way. Quietly enough, the train of modest equipages emerged into Piccadilly from Hyde Park. Those who believed in tradition were sceptical as to whether these unpretentious vehicles could enshrine real maharajahs and maharanees and "pillars of the State" of high degree. The costumes soon dispelled all doubt on the subject. The gold brocades, the harmonious boldness of colour in the rich fabrics of the dress, the barbaric wealth of diamonds and gems, testified that, even in the Victorian age, the East was still the East. We must say frankly that the native Princes had probably no great opinion of the show to which they lent so much *éclat*, and, let us add, to which they gave so much meaning. Elephants bedizened with rupees—even if, as has occurred sometimes in the shows of Rajpoot chivalry, crystal chandeliers were suspended from their tusks—would have produced a vastly more decided sensation than the well-bred English horses and decent English carriages. But it would have been an offence against the whole idea of the pageant had any effort been made to drag in anything exclusive and fantastical. By their dress alone—but most eloquently by their dress—the native Princes showed that if they were loyal feudatories of the Imperial Crown, they were still faithful to the customs of their ancestors. The deputation must be passed over without the full notice due to the loyal service of the ruling Chiefs they represented, and to their own position in their own States as nobles of rank, and administrators of no small renown. The Maharajah of Cooch Behar—it is curious to remark—was the only Prince in the whole procession who was accompanied by his consort. Nothing could have been more easy and more gracious than the acknowledgments made by this lady to the salutations of the crowd, and though the position she occupied showed that her family are fully emancipated from the evil traditions of Hindooism and Mahomedanism with regard to woman's place in society, her appearance in the Queen's Jubilee ought to emphasize and promote the success of the Reform movement in which she inherits so sincere an interest. The Bramo Somaj has had its martyrs; let us hope it has its saints also. Interesting, but in a different way, was the new Ruler of Indore. There is still, says the *Standard*, a great gulf between the conceptions of sovereignty in the East and in the West, but it can hardly be that Holkar will learn no good lesson from the palpable evidence presented to him yesterday that the best way to be great is to be good.

The Indian Procession was constituted as follows:—

FIRST CARRIAGE.

Deputation from his Highness the Rajah of Kapurthala: Kanwar Haman Singh Ahluwalia, C.I.E.
Kanwarani Haman Singh.

SECOND CARRIAGE.

Deputation from his Highness the Maharajah of Bhurtpore, G.C.S.I.
Colonel Gunga Baksh.
Dr. Tyler, C.I.E.

THIRD CARRIAGE.

Deputation from his Highness the Maharajah of Jodpore, G.C.S.I.
Mahraj Sir Pertab Singh, K.C.S.I.
Captain Bruce Hamilton.

FOURTH AND FIFTH CARRIAGES.

Deputation from his Highness the Nizam of Hyderabad, G.C.S.I.
Sirdar Diler ul Mulk, C.I.E.
G. Blathwayt, Esq.
Nawab Amir-i-Akbar Asman Jah Bahadur.
Nawab Zafar Jung Shamsud Dowlah Shumsul.
Colonel Cockburn.

SIXTH CARRIAGE.

The Thakur Sahib of Gondal, K.C.I.E.
Major Talbot, C.I.E.

SEVENTH CARRIAGE.
The Thakur Sahib of Limree.
Colonel Nutt.

EIGHTH CARRIAGE.
His Highness the Thakur Sahib of Morvi.
Colonel Wodehouse.

NINTH CARRIAGE.
His Highness the Maharajah of Cooch Behar.
Her Highness the Maharanee of Cooch Behar, I.E.
R. Bignell, Esq.

TENTH CARRIAGE.
His Highness the Rao of Cutch.
Colonel Goodfellow.

ELEVENTH CARRIAGE.
His Highness the Maharajah Holkar of Indore.
Sir Lepel Griffin, K.C.S.I.

The Maharajah and Maharanee of Cooch Behar and the Maharajah Holkar, whose shoulders were covered with bullion woven into his tunic, were recognized and loudly cheered. But apart from the personalities of individuals, the subject that gave rise to the most excited comment and the greatest amount of wonder was the turban of his Highness the Rao of Cutch, which, when the sun flashed upon it, really blazed with the scintillating lights of diamonds, rubies, and emeralds.

When the Indian chiefs and their suites put in an appearance the somewhat flagging attention of the public in the Abbey began to be aroused and to mark the near approach of the grand and stately ceremonial of the day. The swarthy visages of these Orientals, with their dusky, æsthetic hues of maroon and saffron, and their flashing diamonds, were not more impressive than their stately and solemn gait, which told of a familiarity with ceremonial of which not merely our own Princes but even those of the brilliant Courts of Europe are unable to boast. The deputies and Princes above mentioned entered the Abbey in the order of arrival, last but not least—for state processions are arranged inversely to their natural order of precedence—the majestic Holkar, magnificently turbaned and bejewelled.

ANOTHER PROCESSION.

At 10.30 o'clock a second procession of the following Royal and distinguished guests left the Alexandra Hotel, accompanied by their respective suites, and attended by a captain's escort of the 2nd Life Guards, for the west entrance of the Abbey :—

FIRST CARRIAGE.

His Highness Ab'n Nasr Mirza Hissam us Sultaneh of Persia.
H. L. Churchill, Esq.
Nawab Mirza Hassan Ali Khan, C.I.E.
Mirza Ali Khan.

SECOND CARRIAGE.

His Royal Highness the Prince Devawongse Varoprakar of Siam.
Edward H. French, Esq.
Phra Darum Raksu.

THIRD CARRIAGE.

His Imperial Highness the Prince Komatsu of Japan.
Russell B. Robertson, Esq.
Yoshitane Sonnomiya.

FOURTH CARRIAGE.

Her Majesty the Queen Kapiolani of Hawaii and the Princess Liliyewokalani.
R. F. Synge, Esq.
His Excellency General Curtis Jankea.

On arrival at the Abbey they were received by the Vice-Chamberlain and conducted by the gentlemen in attendance to the Sacrarium, where they were shown by the Treasurer and Comptroller of the Household to the seats prepared for them.—*Overland Mail*, June 24, 1887.

IV.

SIR ASHLEY EDEN.

(LOCAL OPINION IN CALCUTTA.)

After ascribing to Sir Ashley Eden the great quality of magnanimity, it was well said that some who apprehended the weight of his hand lived to feel only the charm of his generosity. Strong good sense went hand-in-hand with steady justice and equal balance of mind. Those who have worked with him have been known to say that if any man wished to forecast Sir Ashley Eden's decision in any matter he had only to inquire what would be the verdict of common sense, and his task was accomplished. He had a marvellous faculty for going straight to the core of any question that he had to deal with; he instinctively put aside the husk and laid bare the kernel. This was the secret of his great quickness in the disposal of business, and of the vigour and terseness with which his decisions were expressed; and it was at once the accompaniment and the result of a natural dislike of affectation or display of any kind, and of all pretence in word or deed. It was this quality which guided him in appreciating and rewarding good service, and which made him the terror of all evil-doers and slovenly workers. Kind and considerate to those below him, a true lover of liberty and fairness, he was an unyielding opponent of all that savoured of harshness, whether between individuals or between Governments. *Parcere subjectis et debellare superbos* was among his mottoes. The fearlessness of his character was more than once displayed in struggles,—and generally successful struggles,—with higher powers for what he believed to be the rights of his province. Fortunately, however, the occasions for these conflicts were comparatively rare. The Imperial Government had so much confidence in his ability and judgment that it readily accepted his views. Moreover, financial sunshine played upon his path, and when there is abundance of money and free permission to spend it, Governors, like other men, are wont to live in sweet contentment.

Sir Steuart Bayley reminded us yesterday (April 15, 1887)

that for the nonce these halcyon days are over for Bengal. The brilliant financial sunshine of Sir Ashley Eden faded into the twilight—and latterly the gloaming—of Sir Rivers Thompson, and if this does not darken into night under Sir Steuart Bayley, it will, we fear, not soon brighten into day. In the beginning of his rule, at any rate, he will apparently have to thread his financial path in a dimness such as wrapped the land of Hades when Odusseus visited the shades. Sir Ashley Eden had ample financial resources at his command, and he made admirable use of them. In one of the last Minutes which he published as Lieutenant-Governor of Bengal he deplored the fact that the rules had restricted him in his expenditure on communications, and compelled him to spend on bricks and mortar much that he would have wished to spend on railways and canals. But his record was still a great one. He did not hide his talent in a napkin, but spent it freely and wisely for the public good. He managed to spend from Provincial funds alone 60 lakhs of rupees on railways and canals, while court-houses, jails, schools, water-works, drainage works, roads, and bridges, testify to his statesmanlike liberality in providing for the wants of the provinces. In his last financial Minute he told us that besides being able to make a contribution of 20 lakhs to the Imperial Government in time of trouble, he had been able to spend 200 lakhs in original works of all kinds. Times are changed now. The spectre of exchange and of frontier defence has beckoned away the rupees from the Bengal treasure chest as effectively as the Pied Piper led the rats from the houses of Hamlin. The drag has been placed on the wheels of progress by the hand of the Finance Committee, and the coach must slacken its speed in the interests of the Empire. Sir Steuart Bayley is entitled to warn us that one of the features of Sir Ashley Eden's administration will be absent from his own. Fortunate will the province be if five years hence he can point to the presence of the rest.

The statue of Sir Ashley Eden (the *Englishman* also informs us) finds an appropriate place by the side of one of the finest of his Public Works. It is carved in marble,—a fitting symbol of the mental strength and vigour of the man. And it is not a little remarkable that, where a pillar once marked the scene of a crime which threatened to extinguish the British dominion in Bengal, should now stand the effigy of one whose name will always be associated with perhaps the brightest chapter in the history of the peaceful development of our rule.

MEETING AT THE NORTHBROOK INDIAN CLUB.

SIR BARROW ELLIS AND SIR ASHLEY EDEN.

[For several reasons it has been thought prudent to publish the report of this meeting entire, for, apart from his Lordship the President's eulogistic remarks on Sir Ashley Eden, corroborating much of what has been said in the sketch, it assembled at a time when the sympathies of India with England were drawn closer together than they had ever been before.]

A luncheon was given on Tuesday, the 12th July, by the members of the Northbrook Indian Club to Mr. F. D. Petit, in recognition of the munificent present of £1,000 to the club by his father, Sir Dimshaw Petit. The Earl of Northbrook, G.C.S.I., presided, having Mr. Petit on his right. Some seventy members of the club were present, including the three Kaulterauni Princes of Morvi, Gondal, and Limri, and the Kaunar Harnam Singh, Sir M. E. Grant-Duff, Sir H. Davies, Sir Owen Burne, Members of the Council of Morvi, Sir Charles Elliot, Chief Commissioner of Assam, Sir Lepel Griffin, G.G. Agent for Central India; besides the above we noticed Mr. Ashburner, the Hon. Dadabhai Naoroji, General Clarke, General Abbot, Mr. D. P. Cama, Mr. Carmichael, Mr. P. Jeejeebhoy, &c.

Lord Northbrook, after reading a letter from Mr. T. H. Thornton, expressing his regret at being prevented from attending, said:—The object of our meeting to-day is to entertain our friend Mr. Petit, and to announce the very munificent donation which his father, Sir Dimshaw Manockjee Petit, High Sheriff of Bombay, has made to the club. He has been kind enough to present to the club £1,000 sterling, for the purpose of forming a library for the club. (Hear, hear.) His wishes are contained in a letter which I received from Mr. Petit. He wishes the amount to be invested in the names of trustees to purchase books, and that in the event of the dissolution of the club the amount should be spent at the discretion of the trustees upon such similar objects as they may deem proper. He desires the donation to be called by his name, so that it may be commemorated in connection with the endowment. These are the terms of the gift. We all know how distinguished our Parsee fellow-subjects have been for their liberality in all matters of public interest. We recollect the munificence of Sir Jamsetjee Jeejeebhoy, of Framjee Conasjee, and of the Camas. Sir Dimshaw Manockjee Petit has earned a name equal to theirs. He has given donations to the amount of something like £150,000 to different institutions of public utility in the Bombay Presidency. Quite recently he has offered £15,000 for the establishment of a Female College in Bombay. I would just mention, in connection with Sir Dimshaw Manockjee Petit, that he is one of the men most identified with the extension of the cotton manufacture in Bombay—an extension which has been of great advantage to the city of Bombay and of India generally, because I think no country can be complete in itself that does not possess some great manufacturing industry. It is more than ten years ago since I left India, and I have been much interested in some figures showing the increase of the cotton manufacture since that time. Between 1876 and 1886 the number of spindles has increased from one million to two-and-a-quarter millions; the quantity of yarn exported has increased tenfold, from 28,500 bales of 400 lb. each to 220,000 bales. At the same time there has been no sensible diminution in the import of cotton manufactures from England to India, so that the increase of the Bombay manufactures has not been detrimental to our manufacturing interests at home. We have great pleasure to-day in entertaining Mr. Petit as the most worthy representative of his father at this club. Hardly any of us to-day can forget that the club and the society to which we belong have suffered two very severe recent losses by the deaths of Sir Barrow Ellis and Sir Ashley Eden; and I should not feel that I had done my duty rightly as representing you at this meeting if I did not say a few words respecting them. I have been officially associated with many Indian statesmen, but there are few for whom I have a higher regard and to whom I feel a greater gratitude than to these two distinguished men. Sir Barrow Ellis was for many years the highest authority upon Bombay questions, and especially upon all matters relative to the revenue. He was for five years a member of the Council of the Governor-General when I was in India, where he showed high administrative capacity, and his advice was of great value to his colleagues. He was remarkable for his strong common sense and his lovable and sympathetic disposition, which endeared him to his own countrymen and to the natives of India of all classes. His cordial appreciation of their high qualities, and his constant desire to advance their best interests, led him, among other things, to take an active part in our club, and his loss will be felt as a personal grief by all of us. Mr. Barrow, his executor, has informed me that Sir Barrow Ellis has left by his will £500 to the Northbrook Indian Association, and a present of books to be added to the club library. Gentlemen, the Indian Civil Service has been rich in able administrators, but I do not think that any Indian gentleman will hesitate to agree with me that we have seen of late years no abler administrator than Sir Ashley Eden. He was a member of the Council of the Viceroy and Chief Commissioner of British Burma when I was in India; while filling the latter office he showed great financial ability. During the Bengal famine it was necessary to buy enormous quantities of rice in Burma and despatch it to Bengal. The business was entrusted to Sir Ashley Eden, who transacted it admirably, and thereby contributed most materially to the success of the relief operations; but it was afterwards, as Lieutenant-Governor of Bengal, that he most particularly made his mark in India. When he left Calcutta five years ago a great meeting was held in his honour, and it was determined to erect a statue to his memory, and last April the statue was uncovered by Sir Steuart Bayley, the present Lieutenant-Governor of Bengal; on both these occasions the expressions of gratitude to Sir Ashley, and appreciation of his high qualities from all classes in Calcutta, were very remarkable. Sir Ashley Eden was distinguished for quickness of perception, for sound judgment, for firmness in carrying out his views, and for his power of securing the confidence of those who served under him. It was said, and very rightly said, at the great meeting at Calcutta that these qualities were rendered still more valuable by "a generous and enlightened sympathy with all classes of the people." Some of us recollect the great troubles in Bengal many years ago connected with the cultivation of indigo. The man who initiated the reform of the abuses of the old indigo system was Sir Ashley Eden. As Mr. Prinsep said, "he courageously stood forth as the redresser of wrongs at some risk to his own career, and was the means of securing liberty and freedom of action to the poorest classes." Sir Steuart Bayley made a remark in his speech which is so true, and at the same time so much in accordance with the objects of the club, that I will venture to quote it. He said that nothing served Sir A. Eden better throughout his successful administration of Bengal "than the genuine and sympathetic friendship of his native friends, who had gathered round him in the early part of his career, and clave to him to its close, and in this respect he offered an example by which, I hope, the younger members of the service, anxious to walk in his footsteps, will not fail to profit." These two distinguished statesmen were also members of the Council of the Secretary of State for India for many years, and I am sure you will agree with me that we not only regret their loss upon personal grounds, but because the country has lost the services of two men whose opinion on all Indian questions was entitled to great weight. Returning from this painful but necessary digression to the real object of our meeting, I propose to you to drink the health of our friend Mr. Petit, and to express to his distinguished father our most sincere thanks for his munificent donation. This club has depended for its initiation, and it now depends for its support, upon the Indian Princes and Indian gentlemen. We should not have been able to meet here now if it had not been for the liberality of several of the Indian Princes, and especially of his Highness the Thakore of Bhownuggur, who gave us a lac of rupees, without which we could not have taken this house or established this club. You well know that the object of this club is to bring Indian and English gentlemen together in every way in which we can reasonably, pleasantly, and profitably do so. In carrying out this object there has been one principle from which we have never swerved, and that is that we should allow no Indian or English politics to be mixed up with the club; and I may say that, although from time to time since we started there have been some questions which excited a keen interest, and upon which many of us differed both upon Indian politics and English, the harmony of the club has not been disturbed. We have from time to time entertained distinguished men connected with India, both English and Indian; we have heard what they had to say, and expressed to them our sympathy with their work and our gratitude for their services. We hope this club has been of service to our younger friends who are studying in England, and that they find here men with whom they can associate with advantage. I think the club is of use particularly to our Indian friends who are studying at the two universities, and who, when they come to London, find themselves quite at home here. These may appear very small things, but I think it is a great advantage, both to England and to India, that there should be some place where those who really take an interest in Indian affairs can meet Indian gentlemen, who either reside in London or, as is the case with many of those present to-day, come from India to visit us for a short time. Believing, therefore, that we are working in the right direction, we all feel deeply grateful to Sir Dimshaw Manockjee Petit, who has come forward to assist us in providing a better library for our club; we will take care to use his liberal donation to the best advantage of the club and to associate his name permanently with the gift. I now beg to propose to you the health of Mr. Petit, and to express on behalf of the club our grateful sense of the munificence of his father, and of the wise way in which he has shown his appreciation of our efforts. The toast was drunk with great enthusiasm.

Mr. Petit in returning thanks said :—Lord Northbrook and gentlemen, I cannot sufficiently express my thanks for the great kindness and honour you have done to my father, Sir Dimshaw Manockjee Petit, by entertaining me to lunch at the club to-day. I have been trained to be a merchant, and do not presume to be either a good scholar or speaker of English, but I assure you that lack of words in me is no lack of grateful sentiments on my part. When I write to my father about this honour that you, Lord Northbrook, and the members of the club have done him, he will feel much pleased to know that what little he has been able to do in a public way has been appreciated by such a distinguished institution as the Northbrook Club, where one can meet all the worthy men who have acquired a name and fame in Indian affairs. My father has always taken a great deal of interest in all questions of education, and he has in his own humble way done his best to promote it as much as possible. He, as also a number of intelligent Indian gentlemen, look upon this club as a most useful institution, which is almost a boon to men coming over from India. I know from my own experience, and that of some of my friends, how useful they have found the club when they arrived first in England, and when their hearts were cheered by meeting at the club their English and Indian friends whom they could perhaps never have met. We Indians are extremely thankful and indebted to you, Lord Northbrook, for establishing this beneficent institution, as also to Sir George Birdwood, Mr. Fitzgerald, and the other members of the committee in promoting it. The club is now all that could be desired, but I hope at no distant date it may be in a position to have a separate home for itself, where accommodation for lodging could be found for temporary visitors to this country. By the facility of intercourse between Englishmen and Indians which this club affords, as also by the great help to the education of Indian young men which the Northbrook Society gives, India is indebted, as a whole, to this institution, and I trust we would have some of our distinguished Indian princes also giving us their support in this matter as his Highness the Thakore Sahib of Bhownuggur has munificently done. I should like to say one word about a great friend the club and a number of Indians and Englishmen have lost in the late Sir Barrow Ellis, whose unexpected death has made us all sad. He was known to us all from Bombay, and his cheerful and genial nature made him a friend of all those who came into contact with him. He was a great friend of ours, and we must deplore much his untimely loss. I thank you again, my Lord Northbrook, and my English and Indian friends, for the kind hospitality and reception you have given me to-day.

V.

HENRY WOODROW

(*Director of Public Instruction, Bengal*).

THE ROYAL VISIT TO CALCUTTA.*

Programme, by Lord Northbrook (Viceroy), of the Undergraduates' Welcome to his Royal Highness, the Prince of Wales.

After leaving the Senate House by the north-eastern door the Procession will stop at the edge of the verandah and will be thus arranged :—

The Registrar. The Syndicate.
The Officiating Director of Public Instruction
[Mr. Woodrow].
The Viceroy. His Royal Highness.
The Vice-Chancellor.
The Ex-officio Members of the University.
The Staff.

The students of the several colleges will be drawn up in an open square. The representatives of the colleges and of the nationalities using the chief languages of these Provinces will be drawn up on the east of the staircase.

They will march by, and will deliver to the officiating Director of Public Instruction scrolls containing the welcome written in English, Bengali, Sanskrit, Hindi, Uriya, Arabic, Persian, Urdu, and Armenian.

The general purport of each welcome is as follows :—

"We, the Youthful Representatives of the (33) millions†

* His Royal Highness the Prince of Wales arrived in the *Serapis* on the 23rd of December, 1875. During the Royal visit the Prince was frequently accompanied by Mr. Woodrow.

† Bengali	33 millions
Uriya	4 ,,
Urdu	9 ,,
Hindi	14 ,,
Aborigines and others	2 ,,
Total	62 ,,

that speak the (Bengali) language in the Provinces of Bengal, Behar, and Orissa, desire to welcome our Future Sovereign, and to thank him for that Education which we enjoy under the British rule."

The officiating Director of Public Instruction will hand to His Royal Highness each scroll, and will mention the language in which it is written, and the population which use that language. His Royal Highness will return them to the Director to keep for him. After the scrolls of welcome have been presented a student from each of the fourteen colleges in Calcutta and its vicinity will pass by, and on his making his bow, the officiating Director will mention the college of which the student is the representative.

The procession will then re-form and will proceed to the Senate House by the north-western door.

The Prince will only march along the verandah. The students will be arranged outside the verandah in the compound, where they will have an excellent opportunity of seeing the Prince, who will halt for a minute in the centre of the verandah, where the officiating Director of Public Instruction will give the scrolls altogether to His Royal Highness.

NORTHBROOK.

ARRIVAL OF THE PRINCE OF WALES IN CALCUTTA.

SIR JOSEPH FAYRER thus graphically describes this interesting and memorable event:—"We did not land till 4 P.M. Prinsep's Ghât* had been splendidly prepared with a landing-place made of pontoons for the occasion. A pavilion and awnings had been erected, and here most of the principal inhabitants of Calcutta were assembled. I met many old friends, and among the ladies Mrs. Morgan and Mrs. J. P. Grant were the first to whom I spoke. The Prince was received on landing by Mr. S. Hogg, and other members of the municipality, and an address was read, to which H.R.H. replied; the address was presented in a beautiful silver casket. The Viceroy, the Commander-in-

* A kind reviewer of our *First Series* (p. 173) reminded us that this famous Ghât is *not* between "Fort William and Baboo Ghaut," but "below the Fort and nearer to Kidderpore and Cooley Bazaar." It is a great thing to have a guide-book before one.

Chief, the Bishop, the Members of Council and the Chief Justice; Scindiah, Holkar, Cashmere, Rewah, Jeypore, Punnah, and many other chiefs were present. After the address a procession was formed, and we drove to Government House, by way of the Ellenborough Course, the road lined with troops, and crowded with people on foot, on horseback, and in carriages. It was nearly 5 P.M. when we left the Ghât, and about 5.30 we reached Government House. I recognized many old friends among the spectators and among the schools drawn up on the Ellenborough Course. I saw my old friends of the E. O. Asylum, with Miss Clarke; I also noticed Woodrow superintending some of the arrangements. The children sang 'God Save the Queen,' and a song in honour of the Prince. It was a beautiful, bright, cold-weather day, and such are very pleasant in Calcutta. It was interesting to see my former home under these new circumstances, and very pleasant to see old friends again. Salutes were fired on shore from the fort and from the fleet. The escort consisted of European cavalry and the Viceroy's body-guard. All the ships in the river were dressed with flags, and on shore decorations of all kinds made a very bright and cheerful appearance. There was no cheering except from Europeans; the Bengalee does not express his pleasure in this way; but still, the greatest interest and enthusiasm were manifested by the dense crowds assembled to meet the Prince. The comparative absence of women was strangely in contrast with Bombay and Madras. The Prince wore Field-Marshal's full dress, with the Garter and the Star of India; the suite were also in full dress."

CONVOCATION OF THE CALCUTTA UNIVERSITY.

THIS was held on Monday, 3rd January, 1876, and was distinguished above such ceremonials in general by the presence of H.R.H. the Prince of Wales. Of course, Mr. Woodrow was a foremost man on this eventful day; for it was no other than that on which the Prince appeared in the academic costume of the University. The Convocation was held in the University Buildings. Sir Joseph Fayrer writes:—"On this occasion I wore my cap and gown probably for the last time as a member of the Senate. The honorary degree of Doctor of Laws was conferred on the Prince; and this was the first honorary degree ever given here." This important matter was submitted to the Senate through Sir Joseph Fayrer's and Dr. Chevers's well-timed joint action. On the present occasion a speech was made by the Vice-Chancellor, to which H.R.H. replied. Sir Joseph also writes:—"I took this opportunity of mentioning to Sutcliffe, the Registrar of the University, the wishes of my Ceylon friends concerning the affiliation of their Medical School to the Calcutta University; and he said he would bring it to the notice of the Senate."

MINUTE ON CONFERRING A DEGREE IN CALCUTTA ON HIS ROYAL HIGHNESS THE PRINCE OF WALES.

Before presenting such an interesting document to our readers—especially interesting where the heir of the British throne is concerned—a word or two may be said about Universities in India, especially that of Calcutta. First, with reference to Mr. Woodrow:—

On the 26th of January, 1855, he received a letter from the Secretary to the Government of India, Mr. (afterwards Sir) Cecil Beadon, appointing him, by order of the Marquis of Dalhousie in Council, a Member of the Committee, for preparing a scheme for the establishment of Universities in the Presidency Towns of Calcutta, Madras, and Bombay. Mr. Woodrow was to receive instructions through Sir James Colville, the President of the Committee. This letter from the Council Chamber was written more than twenty years before the esteemed Director's death; and during that long period he had served under six distinguished Lieutenant-Governors of Lower Bengal:—

Mr. (Sir Frederick) Halliday, his first Chief,
Sir Cecil Beadon,
Sir William Grey,
Sir J. P. Grant,
Sir George Campbell, and
Sir Richard Temple,

who was Lieutenant-Governor at the time of Mr. Woodrow's death, and followed him to the grave at Darjeeling as chief mourner. Of course, such able rulers of so large and important a Province took no ordinary interest in its educational progress. The establishment of the

Calcutta University became a grand fact and landmark in the enlightenment of the people of India.

At length there appeared a "Bill to authorize the University at Calcutta to grant Honorary Degrees."* The preamble begins:—"Whereas, under Act No. II. of 1857, an University was established at Calcutta for the purpose of ascertaining by examination," &c. The first paragraph, referring to the "Power to confer honorary degrees," informs us that—"With the previous consent of the said Chancellor, the said Syndicate for the time being may grant any academical degree to any person without requiring him to undergo any examination for such degree." The pith of the next sentence is embodied in the Minute; and little Mr. Woodrow imagined, during his busy educational life, that his would one day be the first signature (he being President of the Faculty of Arts in the University) of the Syndicate, conferring a degree on the Prince of Wales. The Minute runs thus:—

"16*th December*, 1875.—Act XXI. of 1875, authorizing the University of Calcutta to grant Honorary Degrees, having been passed by the Governor-General in Council, the following certificate, in conformity with paragraph 1 of the Article, was ordered to be placed upon record:—

"*University of Calcutta*.—The undersigned certify that in their opinion H.R.H. Albert Edward, Prince of Wales, is, by reason of eminent position and attainments, a fit and proper person to receive the honorary degree of Doctor in Law in this University.

"(Signed) Arthur Hobhouse, Vice-Chancellor.

H. Woodrow,
A. G. Macpherson,
J. Dyson,
J. B. Partridge,
Charles H. Turner, } Members of the Syndicate.

"My previous consent is hereby signified.

"(Signed) Northbrook."

* Passed by the Governor-General in Council, December, 1875. The Degree was conferred on the 3rd January, 1876. Dr. W. Markby, a learned friend of the Woodrow family, kindly furnished copies of the Bill and Minute. To another friend, Mr. C. B. Clarke, Fellow of Queen's College, Cambridge—a former able and zealous Inspector of Schools in Bengal—the public are indebted for many of the particulars in the "Memoir" of Mr. Woodrow.

NOTIFICATIONS.

"No. 42, of 1876.

"THE CALCUTTA GAZETTE.

"Wednesday, October 18th, 1876.

"ORDERS BY THE LIEUTENANT-GOVERNOR OF BENGAL.

No. 2208, C.S.

"Notification.—The 17th October, 1876.—The Lieutenant-Governor records with great sorrow the sudden death, on the 11th of October, of Mr. Henry Woodrow, M.A., Director of Public Instruction in the Provinces under the Government of Bengal. By this event the Government has been deprived of an able and devoted servant, while the natives have lost a wise and zealous friend.

"H. J. REYNOLDS,
"Officiating Sec. to the Government of Bengal."

"GENERAL DEPARTMENT.

"EDUCATION.—No. 3180.

"Calcutta, the 5th December, 1876.

"RESOLUTION :—

"Read—The General Report on Public Instruction for the year 1875-6.

"'The preparation of this report has been delayed by the lamented death of Mr. H. Woodrow, the Director of Public Instruction. A distinguished scholar, a successful teacher, an energetic Inspector of Schools, and an efficient Director, Mr. Woodrow devoted to the cause of Education, abilities which were at once stimulated by philanthropy and guided by sound judgment. Earnest and conscientious in his work, he displayed at the same time a kindliness and a sympathy which attracted the confidence of all with whom he was brought into contact; and the natives of Bengal, whose best interests he had deeply at heart, will long remember his name with affection and respect. . . . . '

"H. J. REYNOLDS,
"Officiating Sec. to the Government of Bengal."

MEMORIAL TO THE LATE HENRY WOODROW.

A tablet has recently been placed in Rugby School Chapel by a few of the friends and schoolfellows of the late Henry Woodrow, Director of Public Instruction, Bengal, bearing the following inscription:—

M. S.
HENRICI WOODROW
COLL. AD CAMUM GONV: ET CAII
NECNON UNIV: AD GANGEM BENGALENSIS
E SOCIIS.

BONARUM ARTIUM APUD INDOS FAUTOR
DISCIPLINÆ ARNOLDIENSIS
EGREGIUM EXEMPLAR
CHRISTI IMITATOR
SUI ET PRODIGUS ET CONTEMPTOR
NATUS PRID: KAL: AUG: MDCCCXXIII
OBIT A: D: V. ID: OCT: MDCCCLXXVI.

C. C. BARNARD.
Rev. W. BRIGHT, D.D.
EARL OF DERBY.
F. DUMERGUE.
W. J. EVELYN.
W. A. FORBES, C.B.
T. HUGHES, Q.C.
F. L. HUTCHINS.
Rev. T. W. JEX BLAKE, D.D.
Rev. J. LAMB.
Rev. H. A. OLIVIER.
Rev. A. S. ORMEROD.
Rev. C. L. PEMBERTON.
T. C. SANDARS.
W. S. SETON-KARR.
COLONEL EDMUND SMYTH.
T. WALROND, C.B.
Rev. H. T. WHATELY.

May, 1879.

TRANSLATION OF A SANSCRIT ELEGY

BY

RAJAH SOURINDRO MOHUN TAGORE, MUS. DOC.,*

ON

HENRY WOODROW, ESQ., M.A.,

Director of Public Instruction, Bengal, India.

WITH INTRODUCTORY LINES TO HIS MEMORY.

INTRODUCTORY LINES.

'Twas Autumn in his life, and in the year,
When sheaves were garnered in his native land,
The Lord of Harvest, with unerring hand,
Reaped him from earth. Far-ranging Himalaya

* There is also an Indian melody, with verses, composed on the lamented death of Mr. Woodrow, by his friend and admirer, Rajah Sourindro Mohun Tagore, Mus. Doc. The Rajah presented Mrs. Woodrow with a copy of the verses in Sanscrit, enclosed in a silver frame, which she valued most highly. The verses were rendered into English, word for word; and then a talented lady-friend, Miss Nesfield, returned them with English verses, of the same metre, and skilfully composed an accompaniment to the Rajah's Indian melody. It is a beautiful and mournful air expressing grief, which the Sanscrit word "Behâg" is intended to convey. Comparing the two—*i.e.*, the Indian melody and the English version—we find the air is the same, as the melody is unchanged. The amiable and accomplished Rajah continues his friendly acquaintance with Mrs. Woodrow, as the widow of his quondam friend and counsellor; and never was truer or more lasting affection than that he bears to the memory of his old patron. The friendship arose in years gone by, when, through Mr. Woodrow's mediation, the Government of India permitted Sourindro Mohun Tagore to make use of the title of "Musical Doctor," conferred upon him by the University of Philadelphia (America); and he was thenceforth known as Dr. Sourindro M. Tagore. He has had the title of Rajah conferred upon him since that period. His brother is the Maharajah Jotendro Mohun Tagore, a Member of the Bengal Legislative Council. Another kindly action on Mr. Woodrow's part was to assist Dr. Sourindro M. Tagore to resuscitate the "Bengal Academy of Music," to which allusion is made in the sixth verse of the translation of the elegy. For this the Rajah was most grateful, and he always says it was due to Mr. Woodrow that the Academy revived. At concerts of Native music held in Calcutta, Anglo-Indians have listened with interest to the "Vina," and the voices and instruments of fifty performers. The Rajah also possesses a bust of Mr. Woodrow, ordered from England by him—a copy of that unveiled at Calcutta by Sir Alexander Arbuthnot, 15th March, 1879.

Holds what is mortal of him, fitly shrined
Amid those mighty hills, for he was great,
And stood serene, above all strifes of hate
Or jealousy; love filled his heart, his mind
On others' good was bent, a child of God,
He loved his Saviour, loving therefore man;
Alike, the Hindu and Mahomedan
Trusted and honoured him, because he trod
Steadfast *in equity*, nor race, nor creed
Moved him to be unjust in word or deed.

* * * * * *

Who knows not, when a priceless friend has fled
To other worlds, how tenantless is earth
That holdeth him no more, of what great worth
Is aught that speaks to us of him that's dead?
Then marvel not though one, of Eastern blood
And Hindu faith, thus mourns, with kindred tears,
His English counsellor and friend of years,
In language not unworthy brotherhood.

FRANCES E. NESFIELD.

TRANSLATION OF ELEGY.

"Calm of spirit, high of soul,
Benefactor of Bengal,
Henry Woodrow, called from hence,
Merged into the elements.

"Fell the tidings on my brain
With a crushing stroke of pain,
As a thunderbolt were driv'n
Armed with death, from angry heav'n.

"When of that dear friend bereft,
What in all the world was left?
Life was nothingness to me,
Earth one great vacuity!

"Now within my home I set
That which telleth of him yet,
His pale image sculptured fair,
Stands a blest memorial there.

"When to Heaven a fervent thought
Flies, with supplication fraught,
'Tis that he may walk on high
With the Gods, eternally.

"India's muse of song, once wrecked
In the ocean of neglect,
Rescued by his saving hand,
Lifts her voice throughout our land;

"Strikes her lyre's responsive strings,
And a solemn requiem sings,
Sadly chanting the refrain
Called '*Behâg*,' pathetic strain!

"Thus she tenderly condoles
With the grief of stricken souls,
Torn from him, who dwells at rest,
In the City of the Blest."

FRANCES E. NESFIELD.

October, 1879.

THE WOODROW MEMORIAL BUST.

ABOUT the middle of September, 1878, the India Office received, for temporary exhibition in one of its best lighted committee-rooms, the superb marble bust of Mr. Henry Woodrow, the late Director of Public Instruction in Bengal. It will be remembered, according to the *Overland Mail* of 20th September, 1878, that a subscription, to which the natives of India mainly contributed, was set on foot immediately after Mr. Woodrow's sudden death. The esteem for him, which was great among Rugby men who knew him, extended to the native population of India, who recognized his efforts in the spread of education. They raised a fund sufficient to endow a scholarship at the Calcutta University —to be called "The Woodrow Scholarship"—and they sent a commission to England for a marble bust, which was to be erected as a public memorial at Calcutta.

The sculptor selected was Mr. Edwin Roscoe Mullins—an artist of recognized merit, who exhibited five works in the Royal Academy gallery in 1878. "In producing the magnificent bust of Mr. Woodrow, which cannot fail to gratify the subscribers, Mr. Mullins has worked from photographs. We are glad to know that the family and friends consider the bust excellent in every way. It is much larger than life size, and will be placed on a pedestal which waits instructions from Calcutta as to its inscription. Numerous friends of Mr. Woodrow have visited Mr. Mullins' studio, in Montagu street, while the work has been in progress, Mr. Seton Karr and Mr. Tom Hughes—who has an allusion to Mr. Woodrow as a Rugby boy in 'Tom Brown'—among the number. Dr. Guest, the Master of Caius College, Cambridge—the college of which Mr. Woodrow was a fellow—has ordered a copy of the bust for presentation to the college.

"Referring to Mr. Woodrow's career, and his sudden death at Darjeeling in Oct., 1876, a contemporary adds that it was due to Mr. Woodrow that the late Lord Macaulay's minutes on education in India were preserved. Mr. Woodrow discovered these minutes scattered among the records of the office of Public Instruction in Calcutta in 1862, and caused fifty copies to be printed at his own expense. For this he received the thanks of Lord Canning, then Governor-General of India. The minutes are quoted in the 'Life of Lord Macaulay,' lately published by Mr. G. O. Trevelyan, coupled with Mr. Woodrow's name. Mr. Woodrow, when at Rugby, was considered to be a favourite pupil of Dr. Arnold, and he was one of the six who supped with Dr. Arnold on the night of his lamented and sudden death. Thus in the manner of his own death, from its suddenness, Mr. Woodrow resembled his revered master. Dr. Arnold was forty-nine years of age, and Mr. Woodrow fifty-three, and both died in the midst of a career of the highest usefulness. At Rugby Mr. Woodrow was contemporary with Sir Richard Temple, Bart., G.C.S.I.; Dr. Valpy French, the new Bishop of Lahore; Mr. Thomas Hughes; Lord Stanley, now Earl Derby; Mr. Theodore Walrond, Mr. Evelyn, M.P., and many others, whose friendship he there won and maintained through life."

For the exhibition of Mr. Woodrow's bust in the India Office, the public were much indebted to the kindness of the then Permanent Under-Secretary of State, the present Right Honourable Sir Louis Malet, C.B.—the esteemed friend of Cobden—like his great associate always alive to some good action in order to please his fellow-men. It was gratifying to learn that the interest Sir Louis took in this comparatively small matter gave the highest satisfaction to all concerned.

THE LATE MR. HENRY WOODROW.*

UNVEILING OF THE BUST BY SIR ALEXANDER ARBUTHNOT, K.C.S.I.

THE Calcutta *Englishman* of the 17th of March, 1879, contains an interesting account of the unveiling of the memorial bust of the late Mr. Henry Woodrow, Director of Public Instruction in Bengal. The ceremony took place on March 15th, a Degree Day at University College, Calcutta, where the memorial has been erected, and was performed by the Hon. Sir A. J. Arbuthnot, Vice-Chancellor of the University, in the presence of the Bishop of Calcutta, the Lieutenant-Governor of Bengal, General Grant (the famous American President), and many other distinguished persons, including several native gentlemen of high rank. The bust, which is considered to be a good likeness of the late Mr. Woodrow, bore the following inscription :—

"Henry Woodrow, M.A., formerly Fellow of Caius College, Cambridge, Fellow of the University of Calcutta, six years Principal of La Martinière, upwards of twenty years Inspector of Schools, and latterly Director of Public Instruction in Bengal.

"This bust is erected in affectionate remembrance by desire of his Native friends, from funds chiefly contributed by them to perpetuate his memory, and in recognition of his worth and of his devotion to the cause of education in India."

In addition to this memorial a scholarship has been founded, to be called the "Woodrow Scholarship."

"He was born at Norwich, July, 1823, and died at Darjeeling, October, 1876."

The scholarship referred to in this inscription was founded by the Memorial Committee in Calcutta, and is of the annual value of £20. It is to be held in connection with the Calcutta University, and is to be called the "Woodrow Memorial Scholarship." It will be awarded to the best B.A. of the year who does not obtain any other Scholarship. The Committee have also founded an Annual Medal of the value of twenty rupees, to be awarded to the best pupil of the First Grade Vernacular Schools in Bengal, on the results of the competitive examinations held by the Director of Public Instruction. Mr. Woodrow's special attention to the train-

* *Record*, April 23rd, 1879.

ing of native teachers, and his voluntary donations for the encouragement of young men studying in the normal schools, determined the Committee to establish this memorial medal. After the degrees had been conferred, the Vice-Chancellor, referring to the unveiling of the memorial bust in the Senate House, said it had been placed there as a memorial of Mr. Woodrow's long and devoted services to the cause of native education. It is, he went on to say, a melancholy satisfaction that the duty of presiding at that ceremonial and of bearing public testimony to the merits of our valued and lamented colleague, should have devolved upon me; for it so happens that Henry Woodrow and I were schoolfellows [at Rugby]; and although the greater part of our Indian service was passed in different parts of the Empire, we had for many years a bond of union in the fact that we were both employed upon the great work of promoting the education of natives of this land—a work which our lamented colleague performed with zeal and devotion and practical ability that have seldom been surpassed. I well remember meeting Mr. Woodrow on the first occasion of my visiting this city, now nearly four-and-twenty years ago, and renewing the acquaintance of our school-days; and I shall never forget how impressed I then was by the earnestness and the thoroughness with which he had entered upon his new duties. That earnestness and that thoroughness never flagged. They characterized the whole of Mr. Woodrow's useful and active life, up to the closing scene when he was suddenly struck down in the midst of his labours. (Applause.) And there were two other points in his character which we should all of us do well to contemplate, and to which I would invite the attention of you, my younger friends—the newly-passed graduates of this University. I refer to the consistent uprightness and truthfulness of his mind, and to the equanimity with which he bore the trials and disappointments of life. Some of those now present are doubtless aware that many years before his death Mr. Woodrow encountered a severe disappointment in being passed over for the chief office in his department—an office for which he was generally considered to possess the strongest claims. Another person was selected, and Mr. Woodrow had to work on in a subordinate post for another fifteen years; but the disappointment, great as it was, in no way impaired his zeal. He laboured on patiently and steadily, destined at length to attain the goal of his ambition, but, alas! only to enjoy it for a few short months. (Applause,)

VI.

PHYSICAL TRAINING IN INDIA AND ENGLAND.*

Mr. Woodrow selected a most appropriate motto for his excellent pamphlet:—"*The race is not to the swift, nor the battle to the strong.*" Like the great Scottish divine, Dr. Guthrie, in being well-formed, genial, and with "a fine breeze of nature about him," the philanthropic Director of Public Instruction in Bengal sought, not only to improve the Hindu mind, but by art and exercise to renovate his body, never, from the effects of climate, by any means strong. So, then, here we have the "Nestor of Education" in a double capacity; and, again, the two objects of his paper—read at the Social Science Congress, Glasgow, October, 1874—being first to describe the competitive examination in physical training which was introduced by Sir George Campbell into the system of selection for the subordinate Civil Service of Bengal; and, secondly, to urge the expediency of its extension to the competitive examinations in London for the higher Indian Civil Service and for the Army and Navy.

In 1872, Sir George Campbell—now the well-known Member of Parliament, and a fair successor to the gallant and learned Colonel Sykes, who was once M.P. for Hindustan! †—the then Lieutenant-Governor of Bengal, issued instructions for the establishment of Civil Service colleges. The standard on admission was that of entrance to the University of Calcutta, about on a par with the matriculation standard of that of London, and a knowledge of one of the Vernaculars was necessary. In these colleges instruction was ordered in riding and gymnastics, in surveying and drawing, in law and modern science. And it was wisely

* "On the Expediency of the Introduction of Tests for Physical Training into the present System of Competitive Examination for the Army, Navy, and Indian Civil Service."—London, 1875.

† *See* First Series, p. 104.

ordained that the choice of subjects was dictated by the political necessities of the country. The requirements of the public service were considered, as well as the previous training in schools, and the physique of the people. "They," says Mr. Woodrow, "cannot compete with the stalwart men of the North-Western Provinces in thews and sinews, but they are vastly superior to them in brains. For sedentary work, requiring intelligence and steady application, there is no nation in the world superior to the Bengali." Sir George Campbell determined—and it would be well if potentates in Europe gave as much attention to their subjects—that in the Civil Service colleges those subjects should be taught in which the Bengali was least efficient, and consequently "attention was given to gymnastics, by which physical strength might be developed." All intelligent Anglo-Indians will at once admit the strong common-sense of the following passage, which may be taken for India generally, and especially for our new conquest of Upper or Northern Burma:—"Supervision is good for every man, though it is not much liked. It is especially needed in Bengal, where public opinion, except in the large towns, is weak, and where an official of feeble physique is tempted to neglect duties which require active exertion, exposure to the sun, and the endurance of fatigue. In a country where roads are few, adequate supervision over subordinates would imply the power and will to see them at their work, as well as the ability to test the quality of the work. The head of a district should therefore be ubiquitous, for if he stays at his desk he may be certain that duties will be neglected by his subordinates." Sir Alexander Grant—a great authority on all such matters—said that an inspector of schools should be able to ride, with ease, his twenty miles before breakfast, and do a hard day's work after that meal. "In the discharge of my work as an inspector of schools," writes Mr. Woodrow, "I have had to ride, without resting, a distance requiring five relays of horses; but if this power to withstand fatigue is requisite for an inspector of schools, it is even more requisite for magistrates, whether subordinate or chief, entrusted with the administration of a district." Such energy, ubiquity, and administrative talent, as displayed by Mr. Woodrow during his great educational career in India, leads us to think of another distinguished Anglo-Indian (Sir Richard Temple), in considerably higher appointments, and imperfectly sketched in our *First Series.* The names of two such public men suggest the thought, that, were there more of the same kind in the world, what a vast reduction in the national expenditure there would be* at home and abroad! The present complicated machinery of governments might then, in many cases, be reduced to a Governor and his Secretary. But such a consummation will never be, as Temples and Woodrows will ever be rare in the world.† In India, as in England (especially in London), there are men whose trade is perjury; and the grand object is to catch them at once, and bring them to justice. The evidence of circumstances which cannot lie, of course oftener requires far longer riding or travelling in India than in England to pursue it; and hence one of the potent reasons for Sir George Campbell's wisely marking riding as an essential qualification for the public servant, and as one of the subjects to count in the competitive examination. Mr. Woodrow brings this important subject very strongly forward in his pamphlet. A committee appointed (1872) by Sir George Campbell, consisting of the Government Secretary, the Hon. Charles Bernard, the Principal of the Hooghly College, Mr. R. Thwaytes, and the Director of Public Instruction, which appointment Mr. Woodrow then only temporarily held. And he now aptly remarks that "no greater innovation on established notions could be conceived than an examination for Bengalis in riding or gymnastics," especially when some years before Bengali gentlemen thought it derogatory to ride or even walk any distance. In a great school near Calcutta, an application was once made to the manly Inspector for the dismissal of the schoolmaster, because he ridiculed some boys by asking them whether they had feet like Chinese ladies. On inquiry, it appeared that the boys said it was ungentlemanly to incur fatigue, and that no one but a coolie (the patient menial who does the carrying or slave-work of India) would walk three miles.

His Excellency the Viceroy and the Lieutenant-Governor went to Hooghly to see the progress which had been made in the experiment, and were astonished at the success

* Particularly in the way of Office Establishments.

† Having brought the two distinguished names in juxtaposition, we cannot resist here giving the following extract from Sir Richard Temple's "Men and Events of My Time in India," chap. xviii. p. 433:—"Among our Educational officers the most popular was Henry Woodrow, an old schoolfellow of mine at Rugby. His sudden death, shortly after he had been appointed Director of Public Instruction, was lamented not only by his European friends, but also by all classes of educated Natives throughout the country." Sir Richard's interesting work was published in 1882.

attained. In 1873 the award for marks for riding and athletic exercises was determined satisfactorily; and for the first time in India, perhaps even in the world, during modern ages, "physical training counted with mental attainments in determining a candidate's place among the competitors for Government service. The examinations for 1874 were also successful. Sir George Campbell had (1871-2) described the object and progress of his scheme when it was clearly stated that "candidates for appointments of over Rs. 100 a month must show that they can ride at least twelve miles at a rapid pace; candidates for inferior posts must have similar qualifications, or be able to walk twelve miles within three hours and a half without difficulty or prostration." It should here be noted that every candidate was obliged to produce a certificate of character, and a medical certificate of fitness for employ in any part of Bengal.

Good character, health, and physical energy being thus secured, we come to a most important point. "The first test applied is to ascertain whether candidates educated in the modern fashion possess an adequate knowledge of English, or, in the case of other candidates, whether their vernacular education is thorough and good."*

From numerous extracts given by Mr. Woodrow, it is quite evident that Sir George Campbell and other good judges fully believed that, although the Bengali intellect is acute, physical qualities, such as energy, activity and endurance, were the great want. Sir George Campbell was, and, doubtless, still is, quite satisfied that "such tests are good and necessary tests," and he could not have done a greater kindness to the natives of Bengal than by holding out to them such standards, "by which they may gradually fit themselves to emulate Europeans." While on the subject of establishing competitive examinations in physical training in Bengal, for the higher and lower grades of the native Civil Service, Mr Woodrow duly announced the important fact that "the present Lieutenant-Governor,"† Sir Richard Temple, K.C.S.I., had already evinced an active interest in the encouragement of manly exercises.

For those curious on the subject, it may be interesting to state that, at the first examination, in February, 1872, only twenty candidates passed the Civil Service examination.

* From the English examination all who had passed a university examination were exempt.

† 1874-75.

All these men very shortly were appointed to vacancies in the higher branch of the native Civil Service; and for the training of future candidates for these examinations Civil Service classes were opened at both the Hooghly and Patna colleges, "teaching engineering, surveying, chemistry, botany, and riding." A large number of students and candidates for the Public Service at once joined these classes. To check or lessen excessive and unremitting study in a considerable number of Bengali students, gymnasia were opened in 1871–72, at the Dacca, Hooghly and Patna colleges, and elsewhere.

On leaving Mr. Woodrow and the Bengali with his feeble physique, we now turn for a moment to some of his general remarks on the subject of physique with reference to examinations. Never were mind and matter better (or even so well) handled by an experienced educationist before :—

> The early supporters of competitive examination were well aware that moral qualifications could not be tested by papers of questions. They knew that the State needs in its servants such qualities as honesty, sobriety, common sense, sound judgment, discretion, tact, courtesy, high sense of honour, courage, power of command, &c., but they argued that these qualities were as likely to be found associated with mental superiority as dissevered from it. The same assumption was made concerning physical efficiency. Mental qualification only was submitted to the test of examination. Hence, scarcely one-third of the qualifications required in the public servant were tested, and efficiency in the other two-thirds was assumed. This is not only a serious injury to the public service, but has unduly restricted the beneficial influence of the system, by leaving to chance the possession of qualifications that increase the worth of an officer, and that might be ascertained with certainty. It may be granted that nothing but real work can test moral qualification, but the possession of physical efficiency ought not to have been assumed. It can be tested as readily as mental qualification, and it has been so tested.

And now it is asked if India is the only country of the world in which a good physique is desirable? Or, is attention only to be given on the subject to the subordinate Civil Service of Bengal? Although the "Nestor of Education" loves India, he naturally loves the old country more.

Mr. Woodrow proves himself to be a complete master of the whole question when he remarks that all the various branches of the army and navy have need of officers competent both in mind and body to carry out the orders of their superiors. "A general in command of an army," he says, "has less need than his subordinates of strength of arm and vigour of body, but he wants these qualities, in his officers and men, and recent wars show that they are not undesirable even in the general himself."

The logic and common-sense of the following statement are also most convincing:—"The evidence before the Public School Commission showed that the most influential boys in the great public schools were now to be found in the eleven at cricket and in the crews of the first boats, and not, as was formerly the case, high up in the sixth form. Those at the top of the sixth must of course beat those at the bottom. Hence it is worthy of careful thought that the present competitive system, by leaving out of consideration all manly exercises, does not select for commanders over men the persons who when young were the accepted rulers over boys."

And here is more important matter for consideration, when the Rugby boy introduces himself:—

"While head masters and the public are troubled because many boys take too much exercise, they overlook a fact every day becoming more important to the nation—that the most successful boys take too little exercise. The German and Austrian Governments insist on a regular course of gymnastics for every boy in every school. These Governments, from motives of State policy, insist upon the physique of the rising generation being properly attended to, and they demand from school authorities as regular cultivation of the bodily as of the mental powers. It is not found that this inexorable demand gives an undue stimulus to athletic exercises. I fear that such is the perversity of the English boy's nature, that if a course of athletic exercises were declared to be good and necessary, and worthy to count in the award of school distinctions, the zest with which such exercises are pursued would be reduced. If a boy must not go beyond three miles from a certain spot, he has a great desire to go four miles at least; but if he is told he ought to go four miles he would be quite content to go two miles.

"I was at Rugby myself in Dr. Arnold's time. I know what a boy's nature is, and I anticipate that if public schools were to give marks for swimming, running, shooting, and other games, the interest in them would diminish rather than increase.

"The playground is now the English boy's own domain. He can do as he likes there. This constitutes its greatest charm, and much good, with perhaps some evil, is the result. I abhor the French system of continual supervision out of school hours. In fact, many intelligent Frenchmen detest it, and would willingly adopt the English system, but they recoil at the frightful consequences of a change from the excessive supervision of their lycées to the entire freedom of our great public schools."

They think freedom would lapse into license, and license into licentiousness. One acute observer remarked that the change would be a permanent good to France if but one generation could be obliterated, "but that in the first twenty years they would rear a generation of devils." The bookworm is well brought out by the genial writer. He is not troubled with an irrepressible buoyancy of spirits or with intense longing for active exertion. A missionary in

India termed such a successful competitive candidate "a book in breeches." And now it is well said that to change a dashing cavalry officer for "a book in breeches" is a change far from beneficial to the nation. It is quite right to give marks for mental acquirements; but Mr. Woodrow would plead that some few marks should be given for efficiency in bodily exercises, for such a course would handicap the "book in breeches," and bring men whom the army, navy, and India require, to the front. He next considers for what subjects marks should be given. He has shown why marks should be given for riding. The good swimmer also ought to score a few. At Cawnpore, in the Indian mutiny, Thompson and Delafosse saved their lives by swimming, and the former tells us that the best guinea he ever spent was that paid for swimming lessons at the Holborn Baths. The writer of this sketch well recollects the Bishop of Calcutta's falling off some planks, while on his visitation tour, into the Hooghly. The news reached him in Burma nearly twenty-five years ago. And Mr. Woodrow says, in his usual kindly manner, "If Bishop Cotton, whose memory is dear to Rugby, Marlborough, and India, had been able to swim, he might have still been spared to pursue his beneficent course of unhalting, unresting, untiring diligence." And Bishop Selwyn, in New Zealand, showed himself to be a thorough practical divine when he advertised for an Archdeacon who could swim. Truly, some marks ought to be allowed for skill in gymnastics and other athletic exercises. Mr. Woodrow shows his high appreciation of them when he remarks that numerous examples among distinguished Anglo-Indians are furnished of the value of proficiency in manly exercises. "The gallant Outram first gained his people's love as their protector from wild beasts and from oppressors equally fierce and merciless. The heroes who have built up and consolidated the Indian Empire have been as distinguished for physical prowess as for mental powers." Among those living in these particulars may be cited Sir Henry Rawlinson; and again, among those passed away, General Nicholson, who fell at the siege of Delhi. It is well said that India during the mutinies was saved by the Punjab, and the Punjab was saved to us through Nicholson. From his unrivalled skill in all manly exercises, he gained a vast influence over the native mind; for he excelled in all the arts his people valued; and as a horseman or swordsman he was unsurpassed. The brave but simple-minded people of Bunnoo actually believed him to be "an incarnation of the Deity of good fortune, and success was expected to crown his every effort. The ease with which he surmounted difficulties was remarkable. Under his guidance, the followers believed that they marched to certain victory, tempered with just so much danger and difficulty as to make the contest glorious." There is a grand appreciation of the reality of military life in this remark. In fact, we cannot help thinking that Henry Woodrow would have been quite as distinguished as a soldier in the field of war as he was in the great intellectual arena of public instruction. "It may be urged," he says, "that it is difficult to hold examinations in riding, swimming, shooting, fencing, and in athletic exercises;" but really there is no more difficulty in testing them and in awarding marks than in deciding on the best *vivâ voce* translation; and what has been done in Bengal can be done in England and elsewhere. Towards the close of his valuable paper we read that "in whatever way the physical training is to be effected, whether by a term of compulsory military or naval service, or otherwise, there can be no doubt that it is absolutely necessary."* It would be greatly promoted if it counted in Civil Service examinations. "A quarter of a century ago"—now nearly forty years since—Mr. Woodrow tells us, "Macaulay pointed out how wide the influence of the examinations must extend. The interest in the subject of such training would permeate the country through a thousand channels." And, if so, how valuable is physical training which so tends to make a nation manly! This is surely an important subject, especially when every year, as the census shows, the population of the country is being "decanted," as it were, into towns. Such examinations would, above all, prevent evil.

There is a dash of humour in the remainder of Mr. Woodrow's pamphlet. By a mysterious perversion of fate, round men are frequently placed in square holes, and square men in round holes. Regarding a perversity of this sort, he says, with reference to some competitive examinations: "None but an enemy would question the ability, genius, courage, generosity and kindness of heart and high sense of honour that mark the Irish gentleman, but some

* A powerful argument why the Government should regard with favour every effort to encourage and promote manly exercises, is found in the results of the census in 1871, where it is shown that the increase of two millions in the population took place in towns, and not in the country. Again, quoting a London Professor, it is said :—"If, therefore, we have a national system of mental training, surely we ought to have one of physical training."—P. 15.

who are even friends have doubted whether such characteristics as wit, fun and brilliancy are not more common than tact, sound judgment and discretion." And this brings to mind the uncalled-for and rather impertinent remark of a London critic, when, on its being casually stated, in the *First Series* of this work, with reference to a most distinguished Lieutenant-Governor, that with all his brilliant talents Sheridan could never have governed the Punjab, as, lacking the necessary useful qualities above stated, he thought it very clever to assert that "no human being, Anglo-Indian or other, ever thought that he could." But enough of this digression. According to Mr. Woodrow, who leaves no stone unturned in his illustrations, in the British Excise Department there is more necessity for sound judgment and discretion than for brilliant genius; yet he gives the results of examinations fifteen years ago as vastly in favour of the Irish. It is an old story that, in days long gone by, so many Scotchmen got into the directorship of the Bank of England that some were obliged to be turned out by Act of Parliament; so the highly-spirited Irishmen appear to have once carried the day as splendid Excisemen. On a certain occasion, England and Scotland together furnished only 98 out of 240 successful candidates, while Ireland gave 142. And it was thought that if this superiority continued the majority of the future Excise officers in England, Wales and Scotland will be Irishmen.

"This circumstance," says Mr. Woodrow, "will go far to raise cries similar to that of Ireland for the Irish; we may hear Scotland for the Scotch and England for the English. In fact, *Home Rulers may secure for their specific views a much larger following in Great Britain than Ireland itself would approve.*" The italics are ours; and, judging from the state of the great political question of the present day, some may be inclined to add the functions of a prophet to our Anglo-Indian Nestor's other accomplishments. Again, "what has happened in one case may happen again in another. When the Treasury asked for officers for the Excise, men to be distinguished for calmness, sound judgment, and discretion, it received a supply of Irishmen. So when the Horse Guards ask for dashing young cavalry officers it is possible that England, Ireland, and Scotland may perversely send up successful bookworms. An exuberance of animal spirits and a passion for physical exercise are not bad things, either for the army or for India, yet the chance of competition may unfortunately weed out candidates of such proclivities and select in their place the meek, quiet students whose weak frame and pallid cheek tell of unremitted mental toil, and to whom the most dreaded part of the final Indian examination would be the test in riding. From the national calamity of such a selection marks for manly exercises would be a strong preservative.

"It is but justice to admit that the selection for the Indian Civil Service has on the whole been fortunate, and that the successful candidates have with few exceptions possessed a good average physique. This is partly due to the care taken in the medical examination, and partly to the fact that the competition is so severe that a good constitution is required to stand the mental strain."

We now beg leave to think that the paper of which so imperfect a sketch has been given, is an extraordinary one, by a highly-gifted and amiable man. It is a valuable contribution towards the formation of public opinion on a highly-important subject. The writer, among other things, has shown that a system of competitive examination may test a small portion only of the qualifications desirable in a public servant; that physical qualifications having been tested in Bengal, they can be similarly tested in England; that such promote the efficacy and influence of an officer; and, above all, that the army and navy and Indian Civil Service require protection against an influx of mere bookworms, and that he is decidedly of opinion that increased strength would immediately follow the system of selection by competition were the examination extended to physical training. It is pleasing to observe in the present year (1887) that the latter has been more extended to boys, while technical education is receiving increased attention in England.

In the *Daily News* (London), January 23, 1875, after concluding the above sketch, it was pleasing to observe that considerable interest was then taken in the subject. It was thought well worthy of a leading article, in which of course Mr. Woodrow's pamphlet is ably reviewed. He "calculates that probably 50,000 young men are influenced in their culture by the standards of competitive examination. If this is so, it is surely necessary to be very careful that qualities are asked for, and studies encouraged, of the most solid and lasting character and value." Of Competition Wallahs the writer says: "Immediately after the introduction of the competitive system, Anglo-Indians had a natural prejudice against the Competition Wallahs. They did not come of old Indian families, they often did not come of any gently-born family at all; they were accused of all sorts of social peccadilloes, and especially of ignorance of manly sports. 'A Wallah, seeing a musket, thought it was a rifle;' 'a Wallah fell off his horse into a tank,' are concise abridgments of the old scandals about Competition Wallahs." The prejudice is now dying out, but it is not yet quite extinct. The article concludes with the following well-merited compliment: "Nothing but good, we think, can come to both mind and body from the adoption, with proper amendments, of Mr. Woodrow's system."

And again, from our ever active-minded, eminently practical, and gallant Adjutant-General:—

LORD WOLSELEY ON PHYSICAL TRAINING.

Lord Wolseley, on Dec. 12, 1887, opened the new gymnasium and social room just added to the Finsbury Polytechnic, Appold Street.

Lord Wolseley, who was cordially greeted, declared that this institution would not fail to confer great permanent benefit on those who attended it. "He took great interest in physical training, for no matter how one established Board Schools and other means of mental instruction, very little good was done unless the people received bodily training also. What would it matter that the country should teem with scholars and artists unless the men of the country had the courage and the muscle to repel invaders? By looking after the physical training of a people you looked after their health, with which morality went hand-in-hand. In an overcrowded population like this the subject was surrounded with the greatest difficulties, among which was the necessity for sites and funds. It was unsatisfactory that up to the present moment the Legislature had done absolutely nothing to improve the physical training of the people. With every Board School there ought to be an open space or recreation ground for the people, together with a public gymnasium, and he hoped the time was not far distant when this would be the case. It was fortunate that the necessity for athletics had begun to agitate the country, and politicians would do better to take up this subject than to preach long lectures on the franchise, which many people did not understand and cared little about. With regard to temperance, he was not going to insist on water drinking; but believing that immense misery was caused by the public-houses, he rejoiced to think that this institution would act as a counter-attraction. Until similar institutions were established in every district it would continue to be absolute nonsense and humbug to tell working men that they must not enter the public-houses, especially when in many cases their home was only a squalid lodging." What Christian or charitable man in his right senses will deny the truth of Lord Wolseley's remarks?

VII.

THE DUKE OF EDINBURGH IN INDIA, 1870.

A WILD BOAR HUNT.

THERE are no two more remarkable events in the social history of Queen Victoria's reign deserving especially to be noticed, and the chief details presented to the British public in the welcome year of Her Majesty's Jubilee, than the visits to India of their Royal Highnesses the Prince of Wales and Duke of Edinburgh. The distinguished Anglo-Indians who accompanied them, and those whom they met in India, will, it is to be hoped, have rendered the extracts already given not incongruous. The good citizens of London are now tolerably well acquainted—thanks to books and dioramas—with life in Australia, Canada and the great Rocky Mountains, the Nile and all the monuments of antiquity on its banks; but they do not yet pay sufficient attention to the bright land, with a sixth of the human race, over which the Queen-Empress rules; and which, long ere the weary soul thought of Australia, or the mammon-worshipping sons of California—ere civilization was fairly born in the world—was the seat of wealth and grandeur. Ages before Athens and Rome promoted the arts of civilized life and literature, there was India, immortal, solid, and unchangeable.

In 1876, we ventured to write something about the numerous remarkable visits to India, from De Gama, with his gallant crew (1498), down to the most celebrated visit of modern times, which had just been completed with triumphant success. On the title-page of Sir Joseph Fayrer's "Notes" it is distinctly announced that they are "Printed for Private Circulation only." Our distinguished Anglo-Indian says in his preface, "These Notes of my travels in India with the Princes are very brief and fragmentary—a mere diary—but they will, I hope, interest those for whom they were written, as they give some account of where I went and what I did. Both expeditions, happily, proved most successful." And again, "The gracious recognition that I have received from the Queen and Royal Family, assured me that my services, however imperfect, were appreciated. The courtesy and kindness of my companions on both occasions, and the firm support of many during periods of anxiety, made my duty agreeable, and have impressed me with strong feelings of regard and friendship for them all." We now make a retrograde movement and proceed to the diary kept by Sir Joseph Fayrer while with

"Captain H.R.H. The DUKE OF EDINBURGH, K.G., R.N., &c, &c.

THE SUITE:

Major-General Sir Neville Chamberlain, K.C.B., K.C.S.I.
Lieut. Lord C. Beresford, R.N.
Col. Sir Seymour Blane, Bart.
Col. Probyn, C.B., V.C.*
Col. Fraser, C.B., V.C.
Hon. E. Yorke, *Equerry*.
Lieut. A. Haig, R.E., *Equerry*.
Dr. Fayrer, C.S.I., B.M. Service.
Dr. Watson, Staff Surgeon, R.N., H.M.S. *Galatea*.
Capt. J. Clerk.
M. Chevalier, Artist.
Col. Reilly, R.A., C.B.
Capt. Bradford, Central Indian Horse.

"His Royal Highness the Duke of Edinburgh visited Calcutta in December, 1869, and January, 1870.

"The Viceroy, Lord Mayo, deeming it important that an Indian Medical Officer, acquainted with the country, its language, climate and diseases, should accompany His Royal Highness during his travels and tiger-hunting in India, deputed me to perform this duty, and the following are some notes made during the expedition. They are very brief and imperfect, but will preserve some account of the places visited, and of the most interesting incidents of the journey."

From Sir Joseph's "Notes," while with the Duke of Edinburgh, we regret being only able to give—and even this

* Now Lieut.-General Sir D. M. Probyn, K.C.S.I., C.B., V.C., and still (1887) Comptroller and Treasurer of H.R.H. the Prince of Wales's Household. This distinguished Anglo-Indian, with the well-known administrator, Sir Bartle Frere, also accompanied the Prince of Wales to India in 1875–1876.

in an appendix—one incident or adventure; and that is of a sporting character.

The Duke left Calcutta on the morning of the 7th January, 1870, and at Burdwan was received by the Rajah and the Civil Officers of the Station. The party then went on to Nulhattee, and thence, by special train, to Azimgunge, where Mr. Buckle, the Governor-General's Agent, and Mr. Hankey, the Magistrate, were in attendance. After crossing the Bhagirutty, they drove into camp at Dewan Serai, eleven miles from Azimgunge, and twenty-six from Moorshedabad. The camp consisted of a street of double-poled tents, with a large dinner tent,* in front of which, for the first time in India, the Royal Standard floated over the camp of a shikar party. In the morning they were ready to take the field, under the guidance of Major Mylne and other members of the Tent Club. After breakfast the party set out with a line of twenty-eight elephants. The Duke rode an Arab that promised well, although untried to take his rider up to a pig.

A Wild Boar Hunt.

"The beat commenced almost immediately after leaving camp, and lay over level ground, covered here and there with patches of urhur (dhal), grain, linseed, or with more extensive reaches of grass, so long that it reached to the horse's girths. An occasional village, with surrounding jungle of mango, tamarind, bhair, and other trees, varied the scene. There were nineteen riders, besides those on the elephants, and they were divided into parties, with instructions to confine their attention to the particular pigs that the chances of the day might send in their direction. After beating in line for about an hour-and-a-half—during which time there was more than one false alarm—a boar was turned out of the long grass, and made off at his best speed in the direction of the nearest village, which lay just on the outskirts of the plain, where he no doubt expected to find safety, and a shelter he was doomed not to reach. He was first seen from the elephants, for from those on horseback he was concealed by the long grass, and the signal being given, he was soon followed by several spears. He had almost attained the shelter of the trees when he received the first spear from Mr. A. Hills, and so well was it directed that he rolled

* And *shahmianah.*

completely over. He was up again at once, and shaking out the spear, made a charge at the nearest horse, when he was transfixed through and through by Colonel Probyn's long Bombay spear, three feet of which appeared on his other side. A few more well-directed thrusts finished his career.

"Soon after tiffin in a mango tope, the line was again in motion, and before evening, after more than one run in the long grass, two more good boars fell; one to the spear of Major Trevor and the other to that of the Duke. The ground, though level, was somewhat treacherous; the long grass concealed certain blind ditches, in which more than one rider came to grief. Several falls occurred—the Duke had two; but no one was hurt, and the hunt went merrily on till the evening, when, at the death of the last pig, a sad accident occurred, which threw a cloud over all. A gallant little Arab of Lord M. Beresford's got one of his hind feet into a hole, and snapped the leg just above the pastern joint. Even after this he tried to go, and when pulled up the fractured bones protruded through an extensive wound; the foot looked as though attached only by a portion of the skin. As to save him was impossible, he was shot through the head to spare him further suffering, and he fell dead without a struggle, on the ground where he had behaved so well."

After various shikar and other adventures, the move was now to the banks of the Ganges, to cross at Rajmahal, and meet the train for Benares.

The baggage reached the station at Rajmahal only just in time for the special train which had been sent to convey the party to Teen Pahar, where the Viceroy was waiting. At Rajmahal the Duke was met by the Hon. Major Bourke, Mr. Palmer, and others. In a few minutes the station of Teen Pahar was reached, and the train proceeded at once to Jumalpore (16th). On the morning of the 17th, the Duke's party entered Benares.

VIII.

EXTRACTS FROM LORD MACAULAY'S "UNPUBLISHED MINUTES."

BEFORE giving our extracts from the "Minutes"—which differ, in some measure, both in matter and length, from those of Sir George Trevelyan—we learn from his acute biographer, what has already been given in other words, that, at the time of Macaulay's advent,* "there were no Inspectors of Schools, there were no training colleges for masters. The machinery consisted of voluntary committees acting on the spot, and corresponding directly with the superintending body at Calcutta." But he now says of the grand subject of his biography:—"Macaulay rose to the occasion, and threw himself into the routine of administration and control with zeal sustained by diligence and tempered by tact. 'We were hardly prepared,' said a competent critic, 'for the amount of conciliation which he evinces in dealing with irritable colleagues and subordinates, and for the strong, sterling, practical common sense with which he sweeps away rubbish, or cuts the knots of local and departmental problems.'" Regarding the "educational outfit" provided by his learned and brilliant uncle for our Eastern Empire, Sir George Trevelyan says:—"Throughout his innumerable Minutes, on all subjects, from the broadest principle to the narrowest detail, he is everywhere free from crotchets and susceptibilities; and everywhere ready to honour any person that will make himself useful, and to adopt any appliance which can be turned to account." Even a humorous kindness runs through the emphatic condemnation of the "lazy, stupid schoolboys of thirty" of Hooghly College—to be found among the following extracts,† as well as in those given by Sir George Trevelyan—and the acceptance of a large number of the wealthy King of Oudh's

* Nothing resembling an Organization Staff was yet in existence.
† Taken from Mr. Woodrow's work.

"detestable maps!" It is quite evident from the Minutes that Lord Macaulay took a great interest in the study of Geography, probably as much as the great Irish orator, Burke, had done before him. Let us now proceed to the Extracts:—

Mr. Woodrow writes:—"Mr. Macaulay formally gives his assent to the amended instructions issued to Mr. Adams, who was appointed by the Supreme Government to report on the state of Vernacular Education in Bengal. More than a quarter of a century has elapsed since Mr. Adam was instructed to prepare his reports, which he executed in so full and exhaustive a manner that they continue to be the best sketches of the state of Vernacular Education that have been submitted to the public."*

Mr. Macaulay says, with reference to Mr. Adam's second Report:—"Our schools are nurseries of schoolmasters for the next generation."

Mr. Macaulay writes:—"What Mr. Shakespear recommends as to books I highly approve; but as to stipends I cannot agree with him. But I will not argue that question till some distinct proposition is made.

"I would adopt Mr. Shakespear's proposition about the Madrasa at Kusba Bagha. As to the endowments mentioned in the Report, pages 43, 45, I do not think that it would be worth while to take any steps respecting them. There is something so extravagantly absurd in hereditary professorships that we ought not to express any wish to have them revived. Of course, if a man has a legal right to professorship by inheritance, he ought to obtain it. But that is no business of ours. We can interfere only as a board of public instruction, and for purposes of public instruction such professorships are evidently useless. I am a little amused to observe that Mr. Adam, who, in page 45, laments the discontinuance of four of these endowments, and says that the revival of them would give 'an important impulse to learning in the district,' tells us, in page 42, that two of these endowments are still continued. And what is 'the impulse which they give to learning?' 'The present holders,' says he, 'are both mere grammarians, in no way distinguished among their brethren for talents and acquirements. It may be inferred that the endowments

* On the 24th of March, 1835, Macaulay writes:—"I agree with Mr. Sutherland in thinking that Mr. Adam cannot at present be more usefully employed than in digesting such information on the subject of Native Education as may be contained in reports formerly made."

were made for the encouragement of learning only from the fact that the learned teachers are the incumbents.' Here are six endowments of the same sort. Two are continued, and Mr. Adam acknowledges that they are mere jobs. But if the other four were revived, an immense impulse would be given to learning. I am forced to say that I do not very clearly see how Mr. Adam has arrived at this conclusion.

"The important measures which Mr. Shakespear suggests at the close of his minute well deserve serious consideration. I am so much pressed for time at this moment that I can only give my opinion very concisely. I look forward to a time when we may do all that Mr. Shakespear suggests, and even more. But I greatly doubt whether at present, supposing all preliminary difficulties removed and a grant of 78,000 rupees per annum obtained from the Court of Directors in addition to our present funds, we could not employ that sum better than by setting up Thannah Schools. Several plans have occurred to me which, perhaps, persons acquainted with the country may at once pronounce absurd. It has occurred to me, though it is a little at variance with what I wrote a few pages before, that if we had the means of offering so small an addition as two rupees a month to the present emoluments of a village schoolmaster, in every case in which such a schoolmaster should satisfy an examiner appointed by us of his fitness to teach elementary knowledge well and correctly as far as he went, we might induce three or four thousand village schoolmasters to take some pains to qualify themselves for their situation. I may be mistaken, but it seems to me that Thannah Schools such as Mr. Shakespear proposes would be no more than village schools, that the schoolmasters would be no better than the village schoolmasters. It could not be expected, I imagine, that boys would come any distance for such an education as the Thannah Schools would afford. In that case I would rather employ the money, if we could get it, in improving three or four thousand village schools than in establishing six or seven hundred Thannah Schools. At present, however, I think we might employ the money better than on either Village or Thannah Schools.

"I shall be glad to see what gentlemen who know this country better than I do think on this question." (Book J., page 127), 28th September, 1836.

The first opinion of Lord Macaulay in the Book marked

E. is dated the 7th February, 1835. A proposal was made by Mr. Sutherland, the Secretary, to give away a large number of the Committee's Oriental publications to the chief Sanscrit and Arabic scholars in Europe. Macaulay only five days before had remarked in his great Minute :—

"The Committee contrive to get rid of some portion of their vast stock of Oriental literature by giving books away; but they cannot give so fast as they print." On the present occasion he simply states, "I approve of the proposition." (Book E., page 82.)

Benares College.—"As at present advised, I conceive that a sum much smaller than that which Captain Thoresby received would suffice for his successor. That successor ought to take a direct part in the instruction of the English classes. I should be glad to know whether there is now at Benares any gentleman possessed of the requisite attainments to whom 300 or 400 rupees a month would be an object. I say this on the supposition that instruction of a higher kind in English science and literature is at present required in our Benares School. If not, I do not see why we should not save the whole salary. For to pay 750 a month, or a fifth part of that sum monthly, for a superintendence such as that which Captain Thoresby appears to have exercised over the Sanscrit College, seems to me mere waste." (Book C., page 150), 26th February, 1835.

Allahabad School.—"The school seems to be going on in a very satisfactory manner. The evident anxiety of the natives to obtain instruction in the English language must be highly gratifying to those who, like me, look on that language as the great instrument for civilizing and benefiting India. The number of English students at Allahabad has doubled in seven months.

"The merits of Mr. Cook seem to be great, and, as house-rent has risen at Allahabad, in consequence, I suppose, of the political importance which the place has lately acquired, I think that the addition of thirty rupees a month may fairly be made." (Book F., page 54), 26th March, 1835.

The Committee's Stock of Books in London.—"The London booksellers have treated us in a most extraordinary way. I propose that we write to inform them that Professor Wilson is not our agent, and that we expect to hear directly from themselves what they have done with our property." (Book M., page 143), 2nd September, 1837.

Mr. Pereira, Head Master of the Furruckabad School,

proposes to exclude Books on English Grammar from the School Course.—Macaulay concurs:—"I certainly would not approve of Mr. Pereira's suggestions respecting the exclusion of poor students, or the taking of recognizances from those who come to us for education. As to the question respecting Grammar, I would let him take his own way. I am no great believer myself in the advantages which are ordinarily attributed to a knowledge of the theory of Grammar. This indent may, I think, be complied with." Book L., page 75), 23rd November, 1836.

Encouragement of Vernacular Literature.—"I do not believe that any language was ever refined or any literature ever created by any means resembling those which our Committee has at its disposal. Languages grow. They cannot be built. I should be glad to furnish these schools with good Hindee books if there are any. But to create a Hindee literature is an undertaking far beyond our power. We might send an extract to the School Book Society and ask if they have, or are likely to have, any books that would be of use." (Book O., page 63), 25th November, 1836.

The Promotion of Vernacular Literature.—"I am, and always have been, decidedly opposed to the plan to which Mr. Sutherland wishes us to return. We are now following, in my opinion, the slow but sure course on which alone we can depend for a supply of good books in the Vernacular languages of India. We are attempting to raise up a large class of enlightened natives. I hope that twenty years hence there will be hundreds, nay, thousands, of natives familiar with the best models of composition, and well acquainted with Western science. Among them some persons will be found who will have the inclination and the ability to exhibit European knowledge in the Vernacular dialects. This, I believe, to be the only way in which we can raise up a good Vernacular literature in this country. To hire four or five people to make a literature is a course which never answered, and never will answer, in any part of the world. Such undertakings have everywhere a tendency to become jobs, and that tendency is peculiarly to be dreaded in the present instance. For one-half of the Committee do not know a letter of the language in which the books are to be written; and the other half are too busy to pay any minute attention to the way in which the translators perform their task." (Book M., page 140), 30th August, 1837.

The Importance of Geography as compared with a Know-

ledge of the Stars.—"I agree with Mr. Trevelyan that we should procure globes from England; but I cannot agree with him in thinking that we should indent for an equal number of terrestrial and celestial globes. The importance of Geography is very great indeed. I am not sure that it is not of all studies that which is most likely to open the mind of a native of India. But a knowledge of the precise positions of the fixed stars is by no means indispensable even to a very liberal European education. I know many most enlightened English gentlemen who do not know Aldebaran from Castor or Pollux. I would order only one or two celestial globes and twenty terrestrial." (Book G., page 17), 25th March, 1835.

Again, on the subject of globes (6th May):—"I must own, too, that I think the order for globes and other instruments unnecessarily large. To lay out £324 at once in globes alone, useful as I acknowledge those articles to be, seems exceedingly profuse, when we have only about £3,000 a year for all purposes of English education. One 12-inch or 18-inch globe for each school is quite enough; and we ought not, I think, to order sixteen such globes when we are about to establish only seven schools. Useful as the telescopes, the theodolites, and the other scientific instruments mentioned in the indent undoubtedly are, we must consider that four or five such instruments run away with a year's salary of a schoolmaster, and that, if we purchase them, it will be necessary for us to defer the establishment of schools."

Proposal to purchase 100 Copies of Wollaston's Geography.—"I will not object. But I think that we ought seriously to consider whether we are not taking a very expensive course in subscribing to new publications on the elements of science. In England works of great merit may be procured at a very small price, and sent hither to us at a very small additional charge. The price of one of the tracts published by the Society for the Diffusion of Useful Knowledge is sixpence. The same quantity of matter printed in this country would probably cost two rupees. It deserves to be considered whether we ought not to import more and to subscribe less." (Book G., page 22), 28th March, 1835.

Stoppage of the Printing of Oriental Books.—"I should be most reluctant to affront a gentleman for whom I feel so much respect, as I most unfeignedly entertain for Dr. Mill. But we have positive orders from Government, and we surely offer no slight to Dr. Mill by obeying those orders.

"I should be sorry to say anything disrespectfully of that liberal and generous enthusiasm for Oriental literature which appears in Mr. Sutherland's minute. But I own that I cannot think that we ought to be guided in the distribution of the small sum which the Government has allotted for the purpose of education, by considerations which seem a little romantic. That the Saracens a thousand years ago cultivated Mathematical science is hardly, I think, a reason for our spending any money in translating English treatises on mathematics into Arabic. If our proceedings are to be influenced by historical association, it would be easy to refer to topics of a different kind. Mr. Sutherland would probably think it very strange if we were to urge the destruction of the Alexandrian Library as a reason against patronizing Arabic Literature in the nineteenth century. We have, I think, a very plain duty to perform, which the instructions of the Government have, as we have resolved, marked out to us explicitly. The undertaking of Dr. Mill may be, as Mr. Sutherland conceived, a great national work. So is the breakwater at Madras. But under the orders which we have received from the Government, we have just as little to do with the one as with the other. The contracts which we have already made must be fulfilled, and the work of Dr. Mill must, like other works in hand, be stopped." (Book G., page 27), 9th April, 1835.

Stipendiary Schoolboys of Thirty Years old.—"If ever there was a place of education in which stipends were evidently useless, that place is the Hooghly College. We have a greater number of pupils thronging hither than we can find buildings to hold or masters to teach, and yet it is proposed that we should offer bounties to bring in others. As to those who are receiving stipends, I feel some doubt. That men of thirty and thirty-five should be supported in this way seems very absurd, and still more when we find that these have large families, which are subsisting on the funds designed for education. As to the plea of poverty, it will never be wanting under such a system. We make these people helpless beggars by our imprudent relief. Look at No. 10 for example. He has been living on a stipend eleven years. He is near thirty, and we are told that he will not have completed his education for four years to come. Moghal Jan, again (No. 1), is near thirty. He has been paid to learn something during twelve years. We are told that he is lazy and stupid; but there are hopes that in four years more he may have completed his course of study. We have had quite enough of these lazy, stupid schoolboys of thirty. I would tell Dr. Wise that his proposal cannot be listened to. As to the existing students, I would at once strike off all but the four whom Dr. Wise proposes to retain; and those I would allow to remain on the list only as a matter of charity. I would let No. 5, who is thirty, draw his stipend for two years, and the others who are younger, but all above twenty, for three years, and then I would have done with the stipendiary system for ever." (Page 40), 9th September, 1836.

We have omitted from the above selection a rather important and interesting minute on a *Proposal to request Government to compliment the King of Oude on his Liberal Encouragement of Learning.*—"I wish to see native Princes encouraged to bestow on science and literature some portion of what they now waste on dancing-girls and gimcracks; but I cannot approve of Captain Paton's suggestion. In the first place, what the King of Oude has done is quite contemptible, when the amount of his revenue is considered. Many of the native gentlemen who contributed to the Hindu College have, from their private means, expended more on education than this Prince, the richest, I imagine, in India, has furnished from his immense treasures."

Acceptance of the Offer of 200 Copies of the King of Oude's Maps.—The following extract is also given by Sir George Trevelyan:—"By all means" [accept], "though, to be sure, more detestable maps were never seen. One would think that the revenues of Oude and the treasures of Saadut Ali might have borne the expense of producing something better than a map in which Sicily is joined on the toe of Italy, and in which so important an Eastern island as Java does not appear at all." (8th March, 1836.)

Agreeing fully with Mr. Woodrow in "the desire to publish every scrap of Macaulay's writings," we think it advisable to give a few more extracts from the "Unpublished Minutes," which will at once show the extraordinary fitness of the man for the high educational post he occupied, and in which he gained so much distinction. Nothing seems to escape his never-sleeping eye of observation. Fifty years ago we even find him concurring in the dismissal of a schoolmaster for cruelty or ill-timed severity to a scholar. Such a powerful control in India, as in England, even now, is too often necessary.

Regarding the then important educational subject of the Hooghly College, for which Mr. Macaulay had strongly recommended Dr. Wise as the best Principal that could be found, he had also written:—"On the whole I would at once propose Dr. Wise to the General Committee as Principal, without requiring him to give up his practice." (7th May, 1836.)

Mummeries of Heraldry.—"I agree with Mr. Sutherland on almost every point. I could wish that means could be found to avert the necessity of closing the College against new applicants. I think we might with advantage insert after the 10th paragraph, some such paragraph as this:—'The attention of the Committee has lately been drawn to the extreme inconvenience, which in several of the institutions under their care has arisen from the number of holidays. They are desirous to provide against this evil in the Hooghly College at first setting out, as it is one of those evils which it is far easier to prevent than to remedy. They, therefore, request that you will take this subject into immediate consideration, and submit to them as soon as possible what you have to propose.'

"I quite agree with Mr. Sutherland about the arms. Indeed I do not see why the Mummeries of European heraldry should be introdued into any part of our Indian system. Heraldry is not a science which has any eternal rules. It is a system of arbitrary canons, originating in pure caprice. Nothing can be more absurd and grotesque than armorial bearings, considered in themselves. Certain recollections, certain associations, make them interesting in many cases to an Englishman. But in those recollections and associations the natives of India do not participate. A lion rampant with a folio in his paw, with a man standing on each side of him, with a telescope over his head, and with a Persian motto under his feet, must seem to them either very mysterious or very absurd.

"I should have thought, too, that rigid Mahomedans would have entertained religious objections to the proposed device. But on this point other gentlemen are bettter qualified to judge. I quite approve of the plan of going to Hooghly, though I will not promise to go myself. Will Sir Edward Ryan fix a day?" (22nd August, 1836.)

We now proceed to give a few later interesting extracts:—

Concerning the Purchase of Ground for building a College.—"We are greatly obliged to our Secretary and to Mr. Trevelyan for their exertions and for their interesting report. I quite approve of what they suggest as to the internal arrangement of the school and the providing of new masters. Masters should be selected with as little delay as possible. There is little hope that we shall be able to obtain the barracks. We must, therefore, think of building, and here I would recommend that we should neither build nor clear any land for building, till we have purchased all the ground that we shall want. For if we begin to build before we have bought all the land, we shall find that the price will rise enormously, and I fear that the Hooghly College, being an endowment, will not be considered by the Government as one of those public works for which individuals may be compelled to give up their land at a valuation.

"I approve of what is suggested with respect to the visitation of the College, and I do not object to the proposed name." (16th September, 1836.)

Persian Writing Master.—"I shall not object if Mr. Shakespear and Mr. Smith think that this master is wanted and that the proposed remuneration is reasonable. I should not have thought that the scientific drawings of a native of this country were likely to be of any value."

Lodgings and Food for Students not to be given by the College.—"I am against sanctioning the huts, and against building dormitories for poor students. Dr. Wise does not in the least understand our views on these points. I would recommend that he should be distinctly informed that we mean to give instruction gratis, that every rupee laid out in building huts for students, or giving food to students, is a rupee withdrawn from more useful purposes, and that we desire that he will on no occasion depart from this rule, without reference to us."

College Libraries should be open to the Public.—"Dr. Wise's rules seem to have been in the main judiciously framed on the principles laid down by us. With respect to the plan of making our College libraries, circulating libraries, there is much to be said on both sides. If a proper subscription is demanded from those who have access to these libraries, and if all that is raised by this subscription is laid out in adding to the libraries, the students will be no losers by the plan. I should think also that such a system would be beneficial, as it would connect our schools with the best part of the English society at the Mofussil stations. Our libraries, the best of them at least, would be better than any library which would be readily accessible at such a station; and I do not know why we should grudge a young officer the pleasure of reading our copy of 'Boswell's Life of Johnson,' or Marmontel's 'Memoirs,' if he is willing to pay a few rupees for the privilege.

"I will not object to the principle of this part of Dr. Wise's plan. But I do object to his proposal that these subscribers shall subscribe according to their circumstances. I would proceed on this principle, that the object for which the library is established is the good of the students, and that no person should be permitted to take any book thence, unless the students receive from that person a compensation fully equal to the loss which they sustain by being temporarily deprived of that book. I would certainly not fix the subscription at less than one rupee a month for anybody; and I think that everything raised in this way should be expended in adding to the library." (29th October, 1836.)

Maulvis' Place for Prayer.—"What are the objections to allowing the Maulvis to meet for prayer within the College? I think that we can hardly refuse both to suffer them to meet there and to supply them with another place where they may meet, the character of the institution considered. Mr. Sutherland's remarks seem to me generally quite just, except that I do not attach so much importance as he appears to do to the projection of maps, an accomplishment which depends chiefly on manual dexterity, and without which a student may be an excellent geographer." (7th November, 1836.)

"I propose that we should strike off the list of stipendiary students all but the four whom Dr. Wise formerly wished should keep their present stipends for three years and no longer. At the expiration of that period the practice of giving stipends ought to cease altogether." (12th November, 1836.)

Examiner for the Hooghly College.—"Where is a competent person to be found? I shall be heartily glad if any gentleman can suggest one." (1st December, 1836.)

Purchase of Perron's House at Chinsurah.—"Nay, I think that we never expected to obtain the house for less than Rs. 16,000, and if I am rightly informed we may, with perfect prudence, authorize Dr. Wise to go as far as 20,000." (27th December, 1836.)

Suggestions by Mr. Walters and Mr. Samuels.—"We are much obliged to Mr. Walters and Mr. Samuels for the trouble which they have taken, and for the suggestions which they have offered. To the first proposition (the addition of forty-five rupees a month to the salary of the master of the Infant School), I do not object. I am also quite for discharging the useless Pundits. The founder of the College cannot be supposed to have had any particular bias in favour of Brahminical learning. We are therefore perfectly at liberty to deal with that part of the establishment in the manner which may appear to us most useful.

"The second proposition (to buy Perron's house) has already been adopted by the Committee.

"I have great doubts about the third proposition (to establish branch schools in the villages). The advantages of adopting it on a small scale are not very obvious, and we have not money sufficient to defray the expenses of adopting it on the large scale recommended by Mr. Walters.

"The fourth proposition (to establish stipends) has been repeatedly under our consideration. My opinion about it remains unchanged. I altogether dissent from Mr. Walters's proposition about religious books. I would not, of course, keep from the pupils a book which on other grounds they ought to read, merely because it contained information respecting the Christian religion. I would not keep 'Paradise Lost,' or Cowper's 'Task,' or Robinson Crusoe's dialogues with his man Friday out of their hands. But I would not in any school give them books with the object of making converts of the students, and least of all would I do so in a school founded by a zealous Mahomedan, who assuredly would have taken good care to prevent any such use of his money being made, if he could have foreseen it.

"As to the last suggestion of Mr. Walters (to invite tenders for the supply of school books), if it ought to be adopted with respect to the Hooghly College, it ought also to be adopted with respect to all our institutions. Perhaps the whole question had better be referred to the Sub-Committee of School Books, or the Sub-Committee of Finance. The latter Sub-Committee, I think, is that to which it seems naturally to belong." (10th January, 1837.)

What Knowledge of the Vernacular is "absolutely requisite."—"Mr. Sutherland seems to me to have a little misunderstood Dr. Wise. The Doctor does not say that a mere colloquial smattering of Bengali is all that is required. He says it is all that is absolutely requisite; and goes on to add that instruction is given, composition practised, and prizes held out in order to induce the higher classes to acquire a critical knowledge of the Vernacular tongue. By 'absolutely requisite' he seems evidently to mean requisite for purposes of common life, for the purpose of giving orders to the servants, of inquiring the way, of buying and selling in the bazaar, and so forth.

"As to the library, I think that we may expect to receive the books which we ordered from England in the course of a very few months.

"The disbursements recommended may be sanctioned." (20th January, 1837.)

Professors' Duties.—"I should think that in a very few months both Dr. Wise and Mr. Sutherland would find the number of advanced pupils quite sufficient to employ them during at least four hours in the day. I would rather wait a little, than propose at present the arrangement which our Secretary suggests. If it should be found that, at the end of another half-year, Mr. Sutherland has no more to do than at present, I shall be disposed to make some addition to his duties." (20th January, 1837.)

Offer of 30,000 Rupees for Perron's House.—"I cannot agree with Mr. Sutherland. I would give the 30,000 rupees at once, and obtain the house. If we should find the house will do for our College, we shall save ten times 30,000 rupees, for we shall not build a new one for less than three lacs. If, on the other hand, we should determine to build, we shall always be able to part with the house for a price not much smaller than that which is now asked for it; and we shall have the use of it rent-free while we are building. This arrangement cannot be productive of loss to us. It may be productive of very great gain. I would therefore authorize Dr. Wise to offer the 30,000 rupees, and to declare that it is our last word, and that we will not give an anna more." (25th January, 1837.)

The Library.—"I quite approve of what Dr. Wise proposes. I do not think that we need be anxious about the cost. The funds of the Hooghly College will bear a much greater outlay than will be necessary for the procuring of these books. And the sooner the students have a tolerable library the better." (1st March, 1837.)

Purchase of Perron's House for 20,000 Rupees.—"I quite agree with Mr. Sutherland. I would close instantly with the offer." (21st March, 1837.)

Sanction for Punkahs and Punkah Pullers.—"I approve. I would make them physically as comfortable as possible while they are studying." (6th April, 1837.)

Morning School during the Hot Months.—"I agree with Mr. Sutherland in disliking the shifting of hours generally.

But, in this climate, the health and comfort of the students may render such a course necessary. Even in England school hours are generally earlier in summer than in winter. I am inclined to agree to Dr. Wise's proposition." (6th April, 1837.)

Good Salaries for Teachers essential.—"I would give the Rs. 120. It is desirable not merely to keep good masters, but to prevent them from being always on the look-out for better situations. I would try to give them such salaries that they may settle down to their employment as one which is to be the business of their lives. Otherwise we shall have nothing but change. We shall lose every master as soon as he has acquired experience and established a character; and shall have a constant succession of teachers who will themselves be learners. At some of our institutions want of means prevents us from doing all that could be wished. But at Hooghly we are quite able to do all that is necessary to make the system of instruction efficient." (24th April, 1837.)

Proposal that Pupils should purchase their School Books.—"The subject is full of difficulties. Nothing can be proposed which is not open to objection; and there seems to be as little objection to Mr. Sutherland's proposal as to any other." (29th April, 1837.)

Purchase of Philosophical Apparatus.—"I approve. I wish that some of our scientific members would look at the models before we buy them." (2nd May, 1837.)

Periodicals in the College Library.—"I do not see Dr. Wise's letter. I am rather inclined to vote against the proposition as far as I at present understand. How many boys at the Hooghly College will for a long time to come read the *Edinburgh* and *Quarterly Reviews* with any interest? The Principal and the Professor are, probably, the only persons in the institution who would ever cut such works open. And we must never forget that we are forming libraries, not for the English professors, but for the native students." (4th May, 1837.)

SIR LEPEL GRIFFIN AND THE BABOO PRESS.

THE unavoidable delay occasioned in our work going to press, has fortunately enabled the writer, out of justice to Sir Lepel Griffin (who, we are glad to hear, is not yet going to retire from the service), to present the following interesting document to his readers, with reference to the brief sketch or notice of this distinguished Anglo-Indian. It appeared, under the above heading, in a popular Anglo-Indian journal, and, later, under that of "Indian Officials and the Native Press," in one of the great London dailies. where it is written :—

The following official reply to Sir Lepel Griffin's representation to the Government of India on the subject of certain attacks made upon him by the Native Press has been sent to us for publication :—

"Fort William, the 29th March, 1888.

"Sir,—I have laid before the Governor-General in Council the representations you have submitted regarding articles in the *Amrita Bazar Patrika* and other newspapers which reflect upon measures recently taken in the Bhopal State.

"2. You have recommended the criminal prosecution of these newspapers, both in the interests of the Government and on the more personal ground of defence of yourself. In the event of the Government not desiring to institute such proceedings, you ask that you may receive a public and official expression of confidence and approval from the Governor-General in Council. Your observations have been carefully considered, and I am now to communicate to you the following orders :—

"3. The Governor-General in Council is assured that the attitude of the Government in respect of Her Highness the Begum and her country needs no vindication against criticism which evinces a spirit of mere partisanship on behalf of an individual, and complete disregard for the people of Bhopal. The Governor-General in Council therefore holds that the interests of the Government would be in no way served by the institution of criminal proceedings against the newspapers containing the attacks to which you refer.

"4. As far as you are personally concerned, it appears to his Excellency the Viceroy that you also can afford to treat these attacks with indifference. You have the satisfaction of knowing that the policy of the Government in Bhopal affairs was in great measure based upon your advice ; that it has already succeeded in removing serious grievances and introducing valuable reforms ; that your action has been consistently supported by the Governor-General in Council ; and, further, that Her Majesty's Secretary of State has been pleased to express his sense of the vigour, judgment, and discretion you have displayed.

"5. I am to add that you are at liberty to publish this letter.

"I have the honour to be, Sir,

"Your most obedient Servant,

(Sd.) "H. M. DURAND,

"Secretary to the Government of India."

In Memoriam.

SIR ROBERT MONTGOMERY, G.C.S.I., K.C.B.

The death of Sir Robert Montgomery will come home to many an Anglo-Indian. During the mutiny he was, next to Sir John (afterwards Lord) Lawrence, the most prominent official in the Punjab, and his indefatigable exertions were largely instrumental in breaking the neck of the rebellion. But for the levies promptly raised by them in Afghanistan and the Punjab and poured down country, the capture of Delhi could not have been effected as it was before the arrival of a single soldier from England.

Sir Robert's services in this respect were (so it was currently reported at the time) of even greater importance, inasmuch as he was supposed to have strenuously resisted the suicidal policy of withdrawing our frontier to the Indus, which was proposed at this critical moment.—The *Globe*, December 29, 1887.

The *St. James's Gazette* said:—

The late Sir Robert Montgomery served and ruled in the Punjab in days when our *râj* was not so firmly established as it is now. When the storm of the mutinies burst there were only five European regiments to hold the country from the Indus to the Sutlej; and other British troops in the province being quartered, some at Peshawur, the rest in the hills north of Umballa. John Lawrence, the Chief Commissioner, was away at Rawal Pindi; and Robert Montgomery was the highest civil officer in Lahore when the news came of the massacre of Delhi. The sepoys at the cantonment of Mian Mir, a couple of miles from Lahore, were known to be disaffected. It was plain that immediate action must be taken, and Mr. Montgomery (as he then was), in concert with the military authorities, acted with such vigour and promptness that the capital of the Punjab was saved. He was appointed Lieutenant-Governor of the province shortly after the suppression of the Mutiny.

Among other events of his reign may be mentioned the construction of the first line of railway in the Punjab, the opening of the great Bari Doab Canal, and the campaign against the Hindustanee fanatics, wrongly called Wahabees, of the Black Mountain. The district and town of Montgomery, not far from Mooltan, were named after him. For the last nine years of his life Sir Robert Montgomery sat on the Council of the Secretary of State for India. It is to be hoped that the vacancy caused by his lamented death will be filled by some one who knows the Punjab equally well. [This is well said; but it could not be better filled than by Sir Alfred Lyall.]

Sir Robert Montgomery, G.C.S.I.—We regret to announce the death of Sir Robert Montgomery, K.C.B., G.C.S.I., LL.D., member of the Council of the India Office, which sad event occurred on Dec. 28 from bronchitis. The deceased, who was seventy-eight years of age, was a son of the late Rev. S. Montgomery, and was born in Londonderry. He was educated at Foyle College, in that city, and was appointed to the Bengal Presidency, and entered the service of the East India Company in 1828. Having served in various posts, in 1849 he was selected by the late Lord Dalhousie as one of the commissioners for the newly-annexed province of the Punjab, and on the dissolution of the Board, in 1853, was appointed Judicial Commissioner, Superintendent of Prisons, and Director-General of Police for the whole province. During the Mutiny in May 1857, he adopted measures for disarming the large native force stationed at Lahore, and was appointed Chief Commissioner of Oude in 1858, and for his services in aiding the armies under Lord Clyde and restoring tranquillity to the province received the thanks of both Houses of Parliament, and was created a Knight Commander of the Bath. In 1859 he was appointed Lieutenant-Governor of the Punjab, from which he retired in 1865, after service in India of upwards of thirty-six years. He was LL.D. of Trinity College, Dublin, and received the Grand Cross of the Star of India, Feb. 20, 1886. He was appointed a Member of the Council of India in 1868.—*The Overland Mail*, December 30, 1887.

Under the heading of these extracts regarding a really distinguished Anglo-Indian, an appreciative article appeared in *Allen's Indian Mail*, with, perhaps, the usual failing in writers of biographical sketches—that of a proneness to over-do their subject, which, after all, is a fault kind human nature loves to own. There is only one slight error near the commencement, where it is said that Sir Robert Montgomery arrived in India "sixty-six" instead of sixty years ago (1828). The writer proceeds to remark:—

For years young Montgomery passed an uneventful career in the Bengal Civil Service; always ready to do his duty, well spoken of by his superiors, he had made no mark above and beyond his compeers. But in 1849 the second Punjab War left the Sikh dominions at the disposal of the Paramount Power. John Lawrence was called upon as Chief Commissioner to administer the newly-annexed province, and amongst the small but carefully selected band associated with him was Robert Montgomery; and right well the work was done, so that in a comparatively short space of time the North-West Frontier was a model spot within the red line. To serve under "John" was the aim and object of every aspirant to fame and honour. Thus eight years elapsed, till the news flashed from east to west, from north to south, that India was in the throes of rebellion. Then came one of the greatest struggles in which this country has ever taken part. England's sway tottered in the balance, and right nobly did England's sons perform their part. What happened in regard to the Punjab is matter of history; the centre of activity, the centre of danger, was Delhi. If *that* city, the capital of the Mogul Empire, were wrenched from the Imperial diadem; if the insurgents could float the flag of rebellion in place of the standard of Great Britain, then the sun of power would set behind the horizon of annihilation; then every single soul, from the Himalayas to Cape Comorin, would have to fight for dear life. This was a danger which must be averted at all hazards, so John Lawrence determined to denude his province of European troops. No sooner was the decision made than steps were taken to carry it into effect. The disaffected native soldiers were disarmed; every single British regiment was hurried of to the north, and upon the heads of the various districts devolved the duty of keeping the peace of his own domains. All did well, but none better than the subject of our memoir. The crisis was met. India was saved, and nought remained but to reward the doers of the great deed. The thanks of Parliament and a Civil Knight Commandership of the Bath fell to Montgomery's share, to be shortly followed by the succession to the supreme control of the province in which he had won his spurs. For five years Sir Robert Montgomery wielded the sceptre of power; and when he retired after the allotted span a successful career found its closing years happy, peaceful, and honoured in the favoured and coveted post of Member of Council.

The following notice appeared soon after the above, and it deserves not to be omitted from this *In Memoriam*:—

The death of Sir Robert Montgomery is, the *Bombay Gazette* says, the breaking of a link which unites us to some of the most stirring events as well as to some of the most enduring achievements in the history of the empire in India. The schoolfellow of Henry and John Lawrence, their colleague on the Punjab Board, and John Lawrence's *locum tenens* at Lahore in the earlier days of the Mutiny, it would be difficult to recall a name in Anglo-Indian records that has worthier associations. It would be much to say of any man that he had the lifelong regard and affection of John Lawrence. "A fine fellow, brave as a lion, gentle as a lamb," was Lawrence's own encomium upon him, and it was as good as a reputation to have such a thing said of one by such a man. But Montgomery shone in his own light as well as in that which Lawrence's confidence and admiration cast around him. He worked in the Punjab as early as either of the two brothers, and neither of them would have said that he did not work as well. He had done admirable service in organizing the educational service of the Province before he was called on by Lord Dalhousie to succeed Mansel in the Punjab triumvirate. Here he was more than a worker—he was a conciliator. The two brothers did not agree in their view of the way in which the claims of the dispossessed service-tenants should be dealt with. Henry was for yielding nearly everything to the claimants; John was for yielding almost nothing. Montgomery, who was a friend of both, tried to keep the peace between these just men. He was the buffer who, with his conciliatory nature, came between them and prevented many a collision. Here was the gentleness of the lamb which extorted the admiration of John Lawrence. The bravery of the lion was shown years after when, on the news of the capture of Delhi by the mutineers he promptly resolved upon the disarmament of the four native regiments encamped at Mian Meer, and so stemmed the course of insurrection, and made it possible for Lawrence to inaugurate a policy of which the central idea was that India must be saved through the Punjab. His thirty-six years' service in India told lightly upon him. Until very late in life he was one of the youngest looking of old men, well meriting Lawrence's sobriquet of "Evergreen." He was not deemed too old nine years ago for a second appointment to the Secretary of State's Council, and few can have had him, at all events, in view when complaining of the large percentage of men of a bygone time to be found on that body.

At this stage it may be interesting to record the Council of H.M.'s Secretary of State for India as it stood in January, 1887:—

SECRETARY OF STATE,

VISCOUNT CROSS, G.C.B.

COUNCIL.

Vice-President.—Bertram Wodehouse Currie, Esq.

Sir Robert Montgomery, G.C.S.I., G.C.B.
Maj.-Gen. Sir Henry C. Rawlinson, K.C.B., LL.D.
Sir Henry J. S. Maine, K.C.S.I., LL.D., D.C.L.
Col. Henry Yule, C.B.
Robert A. Dalyell, Esq., C.S.I.
Gen. Charles J. Foster, C.B.
Lieut.-Gen. Richard Strachey, C.S.I., F.R.S.
The Hon. Sir Ashley Eden, K.C.S.I., C.I.E., LL.D.
Maj.-Gen. Sir Peter S. Lumsden, G.C.B., C.S.I.
Sir Robert Henry Davies, K.C.S.I., C.I.E.
Sir John Strachey, G.C.S.I., C.I.E.
Gen. Sir Donald M. Stewart, Bart., G.C.B., G.C.S.I., C.I.E.
Col. Sir Owen Tudor Burne, K.C.S.I., C.I.E.

Clerk of the Council.—Horace G. Walpole, Esq.,* C.B., J.P.
Reading Clerk of the Council.—Charles Grey, Esq.

In 1887 the new appointments to the Council were:—
E. Hardie, Esq. (Commercial), Sir A. Arbuthnot, and Sir James B. Peile; and at the beginning of 1888, Sir Alfred Lyall, K.C.B., K.C.I.E.

* Also Assistant Under-Secretary of State.

INDEX TO NAMES

OF

ANGLO-INDIANS AND OTHERS.

A.

B.

C.

D.

R.

S.